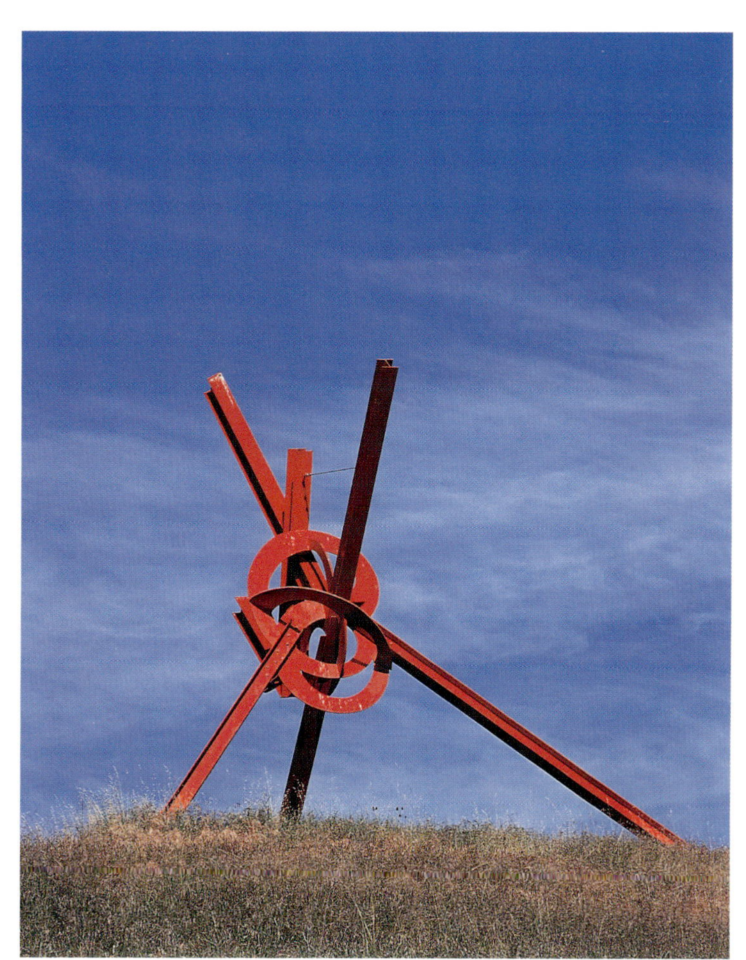

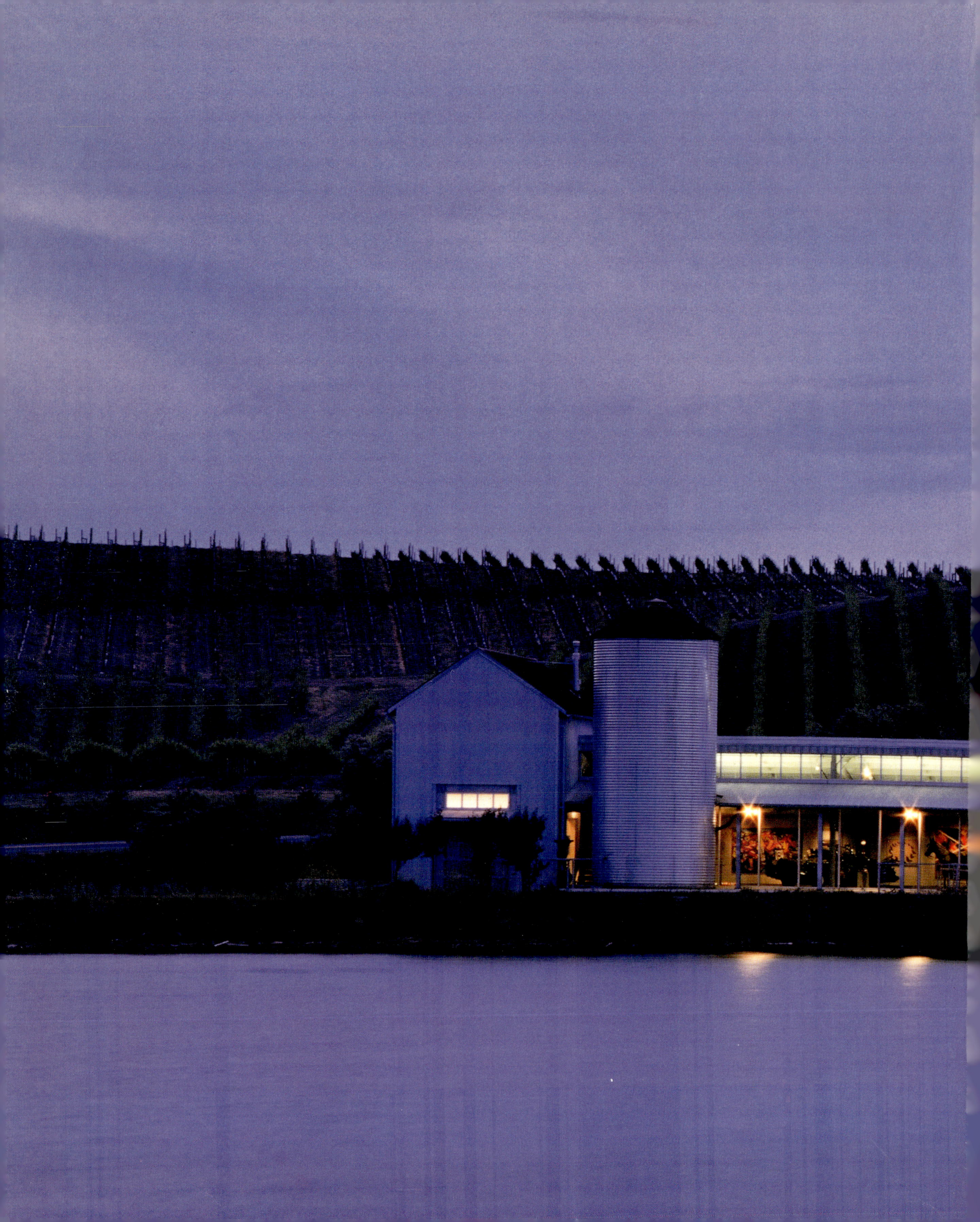

# LOCAL COLOR

## THE DI ROSA COLLECTION OF CONTEMPORARY CALIFORNIA ART

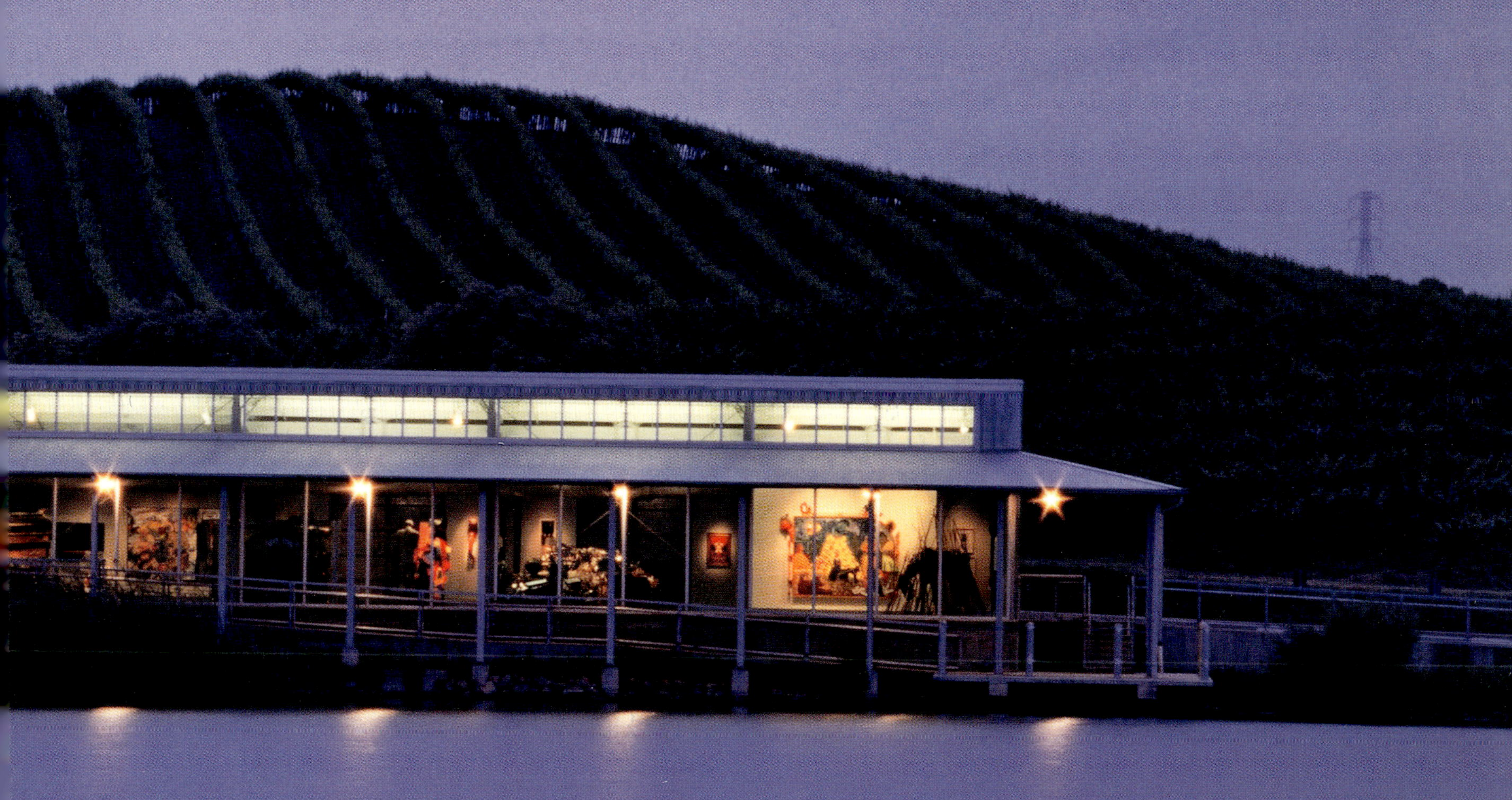

CHRONICLE BOOKS
SAN FRANCISCO

Printed in Hong Kong

Library of Congress Cataloging-in-Publication Data:
Local color : the di Rosa collection of contemporary California art / text by Rene di Rosa . . . [et al.].
p. cm.
ISBN 0-8118-2376-8 (hc) – 0-8118-2377-6 (pb)
1. Art, American–California–San Francisco Bay Area–Catalogs. 2. Art, Modern–20th century–California–San Francisco Bay Area–California. 3. di Rosa, Rene–Art collections–Catalogs. 4. Art–Private collections–California–Napa Valley–Catalogs. I. di Rosa, Rene.
N6530.C22S245 1999
709'.794'074–dc21 98-38931

Design: Susan E. Kelly, Marquand Books, Inc., Seattle

Distributed in Canada by Raincoast Books
8680 Cambie Street
Vancouver, BC V6P 6M9

10 9 8 7 6 5 4 3 2 1

Chronicle Books
85 Second Street
San Francisco, CA 94105

www.chroniclebooks.com

*Photography by Stefan Kirkeby* except as follows:
p. 30 Courtesy of Josephine Alexander Amerigian: Gary Amerigian. p. 49 © 1986 Abraham Aranow: Ruth Bernhard. pp. 90, 155 © James Arkatov: Roy De Forest, Mel Ramos. p. 157 © Ben Blackwell: Alan Rath. pp. 87, 103 © Dona Kopol Bonick: Stephen Davis, Wally Hedrick. p. 70 © Lalo Borja: Enrique Chagoya. p. 33 Courtesy of Braunstein/Quay Gallery: Jeremy Anderson. p. 152 © Kathan Brown: Janis Provisor. p. 72 © Philip Cohen: Gail Chase-Bien. p. 151 © Collection Center For Creative Photography: Jim Pomeroy. pp. 50, 112, 128, 136, 145 © Jeffrey A. Cornell: David Best, Robert Hudson, Tony Ligamari, Jock McDonald, Manuel Neri. p. 80 © 1970 Judy Dater: Imogen Cunningham. pp. 53, 60, 69, 88, 98, 139 © M. Lee Fatherree: Elmer Bischoff, Joan Brown, Squeak Carnwath, Jay DeFeo, Viola Frey, Jim Melchert. p. 74 © Kurt E. Fishback: Van Deren Coke. p. 96 © Gorgoni: Mark di Suvero. p. 29 © Douglas Kent Hall: Terry Allen. p. 148 © Anne Hamersky: Deborah Oropallo. pp. 58, 120, 126, 131, 146, 179 © Leo Holub Photograph: Christopher Brown, Jess, Marilyn Levine, Alvin Light, Nathan Oliveira, Peter Voulkos. p. 140 © Robert Mann: Richard Misrach. pp. 5, 35, 95, 180, 182 © Jock McDonald: Robert Arneson, Veronica di Rosa, Catherine Wagner, William T. Wiley. p. 110 © Mark McGowan: Mildred Howard. p. 162 © Nancy Moran: Raymond Saunders. p. 158 © Fiona O'Connor: Rigo 99. p. 117 © Suzanne Parker: David Ireland. pp. 1, 2-3, 8, 16, 20, 22 © Erhard Pfeiffer. pp. 135, 142 © Nigel Poor: Tom Marioni, Ron Nagle. p. 132 Courtesy of Refusalon: Charles Linder. p. 43 Courtesy of Richard Reisman: Jonathan Barbieri. p. 123 © Schopplein Studio: David Jones. p. 164 © Alice Shaw: Richard Shaw. p. 39 © Juliet Stelzman: Anthony Aziz. p. 77 © Kim Stringfellow: Bruce Conner. p. 104 © Tim Wagar: Mike Henderson. p. 84 © 1994 Julie Weisz: Judy Dater. p. 46 © John Wilson White: Ray Beldner.

*Licensing Credits*

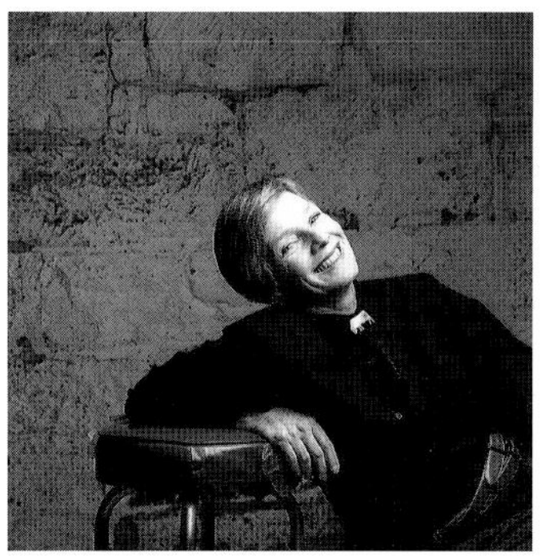

This book is dedicated to the memory and spirit of Veronica di Rosa 1934-1991

*Rene di Rosa* and *the Directors of the Rene & Veronica di Rosa Foundation* give special and loving thanks to *Phyllis C. Wattis* not only for underwriting this volume but for her unending generosity and support of all the arts.

Profound gratitude goes as well to *John P. Axelrod* and *the California Tamarack Foundation* for helping make all this possible.

For their sound advice and diligence, our thanks to the di Rosa Foundation Board of Directors Publications Committee: *Rene di Rosa, James Elliott, Jim Melchert, Richard Reisman, Norma Schlesinger, and Cecile McCann, Chair.*

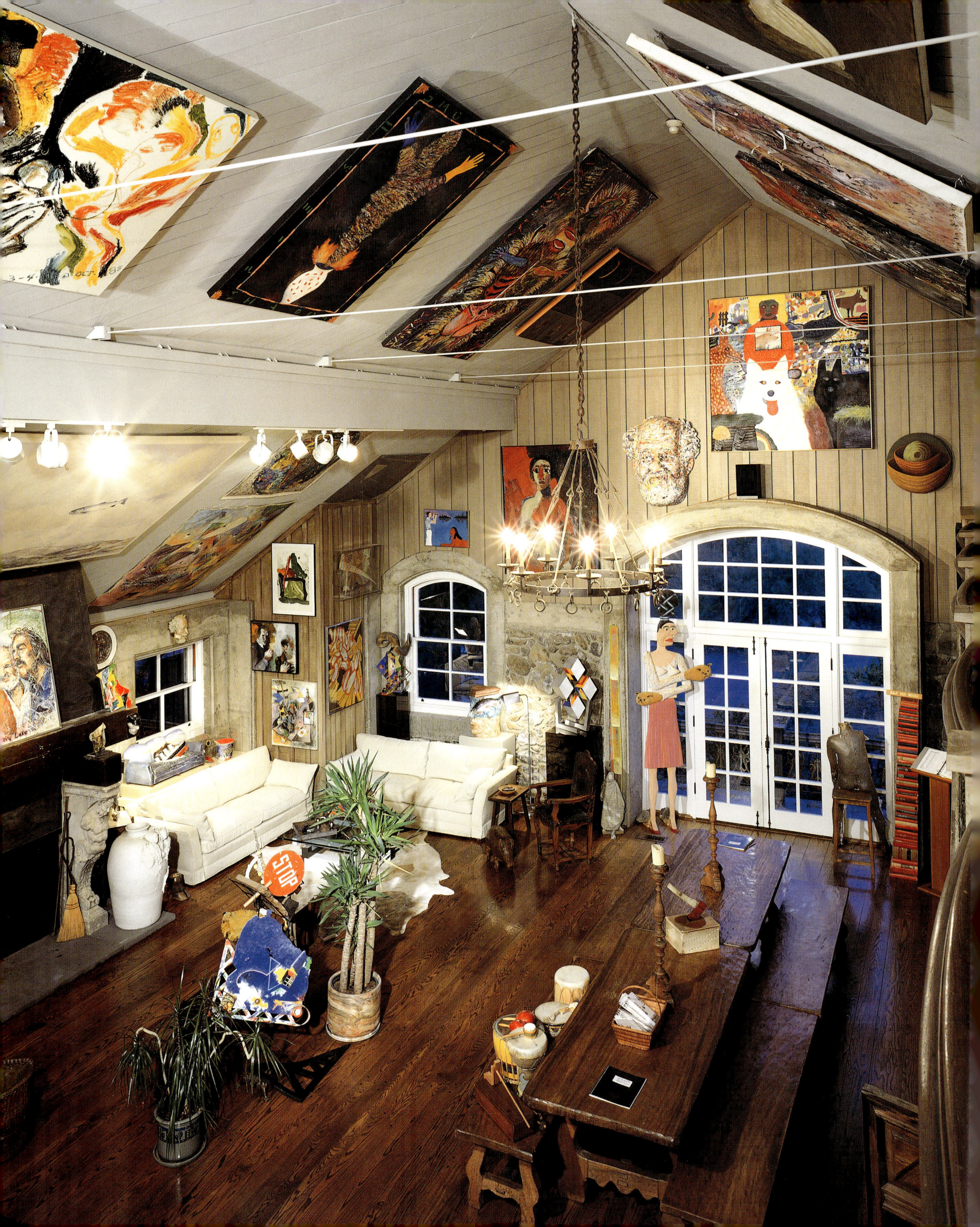
STOP

## CONTENTS

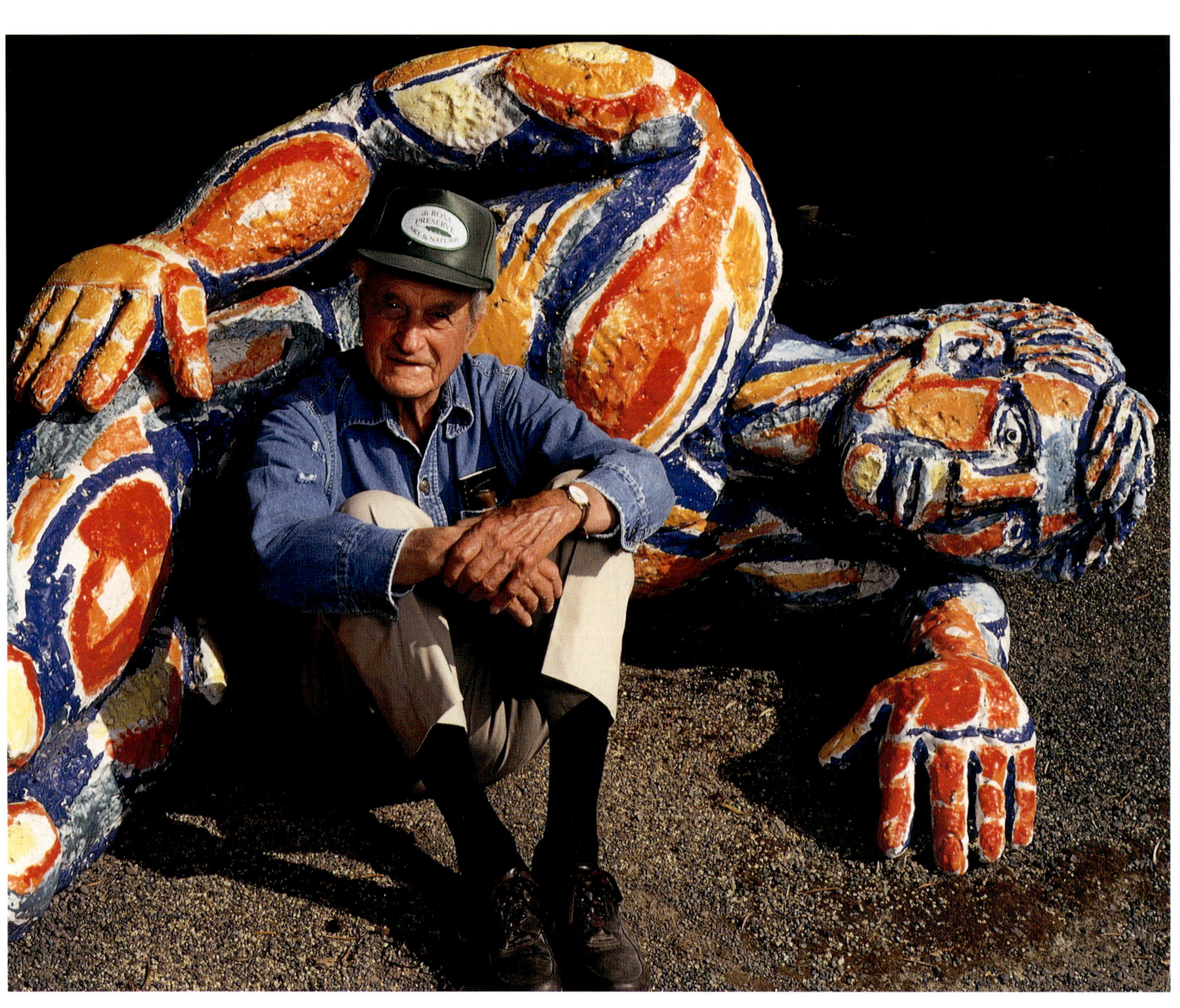
di ROSA
PRESERVE
ART & NATURE

# *Preface*

**RENE DI ROSA, COLLECTOR**
**RICHARD REISMAN, DI ROSA PRESERVE CURATOR**

Hello. My name is Rene di Rosa. I am an artaholic.

*When did you first realize you had crossed the line from harmless interior decor to addic– . . . um . . . magnificent obsession?*

I can't remember when. It's all kind of hazy–like mist on a Bill Allan pond.

*Any hope of a cure?*

Not interested. And none of the artists, dealers, collectors, and plain old art lovers I know are hoping for one either. Art book publishers accept me the way I am.

*You have said that you failed as a writer and wanted to support people who had the talent you lacked. But you were a man of letters. Why did you choose visual artists?*

I like the colors. And I get the words anyway. It would take me another lifetime to read through all those Wileys.

*What kind of art gets your attention?*

Complex. Like a Bob Hudson sculpture. Think it's one thing and then it becomes something else.

*Any particularly favorite medium?*

Couldn't care less. What matters to me is what it's made into, not what it's made out of. Multimedia. Chewing gum, crab claws, hair, bones, bowling balls, feathers, marbles, brooms, boots and shoes, shirts. Pretty much anything–anything that smacks of life. Paint is nice, too.

*You go to pains to point out that you like color and whimsy, that it's OK to laugh. But the collection also contains work that reveals a very dark side of the human condition . . . everything from convoluted politics to twisted sex. What's that all about?*

Wish I knew. Maybe.

*You promote local artists and refer to this as a San Francisco Bay Area collection. But there are different regional artists and aesthetics that are not represented.*

Which shows the creative energies of this region. The Bay Area is the pond from which I fish. It does not define the catch. My personal taste does not include austere abstraction, white on white. I like additive art, not reductive art. I prefer maximal to minimal. I like the figure and identifiable objects that grab your attention through their familiarity. The artists I like use the familiar as a hook to lead you into new realms. The best artists are like shamans who can take us to deeper truths.

*Some have noted that the collection includes several artists not from the Bay Area.*

Mea culpa. But the vast majority are. Most of the rest have at some time lived, taught, and worked here. I have twice gotten caught up by the work of an alien seen in a local gallery. But these are exceptions. I am provincial to the core.

*There are no labels or wall texts illuminating the works in your galleries. Why?*

I wish my memory could credit whoever it was that said talking about art is like trying to French kiss over the telephone. The point is that words can and do get in the way. They distract more than they illuminate. Knowing who did it when and the title can be interesting on some level. But wall labels do not reveal the work and can be insistent distractions. We allow people to spend their time looking and feeling without having to read. If they want to know specifics, they can ask and we will answer. When you walk into a museum and see all that blah blah on the wall, the subtext seems to be "you can't negotiate this without our help." Bill Wiley once said of his own work, "Just because I made this stuff doesn't mean I know any more about it than you do." People bring their own baggage to the viewing experience. We invite them to open that baggage and participate in the conversation between themselves and the art. I believe the absence of labels is empowering. It makes some people nervous, but most enjoy the vacation.

*Before acquiring an art object, you've never asked for anyone else's evaluation of it?*

Maybe I fear getting an educated view before the I-want-it-anyway purchase.

*How do art critics and art academicians view the collection?*

They view it with a curatorial frown. They point to the lack of Abstract Expressionist work and art from the figurative movement that followed it—both of which a museum survey of area art would include. But I'm not a museum. If I like a work, I don't care if it isn't this or that. And so there are a lot of "isn'ts" in the collection—many of them thumbing a whimsical nose at what *should* be in their places.

*How do you presently view the collection?*

I view it as very personal. It is part of me, and many pieces have become part of my life. They almost take the place of the brothers and sisters and sons and daughters I never had. In fact, since the death of my wife Veronica, I've become something of a recluse, with the Preserve as my sustainer. And I've never sold a piece from this almost family collection.

*And it's become a fairly large family, with about 1,600 member pieces: 663 sculptures, 298 paintings, 252 photographs, 236 drawings, 86 prints, 34 collages, 23 films, 12 books, and 5 videos. All these art objects were created by just 640 artists. Doesn't this say that you favored some artists with multiple purchases?*

Yes, I became addicted to the work of various artists and acquired ten or more pieces from the following: William T. Wiley, David Best, Bruce Conner, Robert Arneson, Paul Kos, Tony Ligamari, Jock McDonald, Jim Melchert, Robert Hudson, Roy De Forest, Jim Pomeroy, Viola Frey, Jim Barsness, Tim Cooper, Veronica di Rosa, Bill Dane, and William Allan. Plus five or more gems from Ray Beldner, Joan Brown, Carlos Villa, Alan Shepp, Judy Dater, Ursula Schneider, John Simpkins, Michael Stevens, Earl Thollander, David Anderson, Enrique Chagoya, Stephen Davis, Stephen De Staebler, Squeak Carnwath, Inez Storer, Gary Amerigian, Randy Hussong, Nathan Oliveira, and Richard Shaw.

*Any regrets?*

I don't think it's a regret, but sometimes I wish that I had acquired 1,600 pieces, but each from a different area artist. Because there are hundreds of creators out there who deserve to have their work shown. And how I wish I could get around and view all this emerging talent. Because emerging talent is what has always grabbed me, and now more than ever.

*Perhaps I should insert your quote that the collection's art is divinely regional, superbly parochial, wondrously provincial—an absolute native glory.*

And with its creators living right here among us to give our community a special vitality.

*So is there a problem?*

Yes. Big-city museums everywhere want to be national and then international, with art imported from New York, Europe, and elsewhere grabbing more and more space from what they were formerly showing: art of the region.

*So you're saying that local art is not supported with the same loyalty as a local sports team?*

True. And when trendsetting museums buy elsewhere and display more and more imported art, local galleries find it increasingly difficult to sell the work of area artists, who in turn may be forced to move away, leaving our community without their vitality.

*How would you like a person to feel after visiting the Preserve?*

Perhaps these hopes are a bit lofty. But upon departing I'd like a visitor to feel enriched, entertained, and empowered by what artists of the area can offer them. Because these artists are facing some of the same obstacles we do—and they are striving to overcome.

*Any final hopes that a departing visitor might carry along?*

I'd like to think that visiting a museum that doesn't intimidate and doesn't follow the "correct" preachy-teachy protocols has helped people rediscover themselves and their own creativity. And I hope that now they feel that art is not some lofty "should"—but can be a real part of living. In fact, if creating art is good therapy, then isn't viewing it beneficial—even therapeutic?

P.S. Here's my sing-along for an *incorrect* museum.

Come on out and let go.
To return again while getting to know
that here the art invites a titter
from the free admitter.
Because art here is a healthy remedy
with a laugh at rascality not posing as ponderosity.

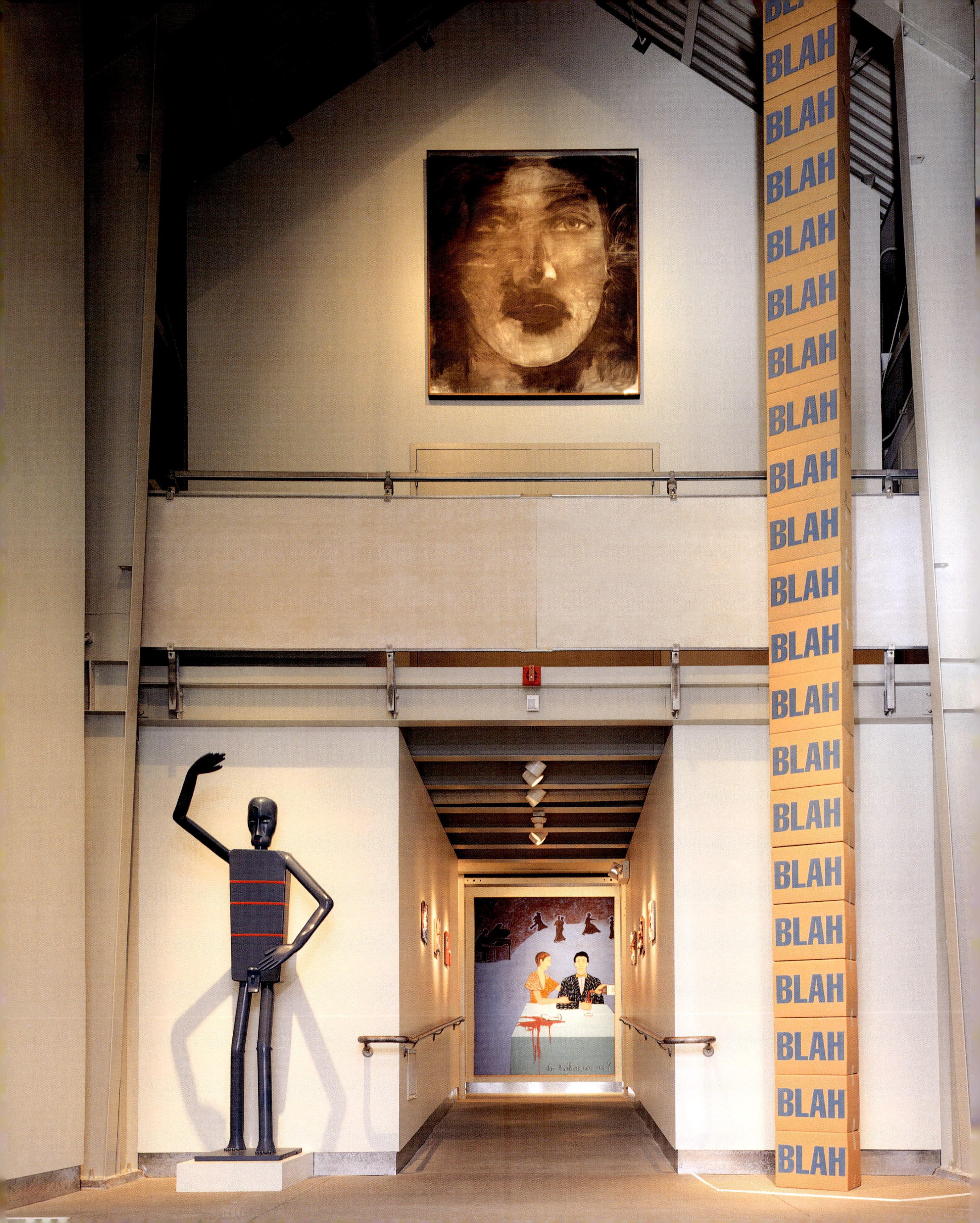
BLAH
BLAH
BLAH
BLAH
BLAH
BLAH
BLAH
BLAH
BLAH
BLAH
BLAH
BLAH
BLAH
BLAH
BLAH
BLAH
BLAH
BLAH
BLAH
BLAH

# *"A Reality Dream": Winery Lake and the di Rosa Collection* **TESSA DECARLO**

*"Art is a reality dream that carries the viewer into an expanded world created jointly by the artist and the beholder."*

—Rene di Rosa

When Rene di Rosa first saw the property that today houses the di Rosa Preserve, it was a working farm in an area so rural that regular phone service had replaced privately operated crank-box "farm lines" only a few years before. Cattle ranged the hillsides, while the fields below were planted with oats and barley. What is today a large lake was then a small pond that provided water to irrigate the fields. The old stone barn that later became di Rosa's art-filled home was used for storing grain and, occasionally, grinding it into meal using a small mill powered by a tractor motor.

In the decades after he bought the property in 1960, di Rosa transformed this rolling farmland into a kind of earthly paradise, a paradise built along the lines of his own whimsical and extravagant nature and consecrated to his own appetite for company, conversation, and, above all, visual beauty. But if the estate he called Winery Lake is a deeply personal creation, it has always had an extraordinarily ambitious public aspect as well. For on these acres di Rosa brought into being two grand enterprises: first, one of the world's most highly regarded vineyards, and second, a nature preserve of spectacular beauty housing the world's most extensive collection of the art of Northern California.

Like the region it celebrates, like the art that fills its indoor spaces and spreads across its hills, like the man who created it, the di Rosa Preserve embraces the clash of public and private, nature and artifice, ego and altruism, cool distance and deep feeling, low humor and high seriousness, seeking in the intersection of opposites what is most dynamic, satisfying, and real. "Give me slashing colors, and I will need a peaceful blending," di Rosa wrote in one of the leaflets he hands out to visitors. "Offer me sweet coloration, then, please, stir me to the strife of life. Yes, awaken me to the yin and yang of living, as reflected in art that mirrors life—my life, my very own life."

## I. EARLY YEARS

Di Rosa's own life embodies that clash of opposites, for this dedicated grape farmer and champion of Northern California had a quintessentially urban and East Coast background. His mother was an heiress from St. Louis, his father an aristocratic Italian who served as that nation's consul general in Boston, where Rene di Rosa was born in 1919. The marriage did not last, but both parents remained close to Rene, their only child, who early on displayed a zest for making grand gestures and cocking a snoot at convention. He arrived at Yale with a string of polo ponies, recalled novelist John Leggett, his college roommate, and made what may have been his first art purchase at the university's art school, where he commissioned a student to paint a female nude to hang in his rooms. The finished picture "had one of the ugliest, coarsest faces I'd ever seen," Leggett reported, "but full-on bare breasts and genitalia. Needless to say, all our fellow undergraduates crowded into the room for a look." In response, di Rosa went out and bought several foxtails of the sort that boys put on their bicycle handlebars. "He affixed these foxtails to the picture's strategic areas," Leggett said, "and announced that the people who wanted to look underneath had to pay a fee."

After graduating in 1942 and serving in the Navy, di Rosa returned to the East Coast, determined to become a writer. He managed to publish a few short stories (one, in a small men's magazine, concerned the amorous exploits of two wine salesmen), but what he has sardonically called "my Great American Novel" eluded him. In the late 1940s he moved to Paris's Left Bank in pursuit of inspiration; although his novel refused to get written, he encountered there an artistic bohemia that deeply impressed him. It was also in Paris that he made his first serious art acquisition, a painting of a green nude with bright red lips that now hangs in the Preserve offices.

Not long afterward di Rosa abandoned Paris and his novel and relocated to San Francisco to take a job as a reporter at the *San Francisco Chronicle,* then one of four daily newspapers in the city. He lived near the Co-Existence Bagel Shop and frequented the City Lights Bookstore and other proto-Beat hangouts. "But I didn't really connect with the bohemia I was seeking, the artists in revolt," he said many years later.

By the end of the 1950s di Rosa was feeling rootless and purposeless. His first marriage had broken up and he had decided that journalism was not his calling. The death of his father left him with a small inheritance, and he decided to use it to escape what he called "the fleshpots of San Francisco." "I wished to investigate an existence closer to Mother Nature and Father Soil," he later wrote. "I searched and searched for real farmland." What he found, and bought in 1960, was the ranch that became Winery Lake.

## II. RENE PLANTS ROOTS

The region known as the Carneros, after the sheep that once grazed there, runs across the southern end of Napa and Sonoma Counties, edging the northern end of the San Francisco Bay. Today it is one of the best-known appellations in California's wine country, but when di Rosa first ventured there the area's rolling hills and gentle valleys were given over to cattle, prune orchards, hay, and grain.

There were vineyards in the area's past, however. In 1855 William Winter bought a ranch carved out of the huge Rancho Huichica land grant and planted seventy acres of grapes. (He planted olive trees as well, quite likely including the venerable olives at the di Rosa Preserve.) In 1884 the property was purchased by two Frenchmen, Michael Debret and Pierre Priet, who renamed it Debret Vineyard and built a large stone winery in 1886.

But the phylloxera root louse that destroyed most of Europe's vines as the nineteenth century wound to a close also devastated the vineyards in California, including Debret's. The land passed into other hands, and grapes were replaced by prunes, tomatoes, and grain. During the Prohibition era the owners kept a few cows for show but secretly hauled grapes to the old winery and produced "moonshine" brandy, reportedly of very high quality. Later the stone building was used to grow mushrooms and then became a granary.

The history of the property excited di Rosa more than its present. Despite the advice of agricultural experts, who warned that the Carneros soils were too clay-hard and the climate too cool, he was determined to return the land to wine grapes and reinvent himself as a farmer.

He embarked on an energetic program of reconditioning the ranch's soils and planting high-quality wine varietals most likely to do well in the Bay-cooled region, mainly pinot noir and chardonnay. He traveled to the nearby University of California, Davis, a world leader in viticultural research, to study modern grape-growing techniques. He expanded the pond to a thirty-acre lake and used the dark topsoil from the pond bottom to enrich the soils of his hillside vineyards. He turned the old stone winery into an imposing house and named the estate Winery Lake.

From the beginning he touted the virtues of the Carneros, and Winery Lake in particular, as a source for outstanding wine grapes. His fondness for showing up at fusty Napa Valley wine events wearing overalls, oversized bow ties, billed caps emblazoned with comical mottos, and sometimes even a gorilla suit fed his reputation as a man willing to flout conventional wisdom, while the quality of his grapes convinced even the skeptics. Winery Lake became one of the first California vineyards prestigious enough to appear on a wine label, and before long di Rosa was able to command some of the highest prices ever paid for California grapes.

## III. ART AND GRAPES

Although he took his new career very seriously, di Rosa often grew bored during the lectures on viticulture at UC Davis. "I resented the science surrounding what I had thought would be a dig-a-hole-and-plant-a-vine exercise, and I found myself wandering off to the art department," he later wrote. As it happened, Davis's art division was a hotbed of emerging talent: among the instructors there in the early 1960s were Robert Arneson, Roy De Forest, Manuel Neri, and William T. Wiley. What particularly appealed to di Rosa was the young artists' exuberant sense of humor. "It's one thing to view an artwork and weep," he wrote later. "It was another, and for me a new sensation, to see a picture that [provoked] a teary feeling, except that here a smile, a chuckle, or a laugh moistened the eye.

"I didn't have the money to collect established artists, but I took satisfaction in helping artists who were then unknown," he recalled. "I wanted to help them become the artist I had failed to become."

Just as di Rosa was one of the first to plant grapes in the Carneros in the 1960s, and a winemaker in the forefront of the Napa Valley wine renaissance of that era, he was also one of only a handful of Bay Area collectors who were then buying work by local artists. In fact, di Rosa became a sort of reverse chauvinist, swimming against the trend of western collectors seeking validation from back East. "Wealthy museum trustees, influenced by their museums' curators, travel to New York to acquire approved art, while many rich New Yorkers still fly to Europe for art," he wrote. "This attitude long ago aroused my desire to support our neighbors, the creative underdogs." Northern California art created in the second half of the twentieth century has remained the focus of his collecting ever since.

Although di Rosa may have failed as a novelist, he was creating a masterpiece of another sort at Winery Lake. He added a stone tower to the house and in it installed a huge church bell he picked up at a warehouse sale of odds and ends that William Randolph Hearst hadn't gotten around to using for his castle at San Simeon. He introduced flocks of peacocks and geese and built an island in the middle of the lake, complete with palm trees. In addition to filling the house with art reflecting his own antic sensibility, di Rosa commissioned sculptures for the gardens and fields all around it. The artists themselves were brought to Winery Lake too, for dinners, picnics, and parties where the host often challenged his guests to discuss everything from the meaning of a particular piece of art to the nature of existence. "There was always plenty of wine and good food and conversation," recalled Jim Melchert, who created the first site-specific work on the estate in 1965. "I had the impression that Rene wanted to make a place that was a paradise—a wonderful place for people to come and gather."

## IV. THE PRESERVE

During the 1980s di Rosa found that art was commanding more and more of his attention, while his enthusiasm for the day-to-day business of grape farming was waning. By that time he was married to his third wife, Veronica, a Canadian-born painter and sculptor. She shared his passion for art, entertaining, and Winery Lake, and the couple continued to add works by old friends and new discoveries to their house and grounds. In 1982 they created the Rene & Veronica di Rosa Foundation with thoughts of someday making their home into an art and nature preserve.

Then in 1986 Seagram's, owners of Sterling Vineyards at the northern end of the Napa Valley, offered to buy di Rosa's vineyards, a total of about two hundred thirty acres, for a price that reflected Winery Lake's immense wine-world cachet. The di Rosas retained two hundred seventeen acres, fifty-three of which now make up the Preserve, including the house and lake. What had been a dream for the distant future was now a real-world possibility.

Their plans had to take into account Napa County's strict prohibitions against building nonagricultural facilities on farmland—safeguards the di Rosas had themselves campaigned for. But supporters of the di Rosas' "art park" noted the importance of the site as a wildlife preserve, home to over a hundred species of herons, coots, terns, owls, woodpeckers, and other birds. In addition, the significance of the di Rosa collection drew endorsements from museum directors all over the United States for a project that David Ross, then-director of the Whitney Museum in New York, called "a great treasure for all of us who love and are concerned about the future of American art."

In 1991, in the midst of the planning process, Veronica di Rosa died in a tragic hiking accident while the couple was vacationing in France. The art and nature preserve thus became a memorial to her as well, and Rene di Rosa pursued the project with even greater energy. He allayed concerns about possible impacts on area agriculture by strictly limiting the number of visitors to the Preserve and granting permanent open-space easements on the property to the Napa County Land Trust. County officials unanimously approved the project in late 1992.

Since the collection had vastly outgrown the di Rosas' home, plans for the Preserve included construction of two large galleries and a tunnel-cum-chapel between the house and the second gallery, designed around Paul Kos's *Chartres Bleu.* But by the time the di Rosa Preserve: Art and Nature opened its doors in the spring of 1997, di Rosa's collecting had outstripped the new facilities as well. The flyers he periodically hands out to visitors must be continually updated to reflect the collection's ever-rising total, and new pieces (many by young artists, some the first works they've ever sold) are constantly appearing in the Preserve's galleries, gardens, and sculpture meadow.

Far from losing its personal character in the transition from private home to public art venue, the di Rosa Preserve remains as idiosyncratic as its founder. The house is still filled with memorabilia of Rene and Veronica di Rosa's lives there, and of their friendships with many of the artists they collected. The lack of identifying labels on the artworks in the Preserve is another reflection of the collector's defiantly anticonventional spirit. "This began with going to museums and watching people glance at the painting and go up and study the goddamn wall label," di Rosa explained. "Without wall tags to read, people have to really look at the art."

Where most collectors would have flattered themselves by presenting only the best-known artists and most valuable pieces, di Rosa, who boasts he has never sold a work of art, has put the entire collection on view (or at least as much of it as there is room for), from outstanding works by world-famous artists to efforts by fledgling unknowns.

"This collection is an artifact in itself, and an adventure in self-discovery rather than connoisseurship, investment gamesmanship, scholarship, or any of those '-ships' that sail from some port other than the heart," explained di Rosa's longtime curator, Richard Reisman. "People can feel the passion that lies behind this place, because it is not just the artists' passion but Rene's."

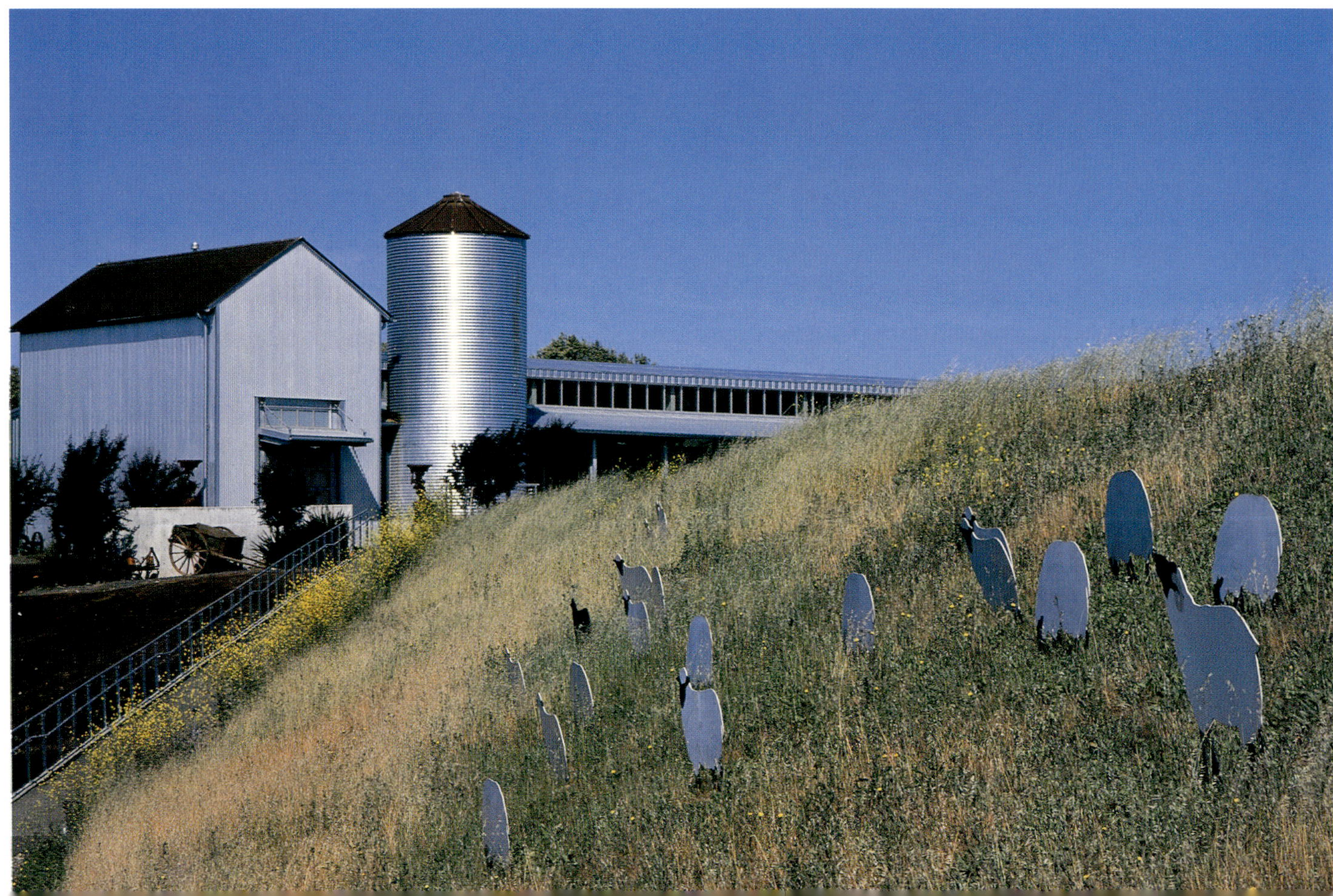

# *An Absolute Native Glory: The di Rosa Collection*

MARIA PORGES

## I. TAKING RISKS

When Rene di Rosa bought land in the rocky southern end of the Napa Valley in 1960, some of the area's farmers thought his plan to establish a vineyard in what was to become known as the Carneros region to be eccentric at best. Carneros had not yet become an appellation world-famous for its long summers of hot, dry days and cool, foggy nights—a climate ideally suited to growing the kind of grapes which, in time, can become a truly great wine.

As it turned out, di Rosa's maverick vision has been vindicated a thousand times over. In the nearly four decades that have passed since then, Northern California has become a center of the wine industry. During the same period, the Bay Area—the urban heart of the region—has also undergone tumultuous change and tremendous growth. This vitality is reflected in the work that has been produced by a thriving local community of artists of all kinds. When di Rosa moved to San Francisco in the mid-fifties, the coffeehouses of the city's North Beach neighborhood were crowded with the members of the Beat Generation. Several cultural revolutions later, painters and sculptors (as well as photographers, videographers, performance artists, and intermedia practitioners of every possible permutation) still move to San Francisco, Oakland, and the surrounding counties every year, attracted by this area's special qualities. Whether they come for the climate, the dramatic scenery, the remarkable social and cultural diversity, or all of the above, some statistics suggest that more artists study and live in the Bay Area than in any other place in the United States, with the single exception of New York City. And as they've graduated from art school, or begun to show their work in one of the Bay Area's many "alternative" spaces, di Rosa has been there at their exhibitions: searching for new objects or images to add to a collection that now numbers well over fifteen hundred pieces. Taking risks, as he has from the beginning of his personal journey as a collector, he has followed his passion for "divinely regional, superbly parochial, wondrously provincial" art.

## II. LOCAL TALENT

Unlike some collectors, whose motivations for accumulating art may have as much to do with status or glamour as with any real attachment to the work they acquire, di Rosa has bought only what he loves (or, in some cases, what thumbs its nose at him). Many of the artists whose work he collected at the beginning of their careers have gone on to international stardom, while others are known only locally or have disappeared into obscurity. No matter how a career has turned out, however, di Rosa has never sold a single piece. Equally important, his attention has been concentrated almost exclusively on work made by artists living (even if only briefly) in the greater San Francisco Bay Area. The resulting accumulation of a wide variety of images and objects functions as a fascinating record of the development of a strongly regional art scene in the area, particularly in the seventies and eighties. During the nineties, the origins of art made in different parts of the country have often been hidden beneath a veneer of universally available pop-cultural sources or references. In contrast, during the period when the core of the di Rosa collection was formed, art made in the Bay Area had a distinctive flavor all its own: a freewheeling, often funny combination of Funk and figuration, seasoned with a liberal use of found materials and clay.

Judging from the collection's holdings, some of that uniqueness persists today, deriving from a profile of qualities that have a powerful resemblance to di Rosa's own personality and tastes: independence, iconoclasm, a certain measure of cultivated eccentricity, a strong sense of humor, and an unwavering focus on the human figure. Certainly the Bay Area's special tradition of alternative venues for exhibition has continued to be strong, offering artists opportunities to show (and, sometimes, even to sell) their work outside of the traditional gallery system. No other city has as rich a variety of these nonprofit, artist-run, seat-of-the-pants spaces where artmakers of all kinds can initiate a dialogue both within their own community and with the art world at large. For di Rosa, the exhilarating pleasure of attending the shows at many of these alternative spaces has been an important part of the process of discovery that builds and informs his collection.

Often, the formation of large private collections is guided by a mixed assortment of motivations, not to mention a host of advisors and art dealers. Works can be purchased as investment, as decoration, or even as a kind of trophylike evidence of the intelligence, taste, and, above all, wealth of their owner. Here, the process of collecting has been a far more passionate enterprise. Certainly, there are galleries from which di Rosa has bought a substantial amount of work over the years, and the collection has had a skilled and dedicated curator, Richard Reisman, for the past twelve years. Still, di Rosa himself has found, examined, and fallen in love with each and every piece before buying it and bringing it home.

## III. FUNK AND THE FIGURE

When asked why he began buying art, di Rosa has responded with engaging self-deprecation that it came about as a result of his own youthful failure as a fiction writer. After stints in New Jersey and Paris spent trying to create his Great American Novel, he moved to San Francisco to take a job as a reporter for the *San Francisco Chronicle.* In the course of his exploratory travels around his new hometown, he began going to galleries and museums, including the de Young Museum, where he remembers being profoundly moved by a Bruce Conner sculpture—a mummified-looking figure ensconced in a high chair. The piece, titled *Child,* caused quite a stir at the time of its inclusion in a San Francisco Arts Association Annual. Radiating a grotesque power, it was intended to function as a protest against an execution at San Quentin prison.

The "funky" creations of iconoclastic individuals like Conner drew not only from art but from music, theater, and poetry as well. For the so-called Beat Generation, the influences of Eastern religion, existential philosophy, and recreational drugs all came together in painting and sculpture that could be seen daily in the coffeehouses and experimental galleries in North Beach, near di Rosa's apartment. But another new style caught his eye as well: a radically new kind of painting that was also, paradoxically, a return to the familiar. In 1950, David Park had rejected abstraction (the ruling style of avant-garde art in the postwar era), reintroducing figurative content to his work. The movement that sprang up in the years that followed became known nationwide as Bay Area Figurative for its combination of recognizable content—landscape, still life, and, especially, the figure—with the gestural brushwork and vigorous paint handling of Abstract Expressionism. Painters now celebrated for their pioneering work in this style include Park, Elmer Bischoff, and Richard Diebenkorn, as well as a second wave of artists, among them Joan Brown, Nathan Oliveira, and sculptor Manuel Neri, all of them represented in the collection.

Purchasing art on a reporter's salary was out of the question, although di Rosa was drawn to some of the work he saw in galleries and museums. Later, he bought Conner's work in depth, eventually acquiring more than thirty pieces, including *CRUCIFIXION* (p. 76), a powerful work from the same period as *Child.* Pieces by others who were working in the late fifties, such as Jay DeFeo and Wally Hedrick, gradually came into the collection as well.

There is no question that the work di Rosa had seen in his first years in San Francisco made a strong impression on him, but his collection begins with another kind of art. The philosophy of both the Beat artists and the figurative painters was a kind of die-for-your-work seriousness that came straight out of Abstract Expressionism: artmaking as an almost religious commitment, intentionally segregated from

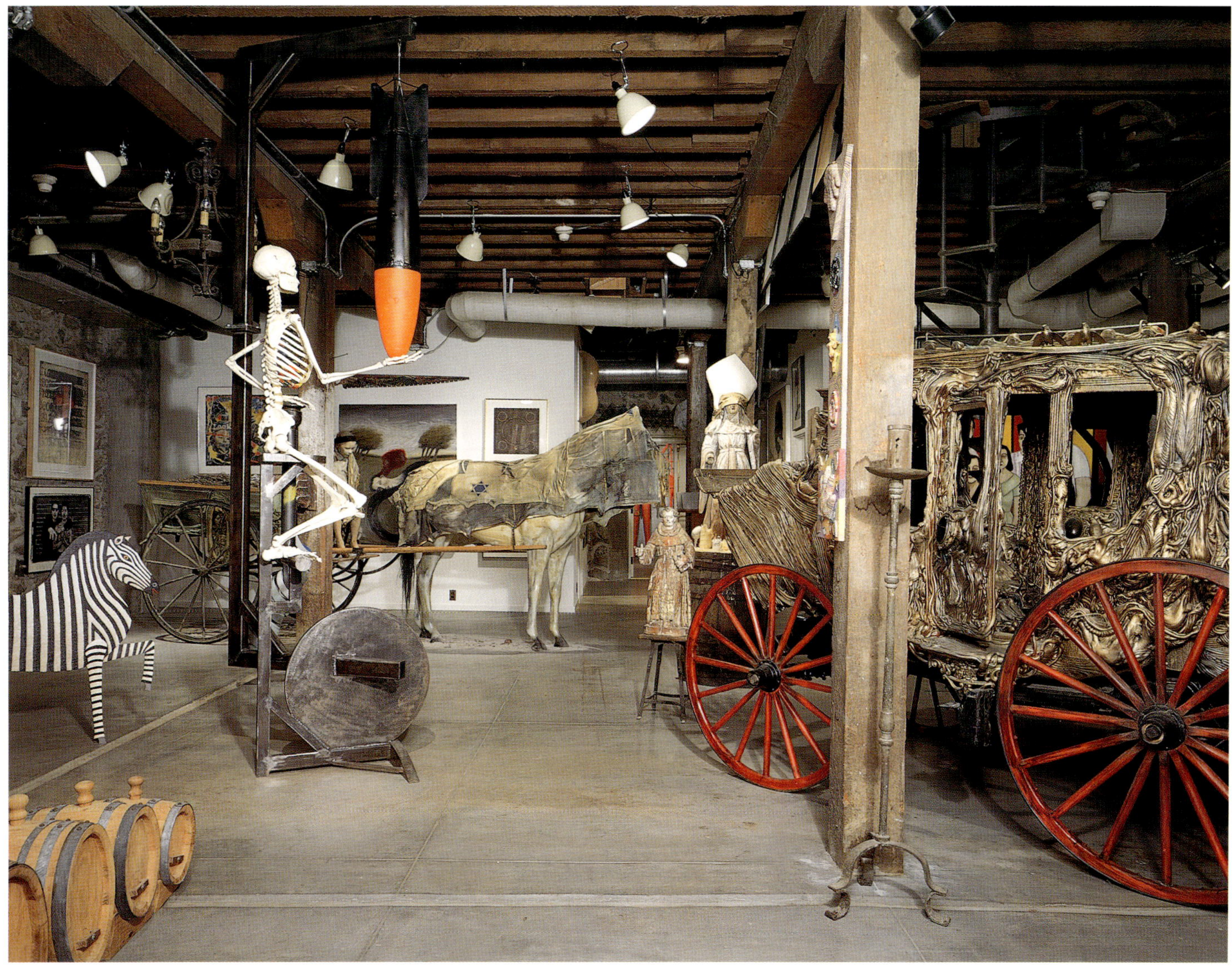

life's mundane, everyday activities. In the sixties, a new attitude emerged, as the culture itself was transformed—by war, by television, and by sheer optimism. As mass media began to homogenize America into a standardized, consumption-driven society, artists rebelled, asserting a regional distinctiveness. Adopting a new set of values, this generation of artists asserted that their work was a part of life—not separated from it—made with a sense of humor, out of everyday objects and ideas.

### IV. MEANWHILE, BACK AT THE RANCH

As a neophyte grape farmer in the early sixties, di Rosa had more enthusiasm than actual knowledge about the finer points of viticulture. He decided to take some classes, driving over the mountains each week to attend lectures at the agricultural extension of the University of California, Davis. He has recalled with wry amusement that going to the university's art department to check things out there was far more interesting than attending talks on soil management or grape diseases. After all, amazing things were happening in the art studios at UC Davis. A surprising number of gifted artists were associated with the school in the sixties and seventies. Deborah Butterfield, Bruce Nauman, John Buck, Richard Shaw, and David Gilhooly were graduate students, learning from Robert Arneson, William T. Wiley, Roy De Forest, Manuel Neri, and Wayne Thiebaud. And di Rosa bought work by almost all of them. One of the first pieces he purchased, in fact, was a sculpture by Arneson that shows Wiley emerging from a pyramid on wheels, dressed in an aviator's suit he was fond of wearing at the time. The work of these two men, who would be among the most influential artists of the sixties and seventies in the Bay Area, embodies the very regionalism that the di Rosa collection would come to celebrate.

Arneson, who started teaching at UC Davis in 1962, had a tremendous impact on art in the Bay Area—not only through his students but also through his use of clay as a serious art material. Because of such artist/teachers as Arneson at Davis, Viola Frey at the California College of Arts and Crafts, and Peter Voulkos, who had come to the University of California, Berkeley, in 1959 to run the "pot palace," as he called the decorative art department's basement ceramics studio, clay sculpture moved to the forefront of the Bay Area's art scene in the sixties and seventies. During this period, di Rosa bought pieces by many talented emerging artists who chose to work with this material, including David Best and Robert Brady as well as Richard Shaw, Ron Nagle, and Jim Melchert, who would themselves go on to become influential teachers at Bay Area schools.

Wiley had come to San Francisco in 1960 from Richland, Washington, to study at the San Francisco Art Institute. Di Rosa remembers that on their first meeting, at Melchert's house, Wiley was wearing the aforementioned aviator's outfit. Although Wiley's early student works were Abstract Expressionist canvases thick with gesturally applied paint, he was adding objects to his paintings by 1962. He soon began to incorporate text as well, and by the end of the decade he was making freestanding sculptural objects out of increasingly rustic-looking materials. It was because of his relaxed attitude (compared to the Abstract Expressionists' total-commitment-to-art seriousness) and his incorporation of chance and accident into his work that critic Hilton Kramer dubbed Wiley's style "Dude Ranch Dada."

While di Rosa was getting to know the faculty and students at UC Davis, he was still visiting galleries in San Francisco. As an early member of the Society for the Encouragement of Contemporary Art (SECA) at the San Francisco Museum of Modern Art, he was involved in bringing unknown but

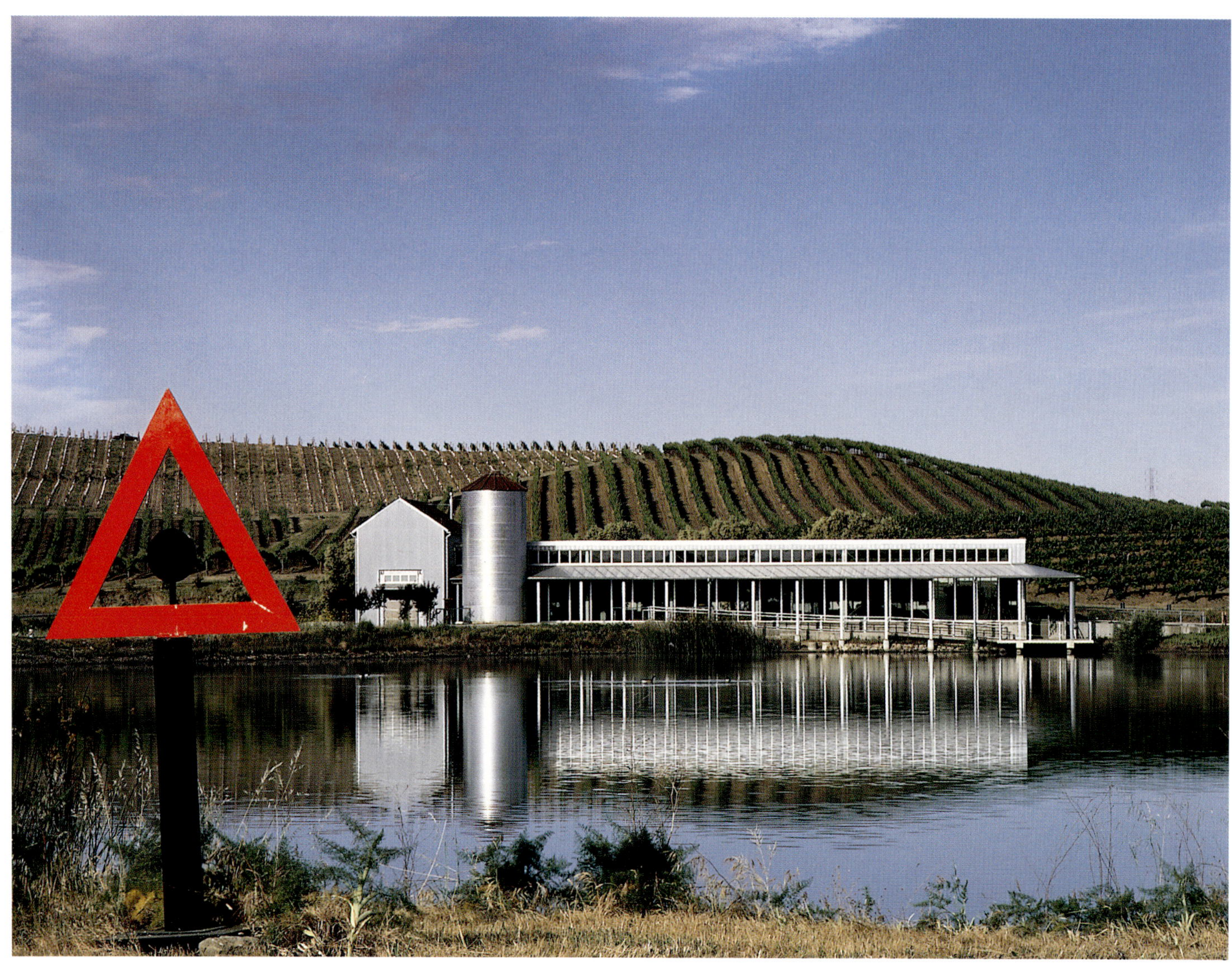

deserving artists into the public eye through exhibitions and awards. He made many studio visits, often buying directly from the artists themselves. He knew faculty and students at the San Francisco Art Institute, having seen the work of some in shows at Wanda Hansen's first gallery on Tillman Place. At one time or another, Hansen represented many of the artists whose work is in the collection, including Wiley, Melchert, Arneson, Joan Brown, and Robert Hudson.

Though he carried on lifelong friendships with some of these painters and sculptors that began back in the early sixties, di Rosa usually met artists only after seeing their work. From the beginning, art was what drew him to these individuals—art, and the belief that he was encouraging their unacknowledged potential. The thoroughness with which he collected some of these artists' work (seventy-six works by Wiley, seventy-two by Best, and thirty-eight by Arneson, to name just three) is testament to the tenaciousness of his affection. At the same time, however, he has continued to add works from every new generation of emerging artists.

## V. "GIVE ME WHAT I SAY I WANT: COLOR, THE HUMAN FIGURE, A TOUCH OF WHIMSY . . ."

Over the years, a certain set of terms has come to be used to describe the Preserve's collection. Words like vibrant, colorful, humorous, and figurative are prominent on this list. In actuality, there are quite a number of nonrepresentational works, both paintings and sculpture, but di Rosa has never been attracted to the cool, minimal school of abstraction. Works like *Elk #4* (p. 31)—Gary Amerigian's brash, almost comical accumulation of giant "brush strokes" of vivid color—fit in perfectly, as do Tony Ligamari's lively, semiabstract compositions of geometric shapes. There is also a substantial amount of conceptually based work. With little exception, however, these pieces embody more than mere ideas. They are as good-looking—and, often, as funny—as they are cerebral.

On closer examination, the humor displayed in many of the works in the collection—whatever their medium—is confrontational, to say the least. In some cases, the political, religious, or sexual subject matter of a number of pieces makes them as challenging as they are attractive. There are numerous skeletons, including one locked in a lascivious kiss; crucified and Last Supper-eating Christs; pictures of Ku Klux Klansmen, homophobes, and a white supremacist. Enrique Chagoya's powerful charcoal drawing *When Paradise Arrived* shows a tiny Indian girl about to be flicked out of the picture by an immense Mickey Mouse-gloved hand labeled "English only" (p. 71), and Judy Dater's feminist photograph of *Ms. Clingfree* portrays the artist herself ironically costumed as a French maid, encumbered by armfuls of cleaning tools and supplies (p. 85). Surprisingly, the impetus behind the inclusion of works with this kind of content seems to be a practical, informal spirituality—a belief in the magic of art and the transformative experience that only it can provide. At times, both Wiley and Best have used the persona of the shaman in their work, and Wiley's *Mr. Unnatural* is surely the wise fool of Eastern philosophy. Certain symbols appear over and over among these works: ladders, for instance—representing the passage from one plane to another, from one mode of being to another—and birds—the messengers, supposedly, of spiritual experience—are everywhere (even outside the buildings, where forty peacocks have the run of the grounds).

Despite the presence of so many religious images and objects, there is nothing particularly sanctified or churchlike about the experience of visiting the Preserve. From the parking lot, a long ramp leads up to a large but wholly unpretentious steel building. Entering through its enormous doors, visitors are greeted by an eclectic assortment of pieces: Jim Barsness's immense transparent drawing of a head (p. 45), a polychromed wooden figure by Jeremy Anderson (p. 32), another large head drawn in charcoal by Christopher Brown (p. 59), Beth Hird's maelstrom of paint and PVC pipe on canvas—and a twenty-eight-foot column of boxes reaching up toward the building's metal-girder ceiling. The word "BLAH," printed in large blue letters on each box, reminds us (somewhat sardonically) of the way in which art, like almost everything else, is in danger of becoming nothing more than a brand-name commodity. This one-word text, repeated in a cascade of rising (or falling) syllables—"BLAH, BLAH, BLAH, BLAH, BLAH"—also takes a humorous poke at all the high-falutin jargon that can stand between museum visitors and their experiences of contemporary art. Stepping past the

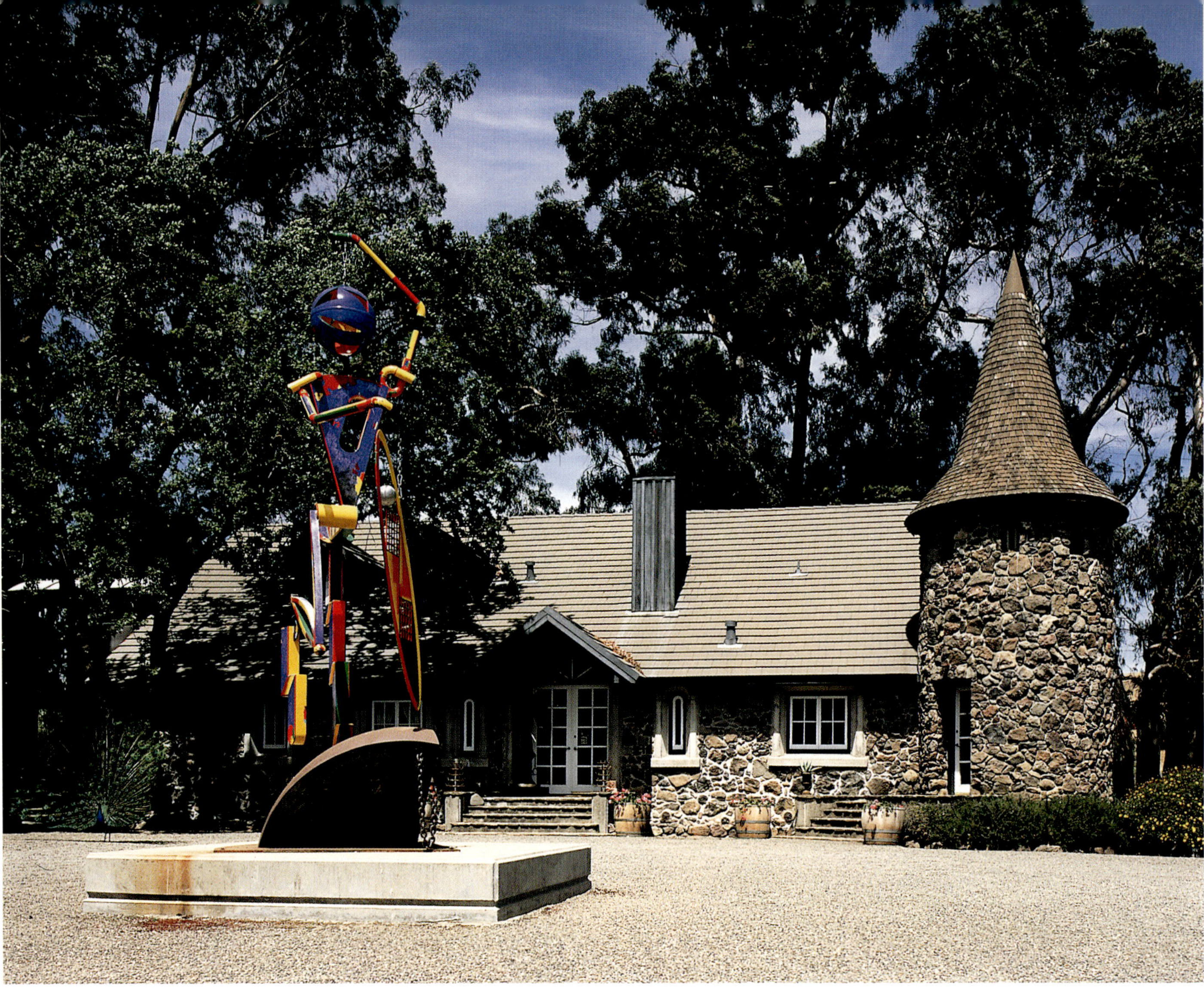

box tower, it becomes clear that there will be no such excess of excruciatingly explanatory language here. In fact, there are no labels anywhere—either in this building, in the main gallery, or in the old stone winery where di Rosa lived for thirty-five years. To find out the name of a particular artist or the title of a piece, one must consult a list that has been placed discreetly in each building.

The absence of any didactic panels or label text causes consternation for some as they begin their tour. Soon, however, the exhilaration of truly participating in the process of interpretation takes over. Freed from the need to anxiously approach each piece to read its pedigree, visitors can stand back and see the relationship between works that may not, at first glance, seem to be from the same metaphorical gene pool. Not knowing what came first, or who influenced whom, allows a process of free association that accomplishes one of di Rosa's most cherished goals. Viewed in this way, the collection embodies a "divinely regional" cohesiveness that goes beyond shared characteristics or materials.

Everywhere, works by artists just beginning their careers hang by those of the Bay Area's current Old Masters. In the gatehouse, Salo Rawet's bow strung with barbed wire from 1992 is a perfect foil for a collaborative drawing called *Indian History Repair* by William T. Wiley and Bill Allan from nearly twenty-five years earlier. In the main gallery building, works by Ray Beldner and Nayland Blake—both in their thirties—hang near those of Paul Kos and Tom Marioni, members of the founding generation of Bay Area Conceptualism. There are startling discoveries, including several large, flamboyant pieces of sculpture by painter Roy De Forest. Large three-dimensional works by this artist such as *One Life to Lead* (p. 88) can be seen only at the Preserve, since it owns virtually *all* of them. In a small room in the lower level of the house, several atypical "stump the experts" works hang together—a cheery floral sketch by Bruce Conner, for example, and a landscape painting by sculptor Fletcher Benton. Throughout the galleries, in fact, surprising early works by now-recognized artists can be found, like Deborah Oropallo's

*Untitled (Fox and Skeleton)* (p. 149). And, as if to confound any expectations visitors may have formed, there *is* a chapel, hidden deep inside the hill below the house itself. Entering through a mysterious doorway set into the slope just behind the main gallery, visitors walk through a tunnel into a narrow room with a high vaulted ceiling. Rows of chairs face what appears to be a tall stained-glass window. This remarkable work by Paul Kos is, in fact, twenty-seven TV monitors, turned on their sides, arranged in three tall stacks. Each one shows a twelve-minute tape loop of a single panel of a famous window at Chartres Cathedral, compressing twelve hours of daylight (p. 124).

Other works by Kos line the stairs to the lower level of the house. There, at one side of a large area crowded with sculptures and paintings, a small room seems to have been di Rosa's office in his grape-farming days. Its walls are covered with memorabilia and photographs, including the honorary degree he received from the San Francisco Art Institute in 1997. A desk in the middle of the floor, empty save for a lamp and a coffee cup, seems as if it, too, must be left over from the past. When approached, however, the desk reveals itself to be yet another work of art, as water pours furiously out of the lamp's glass shade and bubbles up out of the cup. Di Rosa's deliberate placement of Ray Beldner's *Water Table* (pp. 46–47) in a context where visitors can discover its true identity for themselves demonstrates a kind of generosity, mixed with the glee of a born practical joker.

Upstairs, the house—as it was when lived in—is filled almost to the bursting point. Paintings, drawings, photographs, and prints cover every available surface, including the cathedral-style ceiling of the main room. The painting that hangs over the fireplace says a great deal about this place and the objects and images crowding around it. This work by Robert Arneson shows di Rosa, holding an improbably enormous grape, flanked by his old friends Hudson, Wiley, and Arneson himself. Like the dozens of pieces that surround it, this painting of old friends *is* an old friend: a cherished keepsake of an astonishingly creative era.

Many additional outdoor works have been installed over the fifty-three acres that comprise the Preserve. In a grassy field behind the house, Oakland native Mildred Howard's bottle house, titled *Memory Garden, Phase I* (pp. 110–111), stands near works by Alan Shepp and Ray Beldner. A red-painted steel construction on a hilltop nearby is *For Veronica,* by Mark di Suvero (p. 97), who still maintains a sculpture yard in nearby Sonoma County. In front of the house, near the edge of Winery Lake, Viola Frey's immense ceramic figures stand and recline near William T. Wiley's fantastic ten-foot-tall steel harp. Out in the lake, there are more pieces: Veronica di Rosa's cow (cover), seemingly walking on water, and a floating piece by Paul Kos.

As of this writing, most of the collection is on view. Di Rosa's newest acquisitions, from the recent MFA show at Mills College, are already installed in the gatehouse. Ted Troxel's sheep, made principally from sofa-cushion foam, stands before the big bank of windows—equidistant (in more ways than one) from Deborah Butterfield's mud horse (p. 67) and one of David Best's magnificently collaged cars. Near the entrance, David Blott's *Man with Child* shows a delicate baby (an unnervingly lifelike French doll) swaddled in white, supported by a large brown clay hand emerging from a chaotic-looking pile of the same material. These "divinely regional" works have already been placed where visitors can see them and share in Rene di Rosa's affectionate enjoyment of them as part of the collection's magnificent whole.

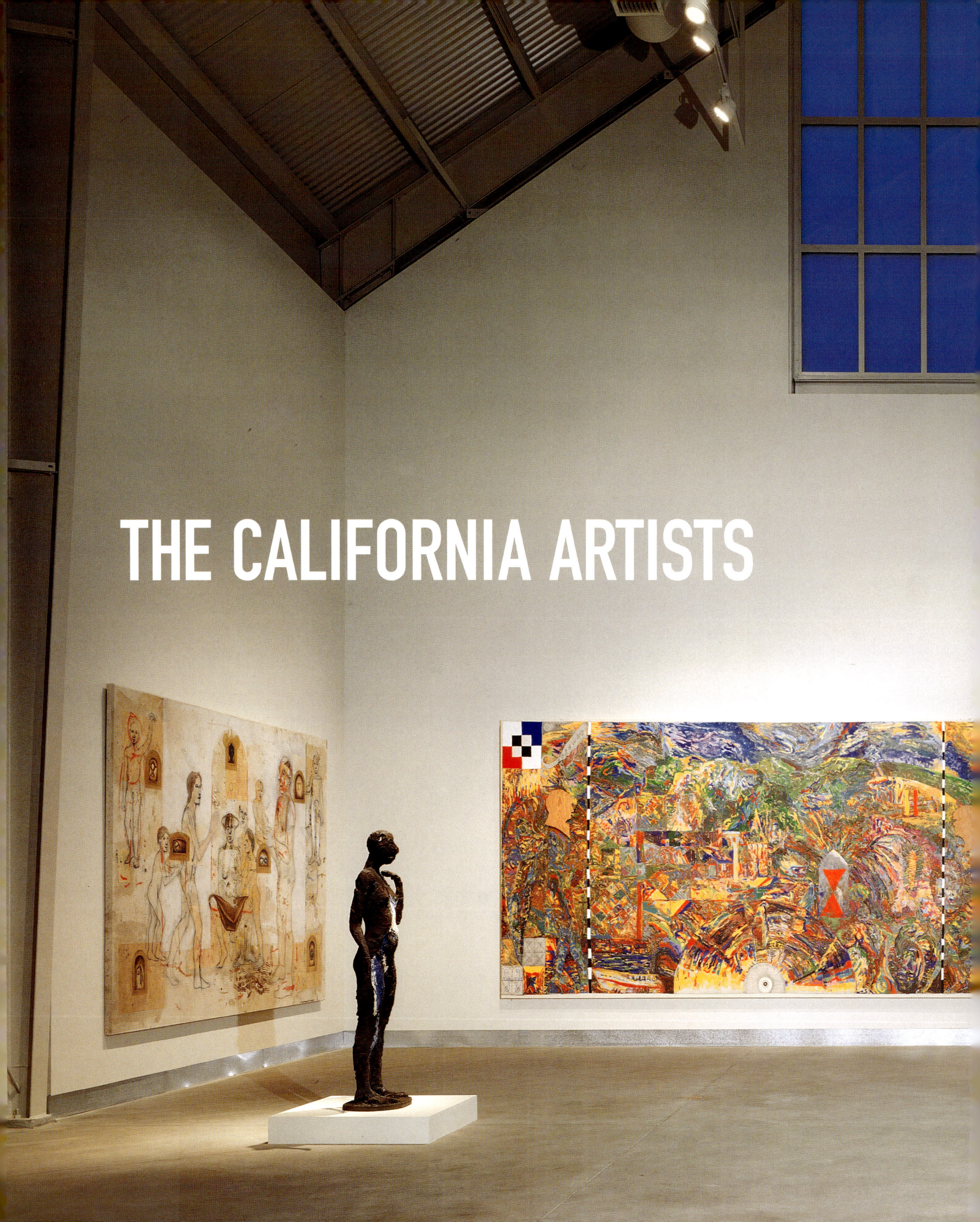

# THE CALIFORNIA ARTISTS

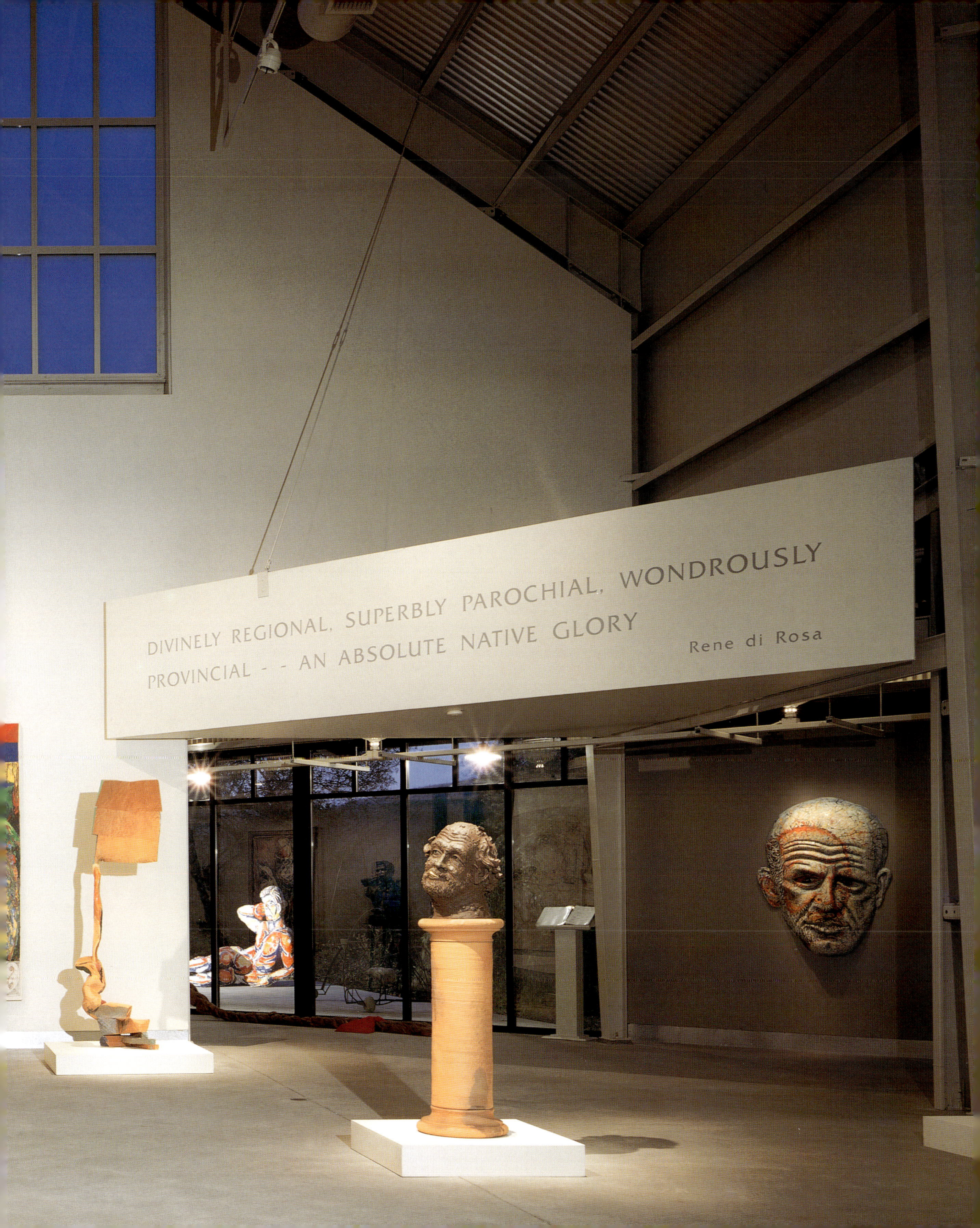
DIVINELY REGIONAL, SUPERBLY PAROCHIAL, WONDROUSLY
PROVINCIAL - - AN ABSOLUTE NATIVE GLORY
Rene di Rosa

# WILLIAM ALLAN

## *Tentative Assault on Mt. Fear*

1971. ACRYLIC ON CANVAS. 74 × 111½

Whatever the formidable artist William Allan presents, he seduces viewers into deeply pondering his poems for the eyes—his mysteries. The prudent recall, however, his statement "I don't want to know anything for sure."[1]

In the 1970s Allan began practicing magical realism in his "story paintings," which featured detailed objects floating absurdly on illusionistic landscapes. He also initiated a number of autobiographical "transient poet" paintings; made lyrically beautiful, realistic watercolors of fish (for Allan, fishing rivals painting as a passion); and painted canvases of skies and waters.

Allan was born in Everett, Washington, in 1936. Along with his friends William T. Wiley and Robert Hudson, he acquired an appreciation of Native American culture through his high school art teacher, Jim McGrath, in Richland, Washington. He graduated from the San Francisco Art Institute in 1958 and helped define Funk in the 1960s, made films with Bruce Nauman, and created Constructions, or narrative boxes. He taught for many years at California State University, Sacramento.

*[*Tentative Assault on Mt. Fear *is about] how to behave. [The jackknife is] for protection, something you send out ahead of you. Before you're ready to climb the mountain, you make a few tries, to get over the dangerous part of it. This painting is about the killer part and the beautiful place, both of which are mixed up. I've thought about how I could justify all the fish I've killed in my life, and also about the fact that I've used the fish as a weapon more than I've used the knife. Most hunters are usually killers, but they're the only people who know what's out there. This is a painting about how to tap the killers, to make them poets.*[2]

1. MARCIA TUCKER, WILLIAM ALLAN, WHITNEY MUSEUM OF AMERICAN ART, NEW YORK, JANUARY 17–FEBRUARY 17, 1974, EXHIBITION BROCHURE, P. 2.

2. IBID., P. 3.

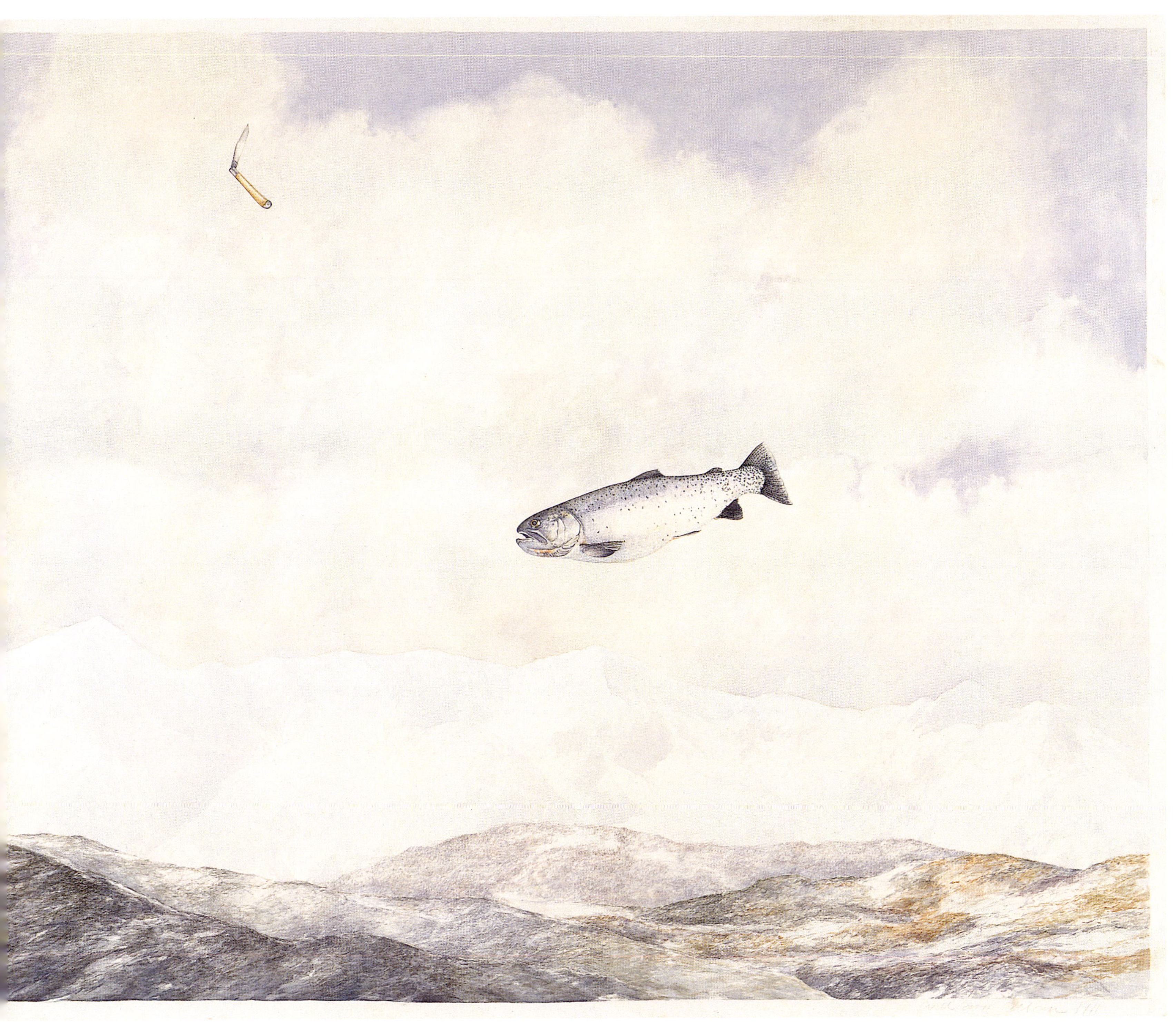

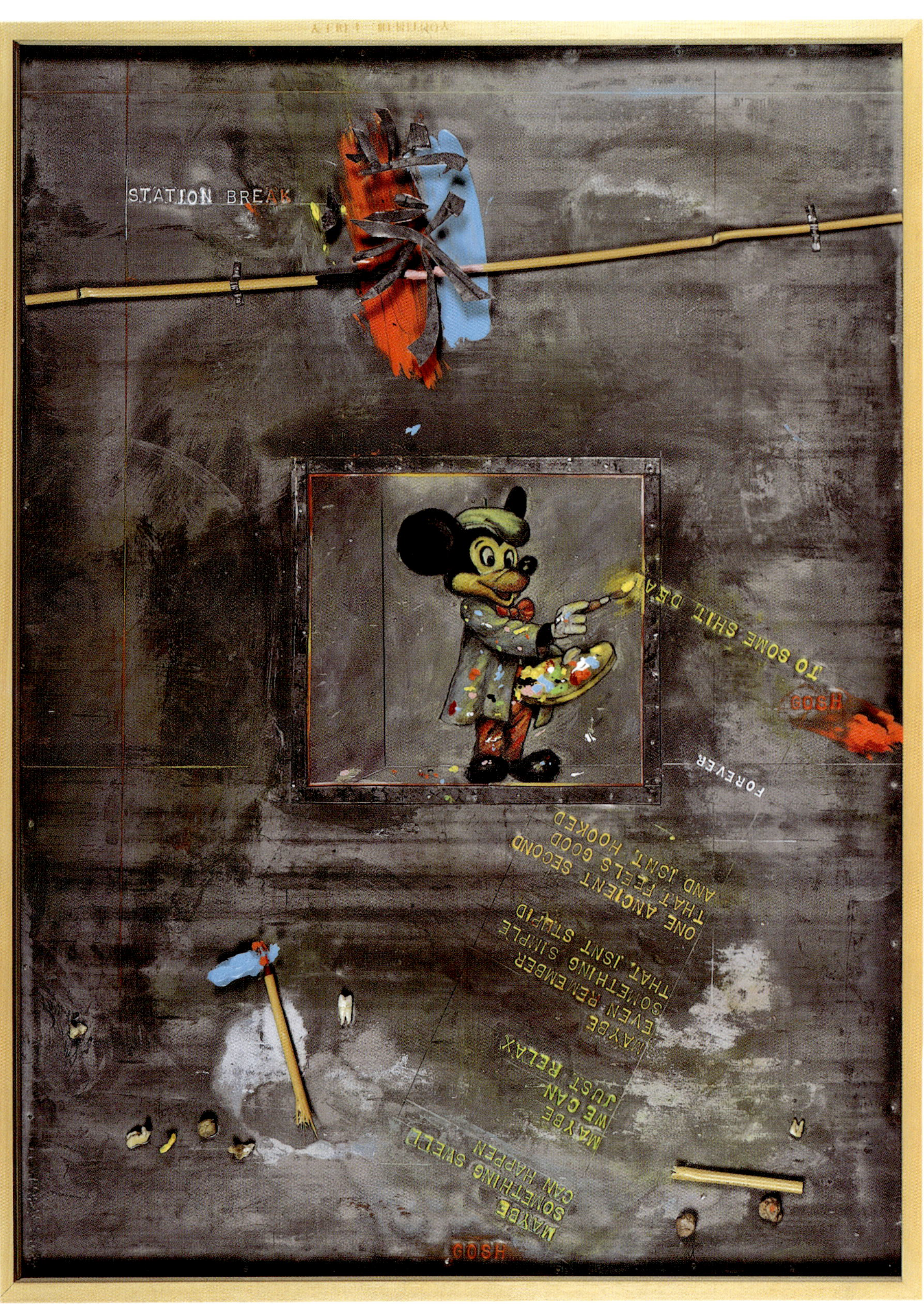


*Station Break*

1986, MIXED MEDIA ON LEAD, 30⅝ × 23

# TERRY ALLEN

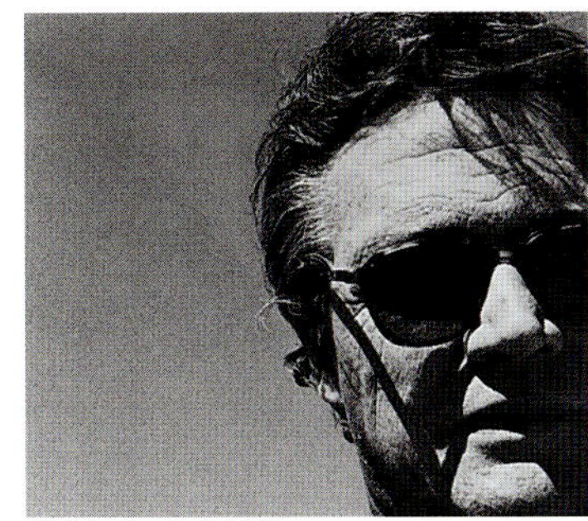

***Shoe***

1991, BRONZE, 32 × 20 × 17

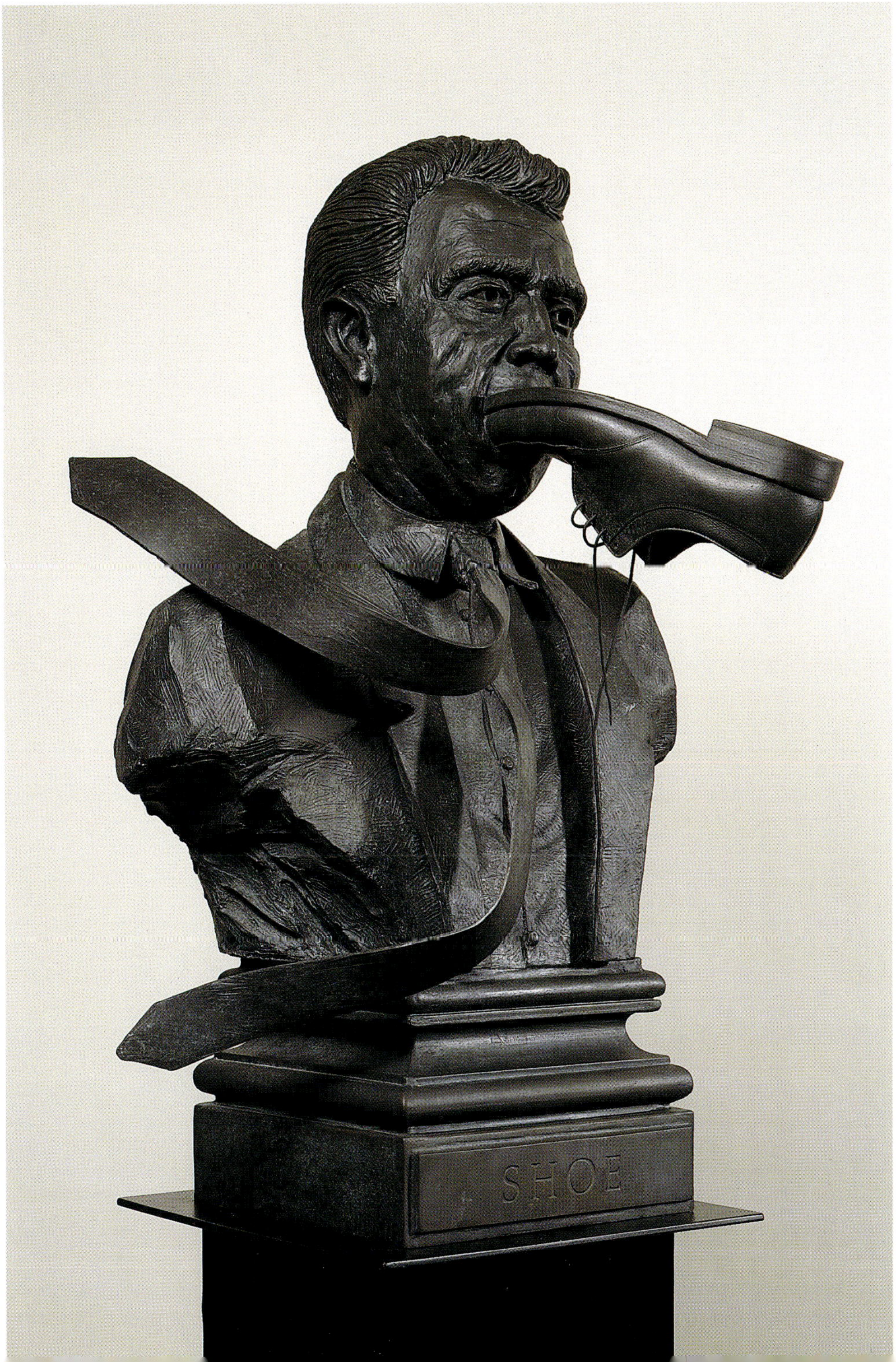

With exceptional versatility, Terry Allen lances the lies we agree upon as our history. In drawings, collages, sculptures, records, videos, assemblages, texts, environments, songs, theatrical works, and performances, he discloses What Is.

Using components appropriated from life, Allen strives for a total engagement of viewers. Working in series, he uses his multimedia pieces as if they were incidents in life to confront his audience. What people accept in life may alienate them in his art, Allen feels—a paradox he considers to be a revelation of their dis-ease with life. Humor appears regularly in his work, but tragedy does not, because he perceives no tragedy in life. Recently he has turned to bronze, a medium laden with historical references, to make ironic statements about contemporary quandaries.

Born in 1943, Allen grew up in Lubbock, Texas, whose culture greatly influenced him. In 1966 he graduated from Chouinard Art Institute in Los Angeles. After teaching for many years at California State University, Fresno, he moved with spouse Jo Harvey Allen, a playwright, actress, and performance artist, to Santa Fe, New Mexico.

Station Break *is part of the* Youth in Asia *series about the aftermath of the Vietnam War—about betrayal. How a country betrays its youth . . . and how programmed they are to be betrayed.*

Shoe *came out of* Corporate Head, *a life-size bronze of a businessman holding a briefcase and bent over with his head stuck in a building's façade. This man on a pedestal has a shoe in his mouth. After the fact of the foot. Or in advance of it. "If the shoe fits, wear it."*

*Our little mirror.*

# GARY AMERIGIAN *Elk #4*

1996. OIL AND MIXED MEDIA ON BOARD. 50 × 50 × 8

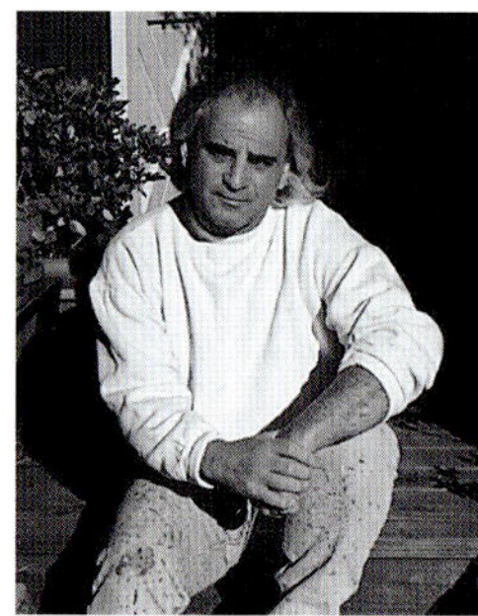

Gary Amerigian labors diligently over his enigmatic "sculpted paintings." But it is the energy of improvisation and the sense of mystical engagement they convey, not the discipline of their fashioning, that compel attention. The artist's definition is an enigma. Having three dimensions (from two to twelve inches in depth), the works could be painted sculptures or sculptural paintings. Are their forms abstractions or immense, illusionistic brush strokes? Such questions puzzle viewers, but they do not detract from the impressiveness of the works. They are what they are.

While improvising his marks, Amerigian simultaneously imagines their colors. Invariably he listens to music—classical, standards, jazz, rock. "Good music is good music. It has the rhythm of the heart," he says.[1] Slowly, consistently, he produces six to twelve paintings per year.

Amerigian was born in Fresno in 1943 and received his BA from California State University, Fresno, in 1968.

*Painting is about the mark. I realized this when I was painting Turneresque landscapes and trying to connect with nature. I felt I was failing, when it struck me that the mark is the means for transposing nature into art. It was totally spontaneous, the revelation that color is everything, the mark is everything. Where the marks meet there is energy, there is a world.*

Elk #4 *[named for the beautiful area of Elk, California] is part of a continuing series of sculpted paintings inspired by the beauty of nature. It consists of spontaneous marks of color coming together to express the nature of pigment. The mark is the painting.*

1. INTERVIEW WITH ROBERT MCDONALD, JUNE 26, 1998.

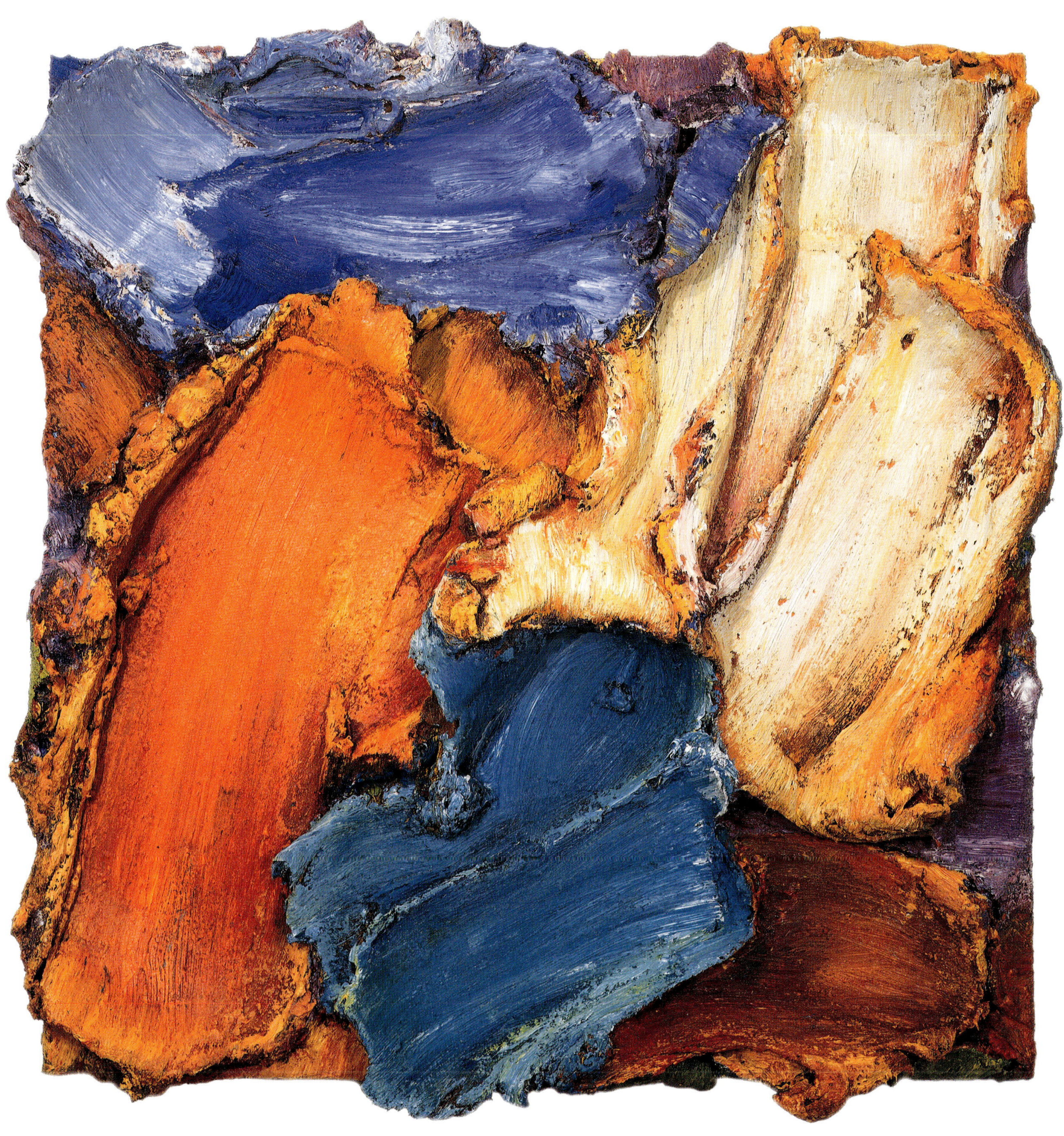

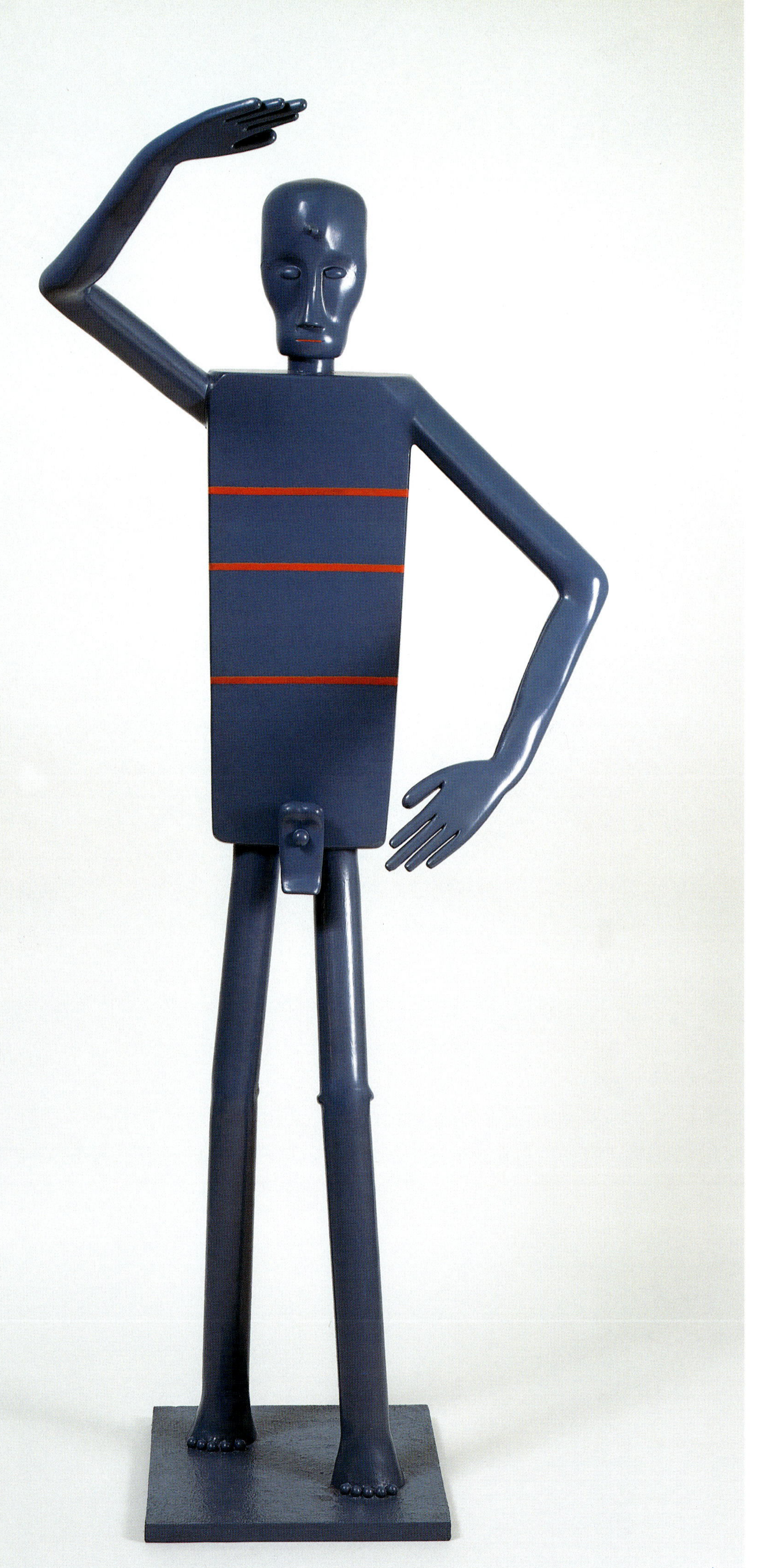

# JEREMY ANDERSON

***Wizard of the North***

1975, REDWOOD AND PAINT, 89 × 36 × 35

Jeremy Anderson played a pivotal role in advancing San Francisco Bay Area sculpture beyond modernism.

Born in 1921 in Palo Alto, California, where his father was a professor of Romance languages at Stanford University, Anderson experienced an erratic education until his instruction at the San Francisco Art Institute (SFAI) from 1946 to 1950, following military service. Surrealism strongly influenced him through sculpture instructor Robert Howard. The megalithic dolmens of Carnac in Brittany, where he traveled on a fellowship in 1950, inspired him with an enduring reverence for the mythical and the mystical. He worked in construction (another influence on his work) to support his family until SFAI hired him in 1958. There his students included William T. Wiley, Robert Hudson, and Richard Shaw. He was an initiator of verbal-visual puns and helped define Funk. Although respected for his instruction through example rather than through words, he lost his position in 1974. He taught at the University of California, Davis, for a year and died in 1981.

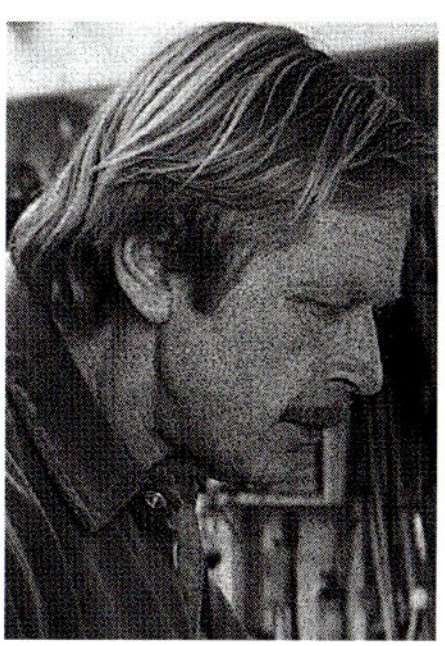

In the 1940s Anderson made primitive forms of magnesite and plaster. He moved on in the 1950s and later to make enigmatic figures, such as the menacing *Wizard of the North,* that were forms and constructions from redwood. He also cast small totems from bronze.

*Sculpture emerges from an endless maze of ideas which it shapes into a new order, a new frame of mind. . . . Taking the world apart is easy; it is getting it back together in an acceptable form that is difficult.*[1]

1. JEREMY ANDERSON, NO DATE.

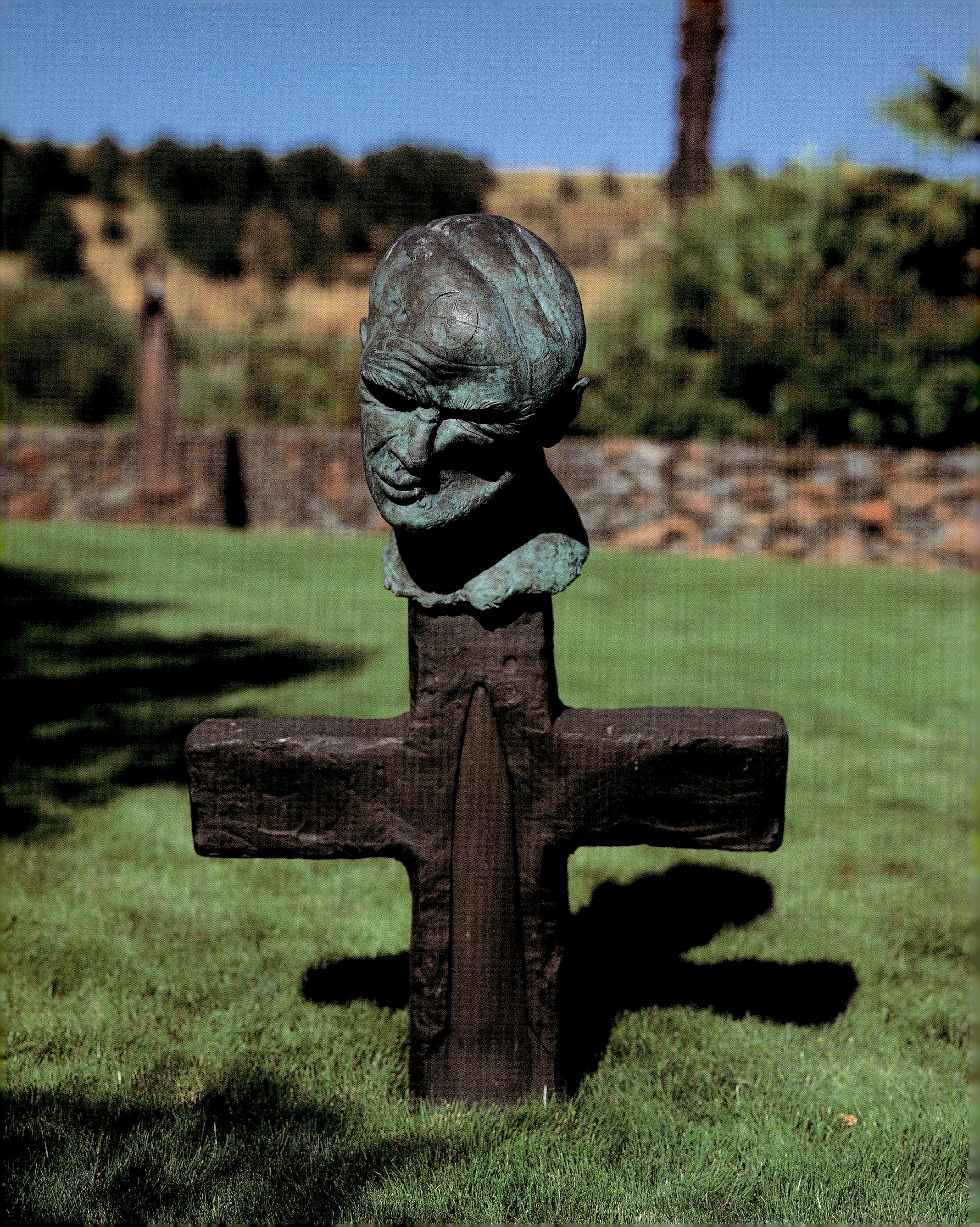

*Minuteman*

1982. BRONZE. 48 × 31 × 15

# ROBERT ARNESON

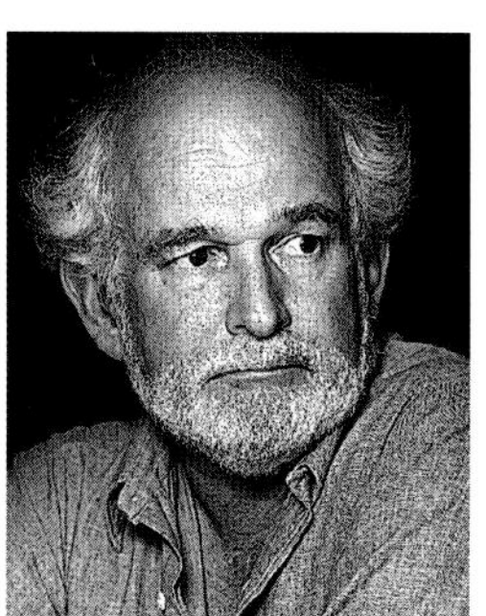

Through his formal innovations and the quality of his work, Robert Arneson advanced the recognition of referential clay sculpture as fine art. He thus complemented and ventured beyond the pioneering efforts of Peter Voulkos, who, in the 1950s at Otis Art Institute in Los Angeles, made expressive clay works that were nonutilitarian, nonobjective, and analogous to action paintings.

Born in 1930 in Benicia, on the Bay delta, Arneson received a BA from the California College of Arts and Crafts in 1954 and an MFA from Mills College in 1958. In 1961, with *No Deposit No Return,* a pot shaped like a beer bottle, he added the imagery of Pop to ceramics, further advancing the idea that objects made in the craft tradition need not be utilitarian. Nevertheless, he maintained some of the elegant tradition of one of his Mills teachers, Anthony Prieto. In pieces such as *Six Pack,* however, Arneson expressed the spirit of Funk in ceramics while demonstrating his penchant for punning—6-Up Pop. His work included imagery such as bathroom fixtures and the home he lived in on Alice Street in Davis; he taught at the University of California, Davis, from 1962 until 1991.

Through art Arneson commented on life, most famously in his 1981 memorial portrait of the assassinated Mayor George Moscone of San Francisco. Having commissioned the piece, the city authorities rejected it because of words and images on the phallic pedestal. In *Minuteman,* part of his *Nuclear Series,* he replaced the traditional helmet with a head. A Minuteman missile appears in relief on the vertical post.

Early in his career, Arneson began creating self-portraits, as in *Balancing Act.* He also made bricks, objectifying his belief in them as the foundation of Western civilization, and bombs, objectifying its destruction. While portraying himself, most recently in bronze in the classical tradition, he commented on all humankind—often with humor, despite knowing that cancer was killing him. His strong drawings and prints enhance the greatness he achieved as a sculptor and as a man.

Arneson died in 1992 in Benicia, where he lived with his wife, artist Sandra Shannonhouse.

## *Six Pack*

1964, GLAZED CERAMIC, 10 × 9¼ × 6½

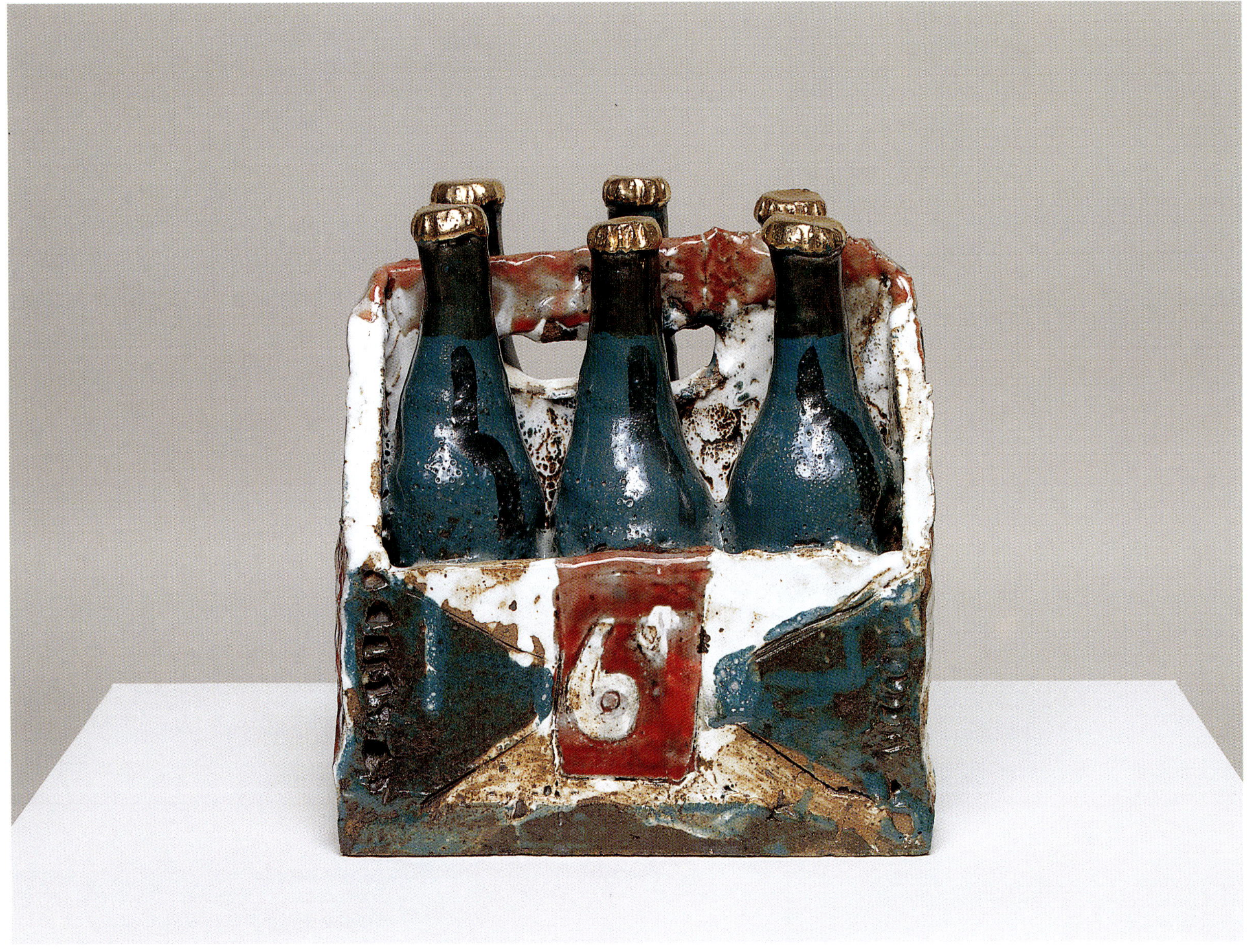

*I've always been a political artist, and I think my work always has something to say. But I never want to be typecast. I don't want to be locked into anything. But I think all the works I'm doing will be more sharply focused than other works. Some will be narrower, some will be broader. All of them will deal with the human condition, and with an imagery that is readable and delves into the American consciousness—that means* my *existence. That's what I mean when I say I'm doing* American *art.*[1]

*You've gotta goof off in art, you gotta play. In any intellectual activity, you've gotta have the space to just play, whether you're a philosopher or writer, just take those dumb risks without anybody being on your* case. *So you don't have to prove anything, but maybe you'll* discover *something.*

*And, as an artist, you have to constantly question yourself and trust yourself. It's okay if part of you is dumb, part of you is smart, part of you is silly, part of you is a great wit, part of you is intellectual—all parts you want to put into the hopper and make a good brew.*[2]

1. KEN KELLEY, "ROBERT ARNESON [INTERVIEW]," SAN FRANCISCO FOCUS 34, NO. 10 (OCTOBER 1987), PP. 50–51.

2. IBID., P. 52.

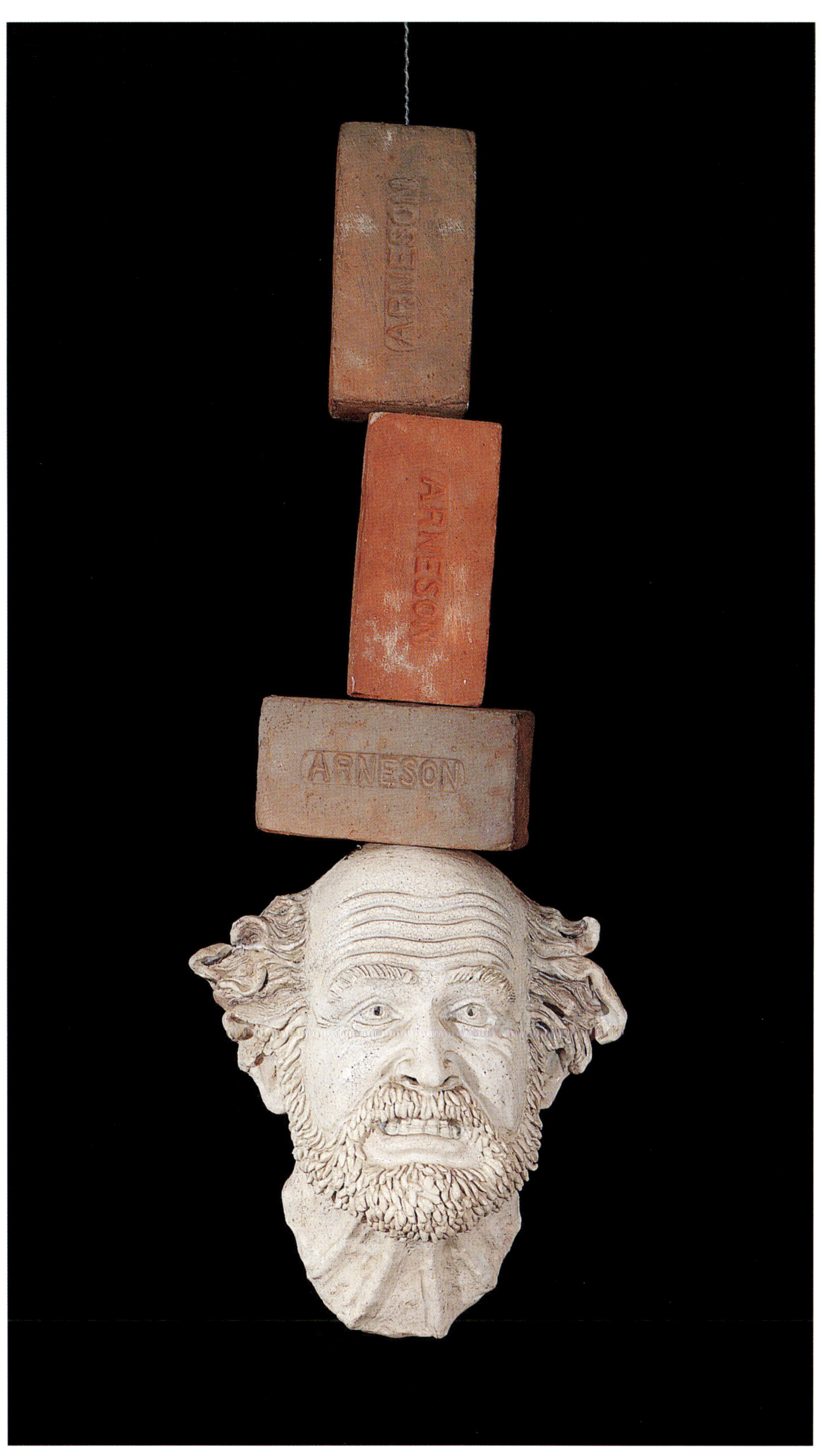


***Balancing Act***

1976, GLAZED AND UNGLAZED CERAMIC, 38 × 14 × 7

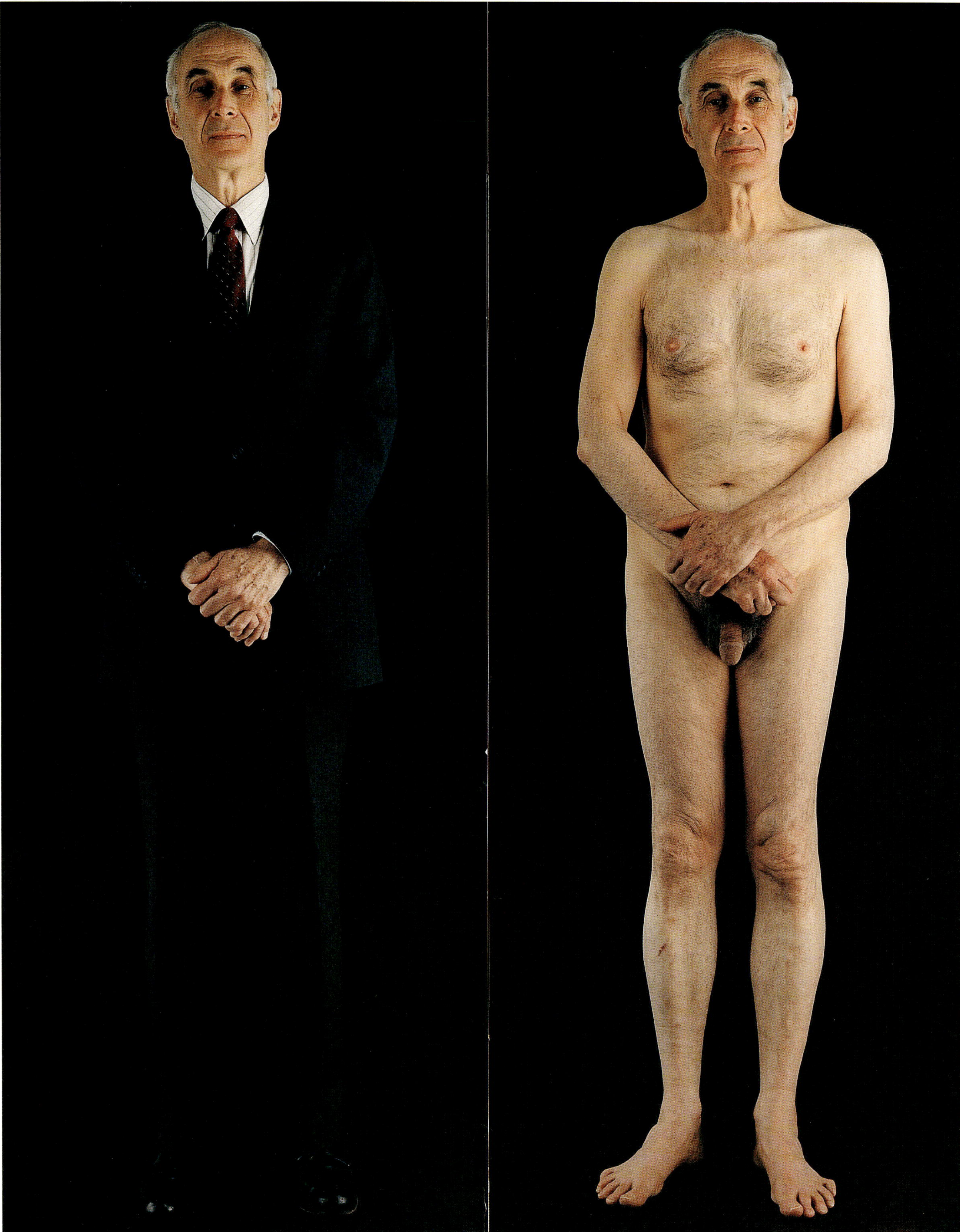

# ANTHONY AZIZ

## *Public Image/Private Sector #4*

1990. TWO EKTACOLOR PRINTS, 72 × 60.
ONE GELATIN-SILVER PRINT, 11 × 8½. ED. OF 3

| | |
|---|---|
| AGE: | 64 |
| HEIGHT: | 6'1" |
| WEIGHT: | 166 |
| FIRM: | Ryder & Lippe, Inc. |
| POSITION: | President and C.E.O. |
| ANNUAL CORPORATE SALES: | $670.3 million |
| NUMBER OF EMPLOYEES: | 9,275 |
| NUMBER OF CHILDREN: | 2 |
| PERSONAL STATEMENT: | "To get ahead in the challenging business climate of the '90s, you have to go that extra mile, creatively set your goals, and then aggressively get the job done. Ryder & Lippe is committed to hunting down and then utilizing the best and brightest talent of America's future." |

Anthony Aziz created *Public Image/Private Sector #4* as part of his MFA thesis at the San Francisco Art Institute in 1990. Each of six diptychs pairs two life-size, frontal, Ektacolor portraits of a white, middle-aged, corporate man: on the left in a business suit and wearing a red "power" tie, on the right in the nude. With ap-

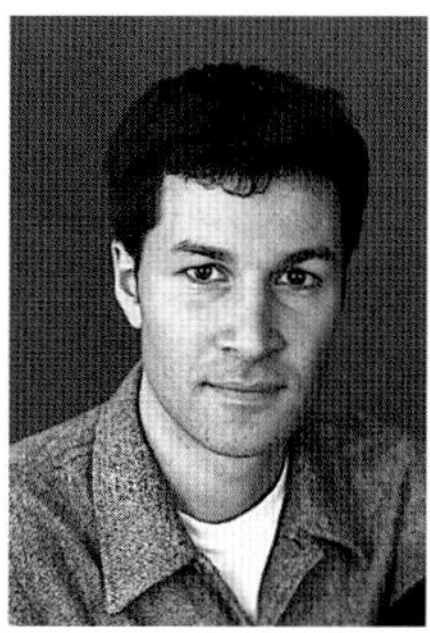

propriate, but fictitious, biographical data accompanying the diptychs, Aziz sought to explore the "masquerade" of masculine identity in North American culture.

The exhibition so impressed fellow MFA candidate Sammy Cucher (from Caracas, Venezuela) that he arranged to meet Aziz. As the creative team Aziz + Cucher, they went on to achieve exceptional success, including being chosen to represent Venezuela in the 1995 Venice Biennale. There they exhibited *The Dystopia Series*, composed of photographic portraits digitally altered to remove facial features so as to suggest the loss of personal identity.

Aziz, of Lebanese and Irish heritage, was born in Lunenberg, Massachusetts, in 1961 and grew up in Boston. Cucher, of Eastern European Jewish ancestry, was born in Lima, Peru, in 1958.

*In 1990 I was concerned primarily with the rhetoric and stylistic conventions of portraiture and the representation of power. In addition, I was interested in how photographic images construct notions of masculinity and identity.*

Public Image/Private Sector, *which includes* Corporate Edge #4, *consists of twelve life size portraits of fictional corporate leaders, both clothed and unclothed, and was inspired by the court paintings of Gainsborough and Goya, as well as by the official images of executives found in corporate annual reports.*

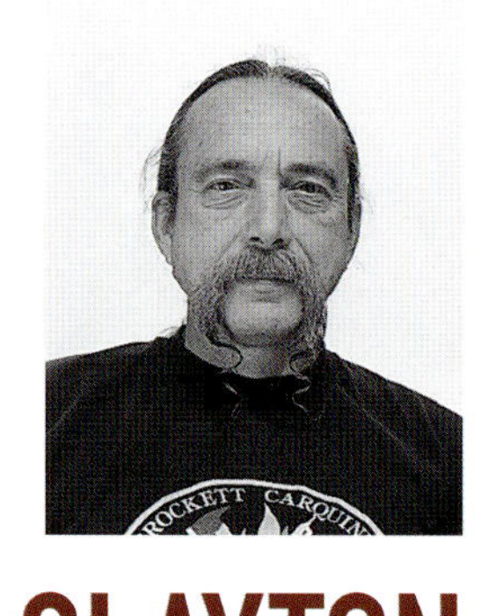

# CLAYTON BAILEY

Clayton Bailey absorbed the influences of Funk and Pop into a unique vision predisposed to satirize society's conventions, especially those concerning art, science, and sex. Most notoriously, in the 1970s he created "Dr. George Gladstone's Wonders of the World Museum" to exhibit fossilized relics from the "Bone Age," actually ceramic sculptures that he had made and, as "Dr. Gladstone," "excavated" and "documented."

Born in Antigo, Wisconsin, in 1939, Bailey earned a BS in 1961 and an MS in 1962 from the University of Wisconsin, Madison. He taught at California State University, Hayward, from 1968 until he retired in 1996.

*I built* Male Chair *to embarrass anyone sitting in it by having male genitalia between their legs. Inspired by Japanese "Haniwa" figures, it was one of a group of salt-glazed creatures and "critters" I made between 1960 and 1963.*

Burping Bowl with Lurching Monster *is a kinetic, hydro-pneumatic object. The creature, periodically lurching up and emitting a loud belching sound, frightens unsuspecting passersby. A thirty- to forty-five-second period between sounds keeps viewers waiting to see what will happen next. The* Burping Bowl *is an alternative to owning a dog or a cat. Owners report that they even have to clean up after them. The* Lurching Monster, *carefully balanced and hinged to the bottom of the bowl, has a hidden flotation chamber that is slowly filled by an aquarium air pump. The air buoys the creature up in the water, and when the trapped air bubble escapes as a belch, the creature sinks to the bottom again. The* Burping Bowl *is an example of "life created from mud."*

***Male Chair***

1963, SALT-GLAZED CERAMIC, 17 × 18 × 18

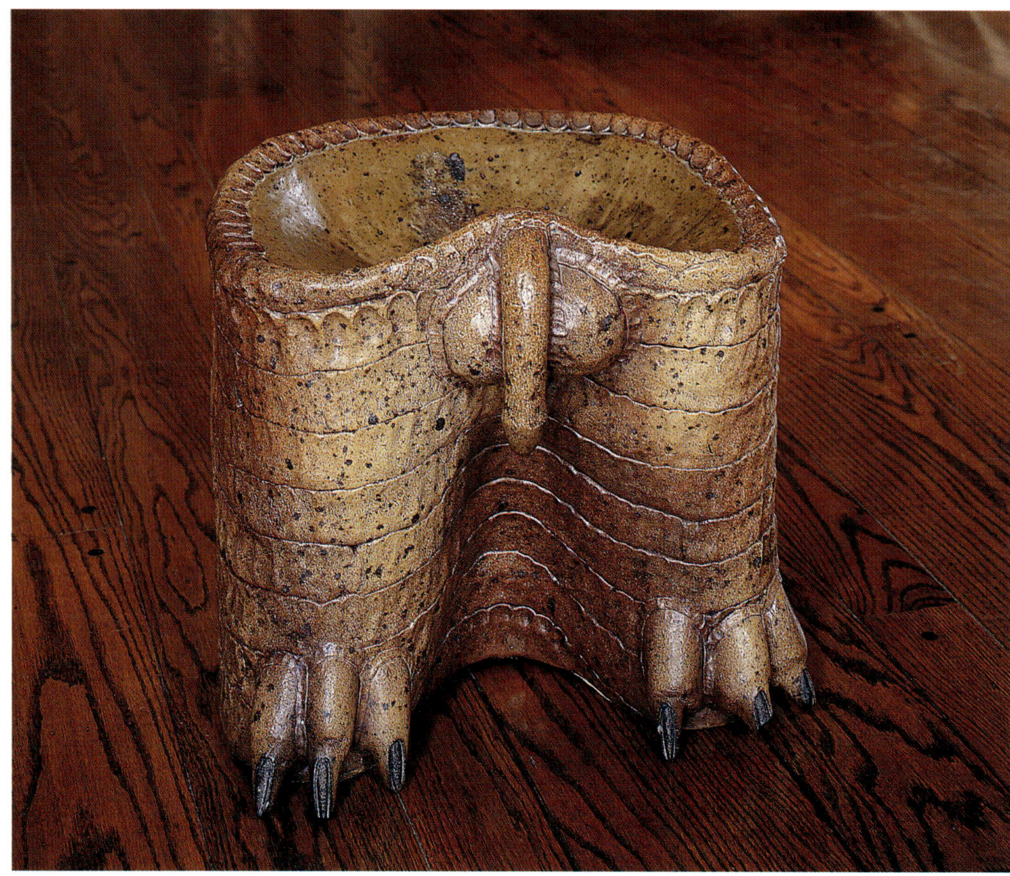

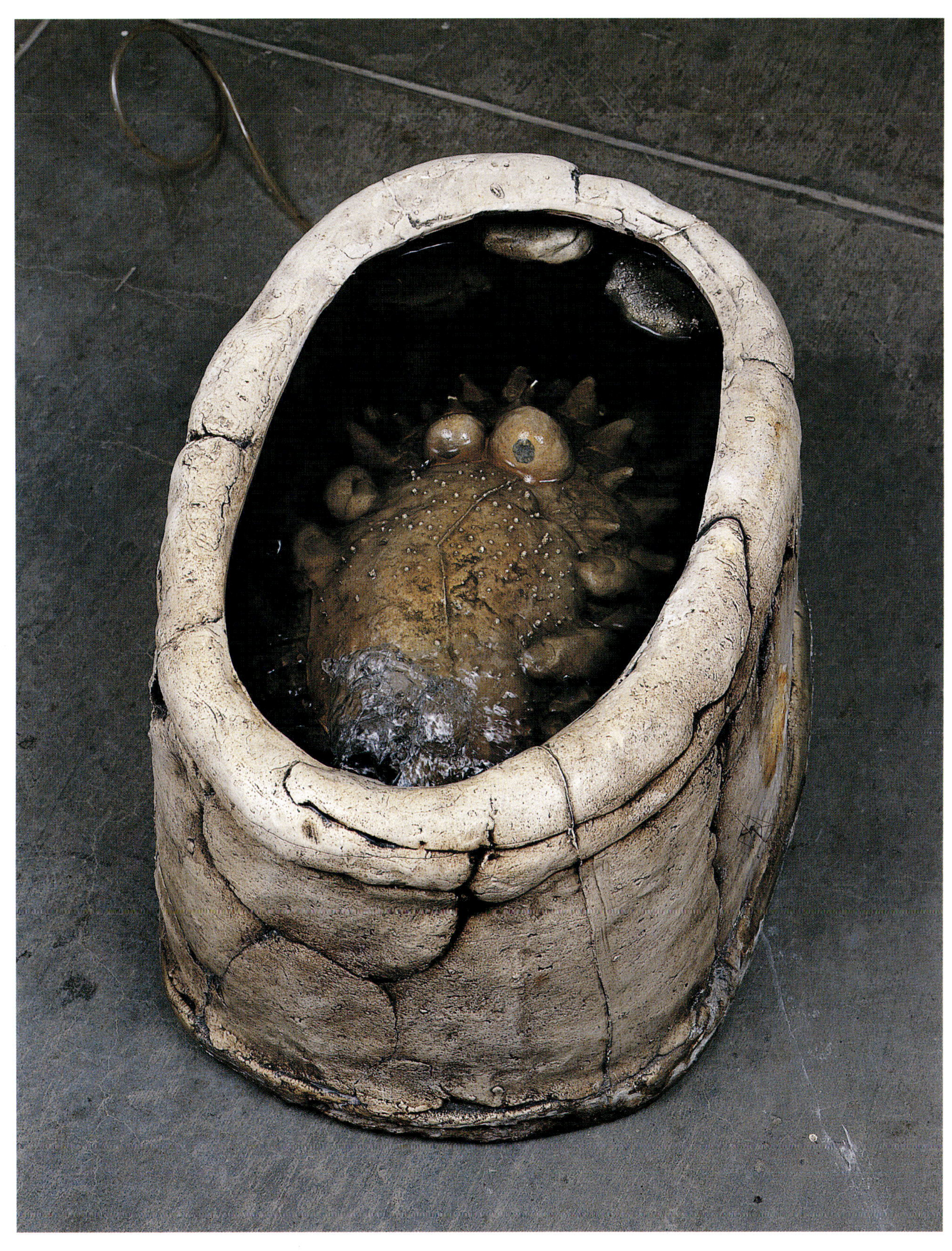

*Burping Bowl with Lurching Monster*

1972, SLIPCAST CERAMIC WITH WATER AND ELECTRIC PUMP, 10 × 12 × 19

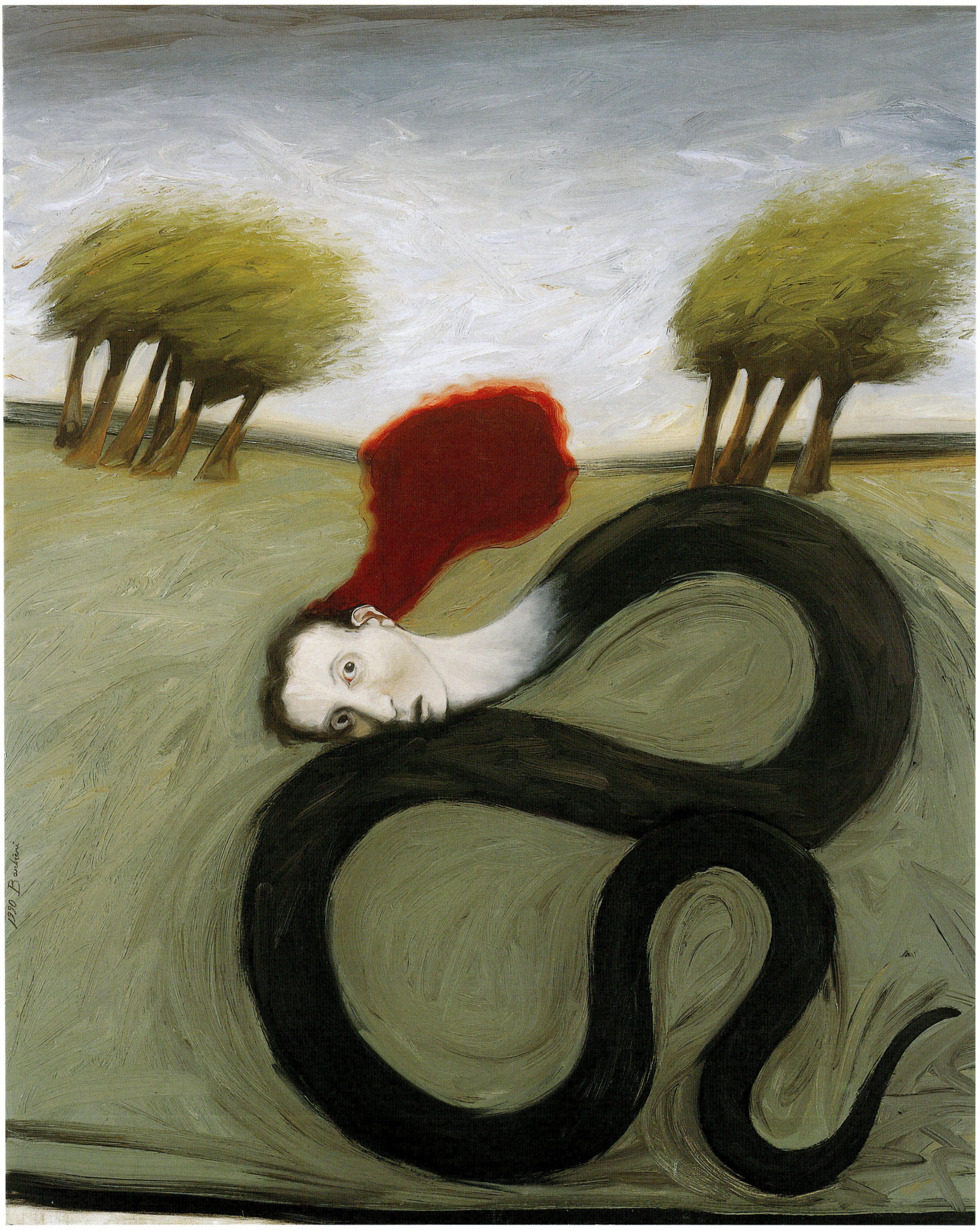
1990 Barbieri

# JONATHAN BARBIERI

## *The Tyranny of Fear*

1990, OIL ON CANVAS, 60 × 50

Jonathan Barbieri was born in Washington, D. C., in 1955. For the years 1977–1978 he was awarded a fellowship for independent study in Guatemala, and in 1978–1979 he studied at the San Francisco Art Institute. He lives with his wife, Lupe, and their two daughters in Etla, Oaxaca, Mexico, and has exhibited in the United States and throughout Mexico.

*When I painted* The Tyranny of Fear, *my wife, Lupe, and I were living in San Francisco's Mission District. Our sagging three-story building was a shopping mall for drugs. But it was home. The aromas of* chorizo, plátano frito, *and* arroz con pescado *recalled lost landscapes, exotic, sunny, dear, and tragic. Food was identity, continuity, an affirmation of human dignity. An act of defiance.*

*Somehow you had to defy the ambulances wailing through your dreams at night, the arson fires, the megaphoned evangelists blasting your mind with hokey-pokey songs about Jesus, the gunshots below your window at two in the morning. You had to defy the fact that the* Barrio *was in your face every minute of every day and every night.*

*Lupe was a social worker organizing support groups for torture victims and refugees whose lives had been shattered by the wars in Central America. Practically everyone I knew through her work had lost someone they loved. Some had found the maimed corpses of friends or family members left in trash dumps or along roadsides.* The Tyranny of Fear *came out of all this.*

*Painting is too big, too deep, to be limited to aesthetic or political doctrine. It belongs to a matrix that extends far beyond the boundaries of an art world fueled by cartoon-sized egos, empty verbiage, and market cynicism. Painting has been part of the evolution of human consciousness since its paleolithic stirrings. Like the food the* señoras *were cooking back then in my building, it reaffirms human dignity. It is an act of defiance.*

# JAMES BARSNESS

## *In Memory of the American Empire*

1990. STABILO PENCIL AND MIXED MEDIA ON COMIC BOOK PAGES MOUNTED ON CANVAS. 94 × 117

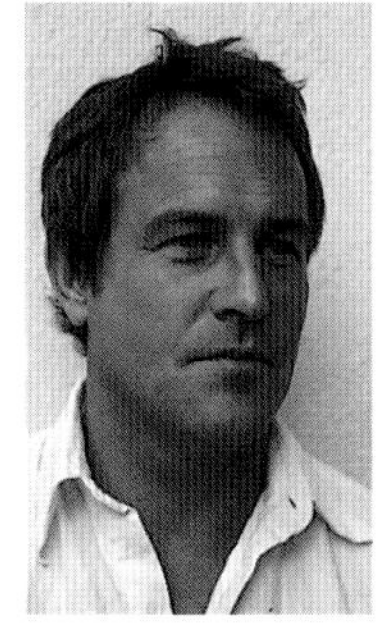

Curators classify James Barsness among Postmodernists and New Traditionalists, meaning he does what he pleases, drawing from *all* traditions, mixing references to Leonardo da Vinci and Hieronymus Bosch with cartoons. He often begins works by doodling with a ballpoint pen.

In the richly suggestive, monumental *In Memory of the American Empire,* Barsness has drawn an immense, androgynous head on a matrix of comics. Promising "I Will Watch While You Sleep," it may represent a society aspiring toward liberty and justice superseded by a society whose highest ambition is entertainment. It may also represent all of Western civilization, symbolized by a combined da Vincian image of Mona Lisa and St. John, superseded by a Boschian hell.

Barsness, born in Bozeman, Montana, in 1954, earned a BA and an MA from Boise State University and, in 1988, an MFA from the San Francisco Art Institute. His wife is artist Didi Dunphy.

*About every three years I succumb to the idea of painting a big head, an idea that I view in general as a bad one. It is in the nature of my work, however, to succumb to bad ideas if they refuse to go away.*

*The big head in* Memory *reminded me of American silver coinage at the turn of the twentieth century, particularly the Liberty dollar and half-dollar, which reminded me of a specifically American kind of generosity of spirit that I grew up assuming to be a fact of life in the 1950s. This attitude, presented most lucidly in fifth-grade social studies class, was that Americans were a tolerant, magnanimous, and mighty people. This seems nowadays to be the most magnificent, simplistic, and brutal geopolitical view imaginable. Still, in making this monument to a bad idea, I wanted to honor the naïve belief that all great things should seem possible.*

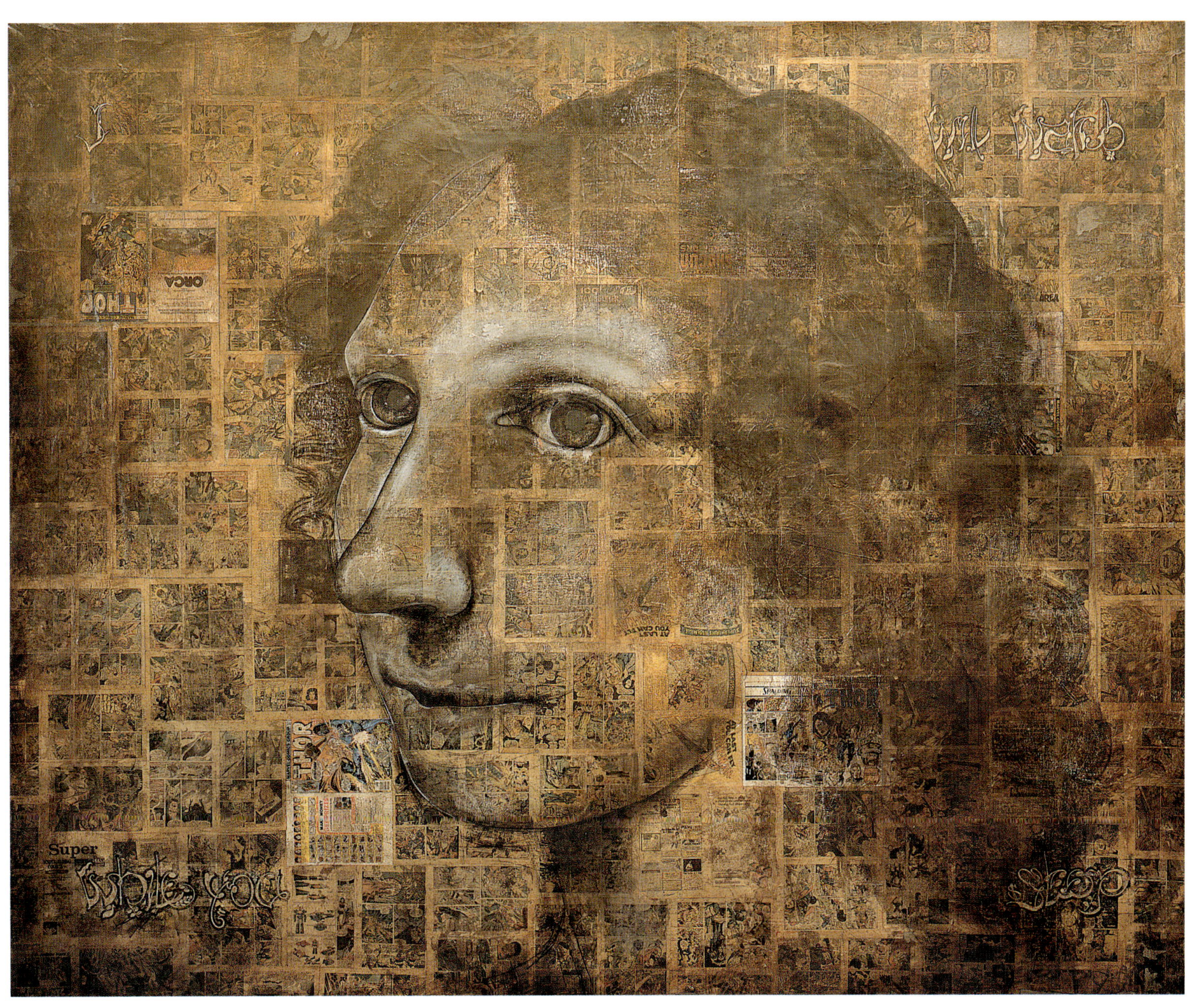
THOR
Super

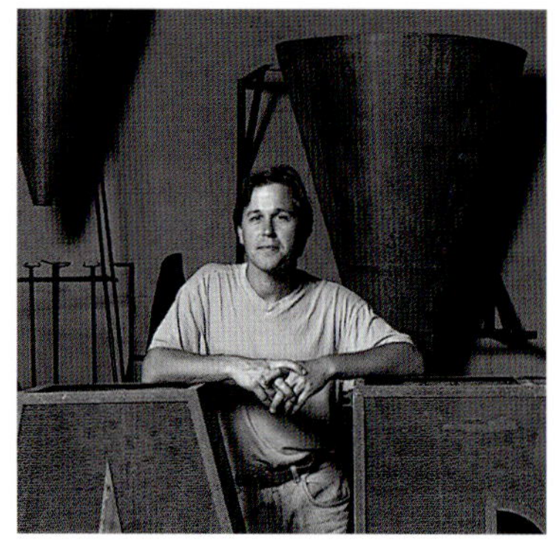

Sculptor and installation artist Ray Beldner was born in San Francisco in 1961. He received a BFA from the San Francisco Art Institute in 1986 and an MFA from Mills College in 1989. He recently completed projects for the cities of San Francisco and Richmond, California, and has taught at the San Francisco Art Institute and the California College of Arts and Crafts.

# RAY BELDNER

***Water Table***

1995, OAK OFFICE DESK, WATER, COPPER PIPING, AND PUMP, 31 × 62 × 36

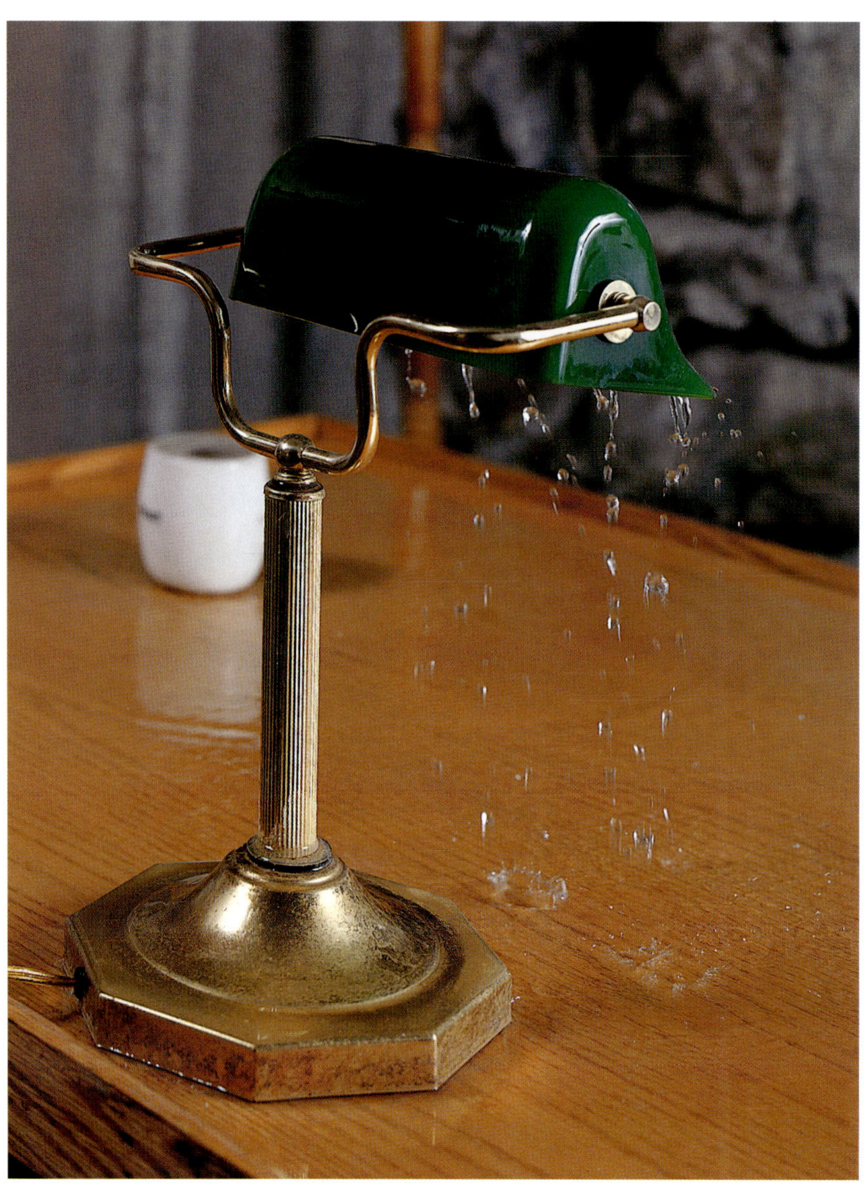

*In exploring issues of landscape—economic, political, personal, and ecological—I use organic and found materials that I combine with video, sound, and movement to investigate the complex relationships between the natural world, human biology, and social systems. My particular interest is in how we alter and consume the landscape (controlling nature by "containing" it), and how we tailor it to mirror our image.*

Water Table, *one of a series of installations entitled* Office Work, *is a commentary about the uneasy relationship between nature and culture. Behind the desk a window frames a landscape. At a visitor's approach, an infrared switch activates a water pump inside the desk. Water flows from the lampshade and bubbles out of the coffee cup, flooding the desktop and collecting in a corner. The water empties into a drain, returning to a hidden catch basin until another visitor activates it and the cycle repeats. Ironically, the flow microcosmically mimics the rise and fall of the hydrologic water table. As a man-made desktop landscape,* Water Table *is a mini-spectacle, both wondrous and sad. It evokes desires it cannot satisfy and recalls an expansiveness it cannot reconstruct.*

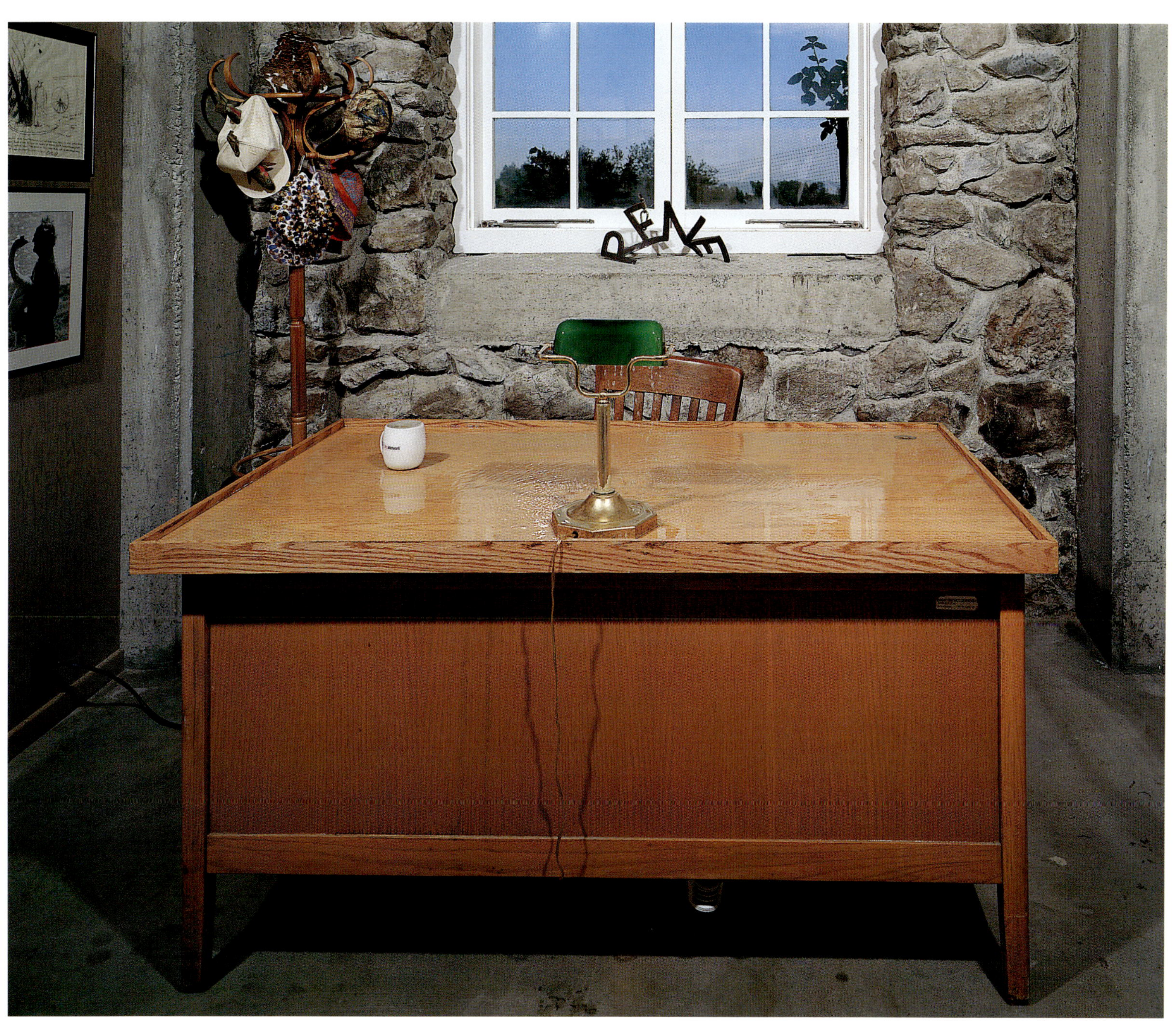

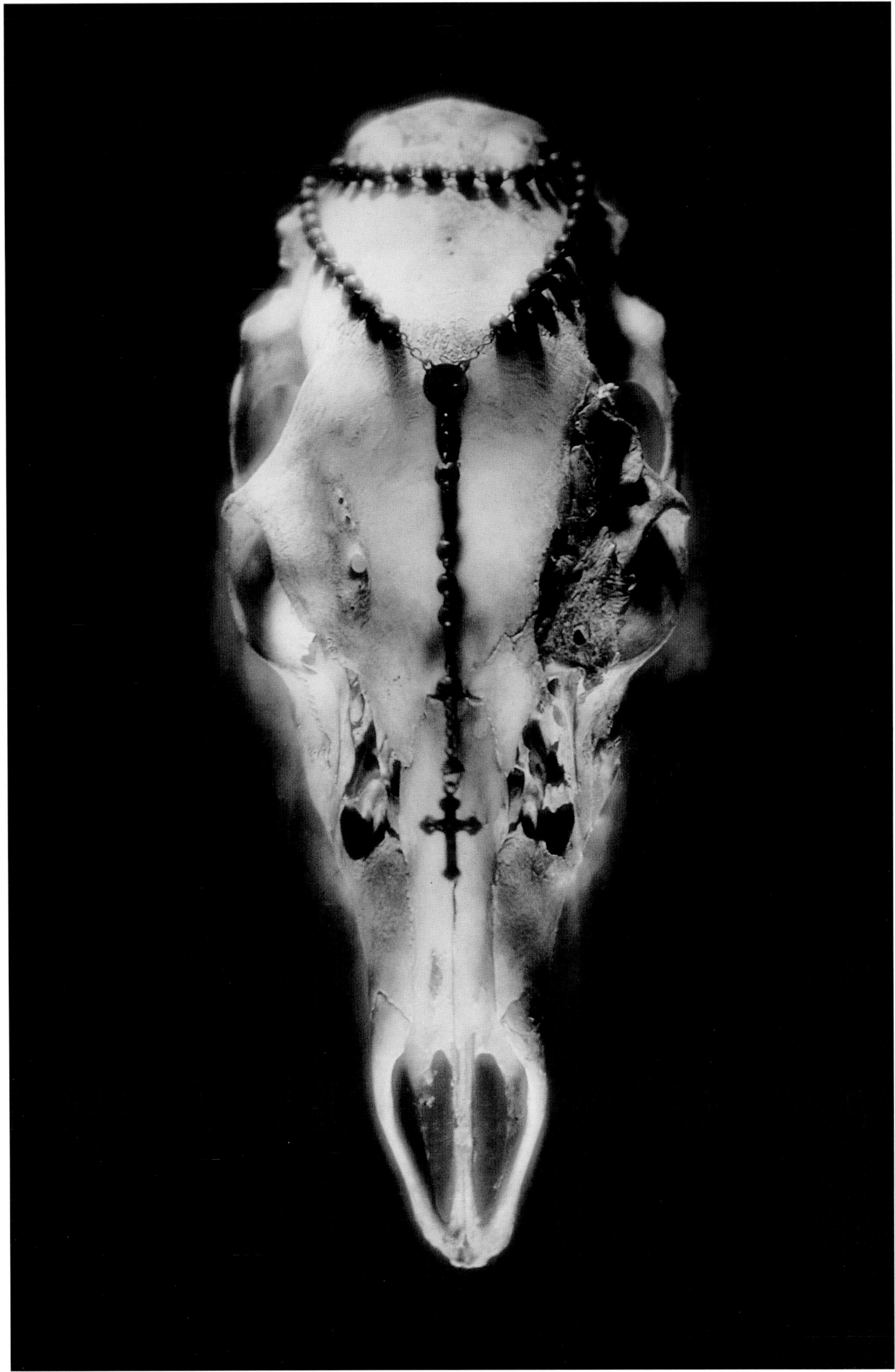

1945, GELATIN-SILVER PRINT (1988), 13½ × 9

# RUTH BERNHARD

## *Skull and Rosary*

Ruth Bernhard's work epitomizes the Middle European humanistic ideal of intelligence guiding the passions to fulfill the yearnings of the flesh and the aspirations of the soul.

Light, which represents the universal and eternal life force, is the medium of Bernhard's art, and her works are, she says, "gifts from the unconscious"[1] whose creation she experiences "as a heightened emotional response, most akin to poetry and music."[2]

In her photographs of female nudes, for which she is internationally acclaimed, Bernhard aspires "to transform the complexities of the figure into harmonies of simplified forms revealing the innate reality, the life force, the spirit, the inherent symbolism as well as the underlying remarkable bone structure."

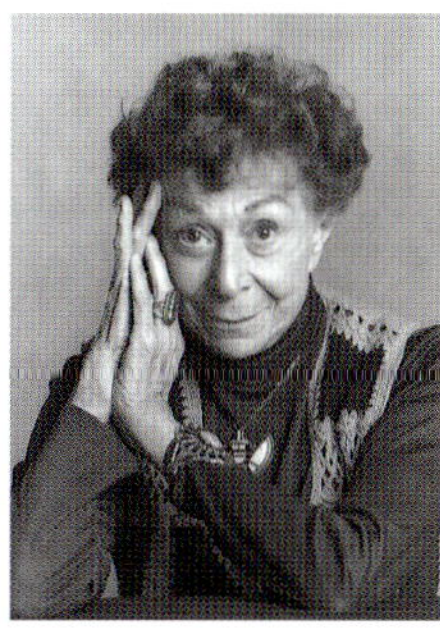

Born in Berlin in 1905, Bernhard studied at the Academy of Fine Arts and then, in 1927, moved to New York, where working in advertising familiarized her with photography. In the 1930s, however, the appeal of the West Coast and its photography milieu inspired her to resettle in California. She has lived in San Francisco since 1953.

*One of my favorite photographs! I've always been interested in skulls because they are the home of the brain, the intelligence. I collect skulls. I regard them as works of art—like Georgia O'Keeffe, whom I knew through Alfred Stieglitz, her husband.*

*People think the skull is dead, but I think everything is connected with life. I felt a connection to myself and didn't question it. That glow around the edges, I thought it was especially for me. I used the rosary also because of its connection with life. After I arrange everything, I make only one exposure—and that's it!*

1. MARGARETTA MITCHELL, "TOWARD THE LIGHT: A BIOGRAPHY OF RUTH BERNHARD" IN RUTH BERNHARD: THE ETERNAL BODY (SAN FRANCISCO: CHRONICLE BOOKS, 1986), P. 15.

2. IBID., P. III.

# DAVID BEST

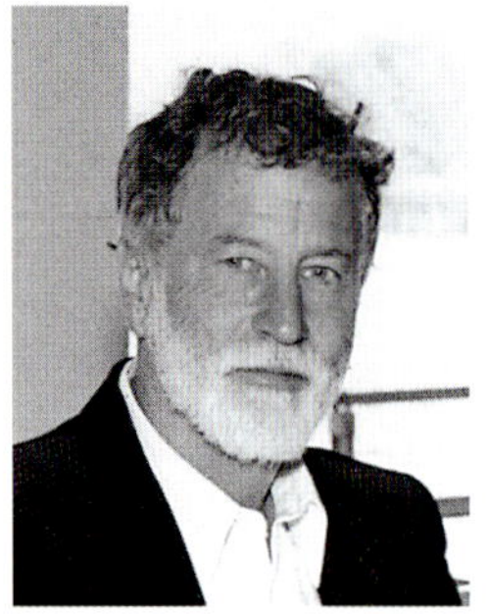

David Best arouses controversy. Praised for his use of complex media and his breadth of vision, he is criticized for showing and trying to say too much—or saying too little. Viewers, in their responses, project onto his art the richness of their own culture, interests, expectations from art, and needs.

"I'm basically a junk sculptor," Best says. "I prefer the term 'junk' to 'found objects.' You have to pay more for *them*."[1] Moving from one to another as he develops several of his works at the same time, he groups them into four general categories:

(1) three- to four-foot-high, fetish-covered plaster and cast porcelain figures, which he calls shamans and magicians

(2) framed works, including drawings, monoprints, and collage-paintings

(3) wagons, such as *Dream of Poland,* which is a little girl's dream staged in an ornate junk wagon, and the gold-painted *Children's Wagon* for transporting youngsters to heaven

(4) cars

Best does not teach, but because he wants to influence people, he solicits their participation in covering old cars with junk. Institutions—museums, alcohol recovery centers, homes for the developmentally challenged, AIDS hospices, and juvenile halls—commission Best as creative organizer and invite the participants. The artist provides the materials, although individuals have donated such objects as a kneecap removed during an operation, false teeth, and a deceased father's boxes of accumulated nuts and bolts. With the artist, they create a kind of public shrine.

"Art helps—it heals, it directs us out of the darkness and shows a way out of madness," Best comments. In response, di Rosa Preserve Curator Richard Reisman writes, "It is important to note that David talks about art showing the way 'out of' the darkness and madness, not 'around' darkness and madness. This means confronting rather than avoiding demons. David's work is, therefore, not a 'diversion.' The work is not art about art, but art directed at the very essence of transformation. It transforms materials in the service of transforming the spirit. The work always speaks to the ultimate journey, beyond the material world, to the highest place. Through darkness and through madness. It is always a bumpy ride."[2]

Best, who was born in San Francisco in 1945, received a BFA from the San Francisco Art Institute in 1974 and an MFA in 1975.

*Elephant and Rider*

1986. STYRENE, CONCRETE, AND MIXED MEDIA. 29 × 24 × 15

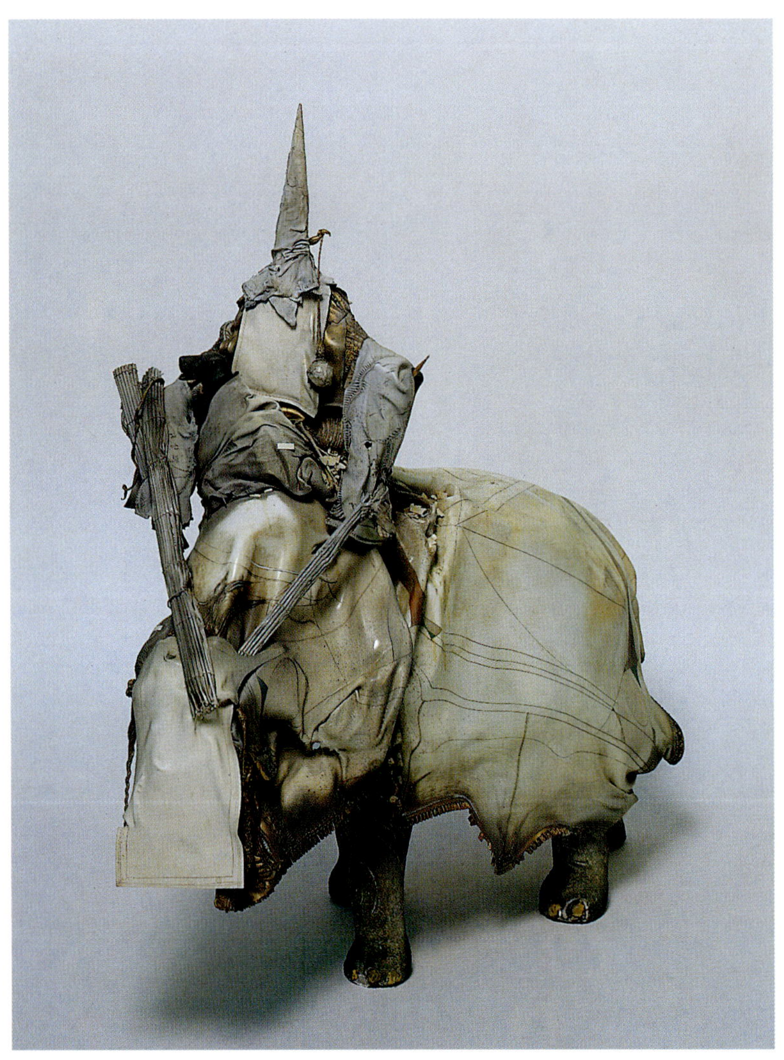

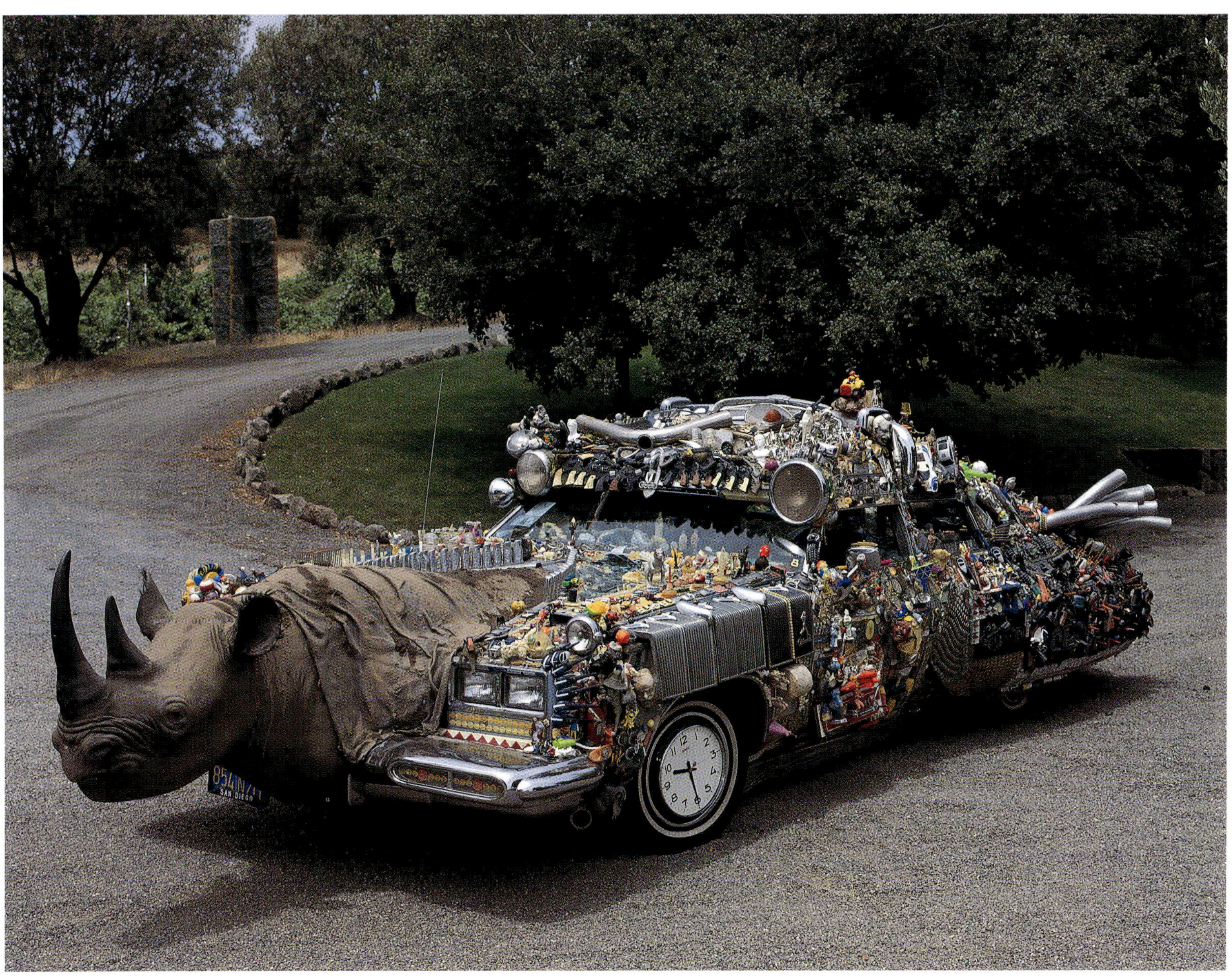

## *Rhinocar*

1985. 1976 OLDSMOBILE AND FOUND OBJECTS. 60 × 276 × 94¾. IN COLLABORATION WITH MICHAEL BISHOP

*Winery Lake is like a family home for the art. The work has not become just stored objects. The collection is more human. It's rough and has flaws, like my work. My stuff is made of junk, has imperfections. There's broken glass in lots of pieces. All my stuff in Rene's collection, except maybe for some drawings, is flawed, imperfect—like me.*

*Cars. I hate the cars. Their batteries die, they're hard to start, difficult to park, don't have registration licenses. I'm not trying to offend anyone. It's just available stuff. The* Rhinocar *[which he organized with Michael Bishop at the Temporary Contemporary in Los Angeles] is just covered with available LA stuff. Anyway, there's no intention to ridicule. It's like archaeology—layers of surviving stuff. The cars have no pain or struggle in them. No soul-searching. They're just automatic—like automatic writing. Just cars with stuff on them. They ask nothing of the observer.*[3]

1. INTERVIEW WITH ROBERT MCDONALD. JULY 14. 1998.

2. RICHARD REISMAN. ORIGINAL MANUSCRIPT. CIRCA 1992.

3. INTERVIEW WITH RICHARD REISMAN. CIRCA 1992.

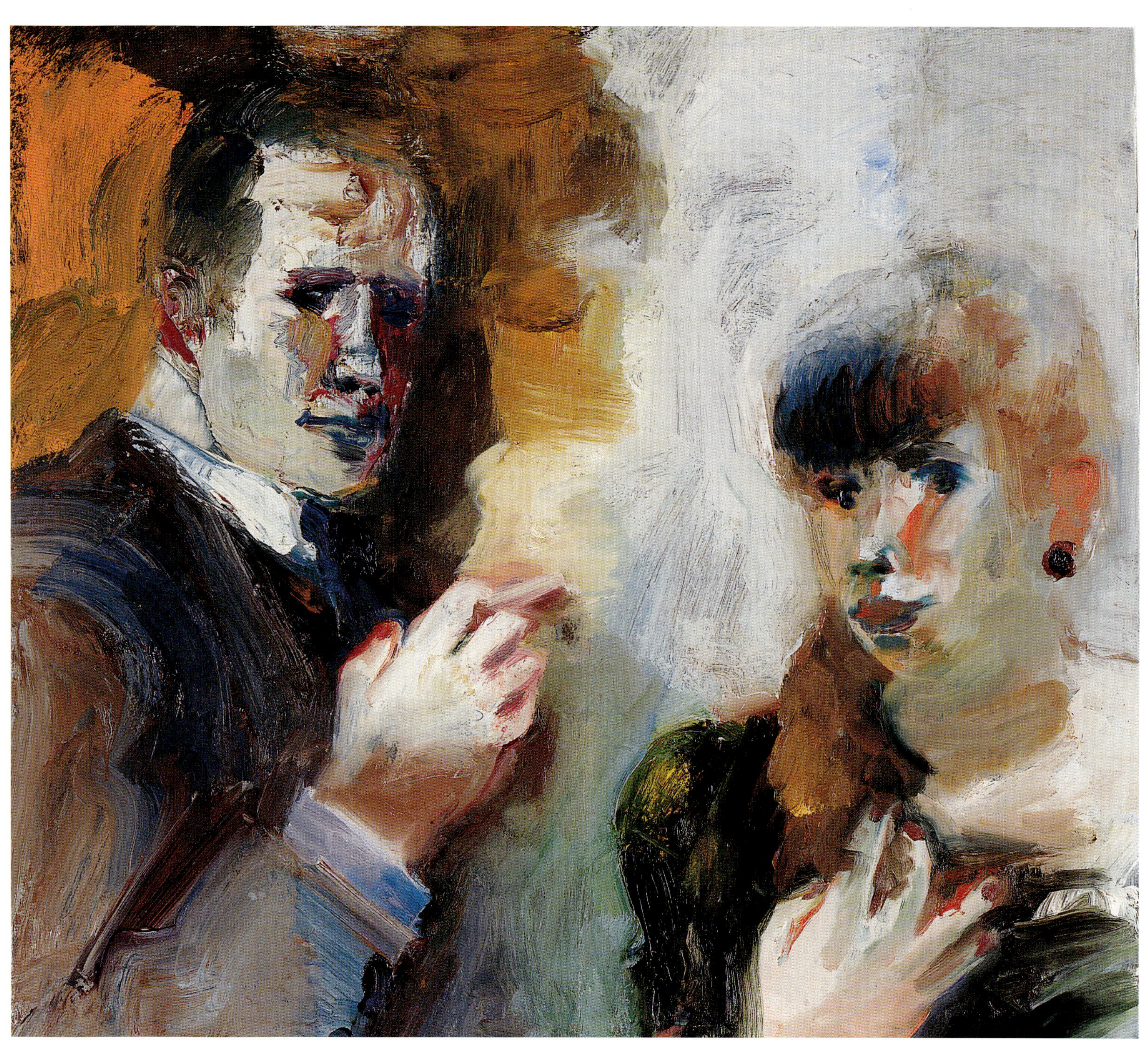

# ELMER BISCHOFF

## *Untitled*

1972. OIL ON CANVAS. 23 × 25¾

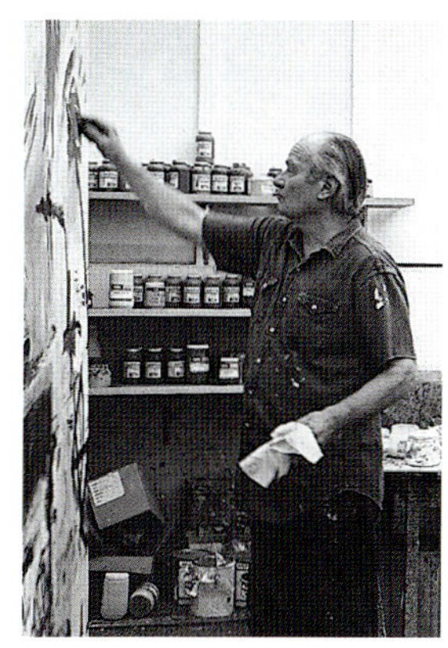

Elmer Bischoff, as a painter and educator, contributed greatly to shaping the San Francisco Bay Area's interest in art during the second half of the twentieth century. With David Park and Richard Diebenkorn, he transformed Abstract Expressionism into Bay Area Figuration. Connoisseurs respect the humanism of his abstract works and the formalism of his figurative works, his use of the light and colors of his environment and, throughout, his romantic poetry.

Born in Berkeley in 1916, Bischoff received a BA in art in 1938 and an MA in 1939 from the University of California, Berkeley. In 1946, after wartime service, he joined the faculty of the San Francisco Art Institute, where he associated with teachers and students such as Park, Diebenkorn, Hassel Smith, and Frank Lobdell. Abstract Expressionism prevailed, but when he resigned in 1952 he had already begun a transition toward figuration. He worked in a painterly fashion, with the mood of his works relating them distantly to those of Edward Hopper.

In 1956 Bischoff returned to the Art Institute to organize and chair a graduate program. In 1963 he joined the faculty of the University of California, Berkeley, where, having returned to abstraction, he remained until 1985. He died in 1991.

*The thing was playing itself dry. I can only compare it to the end of a love affair. When I was in the real grips of Abstract Expressionism, the marks and gestures had a hyper-existence. But it was your own passion that inflamed these things, and there was just a gradual loss of this passion.*[1]

1. THOMAS ALBRIGHT, "ELMER BISCHOFF: BAY AREA FIGURATIVE," CURRANT (DECEMBER 1975–JANUARY 1976), P. 40.

# LEON BORENSZTEIN

## *Farmer Couple, Woodland, California*

1980. GELATIN-SILVER PRINT. ED. 7/30. 17½ × 13¾

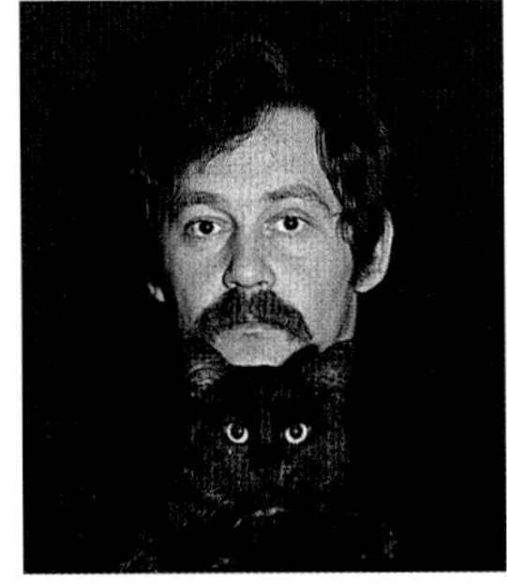

Leon Borensztein, a resident of Oakland whose black-and-white portraits convey a sardonic yet loving humanism rooted in his Eastern European Jewish heritage, was born in Swidnica, Poland, in 1947, to a Polish father and Russian mother. He received a BA in art and geography from the University of Haifa in Israel in 1974, and then an MFA in photography from the San Francisco Art Institute in 1980. In the absence of a fully developed visual arts culture in Israel because of traditional prohibitions against representations of the deity and of human beings created in the deity's image, he has pursued opportunities for a career in the United States. Among other works, he has published books of portraits of handicapped subjects.

Farmer Couple, Woodland, California *was one of my earliest photos from* American Portraits.

*Seeking employment to support my graduate study at the San Francisco Art Institute, I was able to secure a position as a portrait photographer. To combine my artistic goals with my commercial commitments, I used two cameras: one with color slides for the customer and one with black-and-white film for myself. When I took the photographs for myself, I asked people not to smile; then the masks on their faces vanished. Of course, they immediately put on others, but they were easier to penetrate.*

American Portraits *represents a study of families as a microcosm of American society at large. I explore the effects of the American zeitgeist on the individual and how this alters the family unit.*

*I don't believe that the task of an artist is to applaud, flatter, or judge, but rather to question and to provoke.*

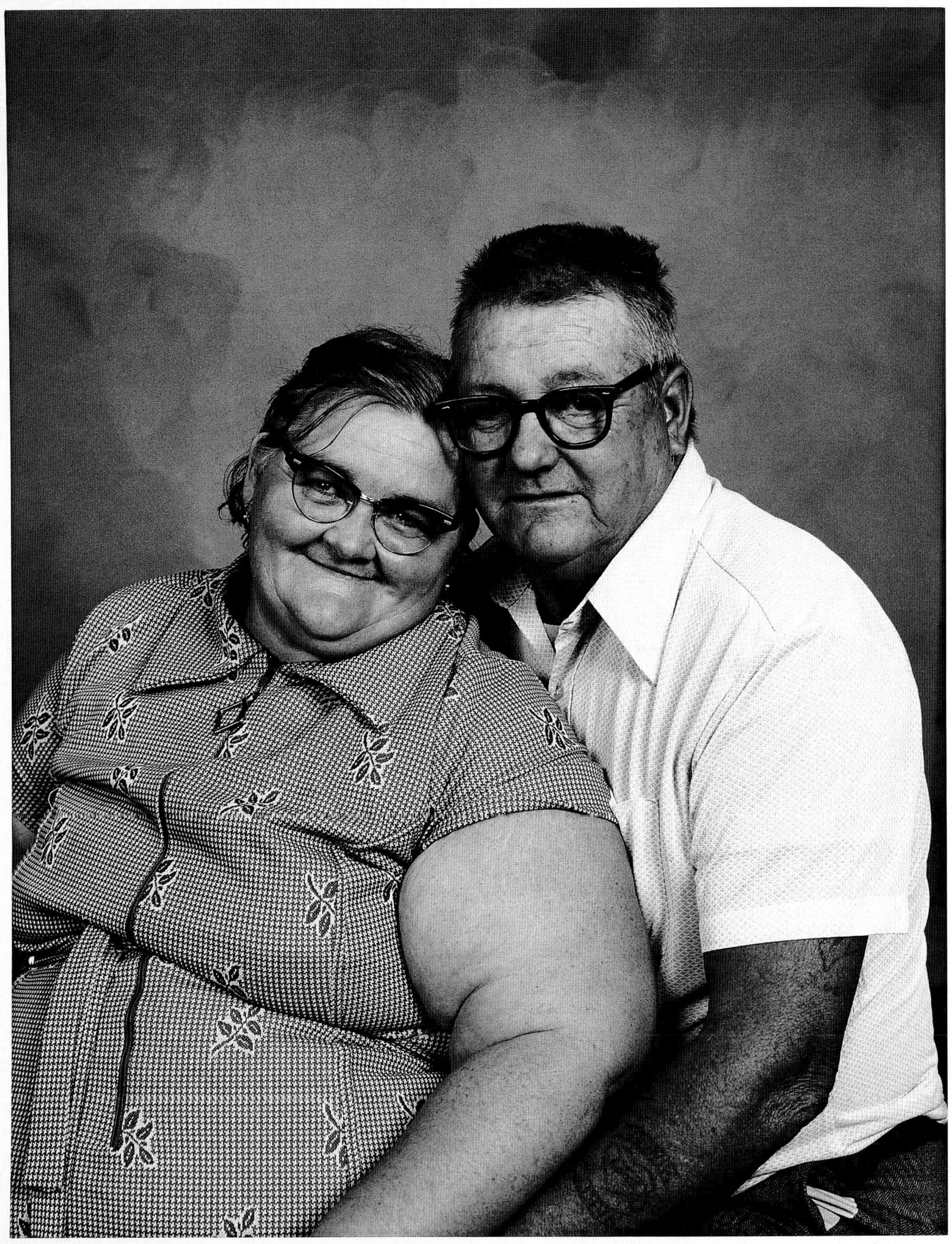

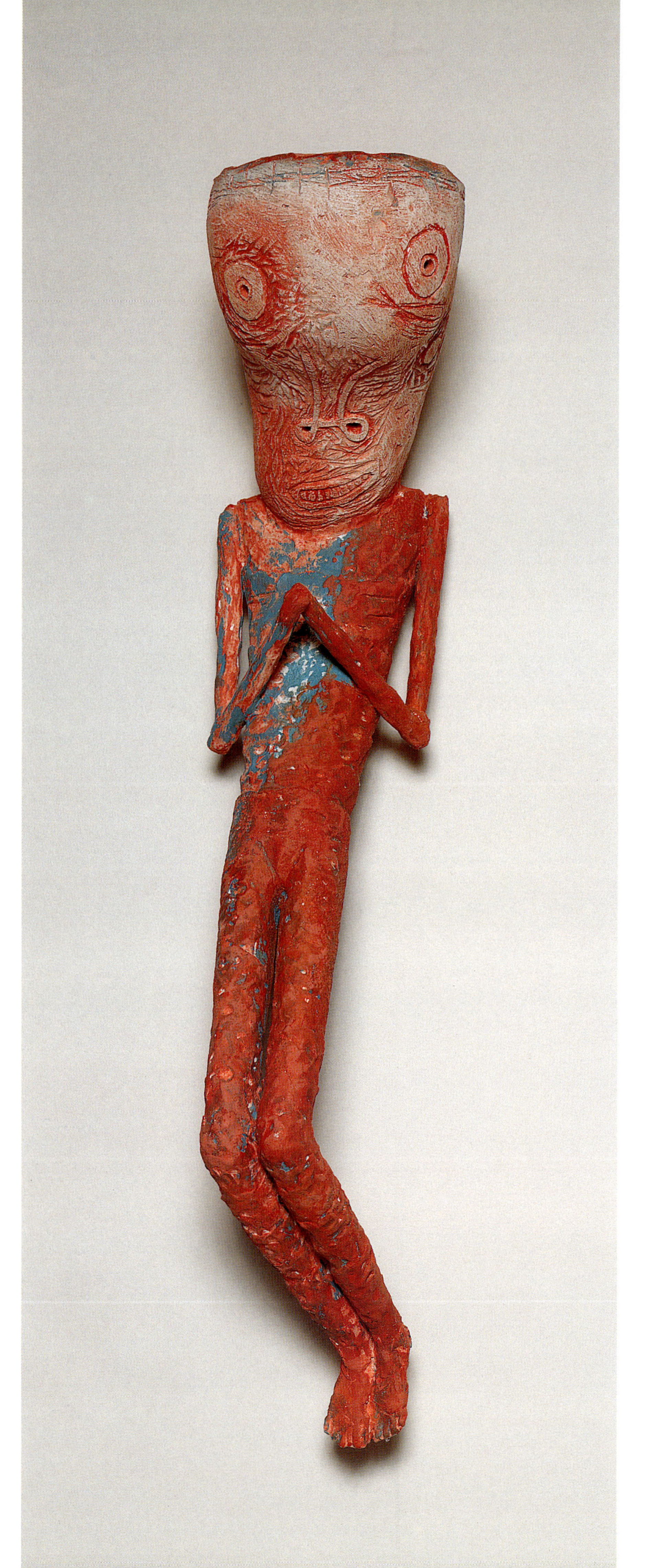

# ROBERT BRADY

***Sherpa*** 1985, STONEWARE, GLAZE, AND PAINT, 43 × 8½ × 13

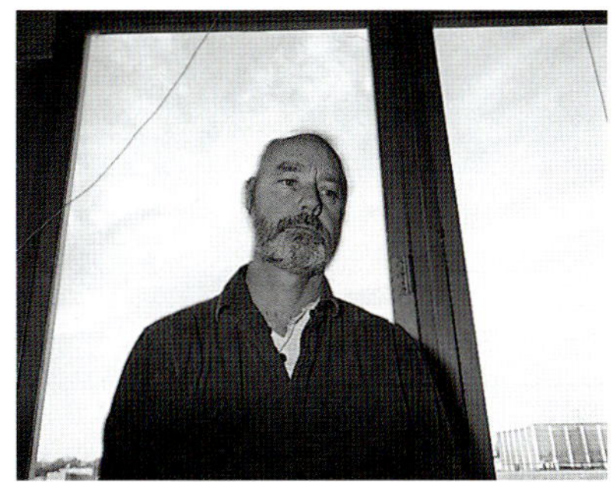

Robert Brady was destined to be an artist the way some people are destined to be saints. His figurative works in ceramic or wood do not address saintliness, however, but explore the poignancy–often grotesque–of being human.

The peripatetic Brady has exhibited works and delivered lectures throughout the United States. He was born in Reno, Nevada, in 1946, received a BFA from the California College of Arts and Crafts (CCAC) in 1968, studied in Mexico under the auspices of CCAC, and in 1975 completed the requirements for an MFA at the University of California, Davis.

*My first serious experience making artworks came in 1964. Since then I have been fully committed to developing as an artist. During the 1970s and most of the 1980s I explored ceramic sculpture using the human figure in scales ranging from smaller to larger than life. In the late 1980s I shifted to using wood and have since then used it for most of my ambitious work. I naturally and conscientiously work from intuition. Despite being art school and university trained, I want to nurture my work with what is close to my heart and to my own life experience, instead of with an academic tradition.*

*My intention is that my figurative sculptures speak about the human condition, history, religion, and myth. Equally important to me is the "conversation" or, even, ritual that occurs between my materials and me during the creative process. Making decisions about ideas, appropriateness, scale, proportions, form, mass, volume, texture, etc., while at the same time hoping to suspend my ego so as to learn, possibly, as much as I impose is something I value and strive for.*

# CHRISTOPHER BROWN

*Dark Head*

1981. CHARCOAL ON PAPER. 72 × 64½

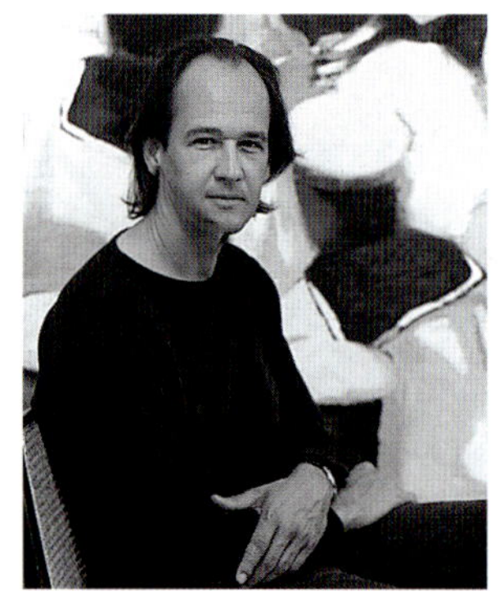

Christopher Brown has been consistent in his use of the human figure and references to it, even in works that appear to be nonobjective. After attracting viewers with recognizable subjects, he instructs them in the technical and abstract beauties of his works in particular and of contemporary art in general.

Charcoal and paper are conservative materials; they do not repel with strangeness. But the scale of *Dark Head,* at six feet by more than five feet, is alarming. While viewers respond initially to an image they recognize, a human face, the overall treatment is such that attention is drawn more to the activity on the surface than to the image. Viewers learn the pleasures of reading the drawing as drawing.

Brown's use of figuration is tied to his beliefs that ideas are as important as methods of communication and that humanistic values are as important as aesthetic decisions.

He was born in Camp Lejeune, North Carolina, in 1951. He received his BFA from the University of Illinois in 1973 and his MFA from the University of California, Davis, in 1976. He taught at UC Berkeley from 1981 until 1994 and now lives in New York.

*Wondering about a statement, I went to eat Chinese food. The rice and vegetables disappeared, but words still stuck in my mouth like gum underneath the counter. Resignedly I cracked open a fortune cookie and read: "A picture is worth a thousand words."*

*As always, it's the viewers' choice, but for me, make it beers with a friend and the grand life of art, and optimism that everything at last will end up in pictures.*

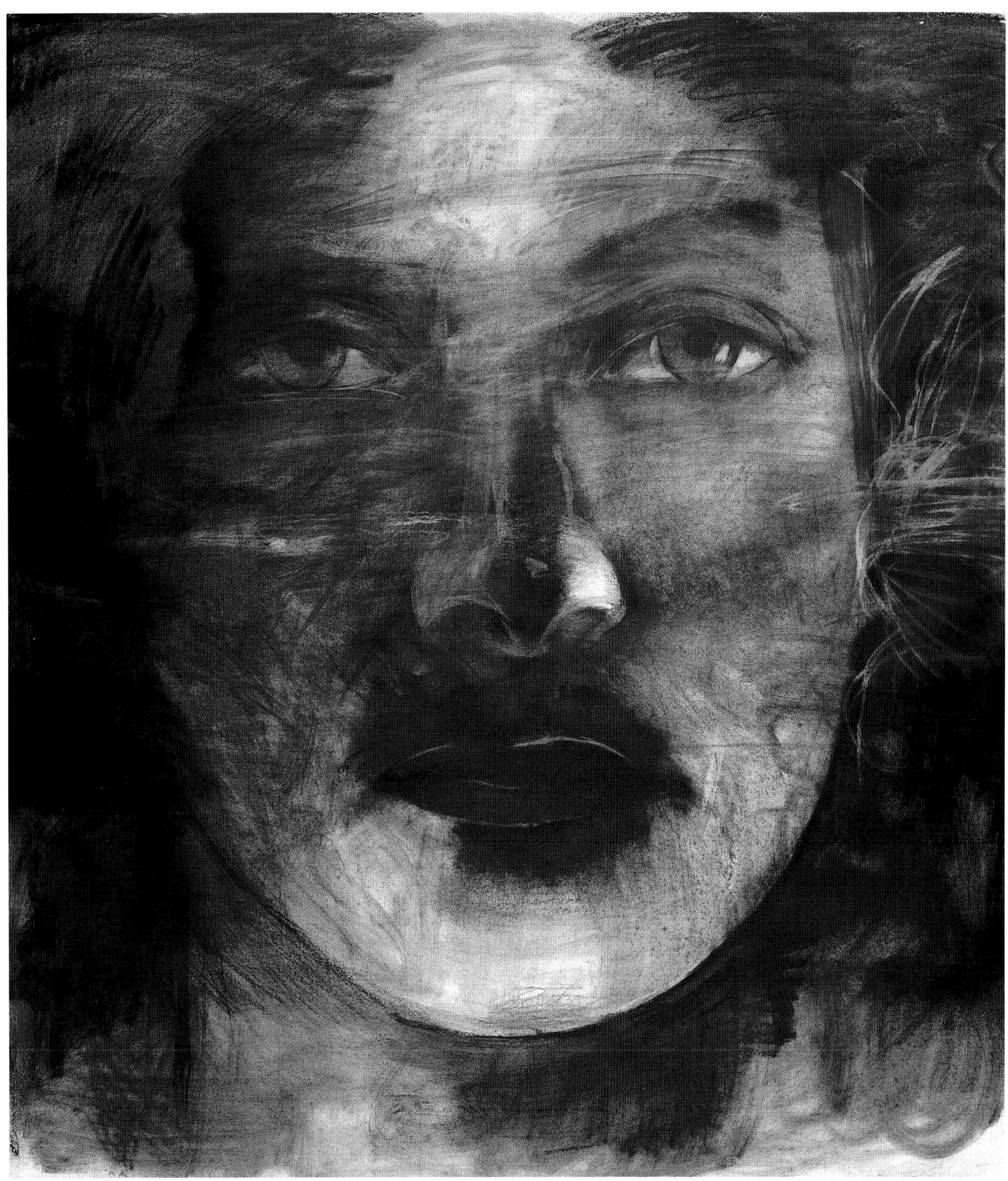

# JOAN BROWN

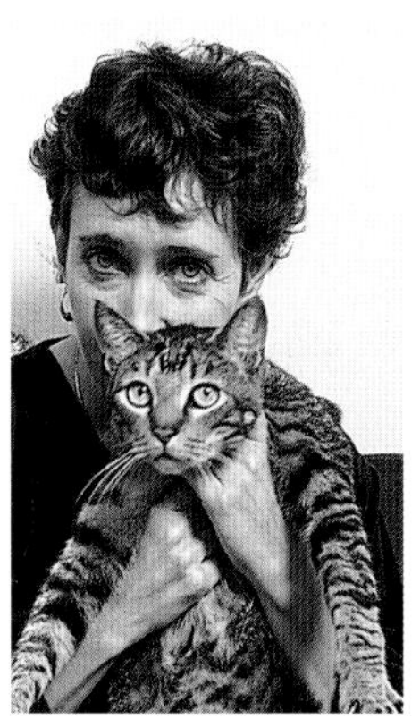

Joan Brown epitomized San Francisco's social and cultural history in the second half of this century. Her aesthetic, beginning in Expressionism, ended in mystical symbolism. Her media evolved from complex, thickly impastoed oil surfaces to reductive enamel paintings, murals, and mosaic obelisks. Her works, whatever their images, engage and energize their viewers.

Born in San Francisco in 1938, Brown enrolled at the San Francisco Art Institute in 1955 to avoid attending a Catholic women's college. She received her BFA in 1959 and MFA in 1960. Four times married, she bore one son, Noel Neri, an artist. She taught at the University of California, Berkeley, from 1974 until 1990, when she was killed while installing an obelisk in Puttaparthi, India. She remains an enduring presence in the art world.

*In my early years as an artist I was very influenced by Expressionism, Impressionism, and the Old Masters—mainly Rembrandt, Goya, and Velázquez. My most influential teacher was Elmer Bischoff.... In the last few years I've been particularly interested in the work of Mark Rothko. Mysticism and Eastern thought have been an influence on my life and my art.*

*I've been to Europe, South America, Egypt, China, and India, and look forward to spending much more time in India. For me, the purpose of travel is to study ancient belief systems and comparative religions. I am fascinated by the similar threads that run through the ancient cultures. Certain images, ideas, and impressions that are particularly meaningful to me appear in my work after my journeys. I'm always surprised to find out what I was most impressed by after I've had a chance to assimilate everything.*

*For several years now I've performed the daily ritual of swimming in San Francisco Bay. I like to do it at the end of the day, near sundown, when the light on the water is very beautiful and peaceful. I depend on this swim. It both relaxes and energizes me. It is actually a form of meditation, and many of my ideas for paintings have materialized while I'm out on the daily swim.*

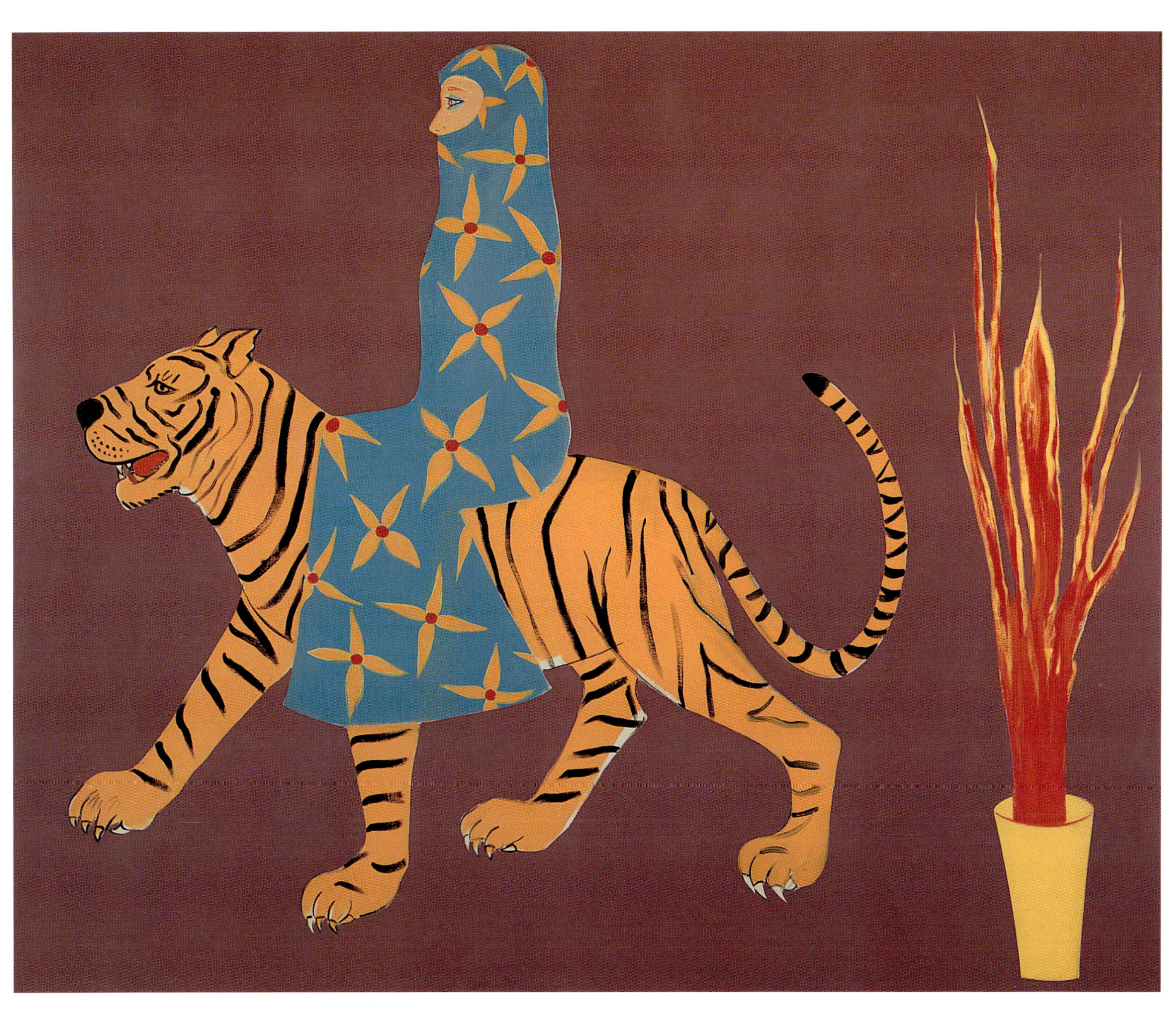

*The Long Journey* 1981, ENAMEL ON CANVAS, 78 × 96

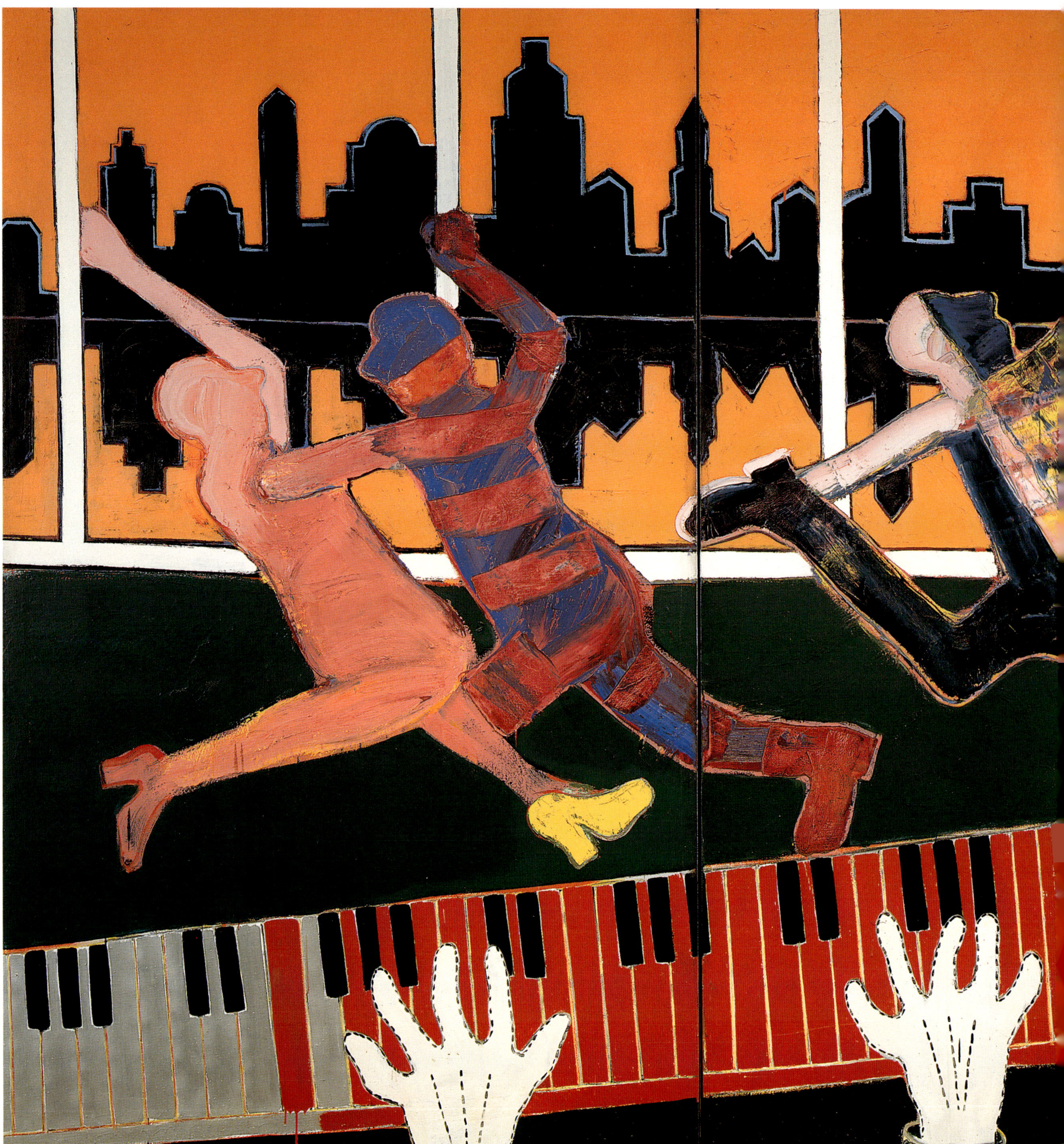

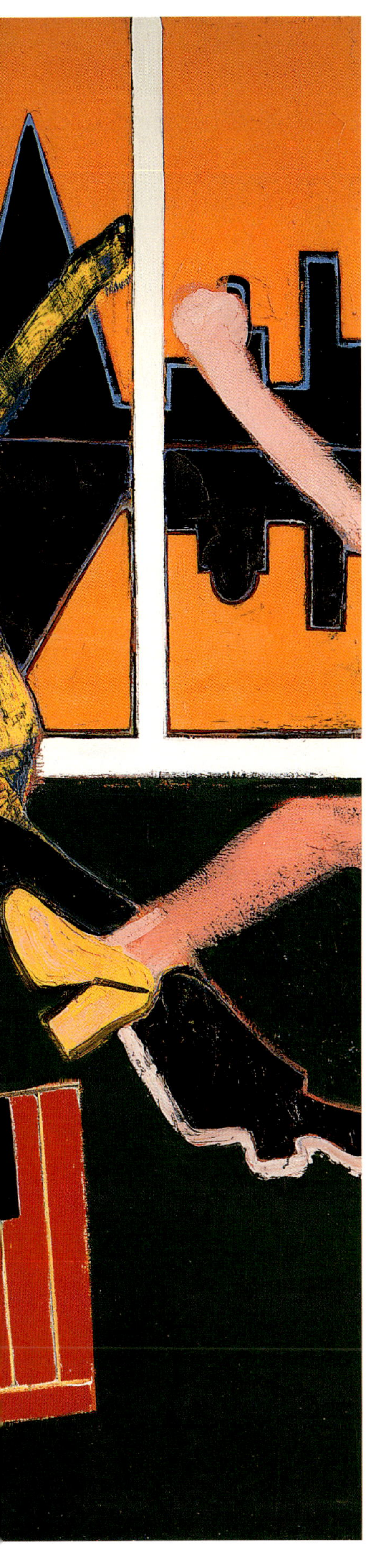

*Dancers in a City #4*

1973, OIL ON CANVAS, 96 × 120

*Throughout the . . . years that I've been painting, my work has dealt with introspection. It can result from observation, actual experiences, feelings, thoughts, ideas, and/or intuition. I strongly feel the need to put this introspection in the form of pictures. I then become the "student" and consciously "study" the content of the pictures I have painted. This is why I choose to keep many of my pictures around me. The form or image varies, but the content is the same. Sometimes it is quite graphic, as in . . . [a] . . . self-portrait. . . . Looking in a mirror, becoming a spectator, literally describing myself, is a very graphic way of being introspective. Other times the work is more narrative. My paint handling changes to whichever technique I feel will best describe what I am trying to express.*

*I strive for that delicate balance between reason and feeling, knowing that sometimes the pictures will lean one way or the other. I'm constantly trying to pull out new information from my intuitive self, which results in the surprises that I discover in my work, and which keeps me ever stimulated.*

*I hope to share with other people who view my pictures my own inward journeys, to which I hope they can relate on some level as being similar to their own.*[1]

1. HENRY HOPKINS, 50 WEST COAST ARTISTS: A CRITICAL SELECTION OF PAINTERS AND SCULPTORS WORKING IN CALIFORNIA (SAN FRANCISCO: CHRONICLE BOOKS, 1981), PP. 34–35.

# JOHN BUCK

1981, WOOD AND PAINT, 96 × 56 × 19

## *The Bridge*

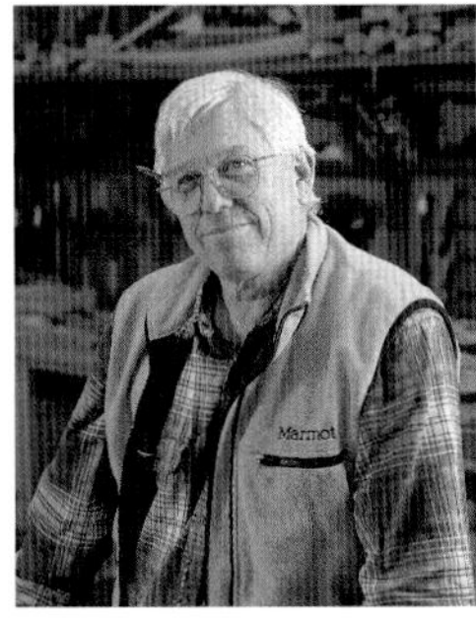

John Buck suspends the psyches of viewers of his works between pleasure and puzzlement, between admiration and alarm. Early on he made zany, low-relief, brightly painted wood sculptures. One piece, for example, portrays a man with a full-frontal torso but a head in profile; his eyes, however, full-face, create a profile with two eyes like a once-upon-a-time Picasso figure study. Buck's later, mixed-media, multiplanar works, with flat, painted, symbolic figures standing in front of unstretched, painted canvases representing environments, are described as autobiographical "metaphors of consciousness."

Buck's intriguing, complex works have antecedents in traditional whittling, naïve painted wood figures, road signs, and carnival art. His mentors include Roy De Forest, Robert Arneson, William T. Wiley, and Jim Nutt of Chicago's Hairy Who (a temporary resident of Sacramento, California, in the early 1970s). He has also worked in bronze and is celebrated for his large-scale wood-block prints.

Buck was born in Ames, Iowa, in 1946. He received a BFA from the Kansas City Art Institute and School of Design in 1968 and an MFA from the University of California, Davis, in 1972. He lives in Montana with his wife, sculptor Deborah Butterfield.

The Bridge *exists on many levels—between people, young and old, places, ideas. This piece was done at a time when my work focused on sculpture that was illusionistic. The figures are shaped to appear round, and the bridge is a dynamic form rendered here as a flat (illusionistic) drawing in space. Like the marks on a doorjamb that measure a growing child, this piece represents a measure of my work.*

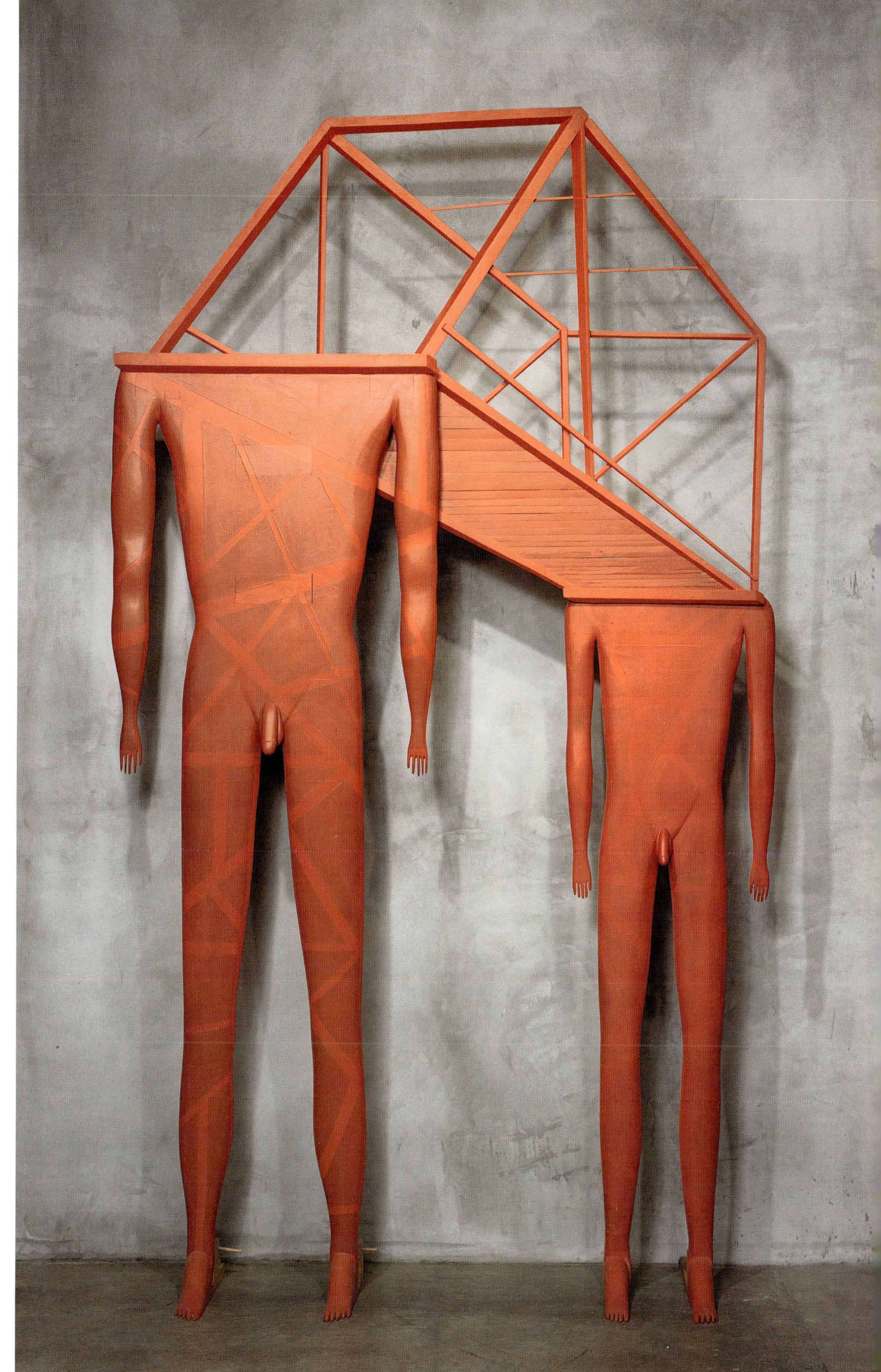

Deborah Butterfield has ridden, trained, and cared for horses all her life. Through art she expresses her love and understanding of them and respect for them. Defying conventional representation, she constructs her sculptures from found materials, both rural in nature–mud, sticks, straw–and urban–automobile parts, bailing wire, tar. More recently, she has been translating some of the more fragile forms into bronze. The authenticity of the poses, however –grazing, whinnying, resting, listening alertly–obviates other considerations. Despite violations of reality, the haunting beauty and presence of these works cause viewers to respond to the antiquity of the companionship they represent. They are unforgettable.

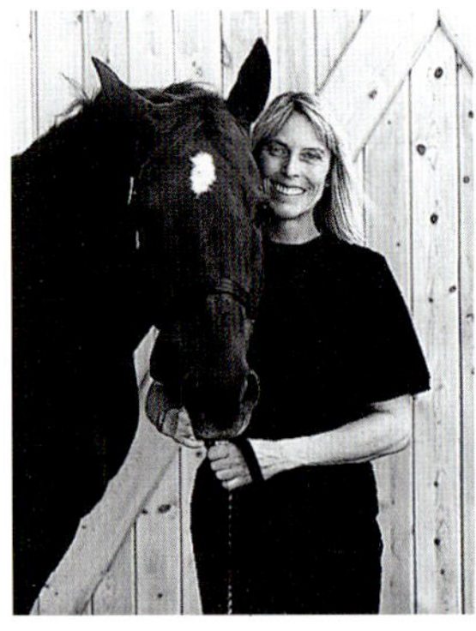

Butterfield considered a career in veterinary medicine before choosing art, which she studied at the Skowhegan School of Painting and Sculpture in Maine and at the University of California, Davis, where she earned a BA in 1972 and an MFA in 1973. Early on, she made life-size ceramic representations of saddles and plaster sculptures of horses. She was born in San Diego in 1949 and lives in Montana with her horses and her husband, sculptor John Buck.

# DEBORAH BUTTERFIELD

## *Horse #7 (Bonfire)*

1978. MUD, STICKS, STRAW, GROUND PAPER, STEEL, DEXTRINE, AND CHICKEN WIRE. 108 × 144 × 60

*These mud and stick horses refer to how horses are closer to the earth than humans–a sort of figure/ground pun. The first pieces in 1977 were reclining mares, which looked like reclining nudes or big piles of brush.*

*In the series that included* Bonfire *I tried to show the space the horses occupied, using the sticks to describe this zone of personal power. I also showed my hand by placing the sticks against the horses to evoke architecture or the architecture of a fire or concealment in the woods.*

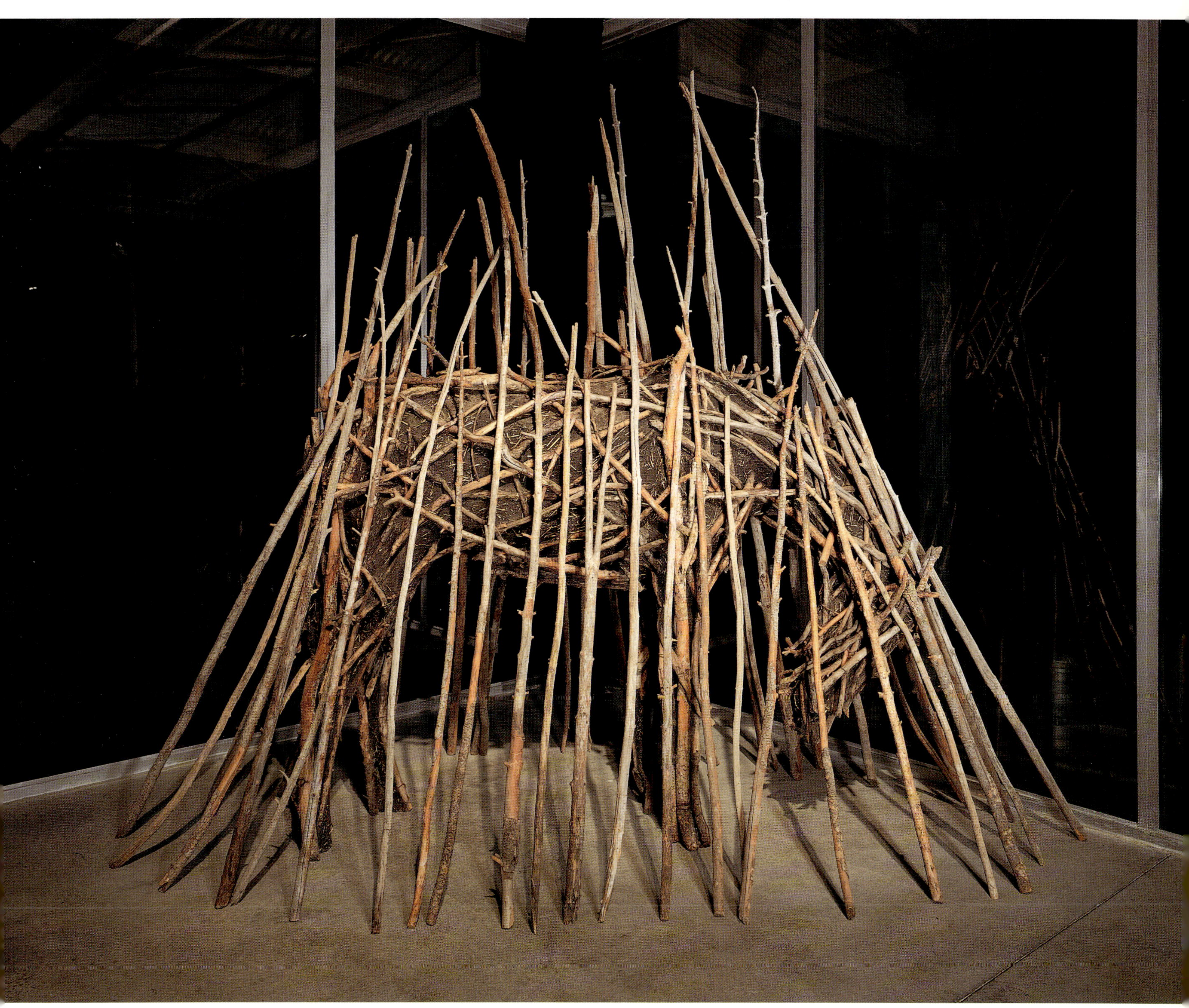

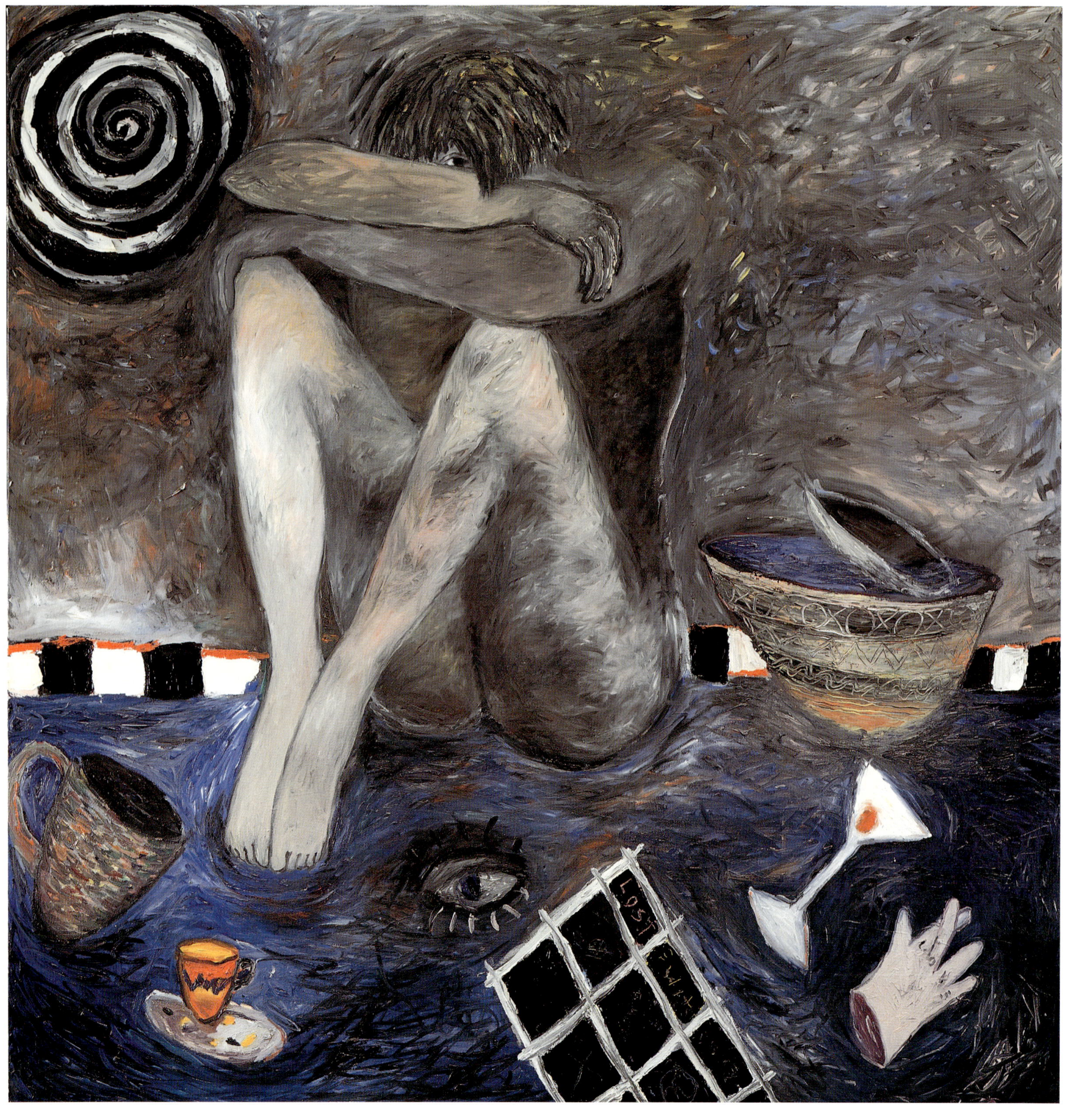
LOST

Squeak Carnwath possesses an exceptional sensitivity to and gift for articulating complex ideas. To study her work, as in *Time Lost,* is to become acquainted with a person.

Born in Abington, Pennsylvania, in 1947, Carnwath first studied at Goddard College in Plainfield, Vermont, but completed work for a BFA in 1971 and an MFA in 1977 at the California College of Arts and Crafts, where her mentor was Viola Frey.

*A SIMPLE LIST*

1. *It's simple really,*
   *to paint is to trust.*
   *To believe in our instincts; to become.*
2. *Painting is an investigation of being.*
3. *It is not the job of art to mirror. Images reflected in a mirror appear to us in reverse. An artist's responsibility is to reveal consciousness; to produce a human document.*
4. *Painting is an act of devotion. A practiced witnessing of the human spirit.*
5. *Paintings are about:*
   *paint*
   *observation &*
   *thought.*
6. *Art is not about facts but about what is; the am-ness of things.*
7. *All paintings share a connection with all other paintings.*
8. *Art is evidence. Evidence of breathing in and breathing out; proof of human majesty.*
9. *Painting places us. Painting puts us in real time. The time in which we inhabit our bodies.*
10. *Light is the true home of painting.*
11. *The visible is how we orient ourselves. It remains our principal source of information about the world. Painting reminds us of what is absent. What we don't see anymore.*
12. *Painting is not only a mnemonic device employed to remember events in our lifetime. Paintings address a greater memory. A memory less topical, one less provincial than the geography of our currently occupied body. Painting reminds us of what we don't know but what we recognize as familiar.*
13. *Painting, like water, takes any form. Paint is a film of pigment on a plane. It is not real in the way that gravity-bound sculpture is real. It is, however, real. Painting comes to reality through illusion. An illusion that allows us to make a leap of faith; to believe. To believe in a blue that can be the wing of a bug or a thought. It makes our invisible visible.*

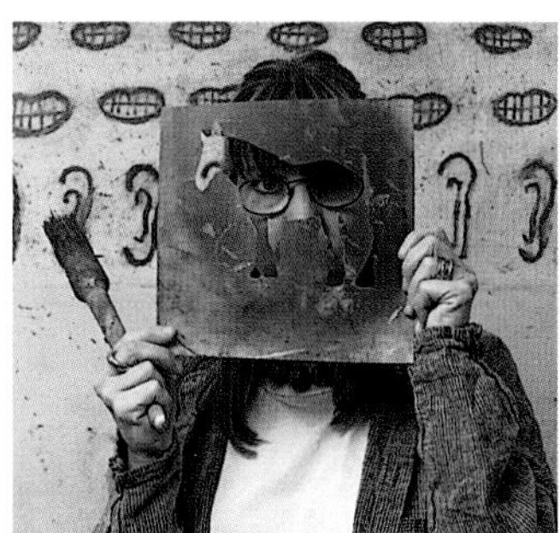

# SQUEAK CARNWATH

1983, OIL ON CANVAS, 60 × 60 ***Time Lost***

# ENRIQUE CHAGOYA

## *When Paradise Arrived*

1988, CHARCOAL AND PASTEL ON PAPER, 80 × 80

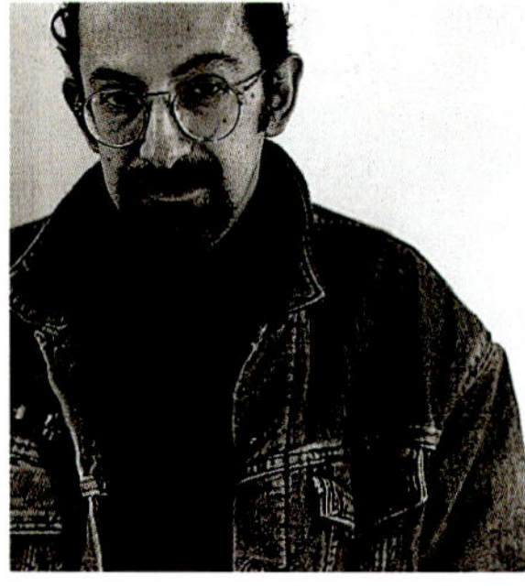

Enrique Chagoya, claiming full participation, significance, and power for artists in their societies, is an existentially engaged artist in the tradition of Francisco Goya, Honoré Daumier, and José Guadalupe Posada. His major works are huge drawings in charcoal and pastel on paper—materials he deliberately chooses for their cheapness. Perceiving human social concerns—justice and injustice, peace and war, free expression and censorship, truth and lies, human follies and cruelties—as multidimensional, he uses grays, not black and white, to represent them.

Born in Mexico City in 1953, Chagoya draws from sources he knows well—the indigenous culture, the Catholic Church, and Walt Disney. Mickey Mouse may be an Everyman observing the sufferings of saints and duplicities of politicians with equal puzzlement, or he may represent fatuousness and evil with a "happy face."

After earning a BFA at the San Francisco Art Institute in 1984, Chagoya received an MA from the University of California, Berkeley, in 1986.

When Paradise Arrived *is about a collision between dominant cultures in North America and the native peoples and/or early Mexicans who inhabited California and the Southwest since before it became the USA. They did not immigrate to this country; this country immigrated to them. The big hand does not necessarily represent any particular cartoon character. It symbolizes corporate culture, official language, dominant politics, etc. Sometimes the interaction is involuntary and violent, and hopefully more often it is voluntary, peaceful, and very rich in positive experiences that transform both the dominating and the dominated in an ever-changing, hybrid new culture.*

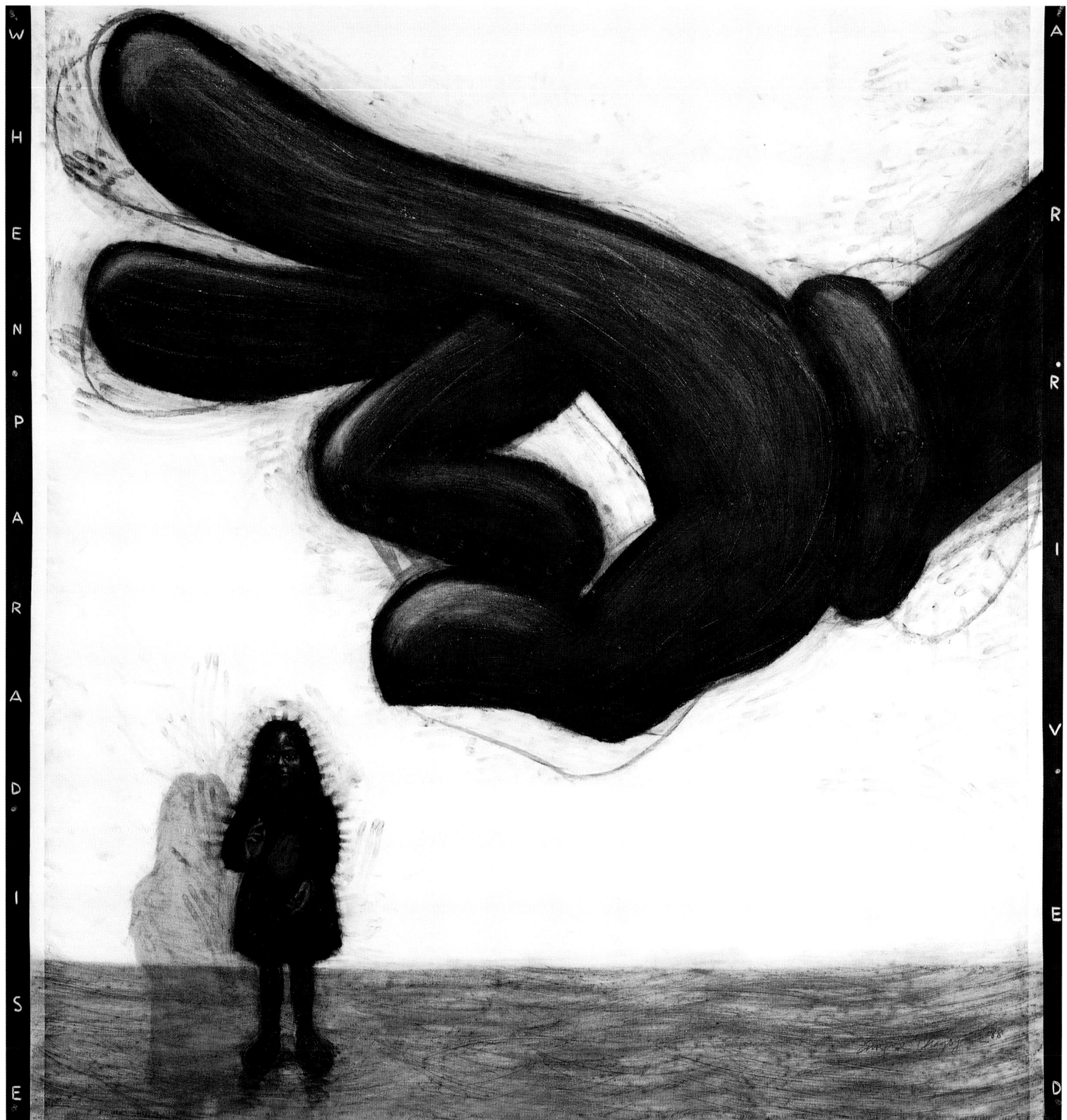
WHEN PARADISE
ARRIVED

## *Arnolfini's Bride IV*

# GAIL CHASE-BIEN

1986, OIL ON CANVAS, 84 × 60

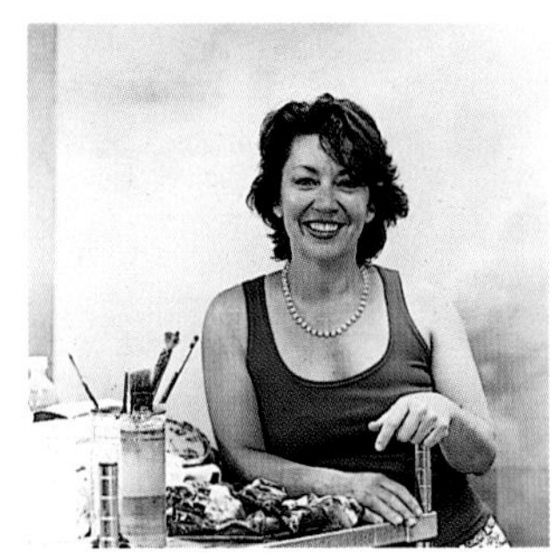

In her masterfully executed five-part series of oil paintings entitled *Arnolfini's Bride,* Gail Chase-Bien boldly "appropriates" imagery from Jan Van Eyck, one of Europe's greatest painters, for rearrangement and reconsideration in commentaries about contemporary life. Parts *I* through *IV* overall reveal the bride emerging, increasingly voluptuous, as her spouse recedes. The doubling of her figure in *IV* represents the plight of women locked in behavior patterns of listlessness and purposelessness. In *V* there is no male, while the female appears in figures both liberated and melancholy.

Chase-Bien was born in Lowell, Massachusetts, in 1946. She received her BFA in 1978 and her MFA in 1980, both with high distinction, from the California College of Arts and Crafts. She lives in Napa, California.

*The* Arnolfini's Bride *series evolved out of my interest in Jan Van Eyck's masterpiece* The Marriage of Arnolfini, *painted in 1434. This Renaissance wedding portrait depicts a groom and his bride in their wedding chamber, about to consummate their marital union. The painting's lavish detail and its atmospheric light create a world of immutability and silence. The couple appear wooden, almost spectral.*

*I wanted to rewrite the script from the bride's perspective and address the hidden emotions of a young woman confined to a prescribed and fixed universe. I attempted to show the bride in attitudes of exhilaration, despair, indifference, and confrontation. The two-dimensionality of the canvas becomes a stage for the emotional duels with herself and her partner, Arnolfini. As the image of Arnolfini slowly recedes from canvas to canvas in the series, the bride becomes the center of the physical universe, free to explore the making of her own destiny.*

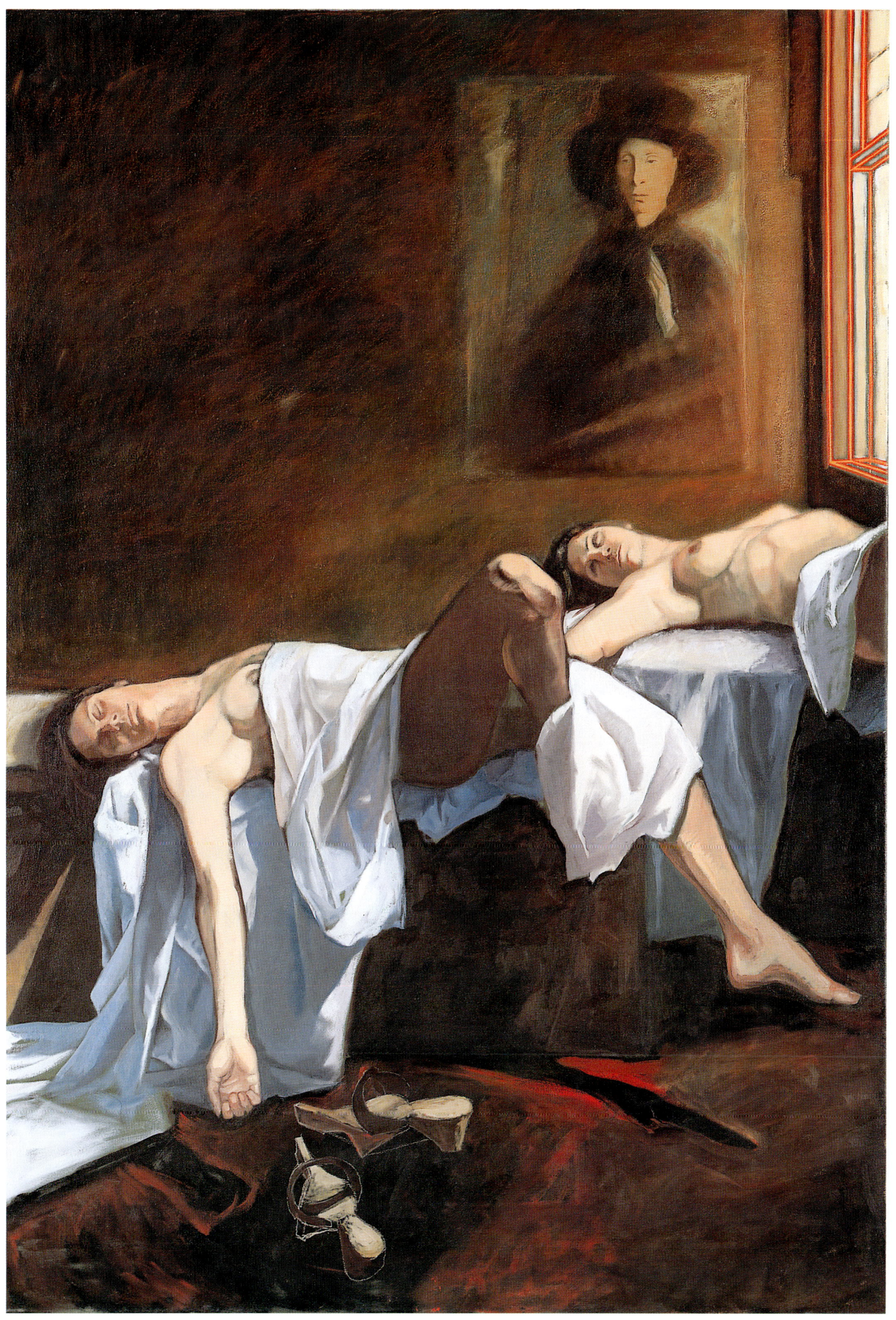

# VAN DEREN COKE

## *Mexico City, D.F.*

1985. CIBACHROME PRINT. 6½ × 10

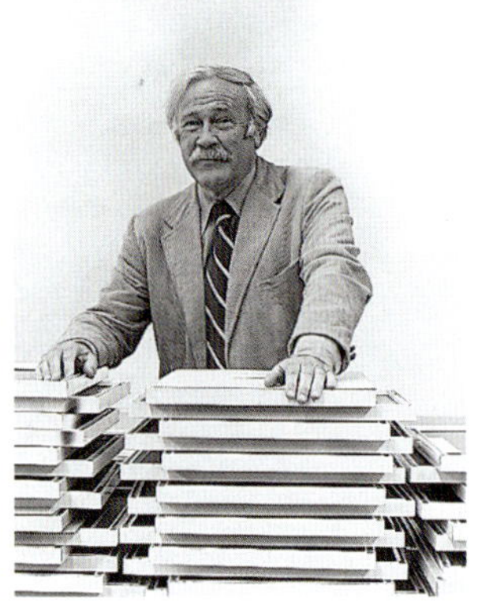

Van Deren Coke's influence on the photography of our time has been incalculable. Born in Lexington, Kentucky, in 1921, at fifteen he became a practicing photographer. He has had a long, exceptionally distinguished career. From 1979 to 1987 he was director of the department of photography at the San Francisco Museum of Modern Art, having earlier been director of the International Museum of Photography at George Eastman House, Rochester, New York. He now lives in Santa Fe, New Mexico.

The straightforwardness of his early works, whatever the nature of their subjects—documentary, figural, serendipitous—reflected the influences of mentors Ansel Adams and Edward Weston. Coke felt it was very difficult to make art with a camera and became a champion for the recognition of photography as a fine art—a matter disputed in some circles until very recently.

Melancholy has characterized much of Coke's work, and his exposure to manipulations of photographic images, such as the rayographs (or photograms) by American surrealist Man Ray, with whom he was acquainted in Paris, allowed him great freedom for self-expression. Proceeding intuitively, he created works without a camera by appropriating and combining images from sources such as newspapers with photographs, placing them on sensitized paper, and exposing them to light. Melancholy accentuated by surreal elements dominates his recent, straightforward Cibachrome prints as well.

Mexico City, D.F.—*Federico García Lorca with red bubble gum on his chin—is a good example of how cultural heroes are treated.*

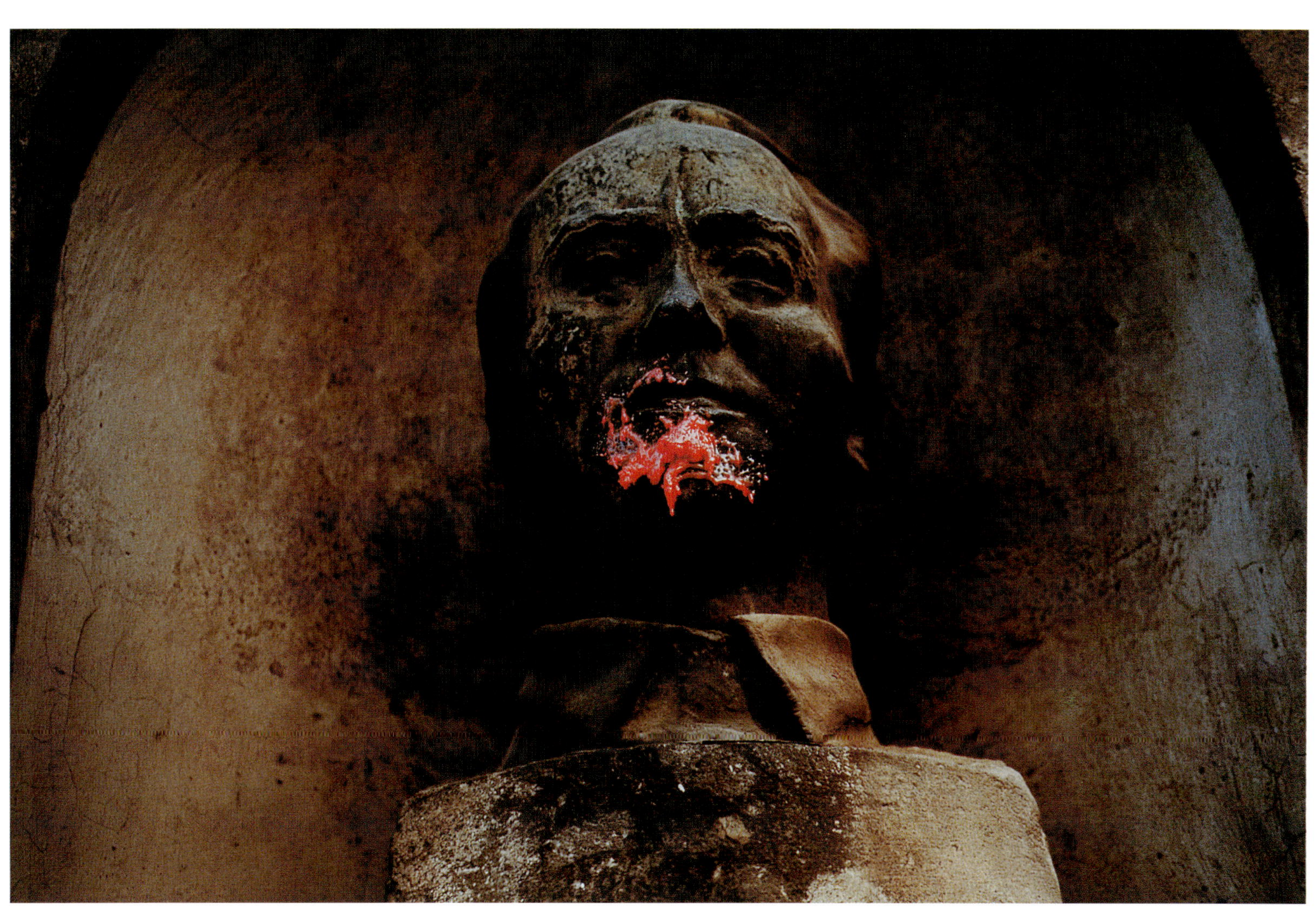

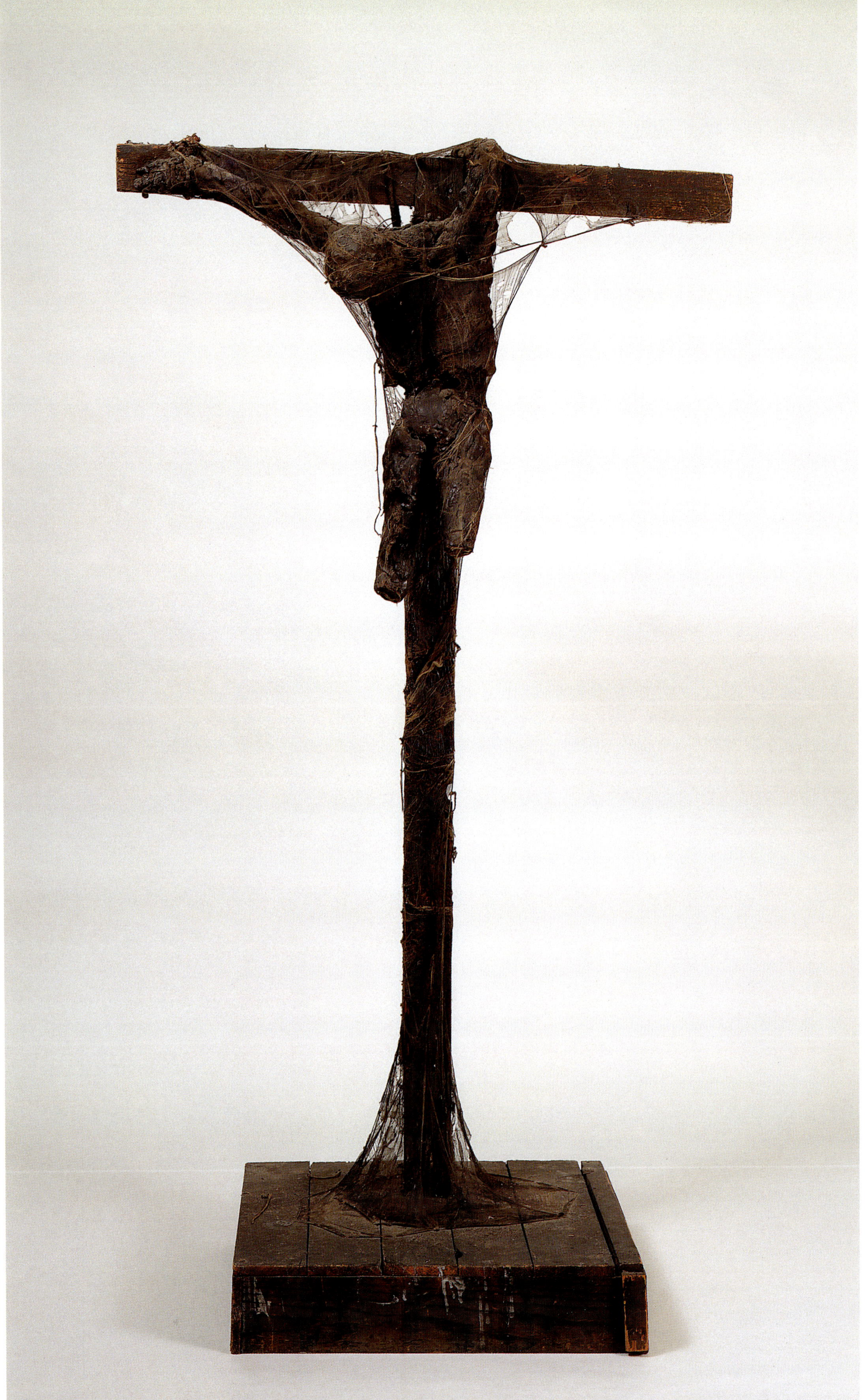

# BRUCE CONNER

1961. WAX, GAUZE, AND WOOD, 85 × 47 × 27½ ***CRUCIFIXION***

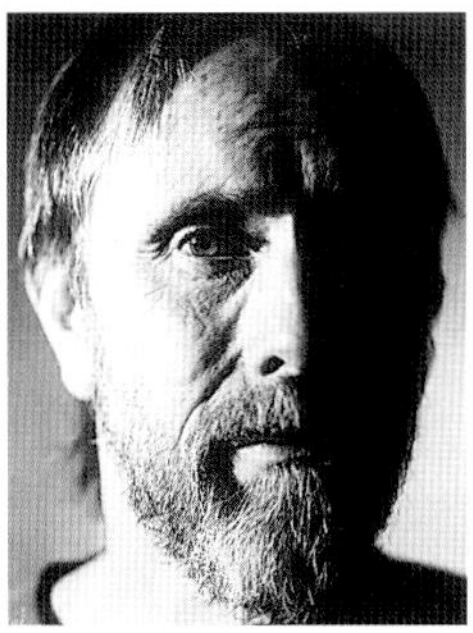

In *CRUCIFIXION* Bruce Conner performs an artistic transubstantiation: his own spirit alters the nature of the materials he uses until they become what he imagines. This assemblage of detritus from life unites the Christian icon of sacrifice (a human form, horribly mutilated) with the Greek ideal of tragedy (pity combined with terror) and contemporary history, creating an event as well as its representation.

Conner, born in McPherson, Kansas, in 1933, studied art at several schools—the University of Nebraska (from which he received a BA in 1956), the Brooklyn Museum Art School, and the University of Colorado. In 1957 he moved with his wife, Jean, a painter, to San Francisco. A pioneer of assemblage, in his early works he characteristically used tattered nylon stockings, which suggest fetishistic sensuality while creating quasi-painterly effects. A dominating presence, he helped define Funk and subsequent developments in contemporary art. He has since realized his vision in many media, usually in black, white, and grays. These later works include intricate, mandalalike drawings on paper, paintings on canvas, prints, photograms (some of them spectacularly beautiful self-portraits), and very important films, some of which can be likened to flowing assemblages.

*I think that one of the themes of [my] work [in general] is an assumption that the creature is good. That the society which we have is alienating to the animal. It expresses power and violence and death and that's its main structure. And the signs of that are in the symbols that we see around us in the arts, in the clothes, in the roles that people play in the society. That people have to deal with this crucifixion of the spirit all the time, and that how well they shine through that is the triumph of those individuals.*[1]

1. REBECCA SOLNIT, SECRET EXHIBITION: SIX CALIFORNIA ARTISTS OF THE COLD WAR ERA (SAN FRANCISCO: CITY LIGHTS BOOKS, 1990), P. 65. [BRUCE CONNER IN AN INTERVIEW FOR ARCHIVES OF AMERICAN ART, 1974.]

# GORDON COOK

*Boat House* 1983, OIL ON MASONITE, 8¼ × 8⅛ UNFRAMED

Gordon Cook's works communicate the power of subtlety. A big man physically, he was also an artist of exceptional philosophical and historical culture. He is best known for the small paintings on which he concentrated obsessively.

The traditionalist prints he made when he arrived in the San Francisco Bay Area in the 1950s earned him a reputation as a retardative artist in a milieu being radically altered by Abstract Expressionist currents from New York City, mediated through the San Francisco Art Institute. Most particularly, Bay Area Figuration in the works of David Park, Elmer Bischoff, and others was emerging.

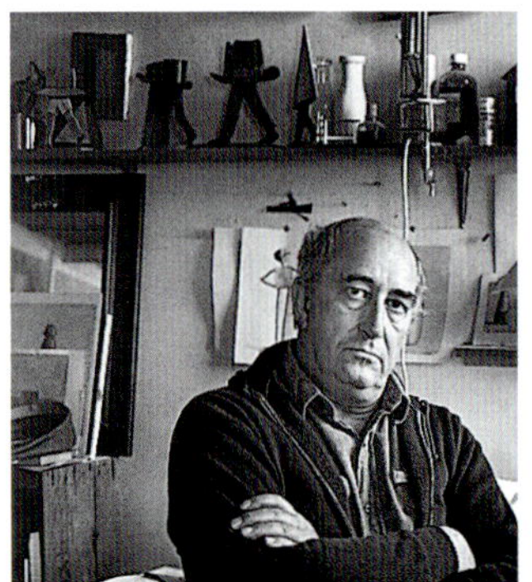

After Cook married painter Joan Brown in 1968, he devoted himself to painting. They were an unusual pair: he was big, she was tiny; he favored subtle representation in small works, she made dazzling, energetic figurative paintings and had achieved some special recognition with her *Fur Rat* sculpture in the *Funk* exhibition of 1967 at the University Art Museum, Berkeley. They did not stay married long.

Although likened to the works of Georgio Morandi for their otherworldliness, Cook's paintings of ordinary objects isolated in space are less architectonic than the Italian master's. His paintings of contrived humanoid forms, while playful, nevertheless represent the melancholy of a Pierrot. As he conveys the ineffability of beauty in his landscapes, no matter how commonplace the scenes, Cook also conveys its permanence, despite the evanescence of its forms.

Cook was born in Chicago in 1927. He attended Illinois Wesleyan University, where he acquired a BFA in 1950 and then went on to the University of Iowa. He died in 1985.

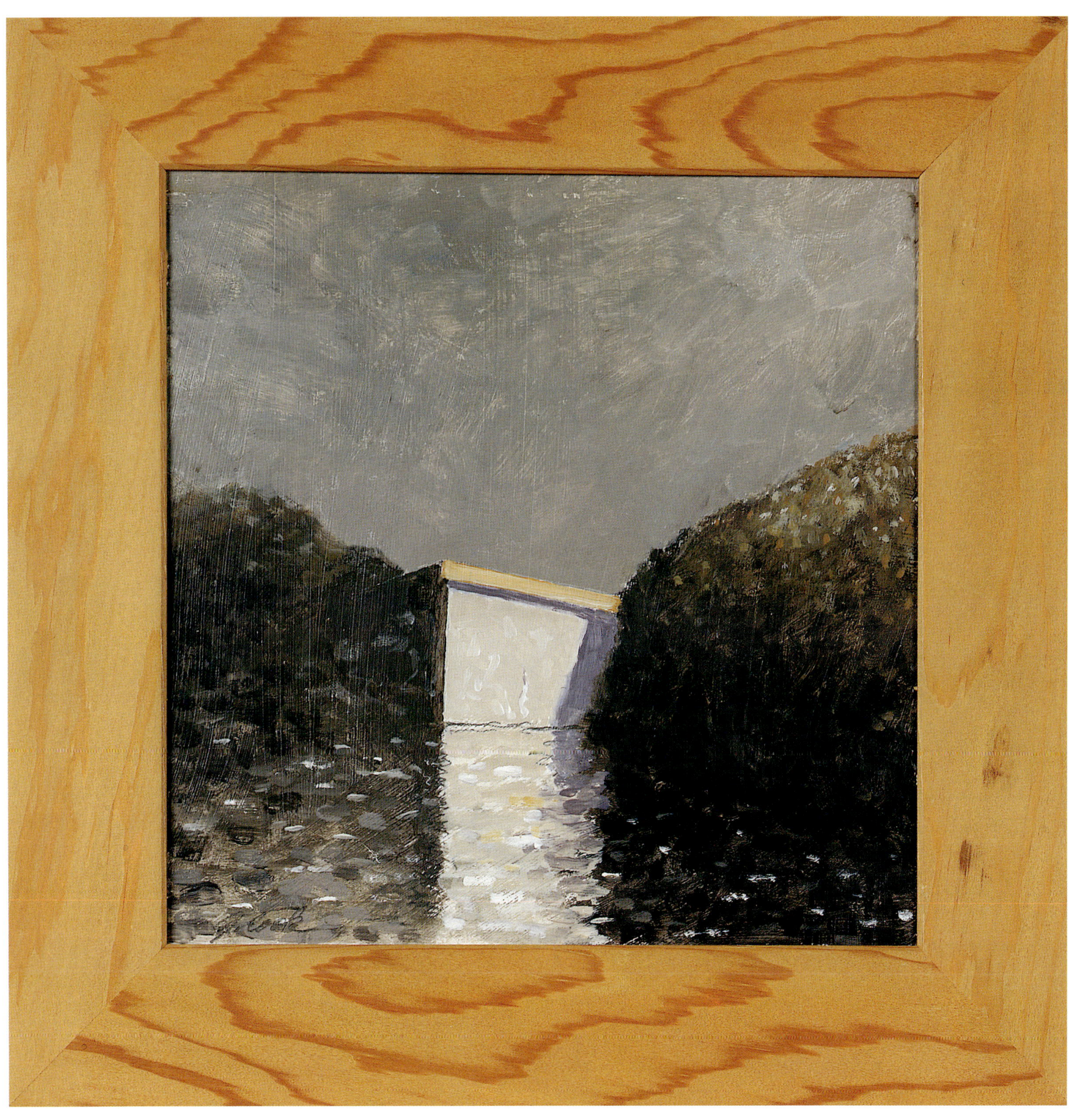

# IMOGEN CUNNINGHAM

## *Coffee Gallery, San Francisco, 1960*

1960, GELATIN-SILVER PRINT, 9¾ × 10½

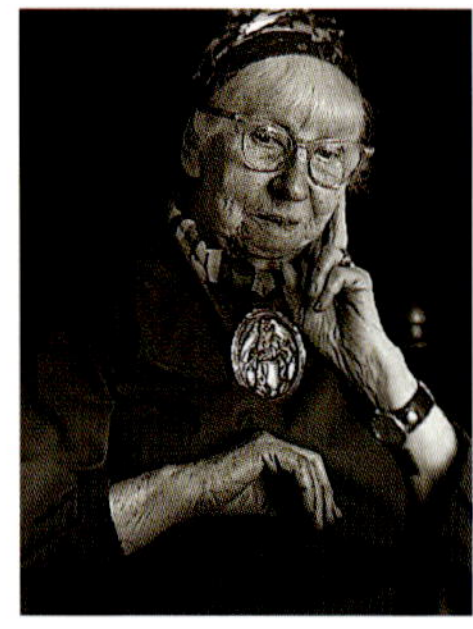

Imogen Cunningham epitomizes the Bay Area's tradition of evangelical, liberal humanism, most unequivocally expressed in her images of people. Her interest in photography began with portraiture but was inclusive, often focusing on flowers. Her works, blending romanticism and realism, are a history of a society and envelop the autobiography of an artist.

Born in 1883, Imogen—as she was always called—grew up in Seattle. In the absence of an art curriculum at the University of Washington, she studied chemistry, graduating in 1907, and then photographic chemistry at Dresden's Technische Hochscule in 1909. In 1915 she married etcher Roi Partridge. They soon moved with their three sons to the Bay Area. In the early 1930s she associated with Group f/64. She and Partridge divorced in 1934. Honored, beloved, and respected, Imogen died in 1976.

*Coffee Gallery* is a serendipitous portrait of a woman called "Linda Lovely"[1] talking with Len Monroe. Richard Lorenz, trustee/curator of the Imogen Cunningham Trust, has written: "As a humanitarian, liberal, and supporter of civil rights, Cunningham produced countless portraits of blacks during the years of segregation. Today it is hard to imagine the power and significance some of her photographs held. Her many images of interracial couples were considered both daring and strident. *Coffee Gallery* . . . was often singled out by critics as reflecting Cunningham's commitment to equality and social justice."[2]

*Have a good life and let other people have one, too. I don't interfere with anyone. I'm not jealous of anybody. I just believe in working, I'm not one of those romantic explainers of my own individual point of view.*[3]

1. MARGERY MANN, IMOGEN CUNNINGHAM PHOTOGRAPHS (SEATTLE AND LONDON: UNIVERSITY OF WASHINGTON PRESS, 1970), P. 17.

2. IMOGEN CUNNINGHAM PORTRAITURE: PHOTOGRAPHS BY IMOGEN CUNNINGHAM (BOSTON: BULFINCH PRESS, 1997), PP. 28, 37 (NOTE 54).

3. IBID., P. 25.

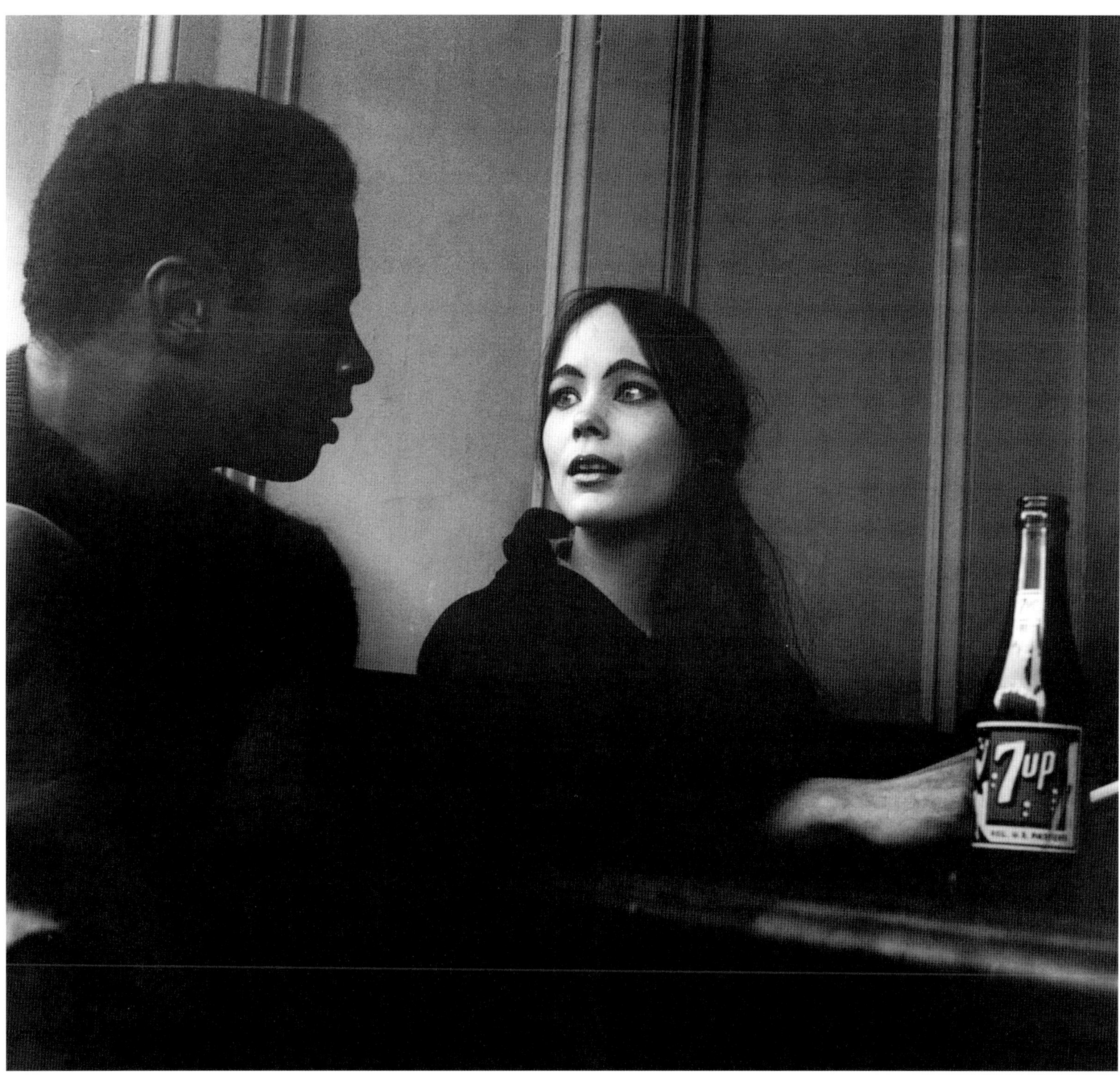
7up

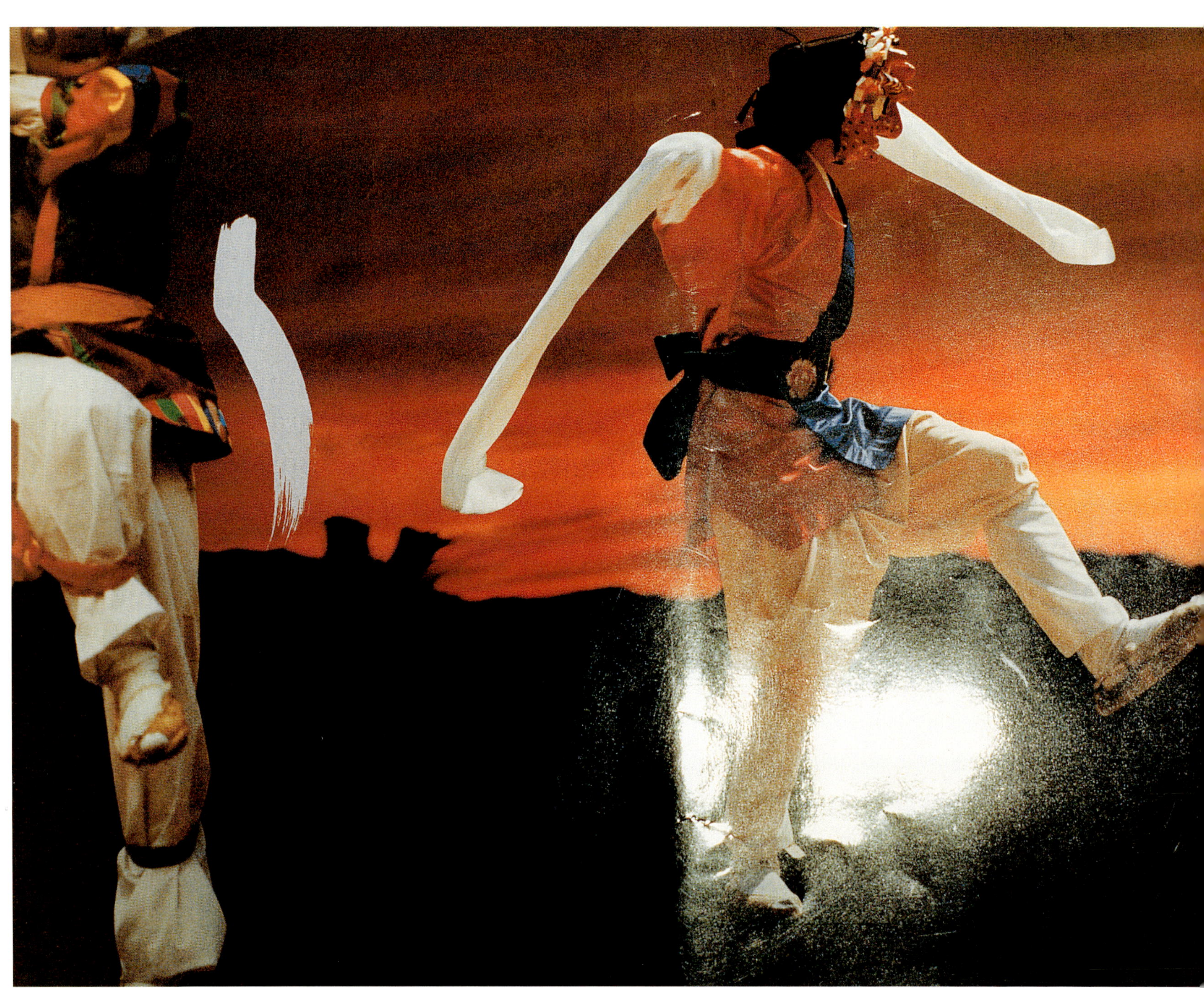

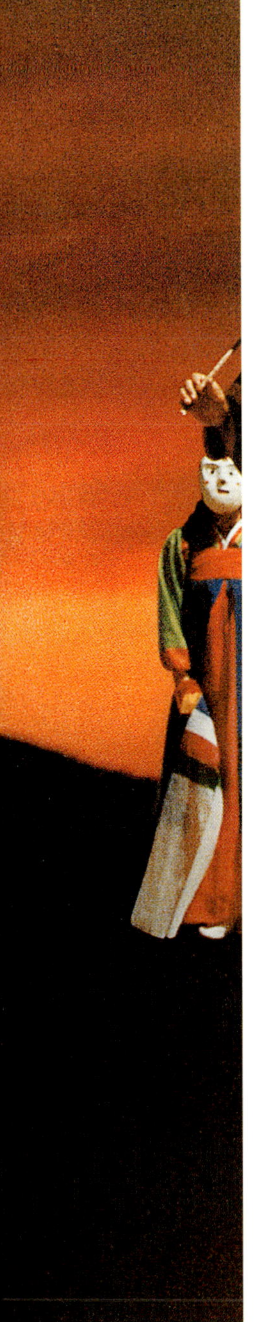

# BILL DANE

1989, EKTACOLOR PRINT, ED. 2/10, 24½ × 36¾

## *San Francisco (Masked Dancers)*

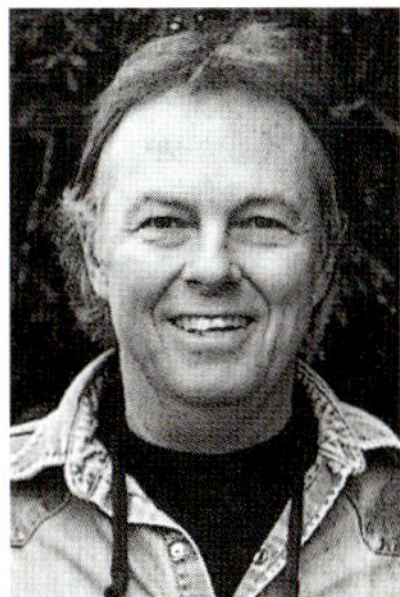

A disaster brought Bill Dane to photography. Fire destroyed his studio and all the paintings in it just before a solo exhibition. Those paintings had been canvases patterned with squares of color, created to focus meditative attention on each surface. Undaunted, Dane prepared new works for the exhibition—gridded, color-field paintings and ethereal, spray-painted, filmy sheets of plastic. Simultaneously, he also began to make photographs: color contact sheets of ordinary images repeated with slight variations—for example, items from his wardrobe.[1] Secure in conventions such as the grid and the commonplace, he began a career creating works that catapult himself, and willing viewers, into the realm of the metaphysical.

Ann Swidler, inspired by an insight of D. H. Lawrence into the American character, links Dane to the American fascination with "evil and the kind of redemption that might come from confronting its mysteries. . . . Dane shows us not an exotic heart of darkness, but the American difficulty in dealing with what we cannot understand, own, or control."[2]

William Thacher Dane was born in Pasadena, California, in 1938. He received BAs in art and political science in 1964 and an MA in painting in 1968, all from the University of California, Berkeley. In 1971 he attended workshops with Diane Arbus and Lee Friedlander at the University Film Study Center, Hampshire College, Amherst, Massachusetts. He lives in Albany, California.

*Taken in San Francisco's Mission District, this photograph, like all of my others, is the result of walking, treasure hunting, exploring the surfaces of our cultures looking for bits and pieces of possible truths. My pleasure.*

1. ANN SWIDLER, "INTRODUCTION," *PHOTOGRAPHS OUTSIDE AND INSIDE AMERICA*, PALACIO DE LOS CONDES DE GABIA, GRANADA, SPAIN, SEPTEMBER 30–NOVEMBER 7, 1993, EXHIBITION CATALOGUE, P. 6.

2. IBID., P. 14.

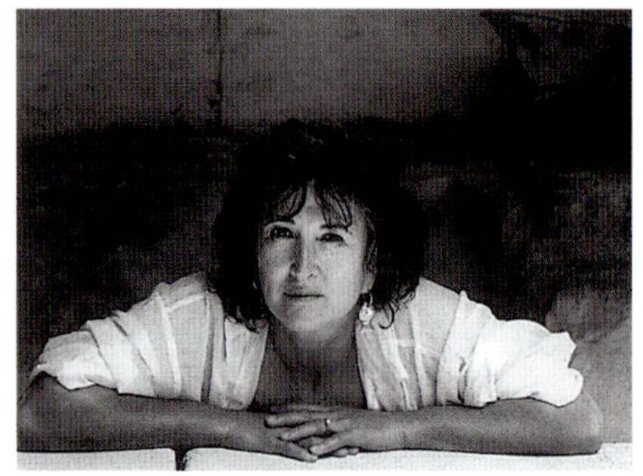

# JUDY DATER

Born in 1941 in Hollywood, where her father owned and managed a movie theater, Judy Dater early on experienced the romance, theatricality, and adventure of film. After initially studying drawing and painting at UCLA, she transferred to San Francisco State University, where she received a BA in 1963 and an MA in photography in 1966. Early in her career, she aspired to be a landscape photographer in the tradition of Ansel Adams. Feeling a compulsion, however, to include a human figure, she eventually realized that she was more interested in the figure than in the landscape. Subsequently she has achieved fame as a photographer of people, although the range of her work is more inclusive. She lives in Palo Alto, California.

Dater's images in this book are self-portraits. As *Ms. Clingfree* she represents the ordinary housewife oppressed by domesticity. She used a timer for *Untitled.*

*The older I get, the one thing I can trust in myself more than anything else is the way I feel about something. When I photograph I try to be as aware of my feelings as I can be and to somehow try and get them out of me and onto the film in terms of the way I am responding or seeing the world. I can then sit back and look at the stuff and analyze it in certain objective ways after it's all done and tell whether or not it works graphically. I can tell if it's good technically, but at the moment when I am actually making the picture, all I can go on is my feelings about things.*[1]

1. DAVID FAHEY, "INTERVIEW," EDITED BY MAXINE WOLF, G. RAY HAWKINS GALLERY, LOS ANGELES, *PHOTO BULLETIN*, VOL. II, NO. 8 (DECEMBER 1979), P. 3.

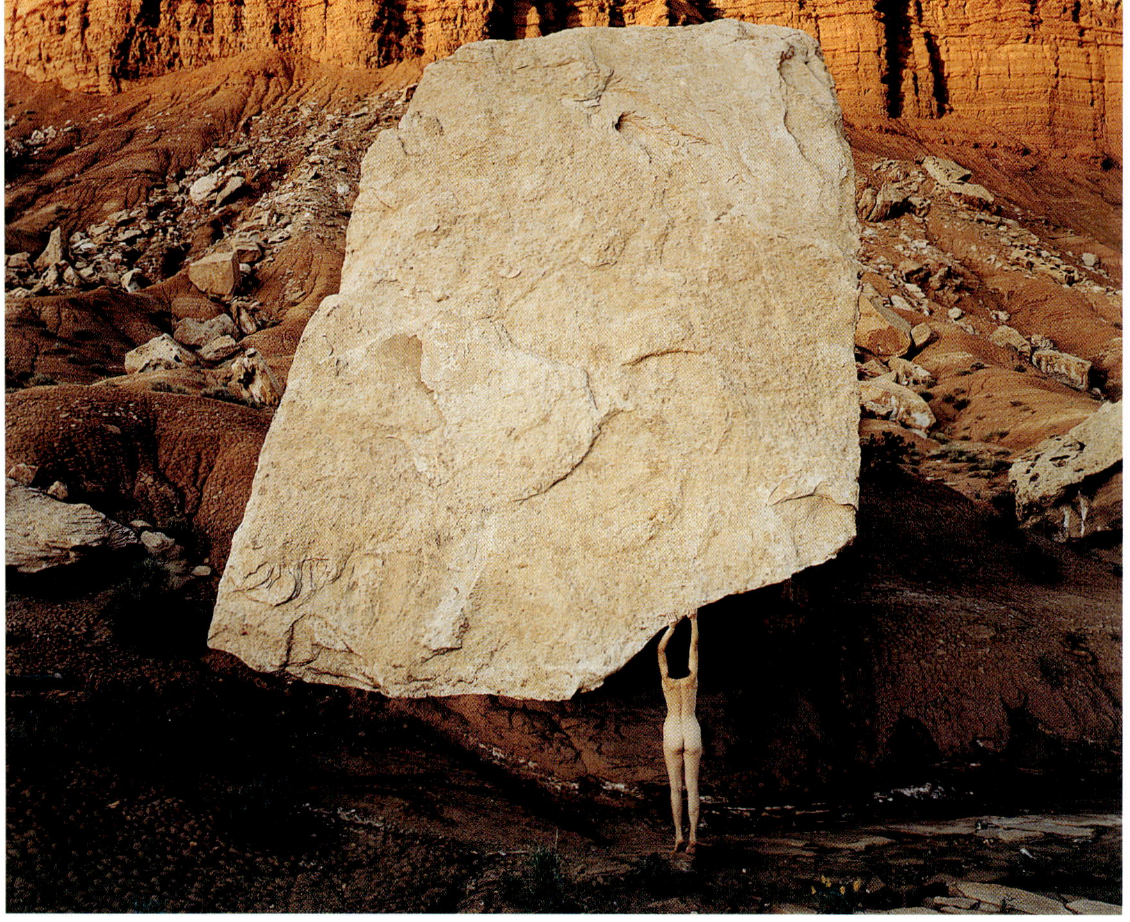

***Untitled***

1983, COLOR COUPLER PRINT, 15 × 19

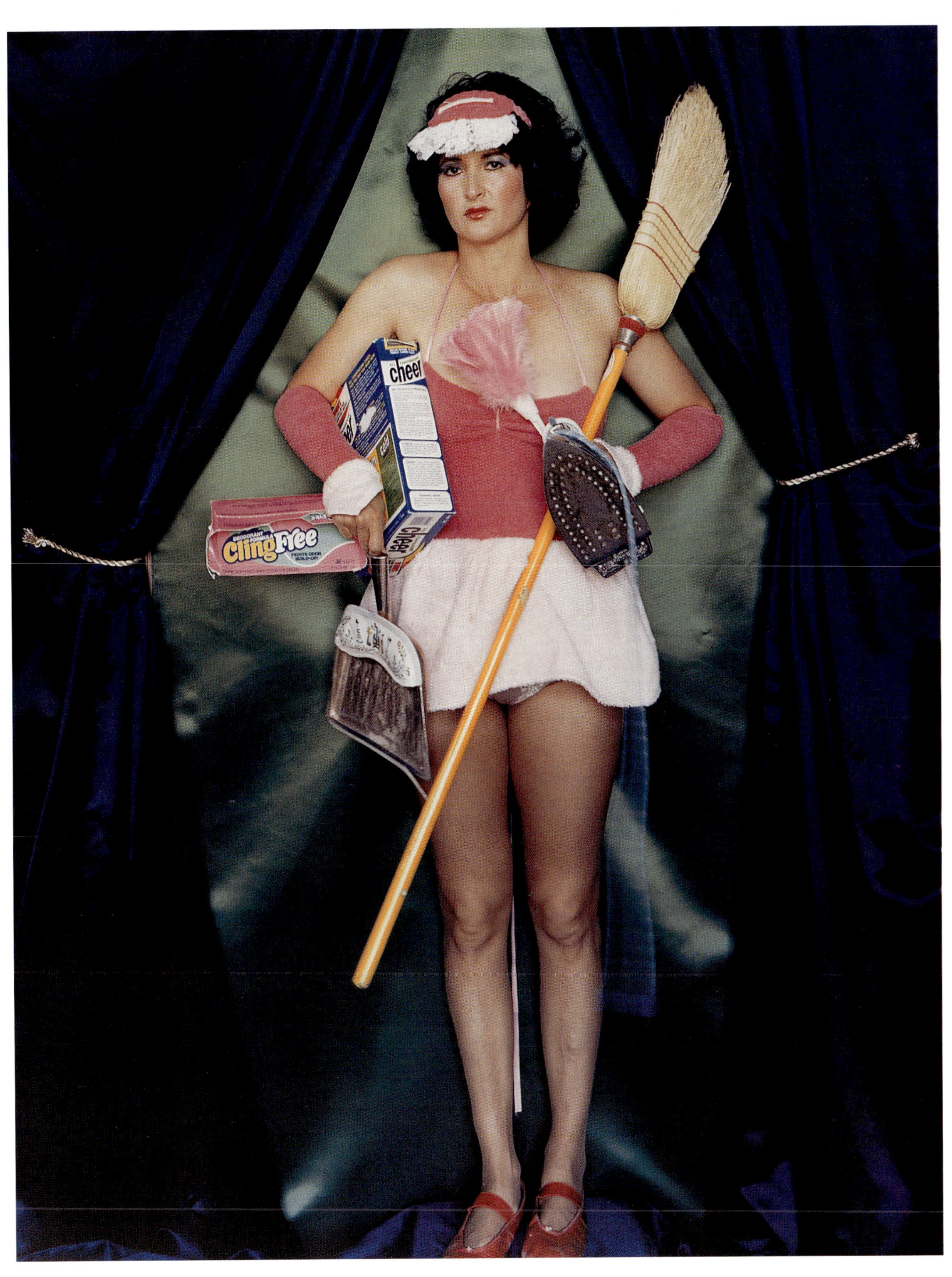


*Ms. Clingfree*

1982, EKTACOLOR PRINT, 17½ × 14

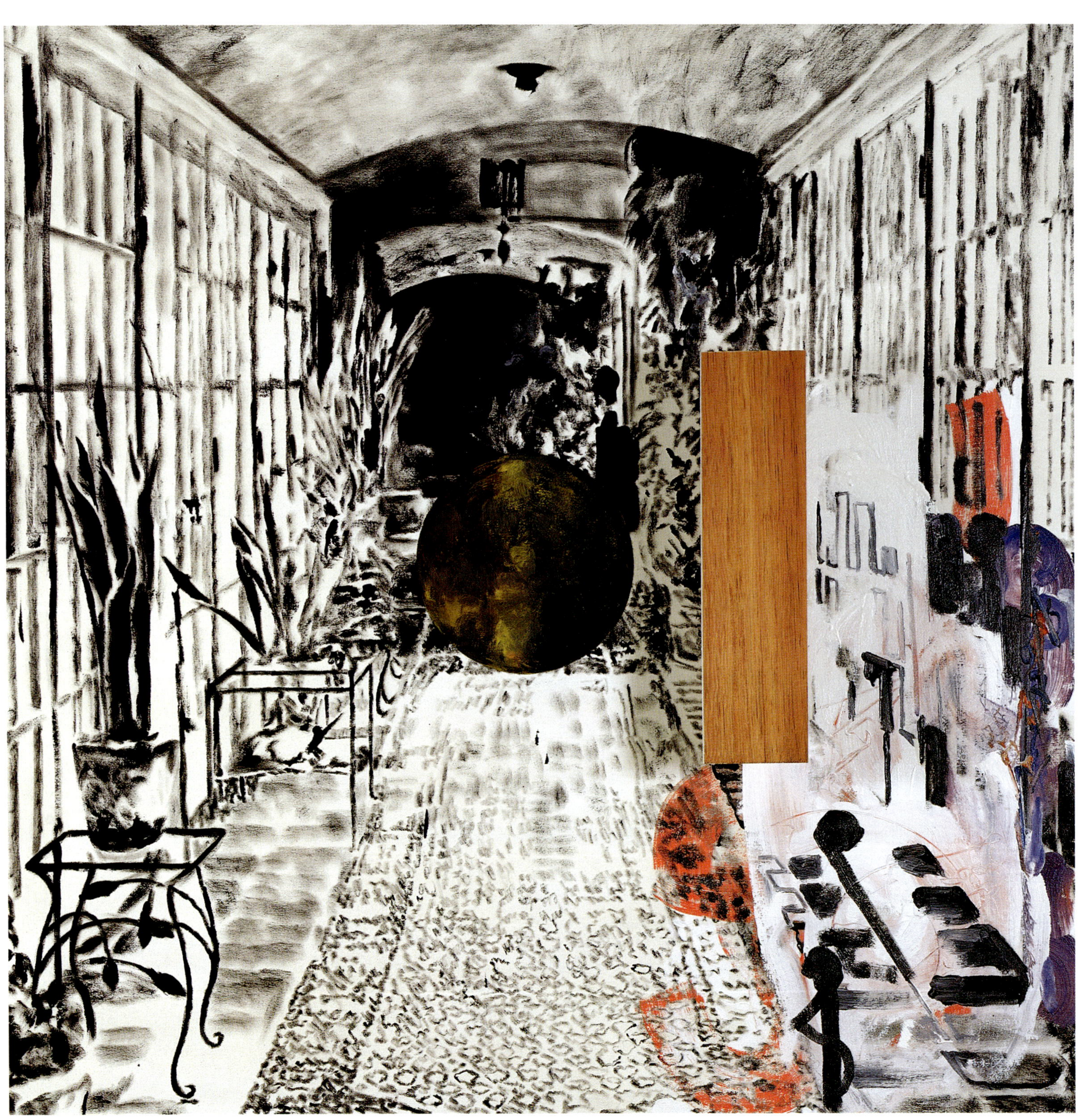

# STEPHEN DAVIS *Corridor*

1986, OIL AND PLYWOOD ON CANVAS, 60 × 60 × 8½

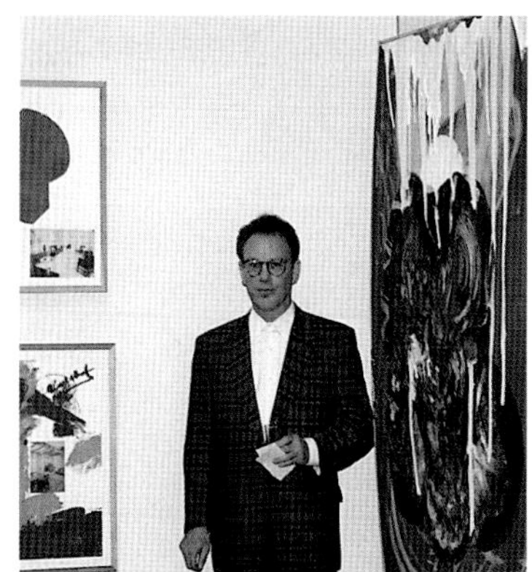

Stephen Davis makes "tough" art. He requires that viewers look closely at his works and think about them, granting them more than fifteen seconds each.

For his paintings of the early 1970s, Davis used large rectangles of unstretched canvas that he covered with dabs of color in a mechanical and ostensibly random fashion to emphasize the paintings' objectness. Later he used smaller, stretched canvases that he painted as monochromatic fields and exhibited as diptychs of complementary colors. In the mid-1970s he created works that came playfully, and literally, "off the wall" using two- or three-dimensional components. In front of wall-oriented squares or rectangles of canvas or Sheetrock, he placed painted mattresses supported horizontally by flowerpots.

Davis still unites humor with seriousness in his recent mixed-media works, about which art historian Mowry Baden writes: "These are among Davis's funniest works. The conventions of spatial represention are forced to live with 'real time' gestural painting and an applied, actual object. After a few minutes of examination, a kind of visual shake-and-bake occurs and all of the carefully delineated conventions begin to lose their stability. The mood changes wildly from work to work. Some are droll, others are mock sinister."[1]

Davis was born in Fort Worth, Texas, in 1945. He received a BA in political science from Claremont Men's College in 1967 and an MFA from the Claremont Graduate School in 1971. He lives in New York City, where he has taught at Hunter College from 1987 to 1993 and from 1995 to the present.

*Comment on* Corridor: *Something from this world and that.*

1. MOWRY BADEN, STEPHEN DAVIS—70'S, 80'S, 90'S, JERNIGAN WICKER FINE ARTS, SAN FRANCISCO, APRIL 29–MAY 30, 1992, EXHIBITION CATALOGUE, P. 2.

# JAY DEFEO

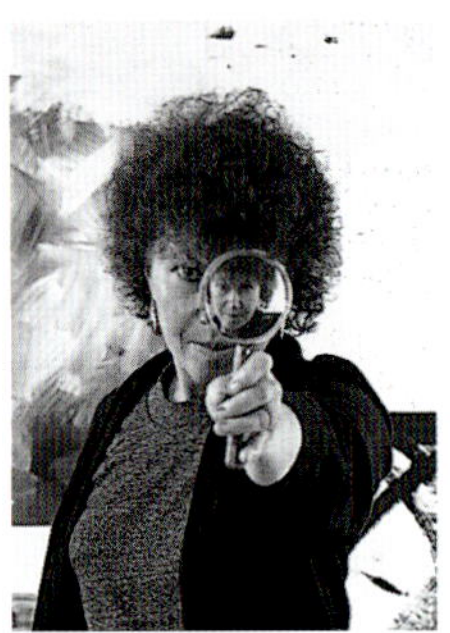

Many remember Jay DeFeo reverently because of her total commitment to art. After receiving a BA in 1950 and an MA in 1951 from the University of California, Berkeley, she traveled for two years in Europe on a fellowship. In 1954 she married Wally Hedrick. Her huge, gray, abstract paintings were remarkable for their sculptural surfaces. The most famous, *The Rose,* a radiating form measuring 129 × 92 × 8 inches and weighing 2,300 pounds, took six years, from 1958 to 1964, to complete. It is in the collection of the Whitney Museum of American Art.

*Isis,* from a later period, exhibits her talent for representation, and *Geisha I,* still later, recalls her early expressiveness, with strong color added.

DeFeo, born in New Hampshire in 1929, grew up in the San Francisco Bay Area. She died in 1989.

*Although I am known as a painter, I have sculptural concerns in my painting and have done sculpture in the past. The medium of oil led to sculptural expression. The change to acrylic and mixed media [as in* Isis*] allowed me a more illusionistic treatment of volume, in the Renaissance tradition. This reflects my concern with expressionism and freely painted surfaces as well as areas treated with refinement and precision.*

*My ideas often emerge in response to materials and elements of chance. I enjoy investigating form, exploring the many possibilities of a visual idea. My early interest in black and white was triggered by Abstract Expressionism. I personally consider my palette to be one of limited color range. I am as interested in texture as in color, and texture is often closely connected to my choice of color.*[1]

1. HENRY HOPKINS, 50 WEST COAST ARTISTS: A CRITICAL SELECTION OF PAINTERS AND SCULPTORS WORKING IN CALIFORNIA (SAN FRANCISCO: CHRONICLE BOOKS, 1981), P. 36.

***Isis***

1972, ACRYLIC AND MIXED MEDIA ON MASONITE, 48 × 24

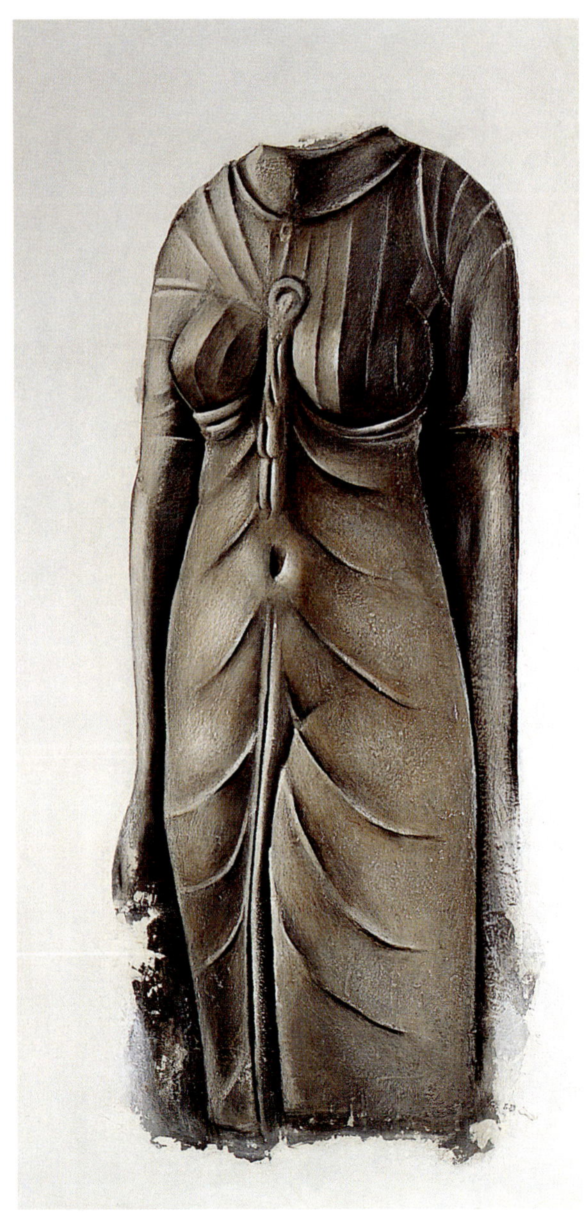

***Geisha I***

1987, OIL ON CANVAS, 84 × 60

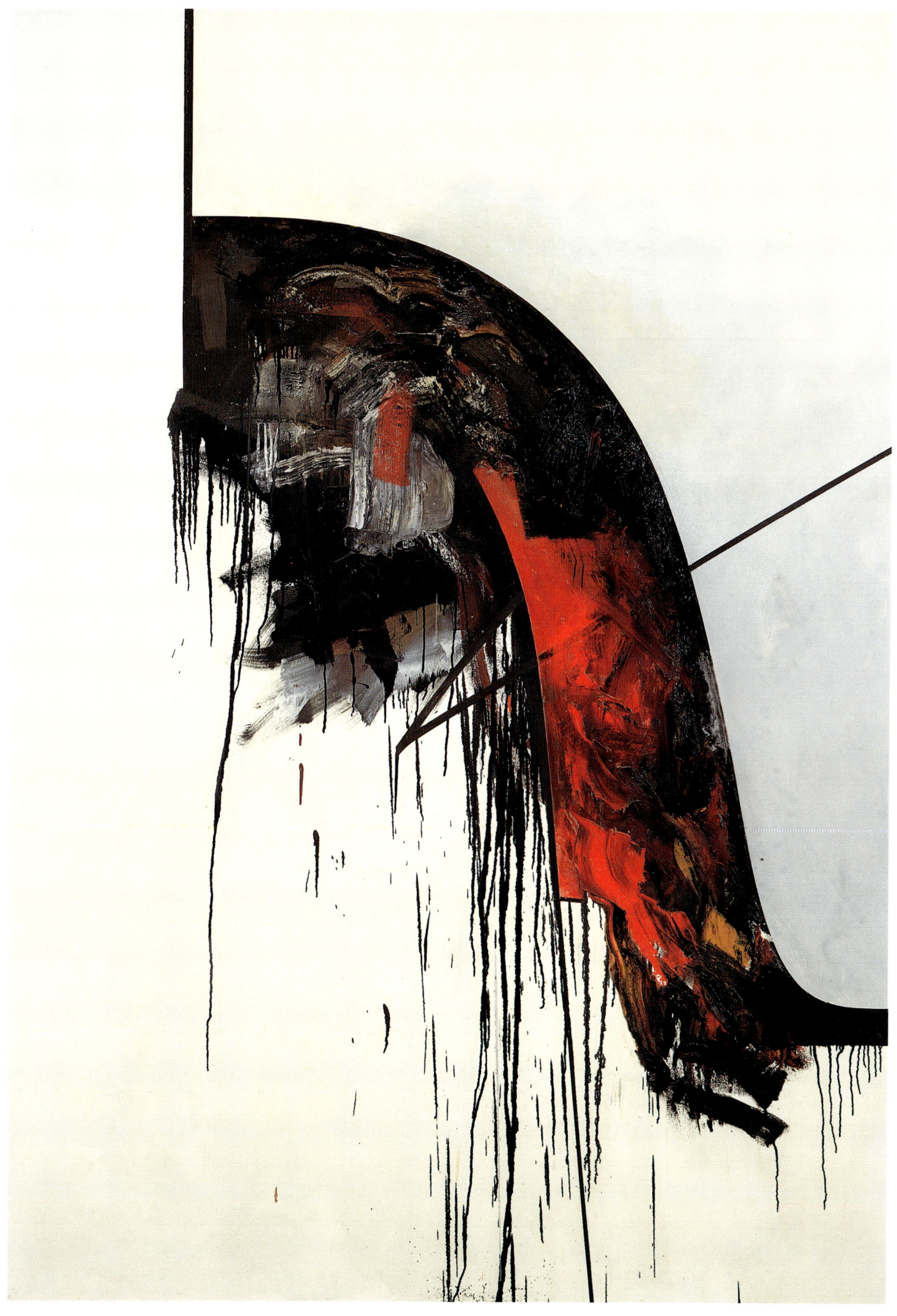

# ROY DE FOREST

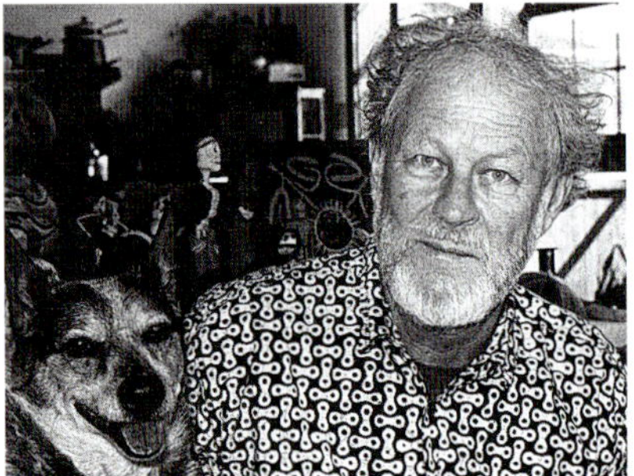

Roy De Forest is a gloriously idiosyncratic artist known chiefly for his paintings crowded with images of humanoid figures, horses, and dogs, seen in fantasy environments that are like amusement-park villages or Henri Rousseau forests. All are on a very flat plane, similar to those used spontaneously by folk artists such as Grandma Moses. Examinations of the meanings of his works, however, could fill tomes. In the French tradition, which the artist acknowledges, while playful and accessible, they are intellectually challenging and serious. The essential points, however, are that human beings are animals related to other animals and, like them, respond to instinct—as the artist does in creating his works.

The bold colors, forms, and lines, the free use of dots of paint straight from their tubes, and, in his sculptures, the ostensibly devil-may-care but invariably harmonious assembling of components all indicate an artist who enjoys his craft.

## *One Life to Lead*

1986. PAINTED WOOD. 60 × 109½ × 24

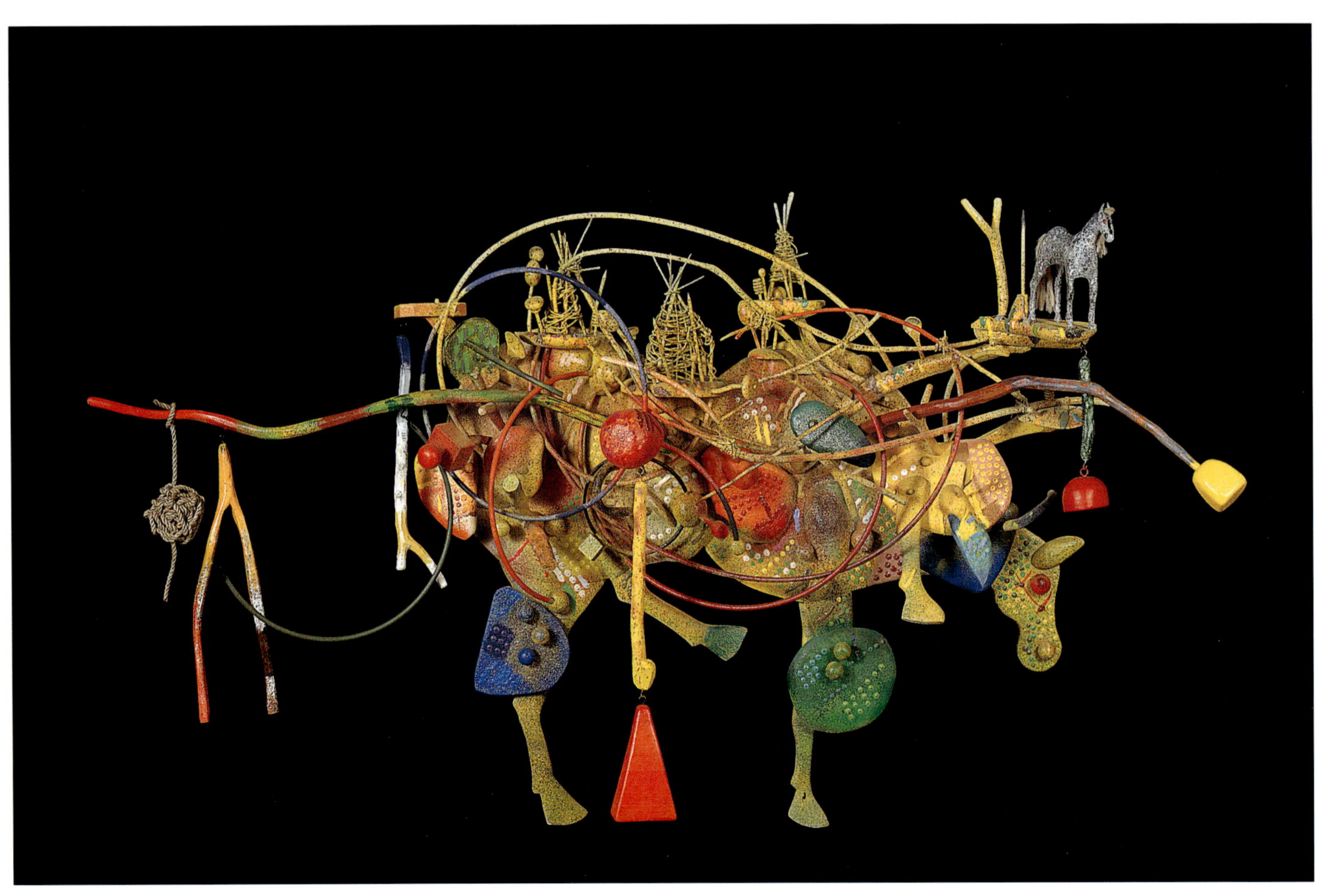

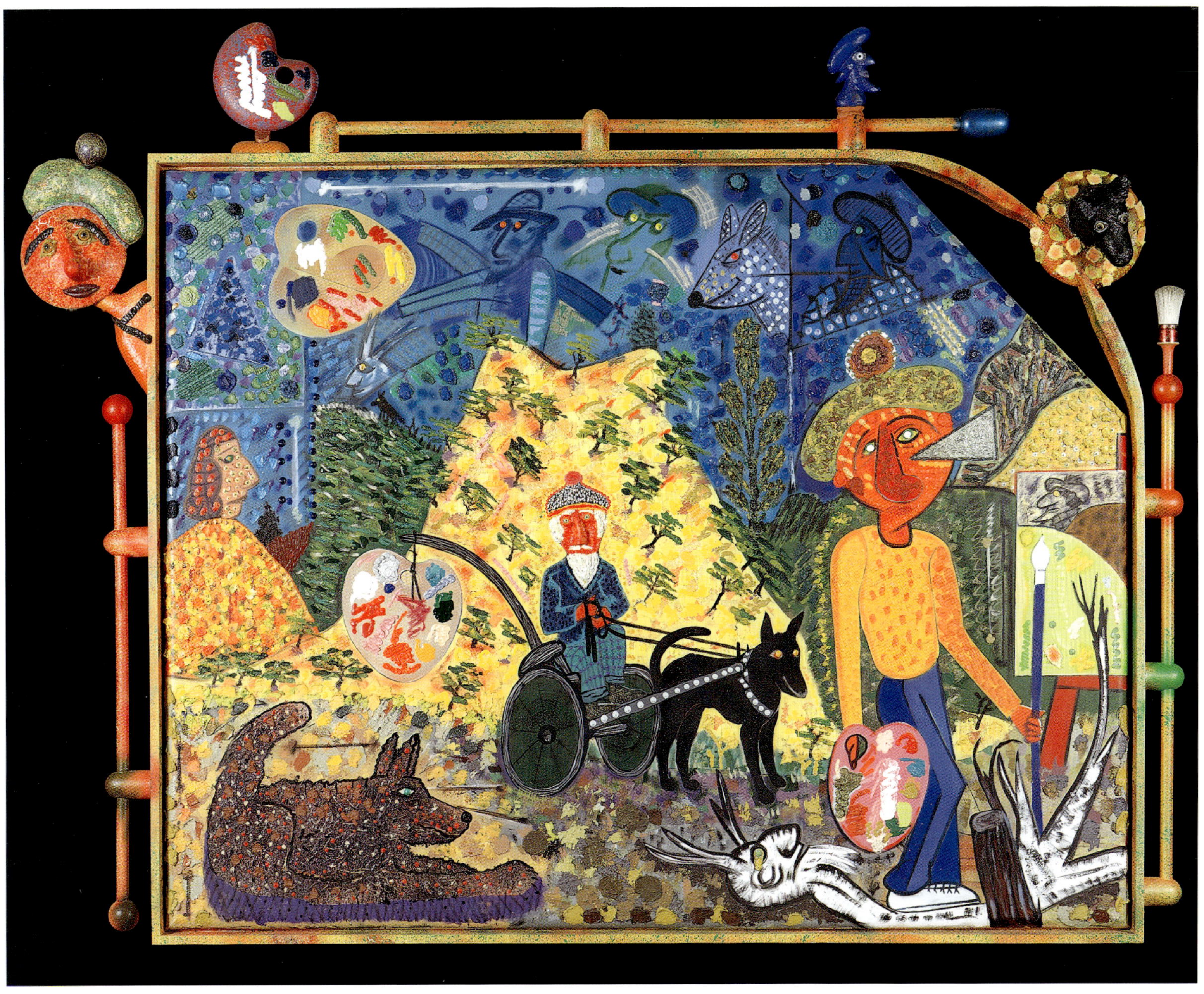

## *Camp of the Landscape Artists*

1991. POLYMER PAINT ON LINEN WITH WOOD AND MIXED MEDIA. 87½ × 116 × 10

De Forest was born in North Platte, Nebraska, in 1930 and grew up on a farm. He lived in Yakima, Washington, before attending the San Francisco Art Institute from 1950 until 1952. He transferred to San Francisco State University, where he earned a BA in 1953 and, after military service, an MA in 1958. He lives in Port Costa, California, and taught at the University of California, Davis, from 1965 until 1982.

*I am an eccentric individual creating fantasy art with the amazing intention of totally building a miniature cosmos into which the artful alchemist could retire with all his friends, animals, and paraphernalia.*[1]

1. PHILIP LINHARES, HERE AND NOW: BAY AREA MASTERWORKS FROM THE DI ROSA COLLECTION, THE OAKLAND MUSEUM, MARCH 11–MAY 8, 1994, EXHIBITION CATALOGUE, P. 18.

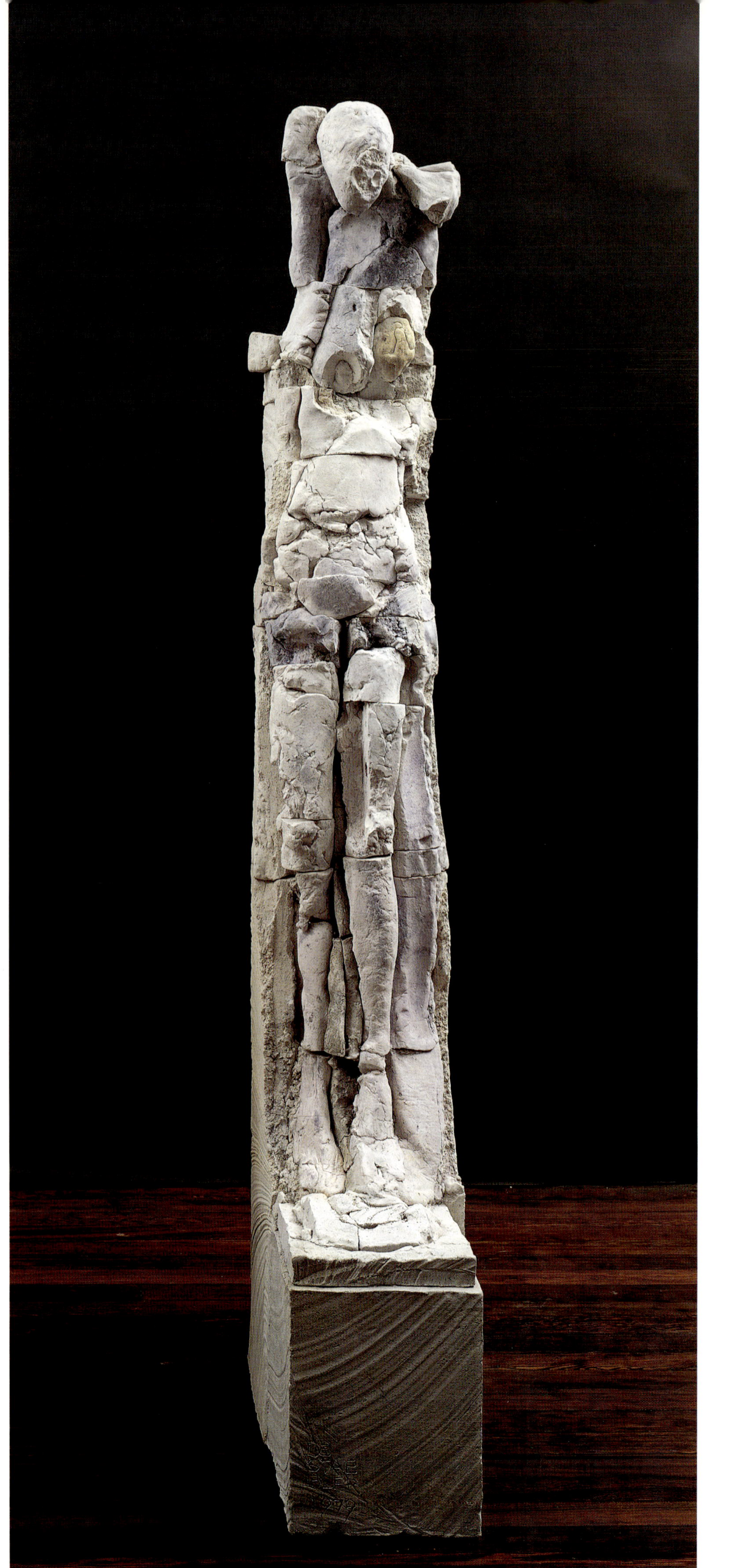

# STEPHEN DE STAEBLER

***Standing Woman with Yellow Breast*** 1979. PORCELAIN AND LOW-FIRE CLAYS. 87½ × 14½ × 26½

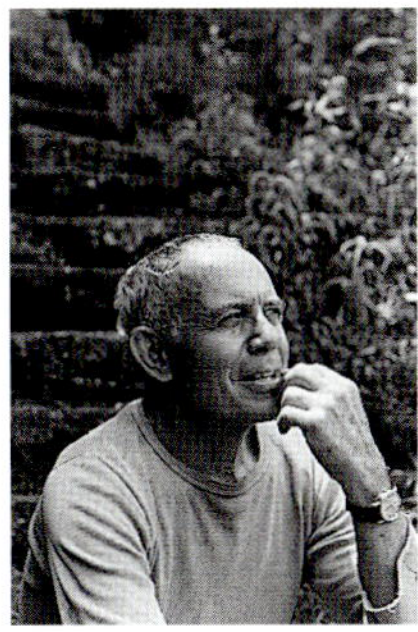

Stephen De Staebler was one of the earliest students to work with Peter Voulkos in the ceramics studio established at the University of California, Berkeley, in 1959. Like Voulkos, he threw himself into the creative process, wrestling with the clay, kicking and punching it in order to incorporate and conjoin the physical force of universal gravity and the personal expressions of human passion. His sculptures thus more nearly represented direct objectifications of universal energy than they would have if they had been formed by the artist's hands and eyes directed solely by his mind. This intimacy with the clay gives his works a palpably erotic charge.

The forms De Staebler has made range from what appear to be admonitory masks, to floor-oriented covers for tombs and shelters from disasters or beds for penance, to rough-shaped thrones for Celtic or Balkan epic heroes. Most memorable, however, are his figurative works (such as *Standing Woman with Yellow Breast*), which are composed of separately fired, tinted, stacked chunks of clay and resemble giant, fossilized human forms and remnants of ancient monuments. His questing, having begun in religion, continues in art.

De Staebler was born in St. Louis in 1933 and attended Princeton University, earning a degree in religion in 1954. In 1961 he received an MA from UC Berkeley.

*The tie between the earth and ourselves is so essential that it is usually obscured by our obsession with separateness. I have tried to find a visual equivalent for our tie with the whole. The earth's landscape has been my starting point, with clay—earth—the medium.*

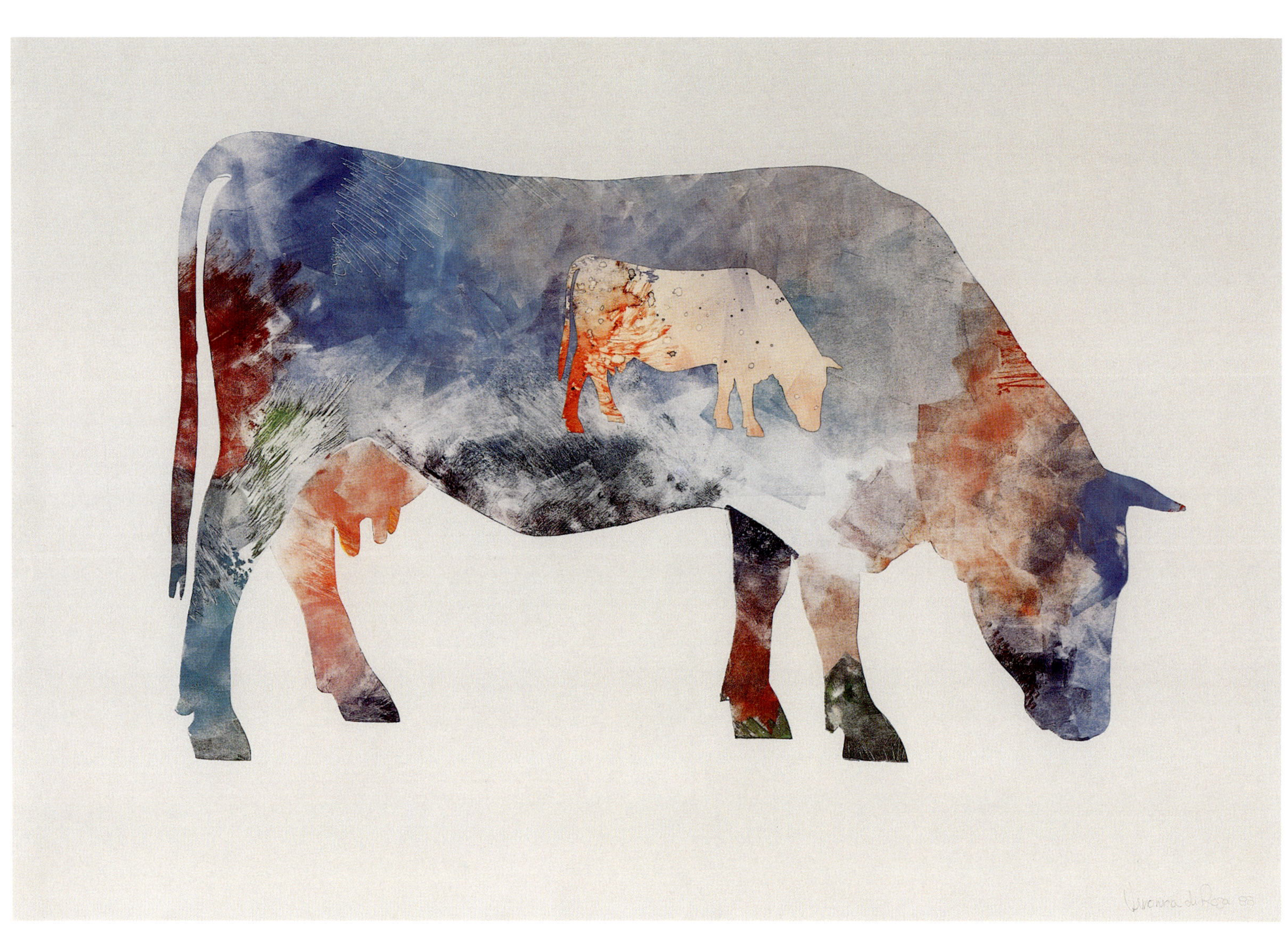

# VERONICA DI ROSA

## *Secondary Cow*

1988, MONOTYPE, 30 × 44½

Veronica di Rosa began working as a fine artist when she was eighteen years old. Through the years, she employed whatever medium she felt would allow her to express her developing artistic vision and life interests, including watercolor, painting, sculpture, printmaking, mixed-media art furniture, assemblage, wine art (labels, posters, brochures, logotypes, and letterheads), and stained glass. She also produced monotypes for Smith-Andersen Editions of Palo Alto, California, and the American Academy in Rome (1988–1990), and a suite of lithographs with narration, *Letters from Henry,* for Limestone Press in San Francisco (1990–1991).

Di Rosa was capable of engaging viewers intimately for a period of time, as in *Travels with Henry,* and of startling and amusing them briefly, as with her flock of steel sheep visible from Carneros Highway on a hillside of the di Rosa Preserve. Her *Secondary Cow* plays several visual jokes.

Born in 1934 in Kelowna, British Columbia, Canada, di Rosa spent a period of time at the Art Center in Pasadena, California, and then earned a BFA at the Emily Carr School of Art in Vancouver, British Columbia, in 1969. From 1980 through 1984 she studied privately with master watercolorist Robert Kinmont. She exhibited nationally in the United States and Canada; her works are in collections throughout the United States and in France and Switzerland. She died tragically in October 1991, falling from a cliff in Normandy while picking wildflowers.

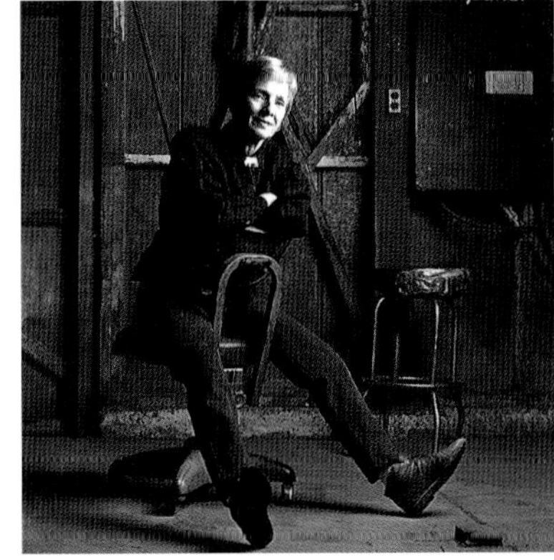

Veronica di Rosa's statement begins with her artwork and extends into her community: it is the tone of the Napa Valley, beginning with its overall visual culture. Among many other interests, she championed the restoration of the Napa Valley Opera House.

# MARK DI SUVERO

*For Veronica* 1987. PAINTED STEEL. 261 × 422 × 468

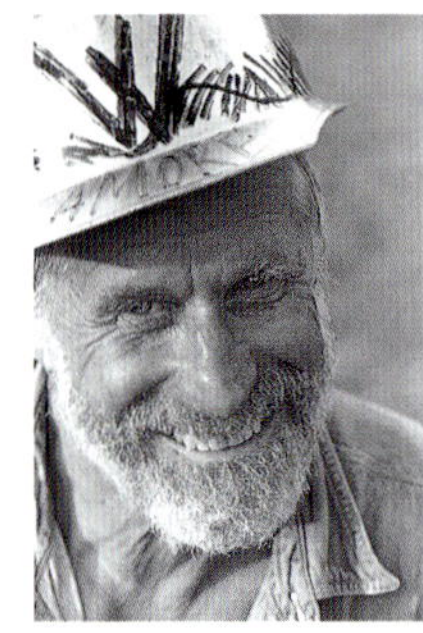

Mark di Suvero is one of the most visible artists working in the United States today. His sculptures are usually monumental in scale, have his signature look, and are often brightly painted. He has an international reputation and is critically acclaimed.

Di Suvero was born in Shanghai, China, in 1933. He moved to San Francisco in 1941, attended San Francisco City College from 1953 through 1954, and then transferred to the University of California, Santa Barbara. After a year he transferred to UC Berkeley, where he received a BA in 1956. The following year he moved to New York City. Since the mid-1970s he has divided his time between New York and the Bay Area, where he maintains a studio in Petaluma. The open space of the western coast may have been an early influence on the expansiveness of his work, as it was for the great dance innovators Isadora Duncan in San Francisco and Martha Graham in Santa Barbara during their formative years.

Di Suvero applies the principles of action painting in three dimensions, using found metal parts and weathered timber beams to create sculptures that resemble the gestural ideograms of Abstract Expressionist painter Franz Kline. Di Suvero can also be playful, however, using rubber tires as seats for viewers to become participants in a kinetic piece. Recently he has moved in the direction of using more pristine materials in structures that are complex and elegant, but nevertheless assertive.

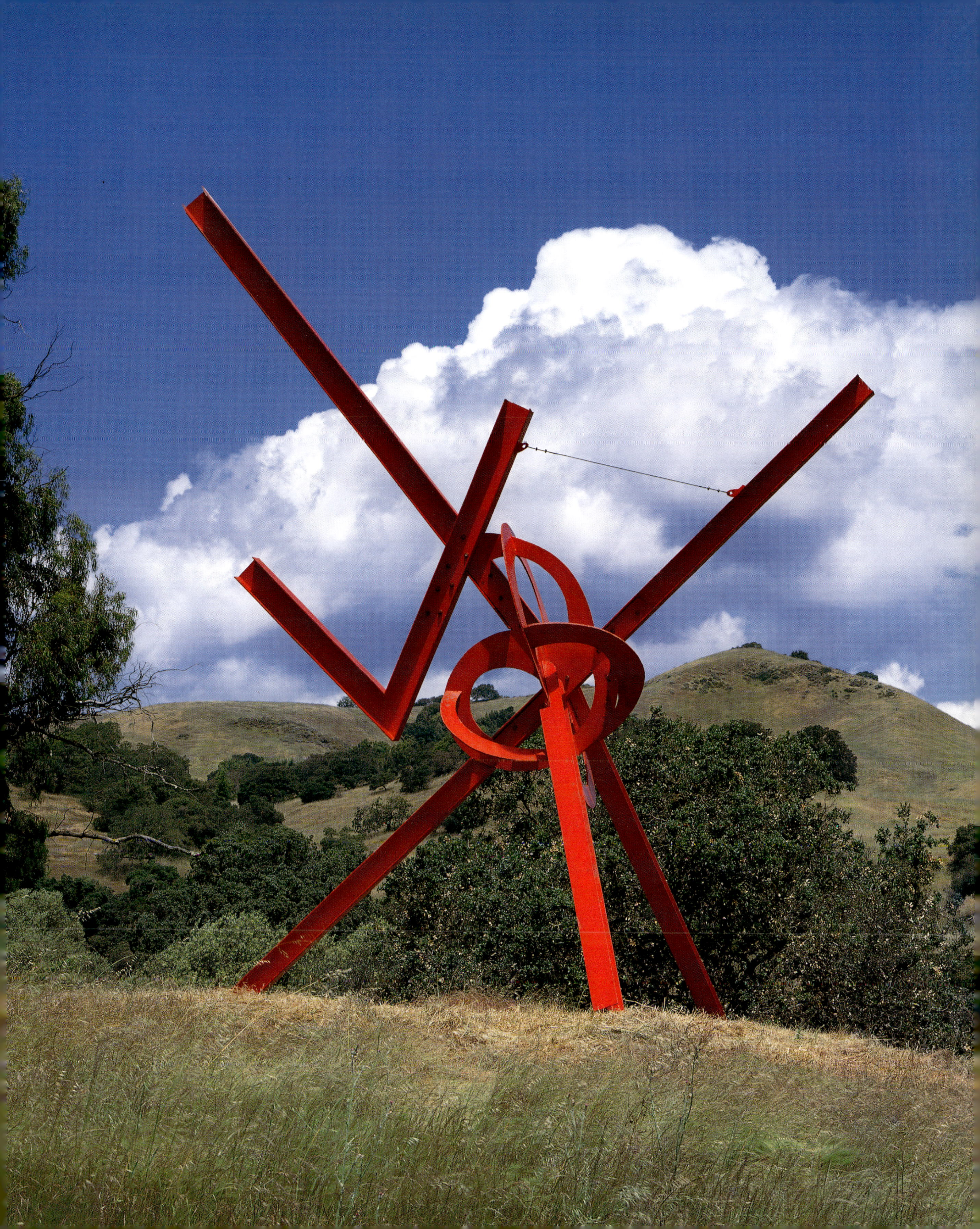

# VIOLA FREY

*Homage* 1987. CERAMIC. 60 × 96 × 84

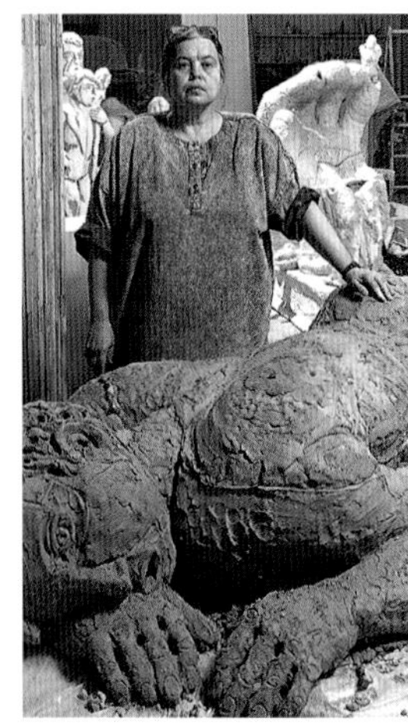

Viola Frey is an aggressively independent artist. In her massive ceramic figures daubed with unusual colors, she puts a Pop perspective on the tradition of Bay Area expressive painting and Funk sculpture.

Frey is a truly idiosyncratic artist who has consistently followed her own vision—liberally appropriating the conventions of traditional American folk art while incorporating contemporary everyday events and everyday people from everyday sources and creating images that seem to anticipate a dumbed-down future.

Her giant sculptures of the 1980s commented on middle-class Americans through their dress and deportment. For example, a 7½-foot male figure, *Power Blue Suit,* is dressed like an executive but has no mouth—a potent image of anomie. She also made a series of sleeping and reclining nude men, such as *Homage,* to address issues of male vulnerability, including AIDS. "Men usually are shown as warriors. Part of the sensibility I bring as a woman artist is not to leave them completely tied into that tradition."[1] In the 1990s she has explored the power relationships between men and women using monumental female nudes sitting, kneeling, and reclining alongside male figures in suits. Through the art of ceramics, Frey unifies all the visual arts and makes trenchant comments about society.

Frey was born in Lodi, California, in 1933. She received a BFA in 1956 from the California College of Arts and Crafts (CCAC) and in 1958 an MFA from Tulane University. Since 1965 she has been one of the most influential instructors in ceramics at CCAC. She lives in Oakland.

*The immediate response of clay is most useful in recording the haphazard, fragmentary character of daily living. This is the now, this noon, this day.*

1. MARCIA TANNER, "VIOLA FREY'S PERSPECTIVES ON POWER," SAN FRANCISCO CHRONICLE DATEBOOK, APRIL 10–16, 1994, P. 27.

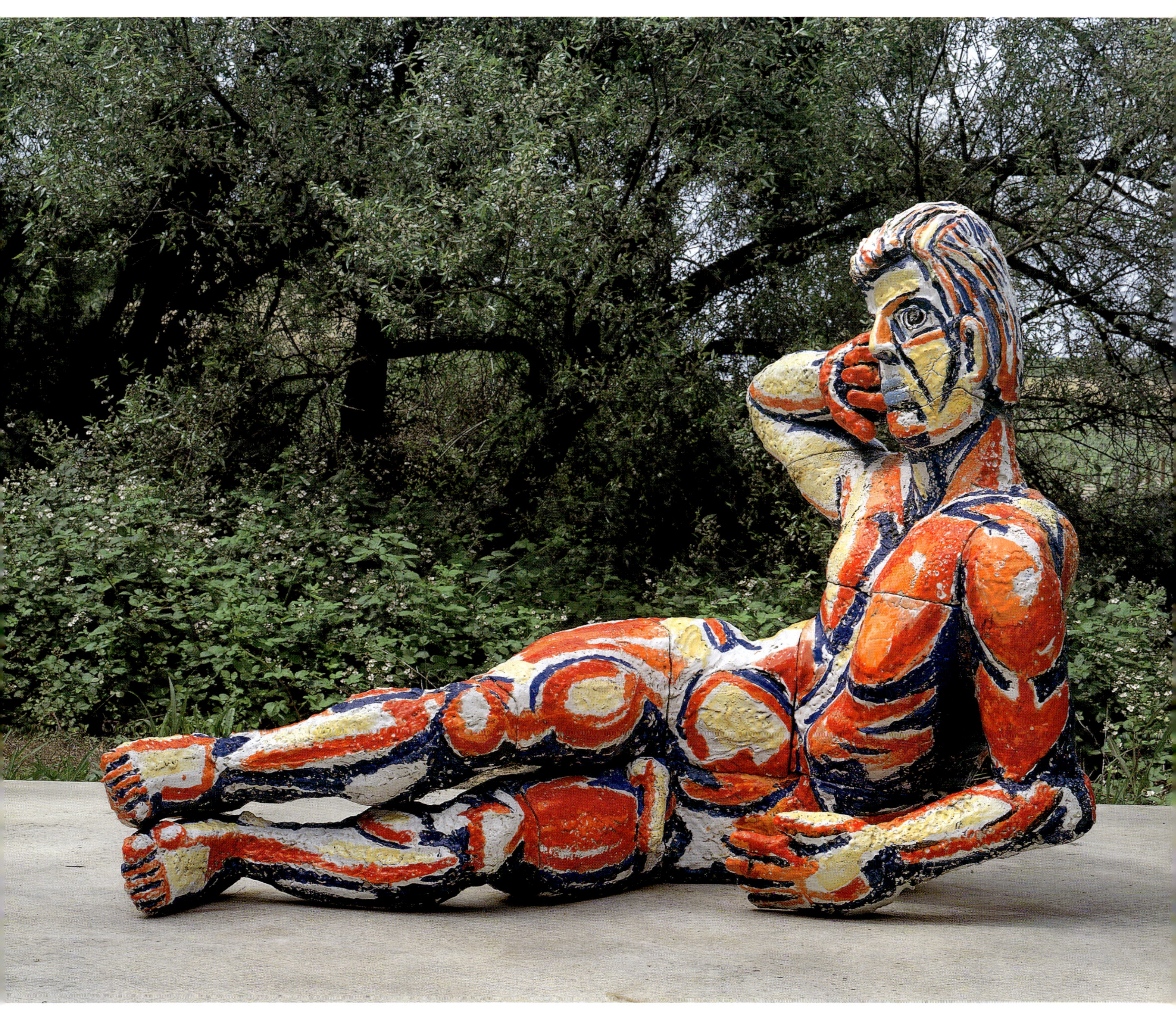

# CHARLES GATEWOOD

*Jennifer & Clint*

1995, CHROMOGENIC COLOR PRINT, ED. 2/25, 18½ × 12½

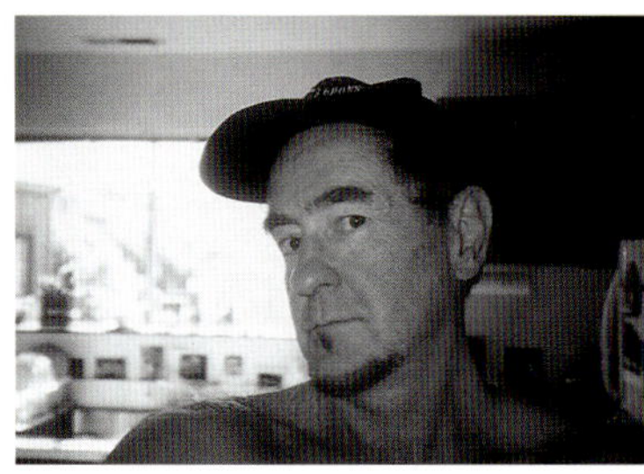

Charles Gatewood was born in Chicago in 1942. He received a BA in anthropology from the University of Missouri, Columbia, which he followed with graduate studies there and at the University of Stockholm. In 1965 he began instructing himself in photography.

In 1966 Gatewood combined the discipline of his academic mode of inquiry with his camera as the tool for carrying out his investigations into America's sexual underground. As much as many other artists, he is joining art with science. His purpose is not only to make beautiful photographs but to reveal realities other than those which society generally agrees upon as *what is real.*

At the time he initiated his inquiries, many citizens viewed Gatewood as an obsessed eccentric whose concerns were extremely marginal. Today, however, as public nudity and other forms of exhibitionism, full-body tattooing, piercing, and various types of sadomasochistic activity have encroached on mainstream American culture, his work appears not only historically significant but also uncannily prophetic.

*Jennifer & Clint* is from *True Blood,* his tenth book (published by Last Gasp Press in 1997), for which Gatewood explored blood rites, rituals, and performances.

Gatewood lives in San Francisco, where he continues his exceptional visual research.

*Two of my* favorite *models.*

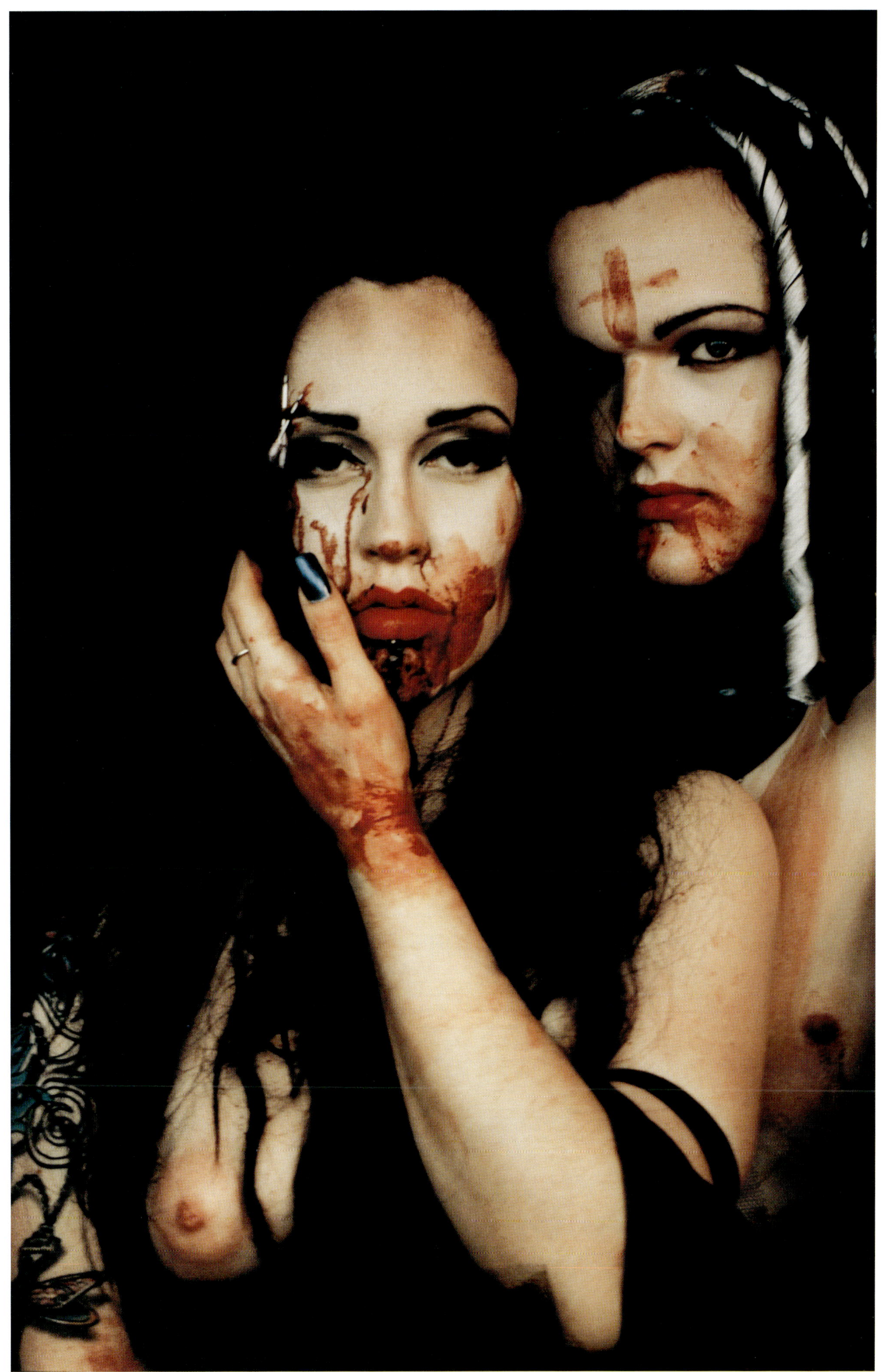

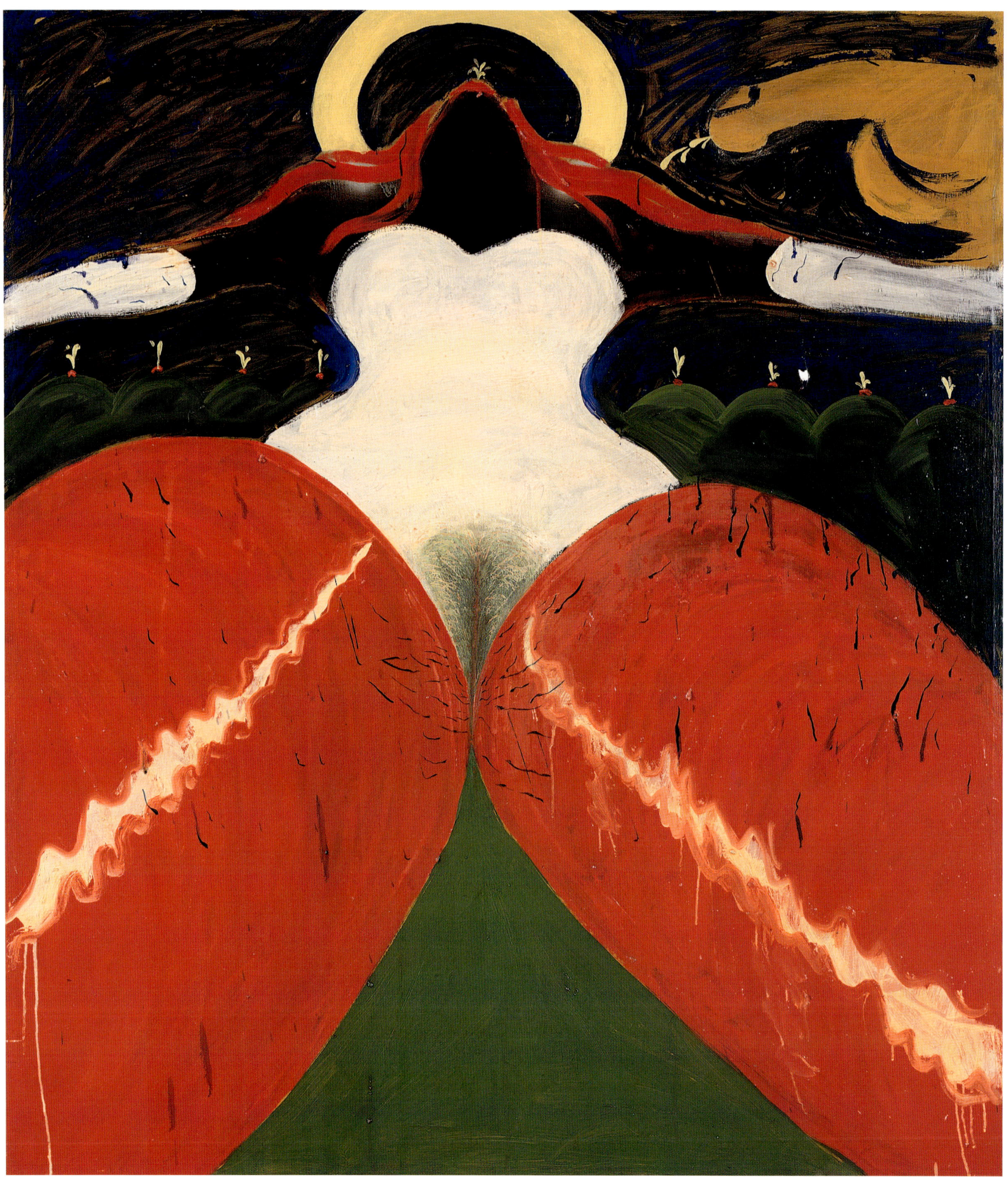

# WALLY HEDRICK

## *The Red Boots at Brown Bag Corral*

1980, OIL ON CANVAS, 62 × 54½

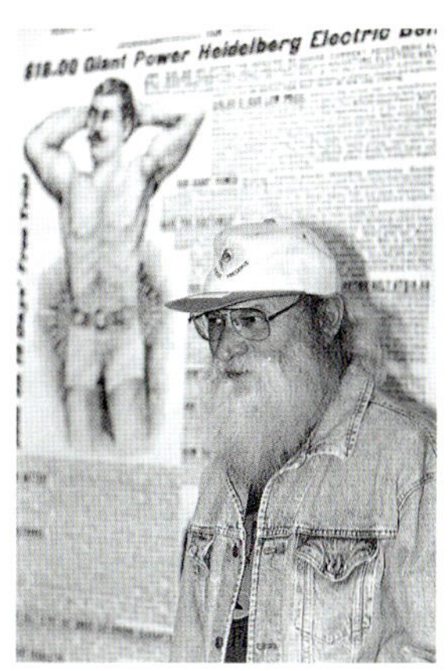


"[W]hat do I know[?] I'm just a kid from Pasadena," Wally Hedrick says of himself. Nevertheless, he was present for and a major contributor to the emergence of San Francisco as a significant center for the visual arts and new literature in the 1950s. His works and ideas, focusing on "sex, politics, and religion,"[1] advanced the definition of Funk and of everything else that has developed from it.

"It is now possible to say Hedrick was ahead of his time," Rebecca Solnit has written, "the first American artist to protest the Vietnam War, the artist who painted flags before Jasper Johns painted flags, who made kinetic junk sculpture before [Jean] Tinguely did. Hedrick was a forerunner of pop art, bad painting[,] neoexpressionism, and image appropriation."[2]

Born in Pasadena in 1928, Hedrick attended the Otis Art Institute in Los Angeles in 1947. After serving in the National Guard and seeing combat in the Korean War, he returned to schooling at the California College of Arts and Crafts in 1954, when he and Jay DeFeo married. He earned a BFA from the San Francisco Art Institute in 1955 and an MA from San Francisco State University in 1958.

*About twenty years ago I was living at Soozie Schlesinger's Brown Bag Farm near Petaluma. Soozie had a poet/writer boyfriend who was mooning around and fell in the pool. When we pulled him out he mumbled that all he wanted in life was to have "Soozie while she was wearing only a pair of red boots and riding her horse around the corral!"*

*Voilà!*

1. REBECCA SOLNIT, SECRET EXHIBITION: SIX CALIFORNIA ARTISTS OF THE COLD WAR ERA (SAN FRANCISCO: CITY LIGHTS BOOKS, 1990), P. 44.

2. IBID.

# MIKE HENDERSON

*Oldies and Goodies*

1988, OIL ON CANVAS, 70 × 70

Using traditional oils, Mike Henderson makes expressive abstract paintings that initiate total experiences with viewers, physically and intellectually. His early works, which protested social injustice from his base in Oakland, gave way in the 1980s to oils conveying a sense of the musical form called blues. He is a proficient guitarist, and some of his paintings are easily read as visualizations of jazz.

Recently, Henderson says, he has been thinking of his works as congruences of time and sound as well as of space and color. "Ultimately," he says, "I would like each painting to be a question rather than an answer—the inner space of the painting as the take-off point for a corresponding inner journey within the viewer."[1]

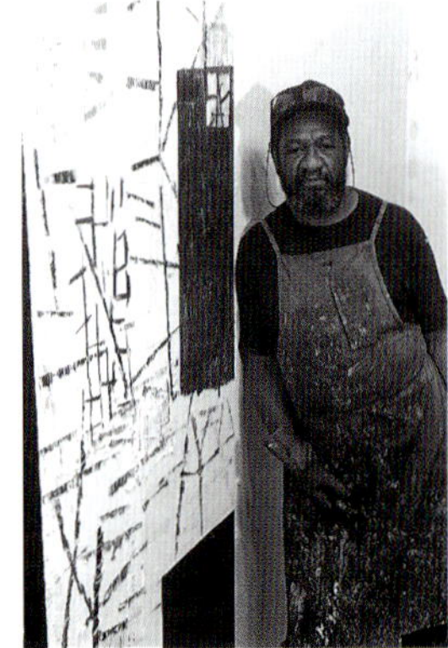

Born in Marshall, Missouri, in 1943, Henderson earned a BFA in 1969 and an MFA in 1970 from the San Francisco Art Institute.

*I believe that an artist must be free of culture, geography, self, philosophies, theories, goals, tools, history, and all preconceived ideas. However, the artist must know all of these things in order to be free of them. I believe that being an artist is like every occupation. What I paint comes from the freedom this idea brings.*

*I am currently working with paintings that are influenced by light, sound, and space. I am trying to make a painting that doesn't have an immediate impact but attempts to engage the viewer in a conversation and thereby, over time, will reveal its emotions.*

Oldies and Goodies *is about not looking backward or forward but only looking straight ahead.*

*Straight ahead with every step.*
*Straight ahead with every fall.*
*Straight ahead with every success.*
*Straight ahead and face it all.*
*For only time creates* Oldies and Goodies.

1. UNDATED CORRESPONDENCE WITH RICHARD REISMAN, SPRING 1998.

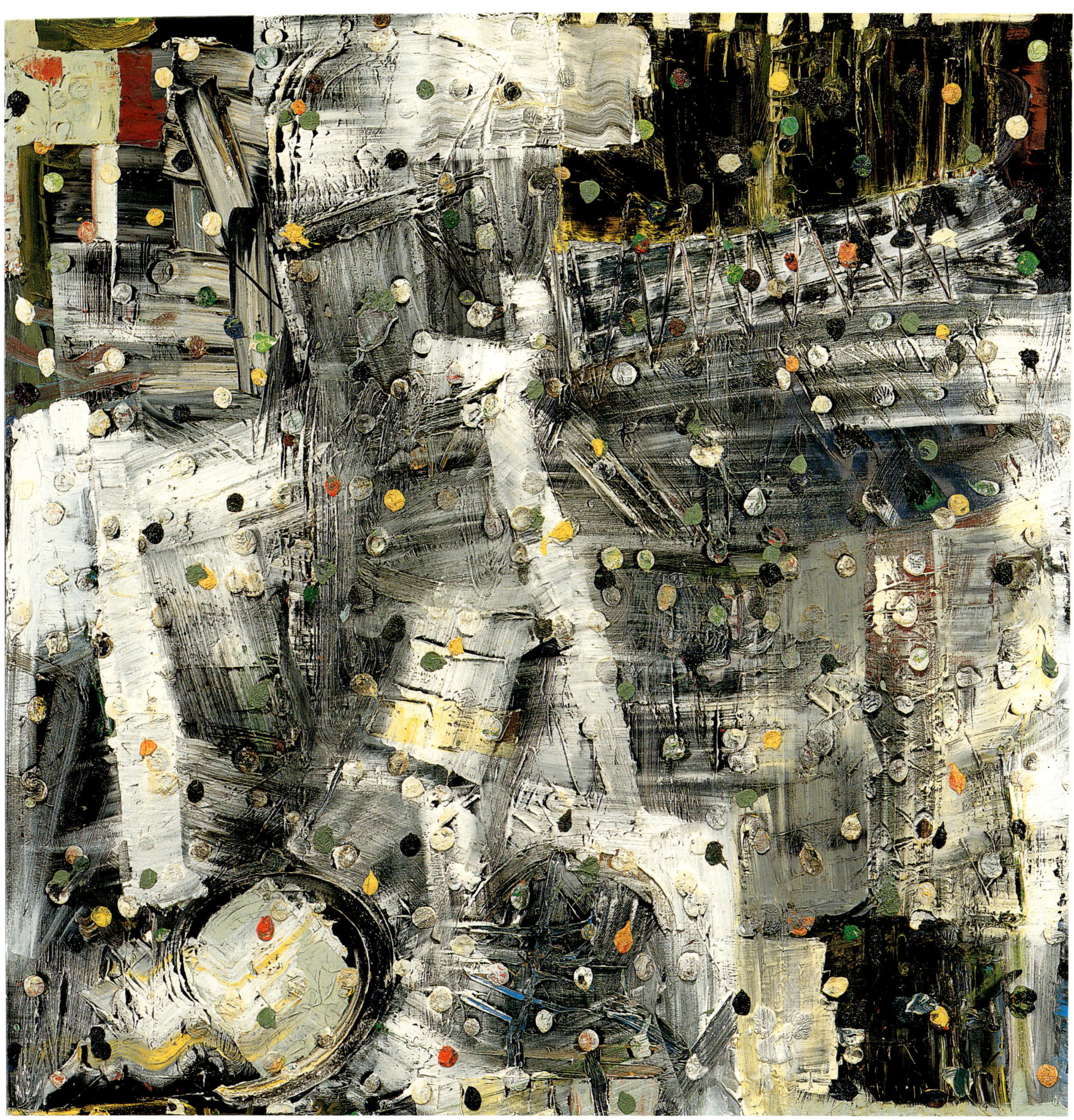

# LYNN HERSHMAN

## *Constructing Roberta Breitmore*

1975. CHROMOGENIC COLOR PRINT. 19¾ × 12¾

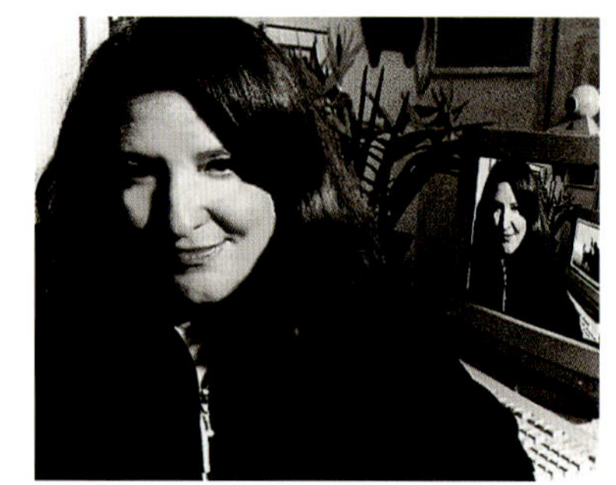

Conceptual artist Lynn Hershman staged her most dramatic installation at the Dante Hotel in San Francisco's North Beach beginning on November 30, 1973, and lasting for nine months: it gave the appearance of two dead women in a bed. (An uninformed visitor called the police.) In 1975 she began the creation of a fictitious woman, "Roberta Breitmore."

Hershman, one of the most brilliant and versatile artists identified with the San Francisco Bay Area, was born in Cleveland in 1941. She received a BS from Case Western Reserve University in 1963 and an MA from San Francisco State University in 1972.

*When the Dante Hotel room closed it seemed important to liberate the person who could have lived there. Thus began a ten-year project,* Roberta Breitmore, *a private performance of a simulated person. Her first act was to advertise for a roommate. People who answered the ad became participants in her adventures. As she became part of their reality, they became part of her fiction.*

*Roberta had credit cards and checking accounts. Her profile was animated through cosmetics applied to her face as if it were a canvas. She participated in EST and Weight Watchers, saw a psychiatrist, and had her own language, speech patterns, handwriting, apartment, clothing, gestures, and moods. Most significantly, she witnessed and documented the alienation of her time.*

*People assume that I was Roberta, but she was her own person with defined needs, ambitions, and instincts. Roberta represented a part of me as surely as we all have within us an underside, a dark, shadowy cadaver that we try with pathetic illusion to camouflage.*

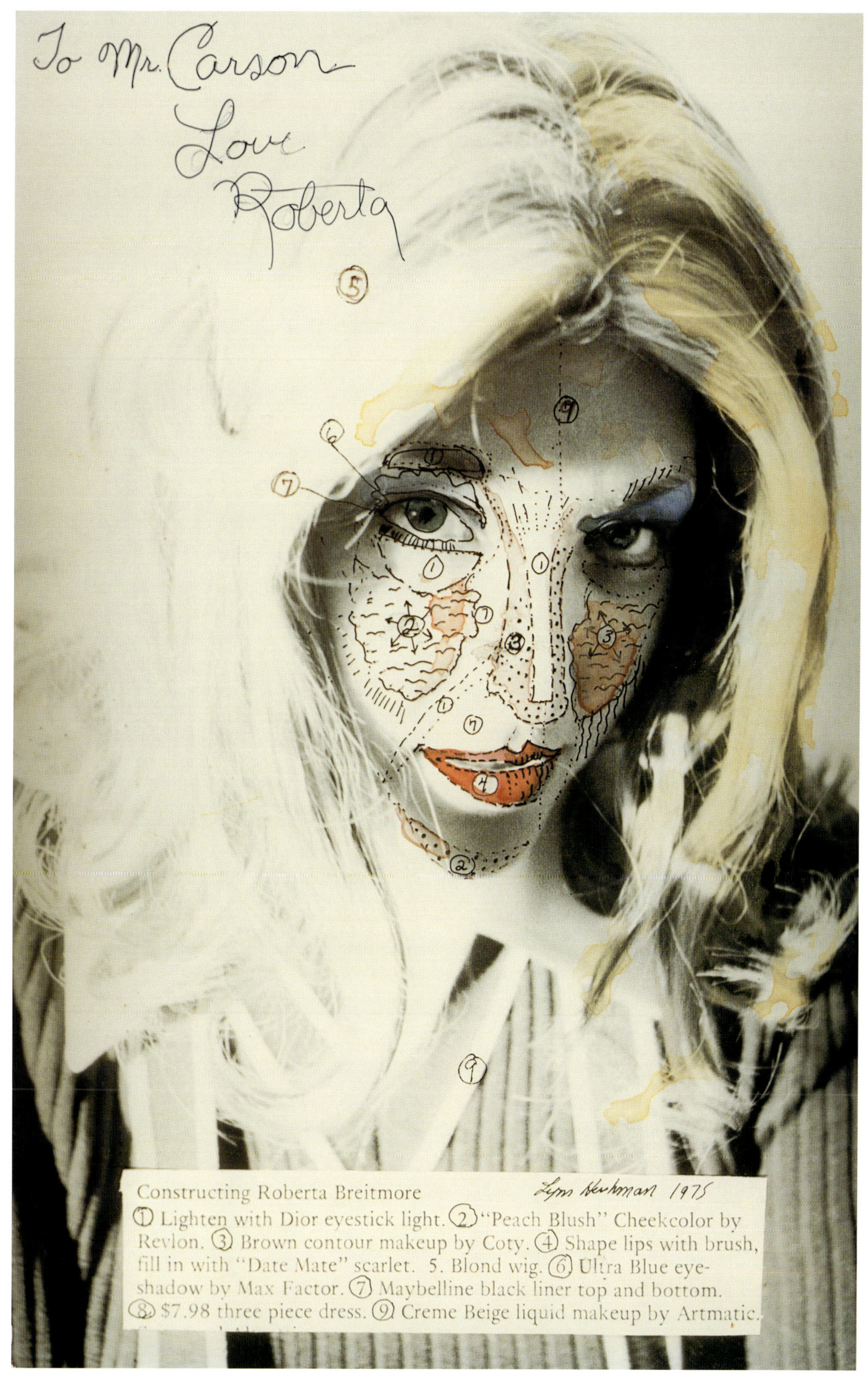

To Mr. Carson
Love
Roberta
Constructing Roberta Breitmore
Lynn Hershman 1975
① Lighten with Dior eyestick light. ② "Peach Blush" Cheekcolor by
Revlon. ③ Brown contour makeup by Coty. ④ Shape lips with brush,
fill in with "Date Mate" scarlet. 5. Blond wig. ⑥ Ultra Blue eye-
shadow by Max Factor. ⑦ Maybelline black liner top and bottom.
⑧ $7.98 three piece dress. ⑨ Creme Beige liquid makeup by Artmatic.

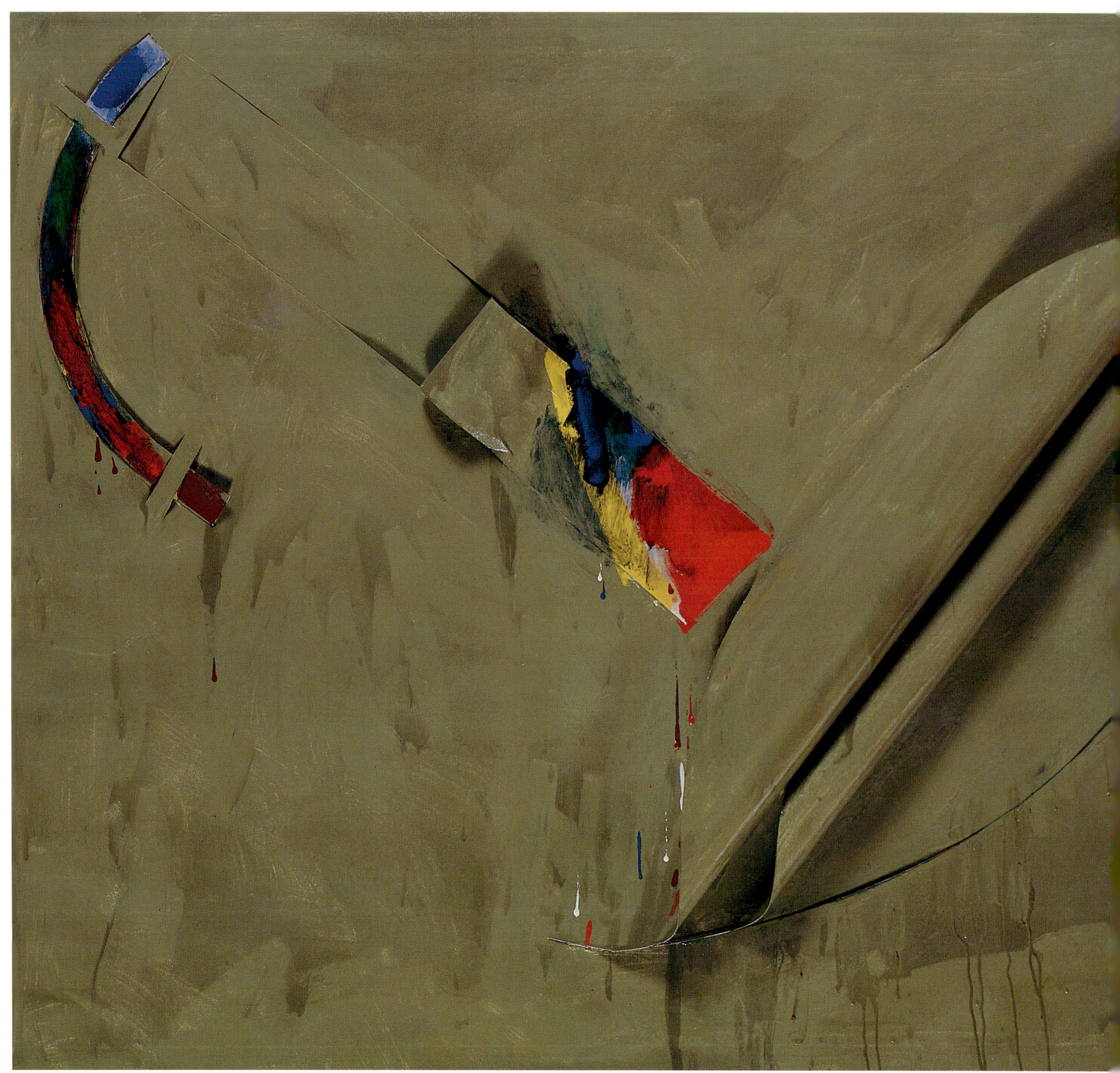

# TOM HOLLAND

1978, EPOXY ON PAPER, 35 × 45 × 2¾

## *62nd Street Series #43*

Although he has moved beyond two-dimensionality, Tom Holland has always identified himself as a painter. He was born in Seattle in 1936 but grew up in California. He attended Willamette University in Salem, Oregon, from 1954 until 1956 and then transferred to the University of California, Santa Barbara, in 1957, but

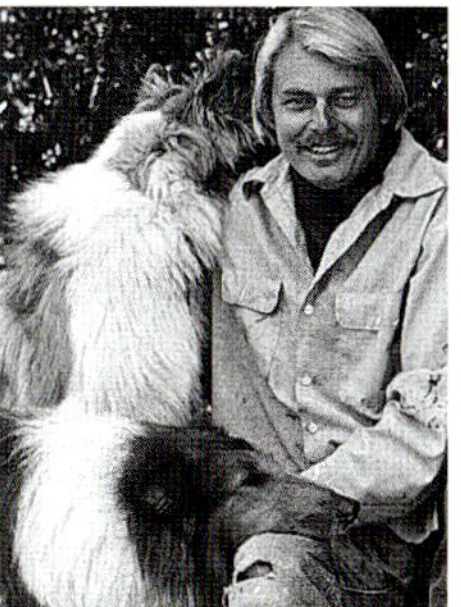

quickly moved to UC Berkeley, where he studied until 1959. A Fulbright scholarship in 1960 took him to Santiago, Chile. He briefly used an earthy palette and forms resembling airplanes and alligators in thick surfaces.

He experimented for some years with anti-form violations, tearing canvases and modifying their shapes. While teaching at the University of California, Los Angeles, between 1968 and 1970, he used a kind of Funk-Pop imagery, including palm trees. He also experimented with fiberglass strips woven into grids or grouped in loops, on which he spattered juicy, LA finish-fetish colors. His works were not cool, however, but expressive—even dancing. Since then he has generally constructed his signature forms out of layered, geometrically cut aluminum sheets, fiberglass, or paper, saturating them with lush epoxy pigments and preserving drips and gobs.

Holland brought painting off the wall and incorporated volume and space into it, making it a passionate, three-dimensional experience.

He taught at the San Francisco Art Institute from 1963 until 1967 and at UCLA and elsewhere from 1970 until 1982. He and his wife reside in Berkeley. They have three sons.

*My mother was a painter and my father was interested in nature and photography. . . . The artist David Park has influenced me personally. Many others have influenced me through their work.*[1]

1. HENRY HOPKINS, 50 WEST COAST ARTISTS: A CRITICAL SELECTION OF PAINTERS AND SCULPTORS WORKING IN CALIFORNIA (SAN FRANCISCO: CHRONICLE BOOKS, 1981), P. 44.

1990, 4,000 BOTTLES, TEXT, AND MIXED MEDIA, 132 × 120 × 96

# MILDRED HOWARD

## *Memory Garden, Phase I*

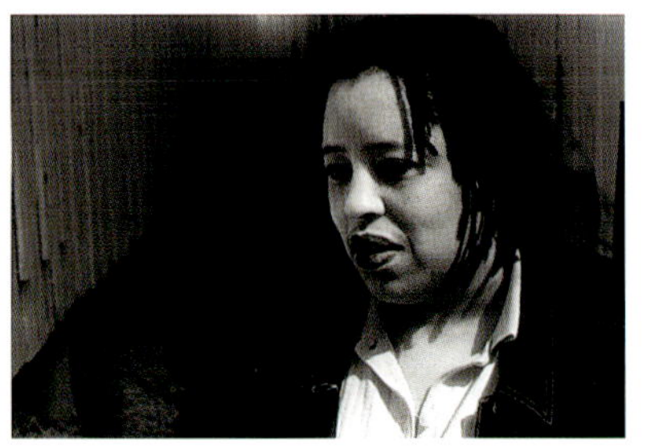

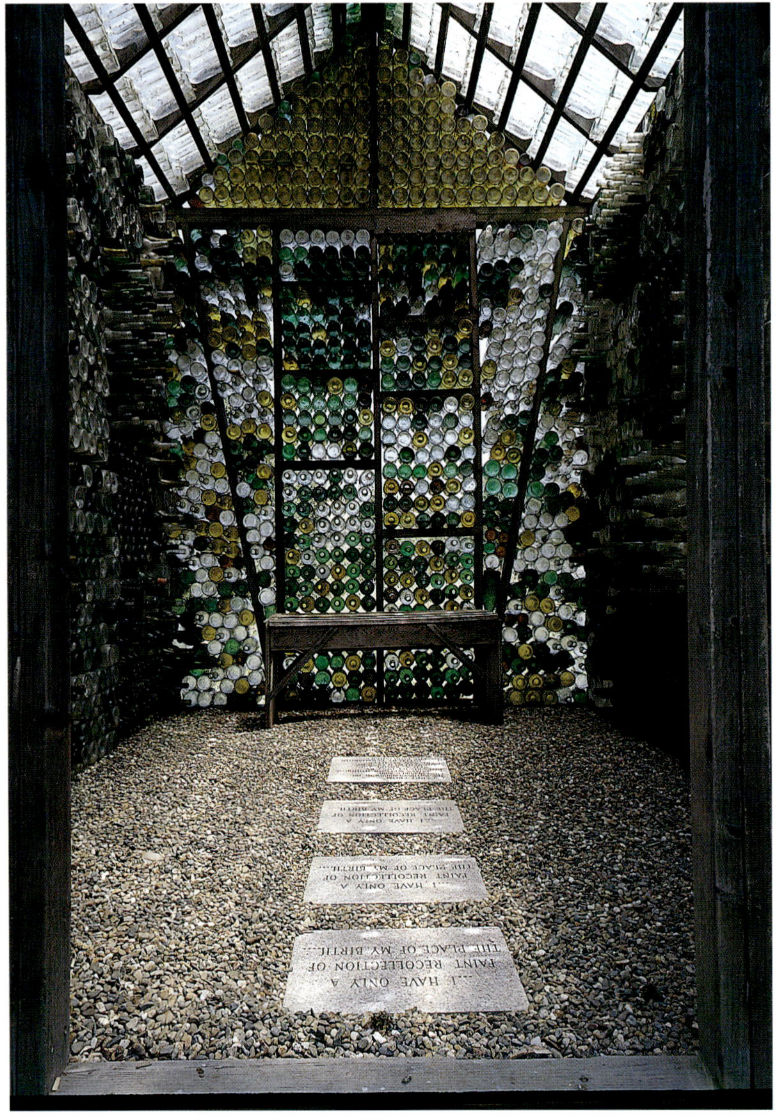


Mildred Howard makes artworks rooted in all aspects of human experience. Although she was born in San Francisco in 1945, Berkeley is her home. She earned an MFA in fiberworks from John F. Kennedy University in Orinda, California, in 1985.

*The idea of the bottle house came from James Weldon Johnson's* Autobiography of an Ex-Colored Man, *about a man of African ancestry who passes for white. He longs to connect with his origins but fears exposure.*

*Johnson's description of a garden where bottles are stuck in the ground neck down reminded me of African Americans' use of bottles in gardens and on trees to banish evil spirits. I used them to build a sanctuary of memory. I use memory, place, history, family, and identity to stimulate my creativity. Using selected objects to commingle past and present, I create a model of the world to stir emotions, to question beliefs and misconceptions about how different people view the world. I use everyday objects beyond their original purposes to express connectedness to and respect for ancestors personally and collectively.*

*What fascinates me is the spatial presence and feeling of congregation—a group, a choir, or an idea about issues of race, gender, culture, and religion. Often the anticipation of these groups is not present in the real world but [exists] as a memory of the past or an anticipation of the future.*

*Standing in the house, you see fluttering fragments of passersby in the spaces between the bottles. You identify with the outside world, but the reality of the interior fragments you. You perceive the outside world, but it is colored by your feelings, beliefs, and emotions.*

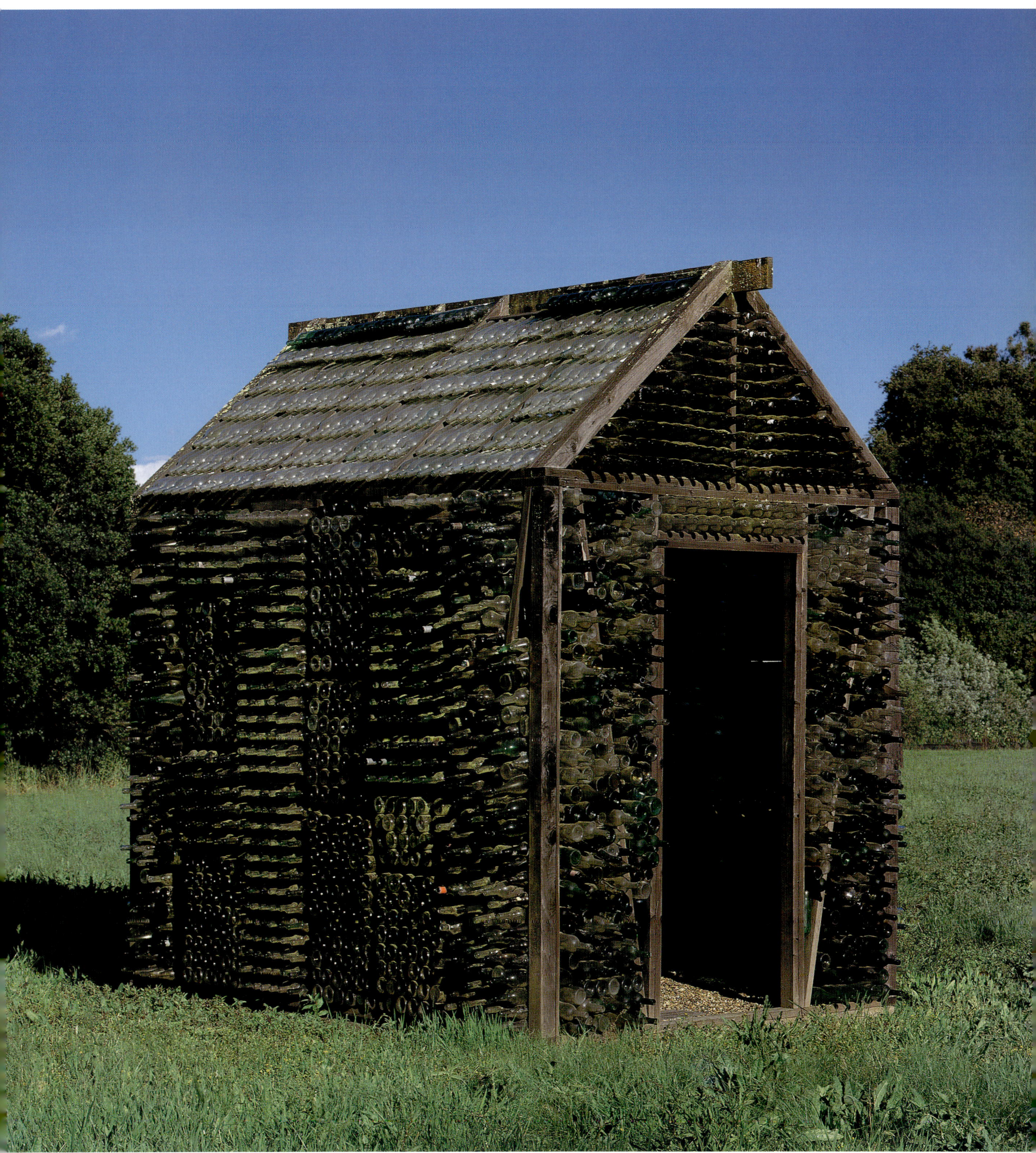

# ROBERT HUDSON

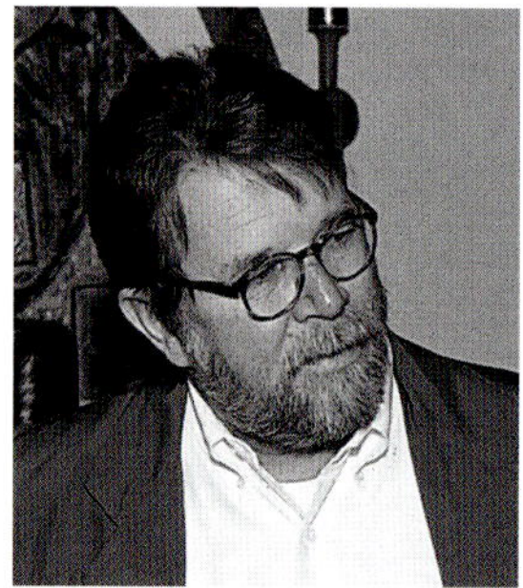

Robert Hudson makes bizarre sculptures whose seemingly inharmonious elements work together to form statements whose authority equals that of other major contemporary artists. And yet he seems to be a figure on the periphery of the official art scene, a status that gives him a freedom many artists lose once they achieve conventional success. Critic and scholar Lucy Lippard has defined his works as fitting under the rubric of Eccentric Abstraction. They might be more accurately classified, however, by the term Magical Abstraction. They are supremely disorienting and never lose their power.

Although born in Salt Lake City, Utah, in 1938, Hudson grew up in Richland, Washington, near the Yakima Indian Reservation. As a boy, he made drawings and paintings and totem poles. In Richland he knew William T. Wiley and William Allan, who, like him, were profoundly influenced by Native American art and culture through their high school art teacher, Jim McGrath. Hudson, like Wiley and Allan, left Richland to attend the San Francisco Art Institute, where he earned a BFA in 1962 and an MFA in 1963. Their friendships and mutual influences have continued in the San Francisco Bay Area.

## *Teapot, 1972 (Ceramic #19)*

1972. PORCELAIN WITH UNDERGLAZES AND CHINA PAINT. 17½ × 12¼ × 8½

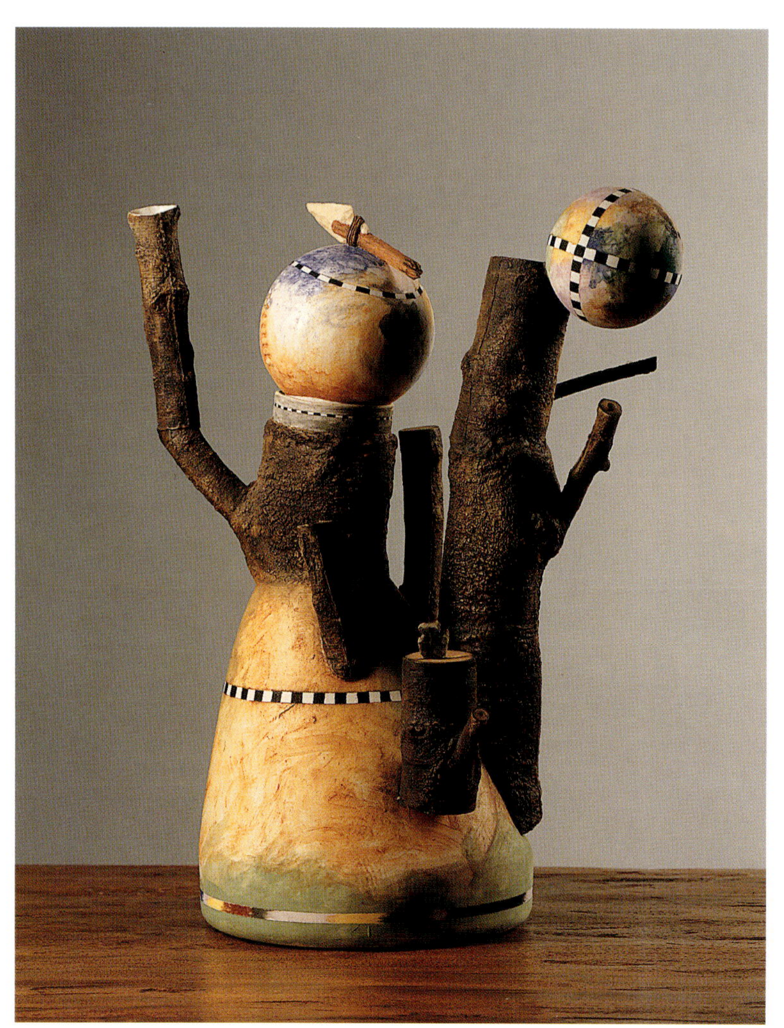

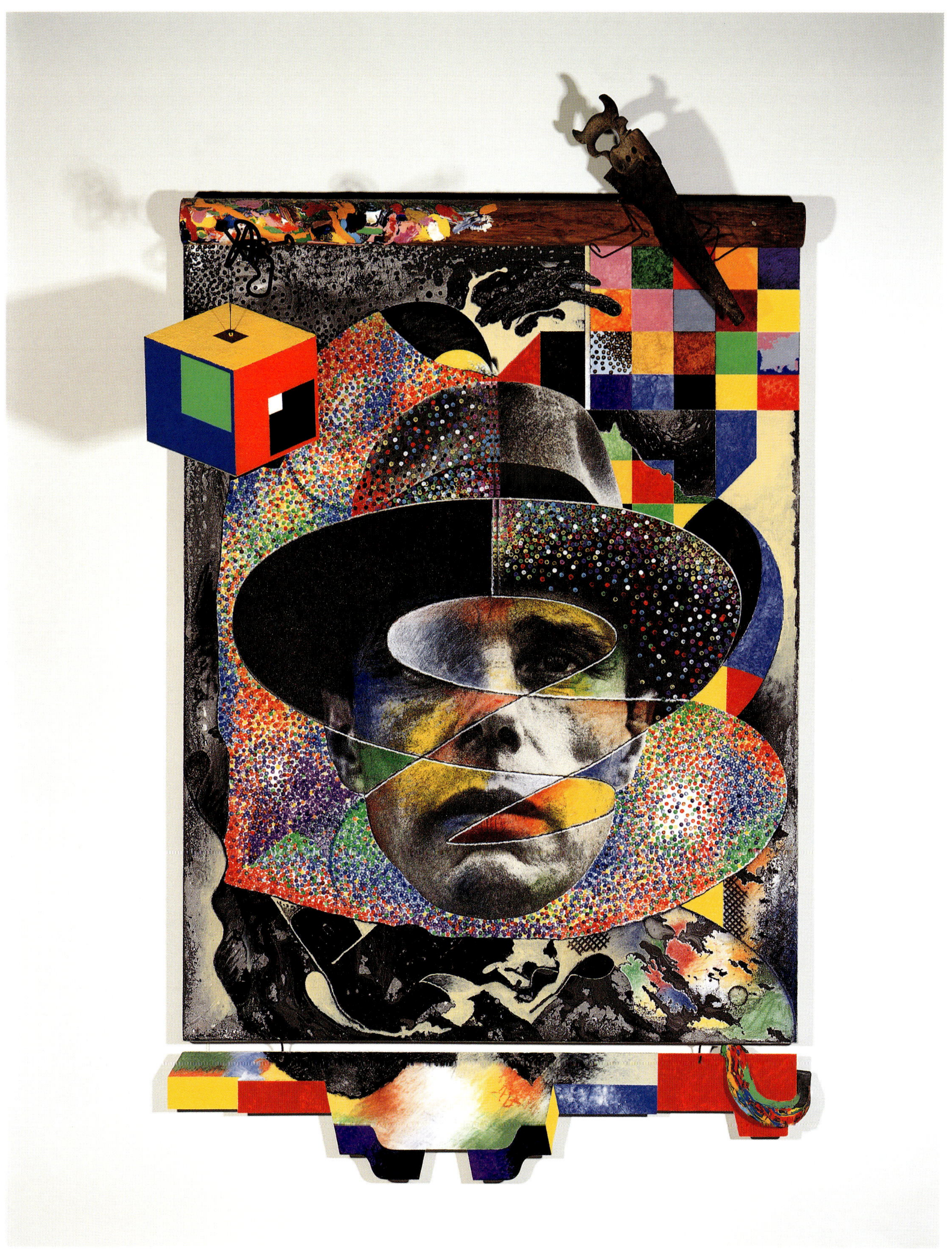

*Untitled*

1980–1981. ACRYLIC, CHARCOAL, ENAMEL PAINT AND COLLAGE ON CANVAS, WOOD, MASONITE, TIN, FINISHING SAW, AND WIRE, 76 × 46 × 21

Hudson favors wildly unusual materials—for example, a stuffed buck deer in a sculpture and grid-stitched cotton batting in a group of paintings—and eccentric combinations of forms in dazzling colors and bold patterns, as in *Figure of Speech.* For eighteen months in the period from 1971 to 1973, he worked with ceramist Richard Shaw to produce such works as *Teapot, 1972 (Ceramic #19).*

*The thing I like . . . is making flat things go round with paint. Just being able to have an object be what it is and then also be something else—like a whisper or a dance.*[1]

1. JAN BUTTERFIELD, "PERCEPTUAL ALCHEMY: THE PAINTINGS OF ROBERT HUDSON," ROBERT HUDSON: A SURVEY, SAN FRANCISCO MUSEUM OF MODERN ART, JUNE 27–AUGUST 18, 1985, EXHIBITION CATALOGUE, P. 25.

*Figure of Speech*

1984, WELDED AND PAINTED STEEL, 170½ × 104 × 62

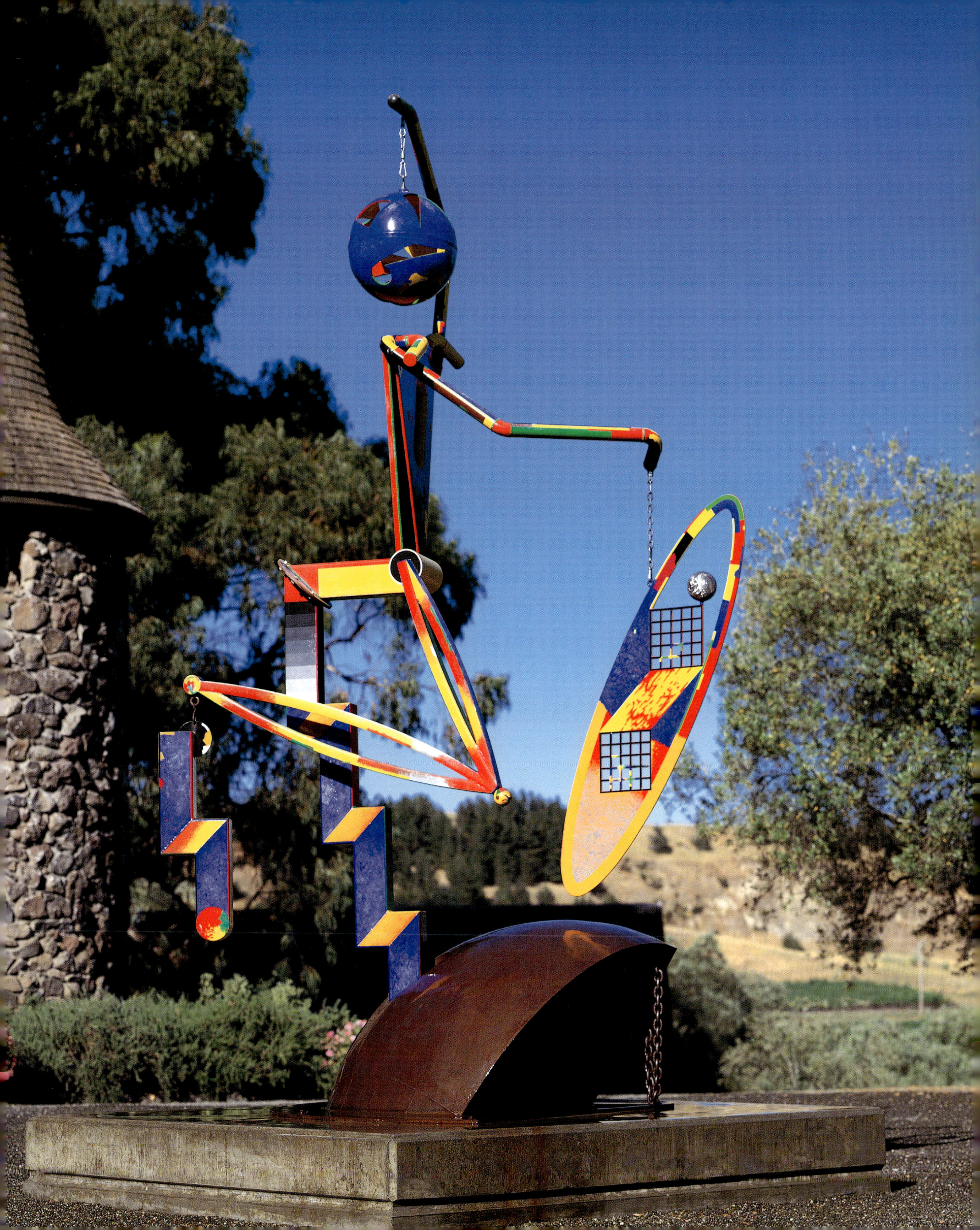

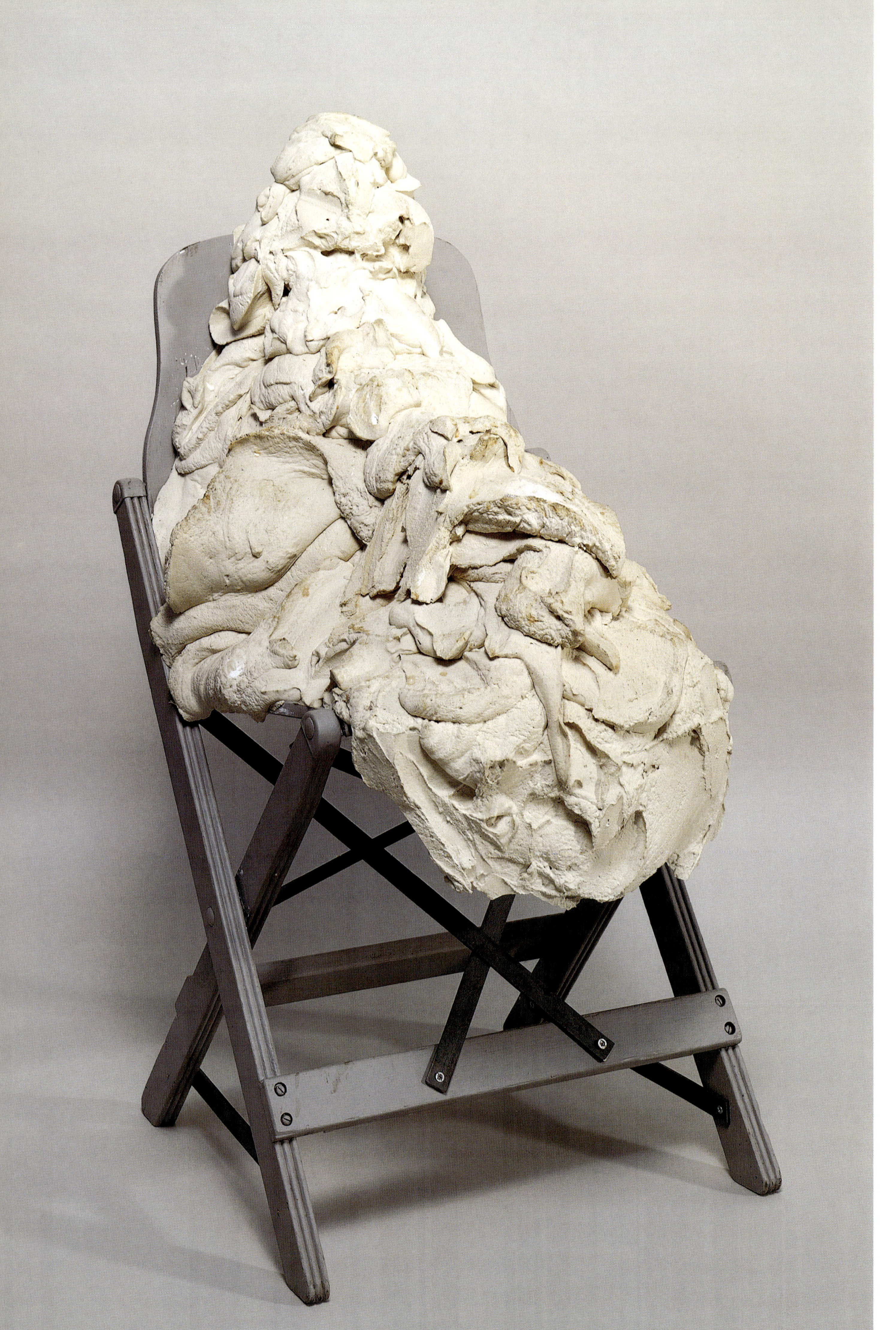

# DAVID IRELAND

1994. WOOD, METAL, AND FIXALL, 35 × 20 × 17 *Untitled*

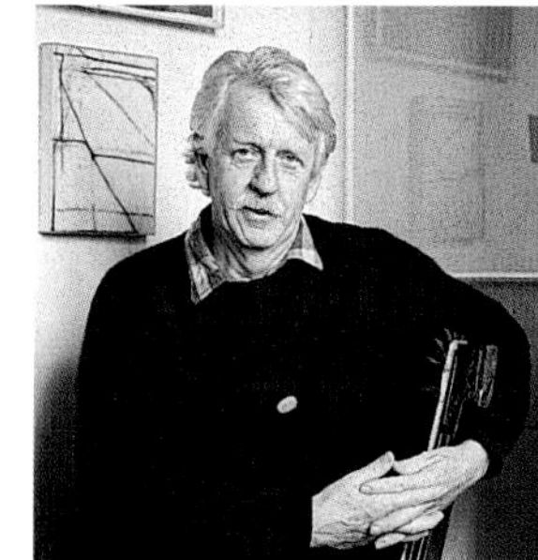

Conceptualist David Ireland promotes the subversiveness of art, teaching viewers that art that is able to change their perceptions also changes their values. He came to contemporary art haltingly and indirectly, committing himself fully only when he was already mature.

Ireland was born in Bellingham, Washington, in 1930. He received a BA from the California College of Arts and Crafts in 1953, then worked as an architectural draftsman and, later, a safari guide in Africa. After traveling throughout the world he returned to school in the early 1970s, completing an MFA at the San Francisco Art Institute in 1974.

Ireland is particularly recognized for two structures in San Francisco: his own house and another house that is its antithesis. He did not renovate or restore the distressed Victorian building that he chose for his home in San Francisco's Mission District. Instead, he stripped it down to its essentials, leaving them as he found them, and painted them with contemporary preservatives, thus maintaining the structure with its history. He used the residual materials for making works of art. Nearby at 500 Capp Street, in 1983, he completed a minimalist corrugated metal and Sheetrock building that would earn a legendary reputation as a work and performance space for artists.

*I'm using the chair because of its multiple implications: the throne, the symbol of authority; "going through the chairs," the symbol of fraternal organizations; and the chair, a symbol of home. It is also the micro-architecture.*

*I use the concrete because it is one of many materials that have a liquid-to-solid characteristic. It flows. It is universal. It is strong. In this instance, it is no longer a chair. It is more than a chair.*

# OLIVER *Untitled No. 6* JACKSON

1985. OIL PASTEL ON LINEN. 57 × 70

In pursuit of his artistic vision, Oliver Jackson uses the media and techniques he feels are necessary for its realization.

Jackson, who was born in St. Louis in 1935, feels that he learned much through his associations with jazz musicians in his hometown: "A musician knows when he is losing the attention of his audience right away. . . . Working with musicians taught me about the whole matter of *time* in a painting, the need to eliminate the dead spots, the parts that don't move. From musicians, I learned how to get into a painting, to find an opening. And the most important thing you learn from the best musicians is: just play the tune. There are some tunes, certain thematic ideas, that call for lots of notes and speed and intricacy. Others have to be done with very few, and very simply. The same is true of a painting."[1]

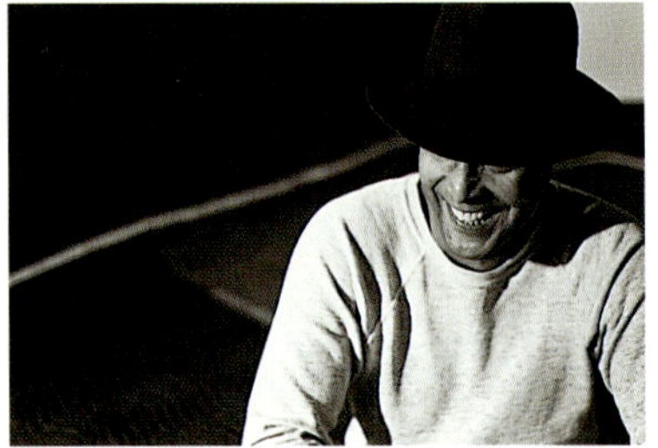

Jackson received a BFA from Illinois Wesleyan University in 1958 and an MFA from the University of Iowa in 1963. He has taught at California State University, Sacramento, since 1971.

*The aesthetics are the artist's vehicle. They are the syntax to get the spirit to move. But for the viewer*—this is not his business. *The business of the viewer is to have an experience (and the artist must be so good at his syntax that the experience is there) and there is nothing between him and the art—no hype, no intellectual nonsense. The power of our experience will tell us who the great artists are, and the beauty of the work will be known through its power.*[2]

1. THOMAS ALBRIGHT. "OLIVER JACKSON." OLIVER JACKSON. SEATTLE ART MUSEUM. SEPTEMBER 17–NOVEMBER 7. 1982. EXHIBITION CATALOGUE. P. 7.

2. JAN BUTTERFIELD. "INTERVIEW." OLIVER JACKSON. SEATTLE ART MUSEUM. SEPTEMBER 17–NOVEMBER 7. 1982. EXHIBITION CATALOGUE. P. 29.

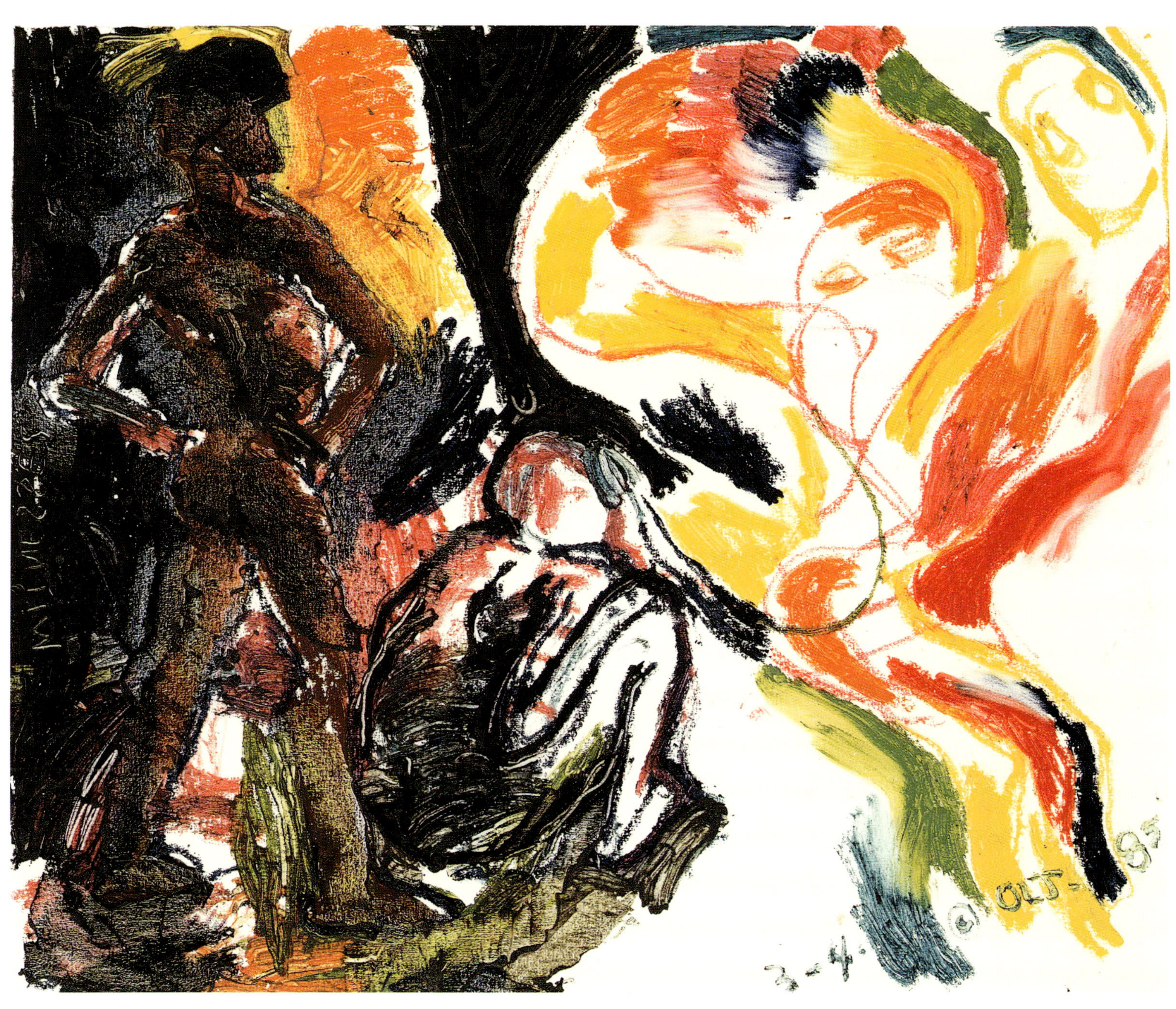

# JESS *And It's Jung by a Gnose*

1955. PHOTO COLLAGE. 13 × 21

Jess Collins, known solely by his given name, epitomizes eccentricity in art. More important, however, he represents integrity.

Burgess Franklin Collins was born in Long Beach, California, in 1923. From the age of seven he knew what his true vocation was. Nevertheless, he followed his family's direction and enrolled at the California Institute of Technology where, after an interruption for military service working in chemical warfare, he earned a BS in chemistry in 1948. A Jungian Big Dream of a world incinerated by an atomic bomb pushed him to rebel and attend the San Francisco Art Institute from 1949 until 1951.

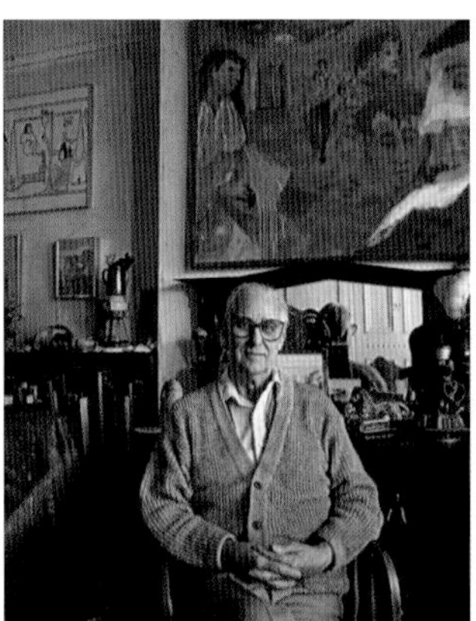

From studying action painting, Jess learned to work with a "field in flux" until the work of art makes itself. Feeling that he lacked the skills to create representational images, he turned to the use of images from existing sources, including magazines, books, comic strips (especially *Dick Tracy*), and puzzles, which he saves until "they ask to be used." Pinning the components onto a surface before pasting them down, so that the composition can remain in flux, he intuitively follows his stream of consciousness until the images arrange themselves in works rich in visual and literary associations.

*And It's Jung by a Gnose* is a classic work of the period when San Francisco's Beat culture was flourishing. In the following years, living reclusively with his lover, poet Robert Duncan (who died in 1988), Jess went on to develop other art forms, such as Translations and Salvages (thickly impastoed paintings), and Assemblies (three-dimensional groupings). Jess dropped his surname to mark his repudiation of his family's values.

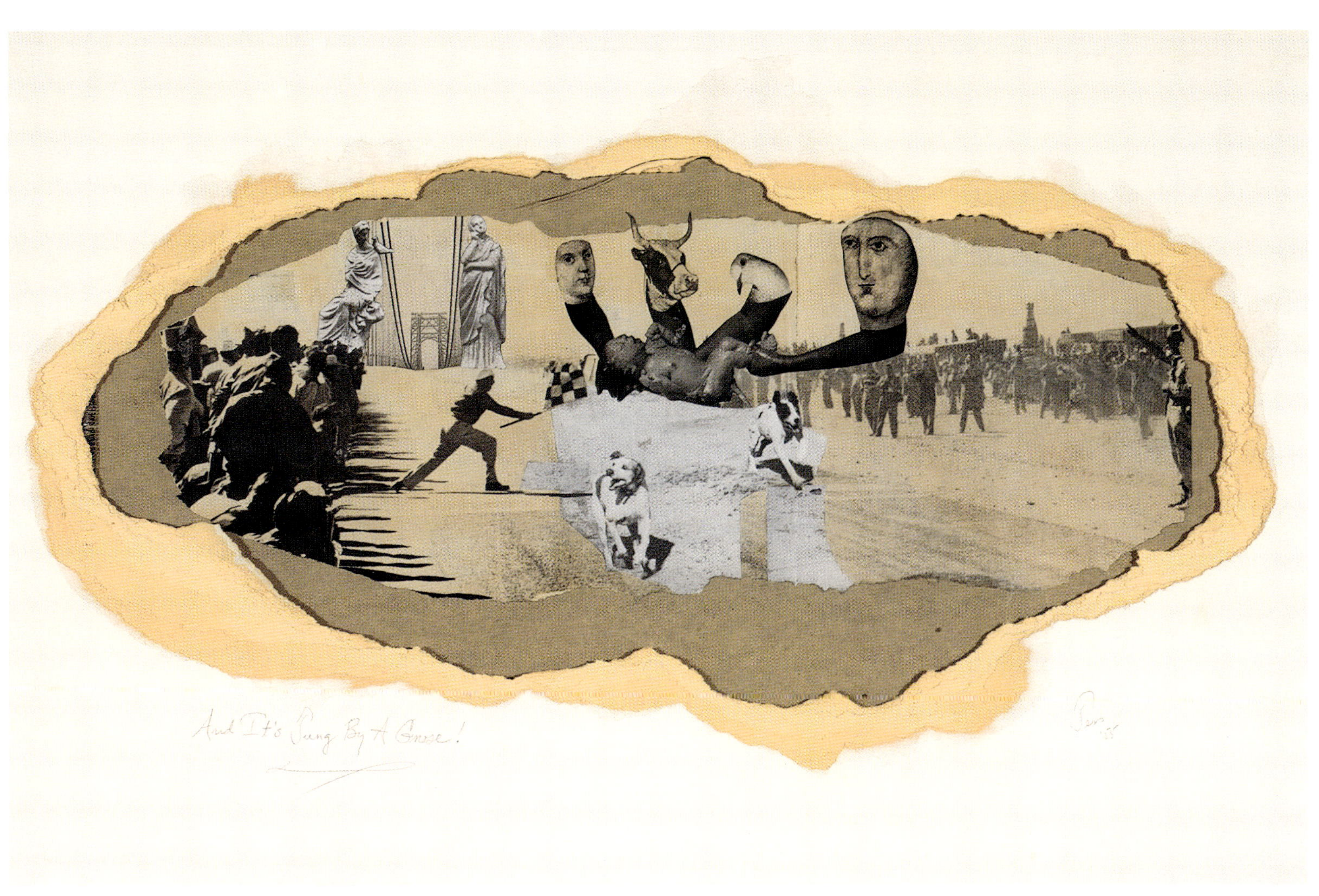
And It's Sung By A Goose!

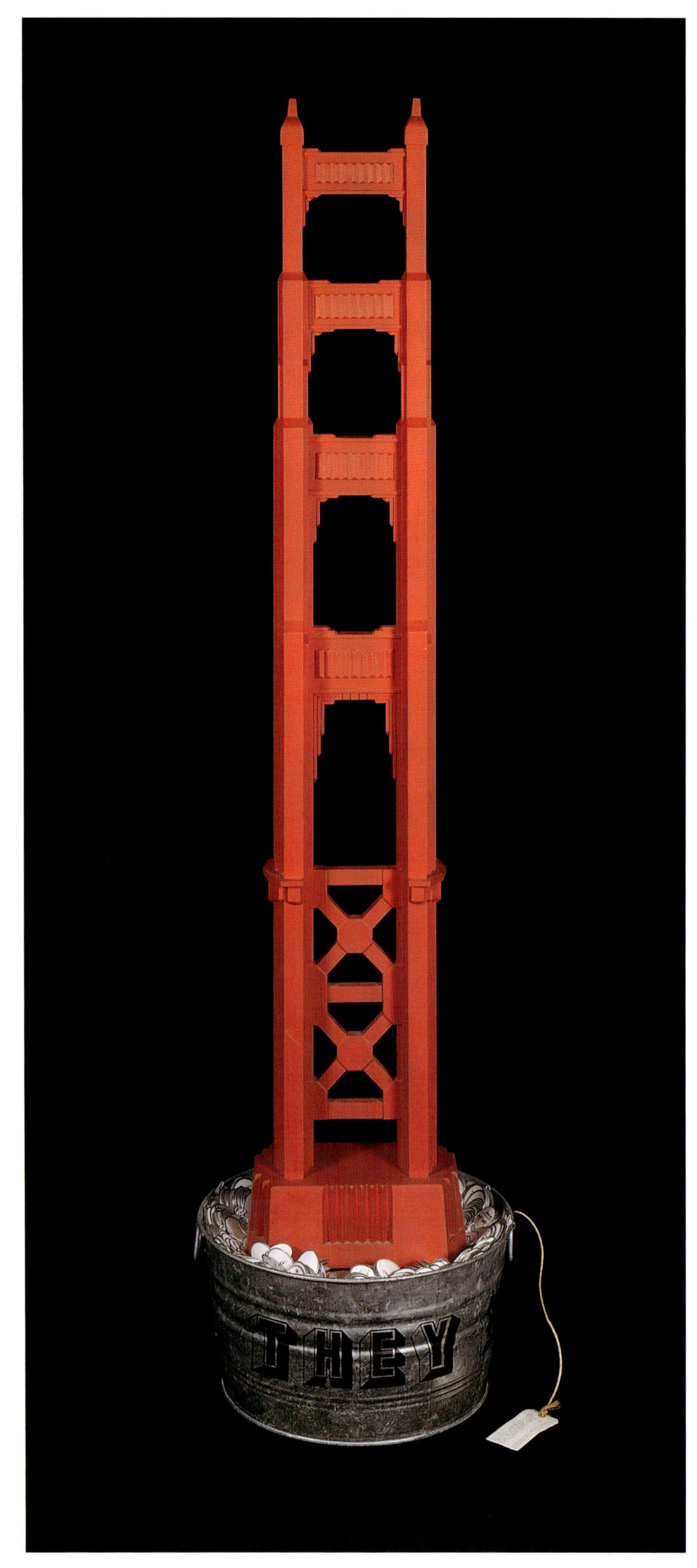
THEY

## *They Who Chose*

1987, MIXED MEDIA, 89 × 23 × 23

# DAVID JONES

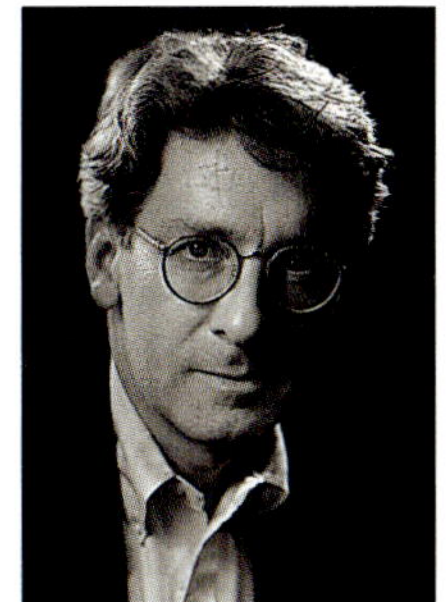

David Jones was born in Columbus, Ohio, in 1948. He earned a BFA from the Kansas City Art Institute in 1970 and then moved to California, where he received an MA in 1971 and an MFA in 1973 from the University of California, Berkeley. He lives in Emeryville, California.

*With my works I prefer to: create the fundamental paradox that results when abstraction and representation coexist equally and simultaneously; feel free combining and shifting from one source, material, and idea to another, thus carrying with them the temporal referent of their present physical circumstance and creation; elicit the literary effect either with or in the absence of words; circumvent the linear mind-set for the intuitive ramble; and embrace paradox and contradiction as conditions of my work.*

*SIDE THOUGHTS* [from the shipping tag attached to *They Who Chose*]

*The challenge of the familiar is perceiving in unfamiliar ways.*

*Some may perceive the G.G. Bridge as a symbol of the "California Dream."*

*Some may perceive the G.G. Bridge as an engineering triumph.*

*Some may perceive the G.G. Bridge as a symbol of man's conquest of the elements.*

*Some may perceive the G.G. Bridge as a signpost to the broad Pacific.*

*When I see the G.G. Bridge, which I do most mornings, I think of all the artists who are here and those who left, all making contributions to the Bay Area's cultural heritage. They are* They Who Chose: *committed to living in the aesthetic waters, so to speak, and this is my dedication to them.*

*There are approximately twelve hundred artists' names included in the aesthetic waters.*

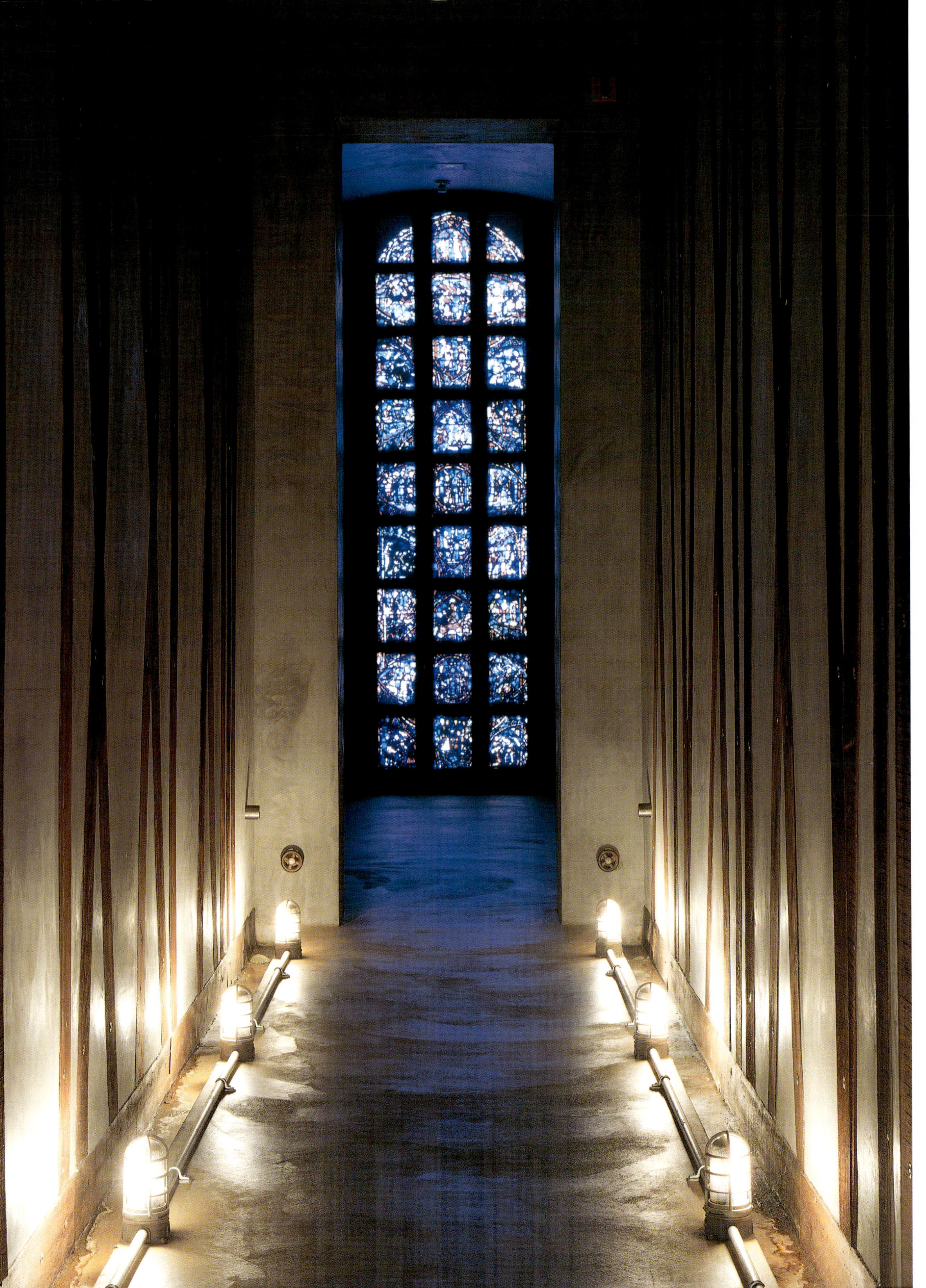

# PAUL KOS

## *Chartres Bleu*

1986/1996. LASER DISCS, PLAYERS, MONITORS, AND ELECTRONICS.
180 × 57 × 19

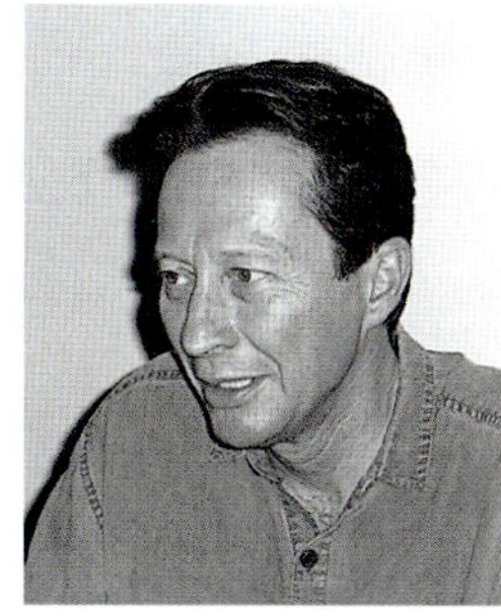

Conceptualist Paul Kos makes works that are as intellectually challenging as they are physically engaging. For example, in 1969 he created an installation imitating sixty-four square feet of Yellowstone National Park, including bubbling terrain and sulfur smells. In 1971 in downtown San Francisco, in a building designed by Frank Lloyd Wright with an interior ramp, he installed a ton of sand that sifted through a small hole in the main floor onto the basement floor below. As a negative funnel developed at street level within a flawless volcano form, a positive cone developed below ground.

For *Chartres Bleu* Kos used twenty-seven television monitors and laser disc players to replicate a stained-glass window of Chartres Cathedral. Using current technology, he re-creates a fragment of one of the sublime masterpieces of Western European art and a triumph of the technology of its time. The artist's *Tunnel/Chapel,* with the fourteen Stations of the Cross represented by Roman numerals, is the approach to the piece.

Kos was born in Rock Springs, Wyoming, in 1942. He earned a BFA in 1965 and an MFA in 1967 from the San Francisco Art Institute, where he has taught since 1978.

*I work under these precepts:*
*Reveal slowly.*
*Prove metaphor is more.*
*Heed site or be shortsighted.*
*Respect simple, humble materials.*
*Prefer art that* is, *to art that is* about. . . .
*Demand double duty of chosen elements.*
*Strive for equilibrium in message and messenger.*
*Value the Spanish* aquí, acá, allí, allá *for their sense of form.*
[artist's translation: here near, here far; there near, there far]
*Opt for, but never expect, "partly cloudy, becoming mostly sunny."*

# MARILYN LEVINE

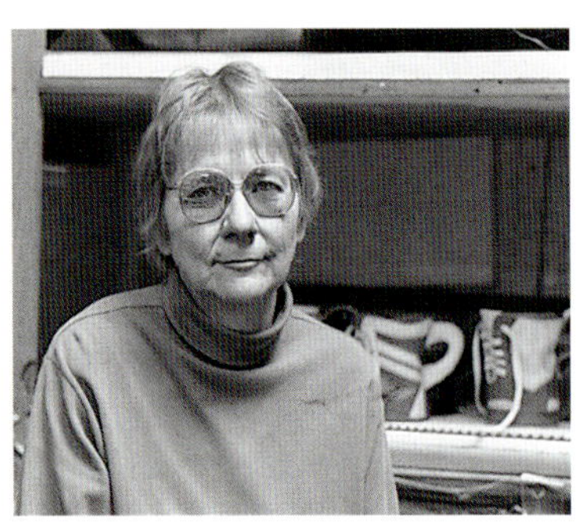

Marilyn Levine's life has united science and art. After earning a BSc in 1957 and an MSc in 1959 from the University of Alberta, Edmonton, she worked as a chemist. She had also studied art, however, and earned an MA in 1970 and an MFA in 1971 from the University of California, Berkeley.

Although initially influenced by Funk, Levine has consistently pursued her own vision. Her sculptures of commonplace subjects relate to Pop, but even more to American trompe l'oeil and to photo-realism. Uniting her skills as artist and scientist in her replications of leather objects, she satisfies her attraction to the personal histories embodied by her models.

Levine was born in Medicine Hat, Alberta, Canada, in 1935 and lives in Oakland.

*While drawing a trilobite fossil in a geology class, I carefully modeled the legs with shading and highlights. But a lab instructor came around and pointed out that my trilobite had the wrong number of legs. I had been so involved with illusion that I had sacrificed accuracy.*

*Sixteen years later, having ended my career in science and briefly experimented with hard-edge abstract sculpture and Funk art, I returned to my obsession with illusionism. As with my drawing of the trilobite, accuracy to me was less important than illusionism—the illusion not only of the object itself but of its history with humans. Moreover, the details of the history are less important than a sense that there had been a history.*

Blue Hat *was a transition piece between my experimentation with Funk and my current obsession with illusionism.*

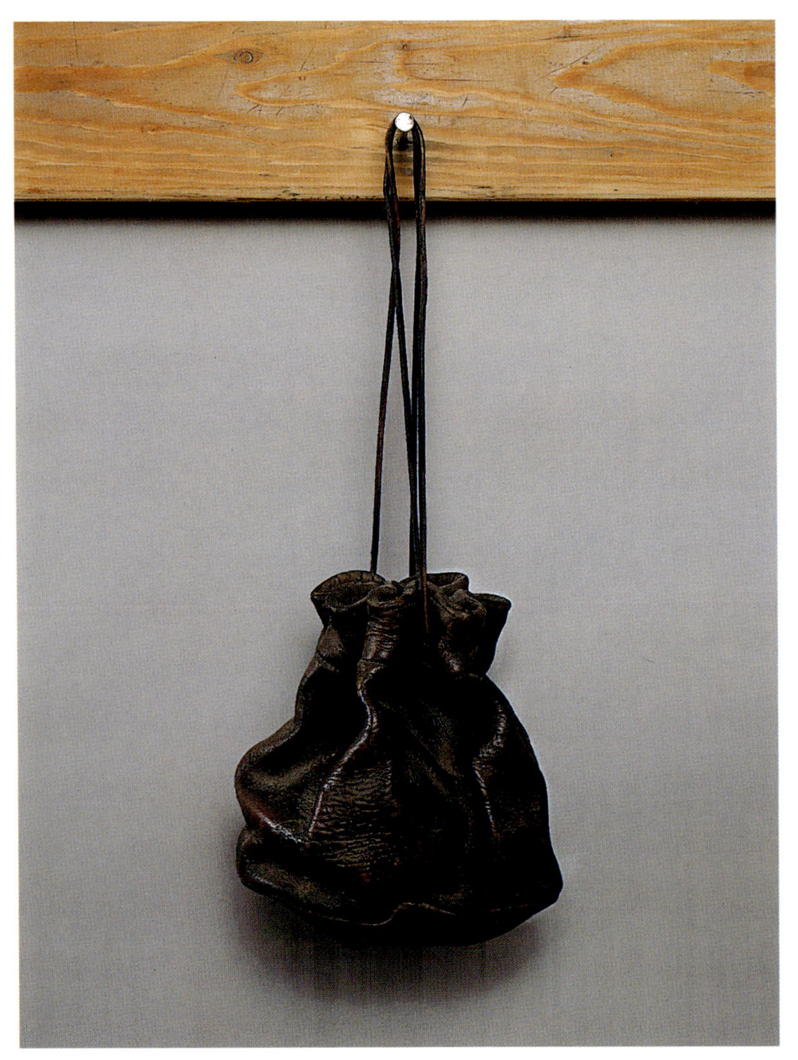

***Brown Drawstring Bag***

1980. HIGH-FIRE CERAMIC WITH LEATHER LACES. 6½ × 5½ × 4½

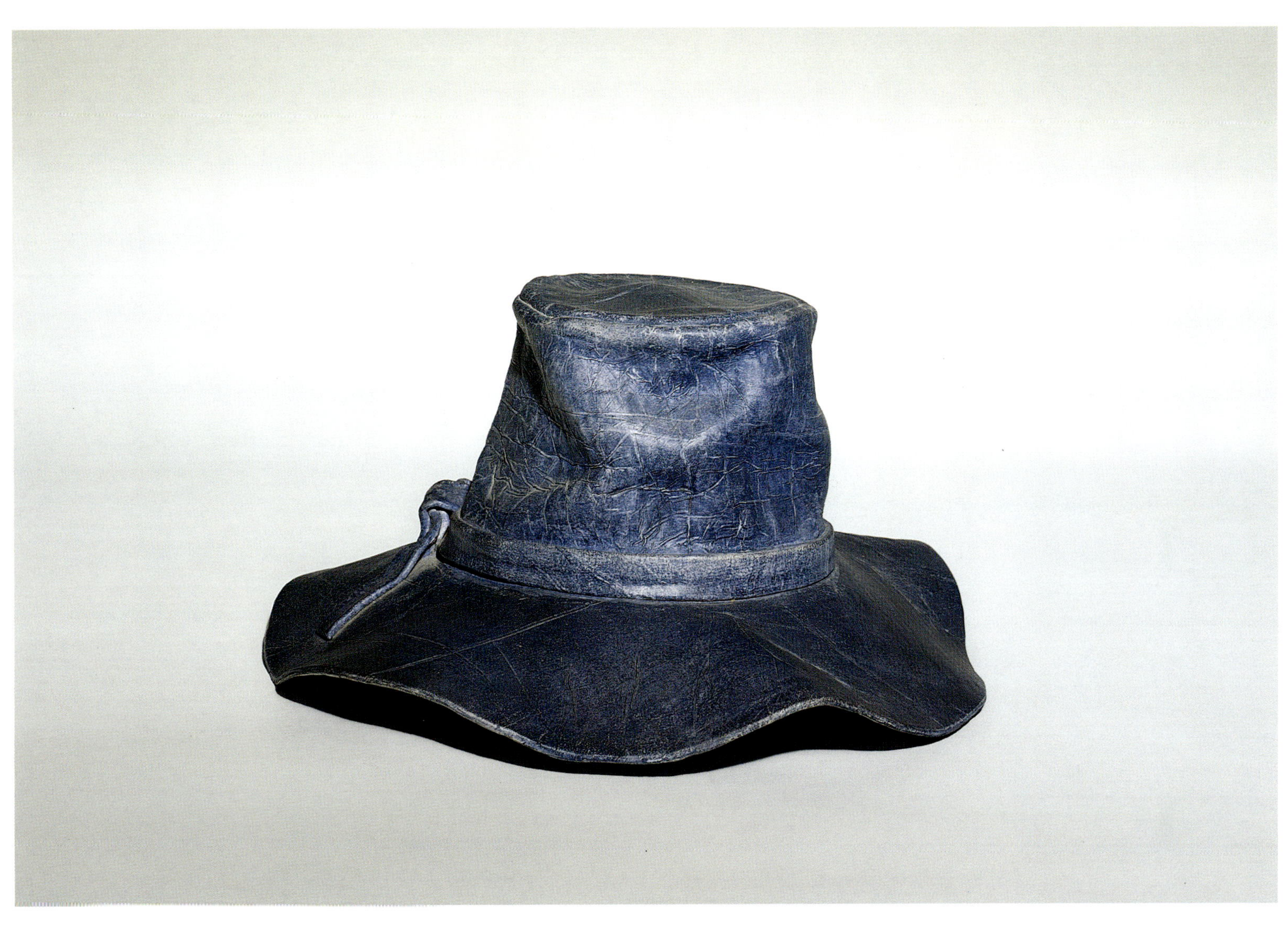

*Blue Hat*

1971, UNGLAZED LOW-FIRE CERAMIC WITH BLUE ENGOBE, 8 × 16 × 15

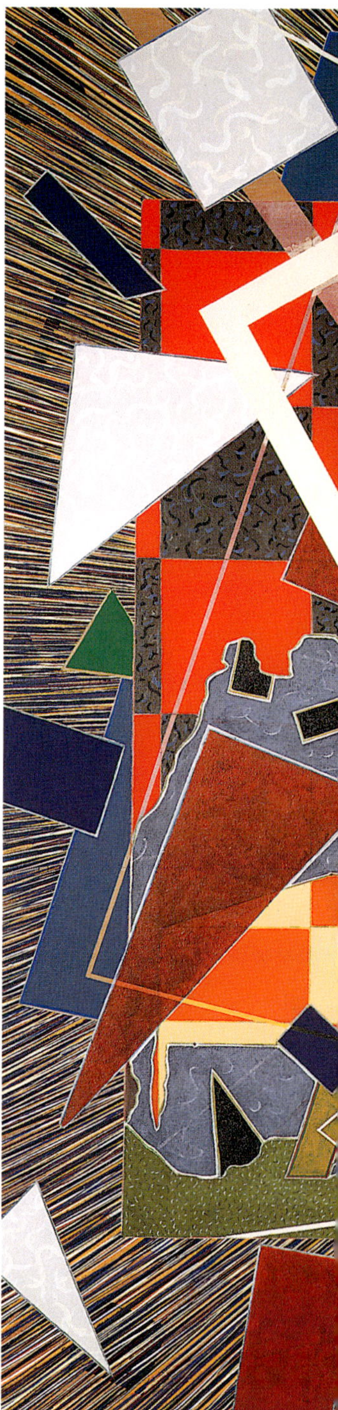

1991. MIXED-MEDIA PAINT ON UNPRIMED COTTON. 78 × 120 *Last Supper*

# TONY LIGAMARI

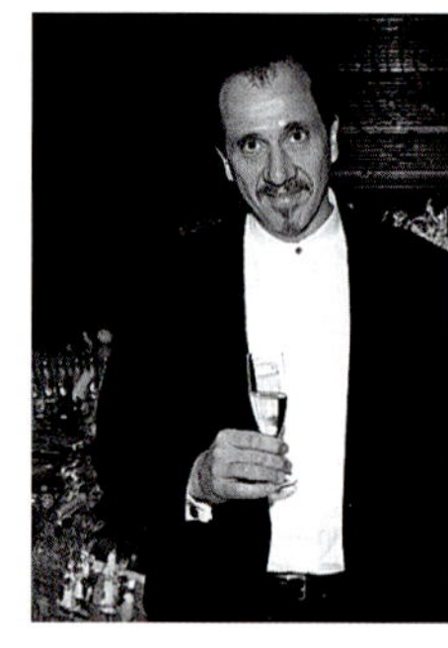

After enrolling as a painter at the School for the Visual Arts in New York City in 1970, Tony Ligamari turned to video. When he turned back to painting, he kept from video the use of "scan lines" for plotting. He begins with masking tape and raw canvas on the floor, frequently reconfiguring as he intuitively proceeds, adding layers of pigment with household brooms. "When in doubt, make a mess!" he says.[1]

Ligamari has made series of religious works—the Stations of the Cross and ten paintings constituting a chapel—which he views as art projects, not expressions of faith. He left Roman Catholicism decades ago.

Ligamari was born in Poughkeepsie, New York, in 1952. He received a BA in 1982 and an MFA in 1984 from the San Francisco Art Institute. A summer at Skowhegan School in Skowhegan, Maine, in 1983 and a year in Europe traveling on his "personal Art History 101 course"[2] were epiphanic. He lives with his wife, an attorney, and their two children in San Francisco. He takes occasional art jobs but concentrates on painting in his Berkeley studio.

Last Supper *was a painting I always knew I would do. I actually copied it, gridding it out pretty close to scale, and discovered that da Vinci had used very complex mathematics. For one thing, I found that all the heads were in a single horizontal band, except for one, and that was Judas.*

*I started* Last Supper *in Loomis [California] and finished it in Berkeley. It went quickly—but it still took six months.*

*I have no religious feeling about it. It's art history.*

1. INTERVIEW WITH ROBERT MCDONALD, JULY 28, 1998.

2. IBID.

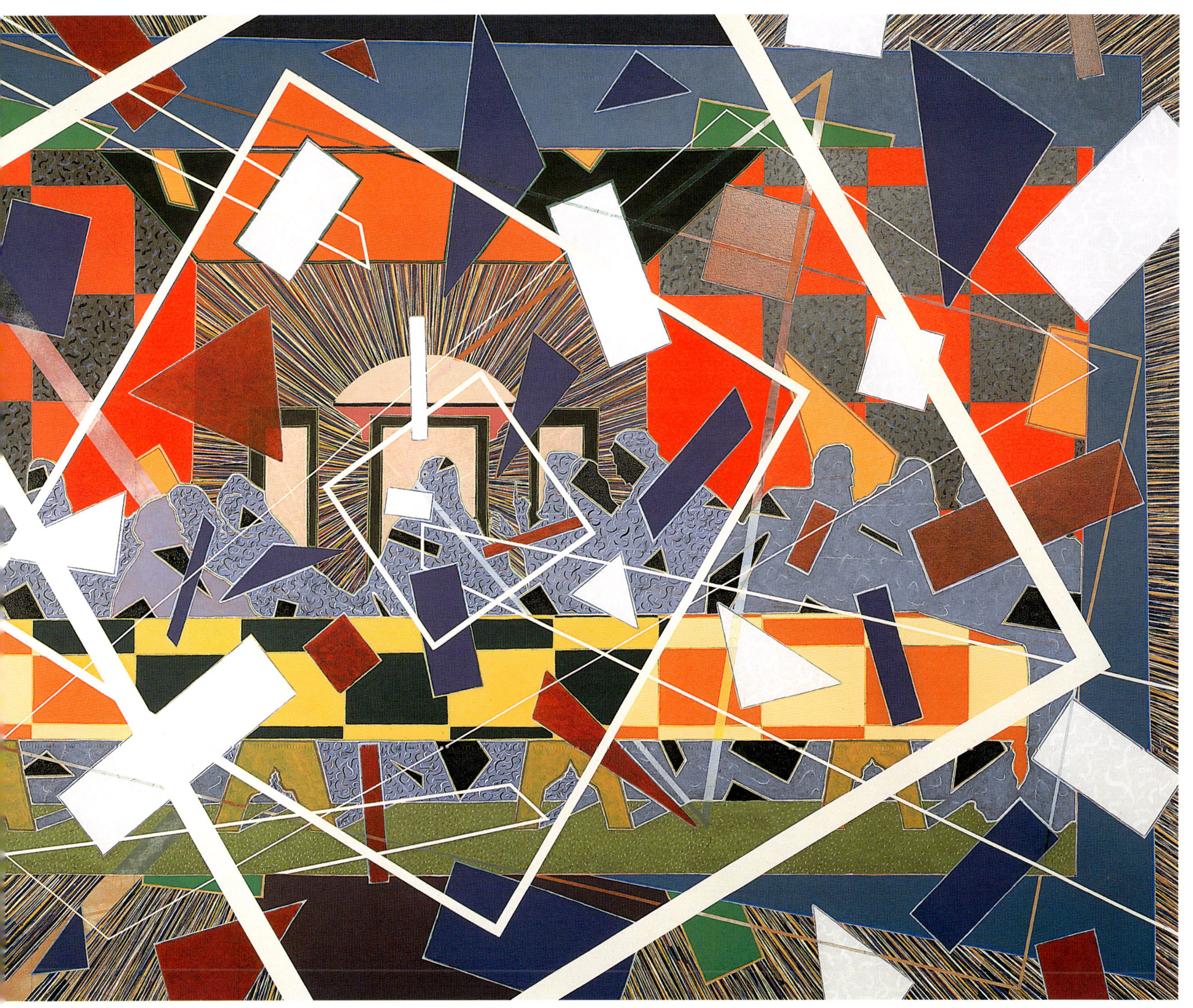

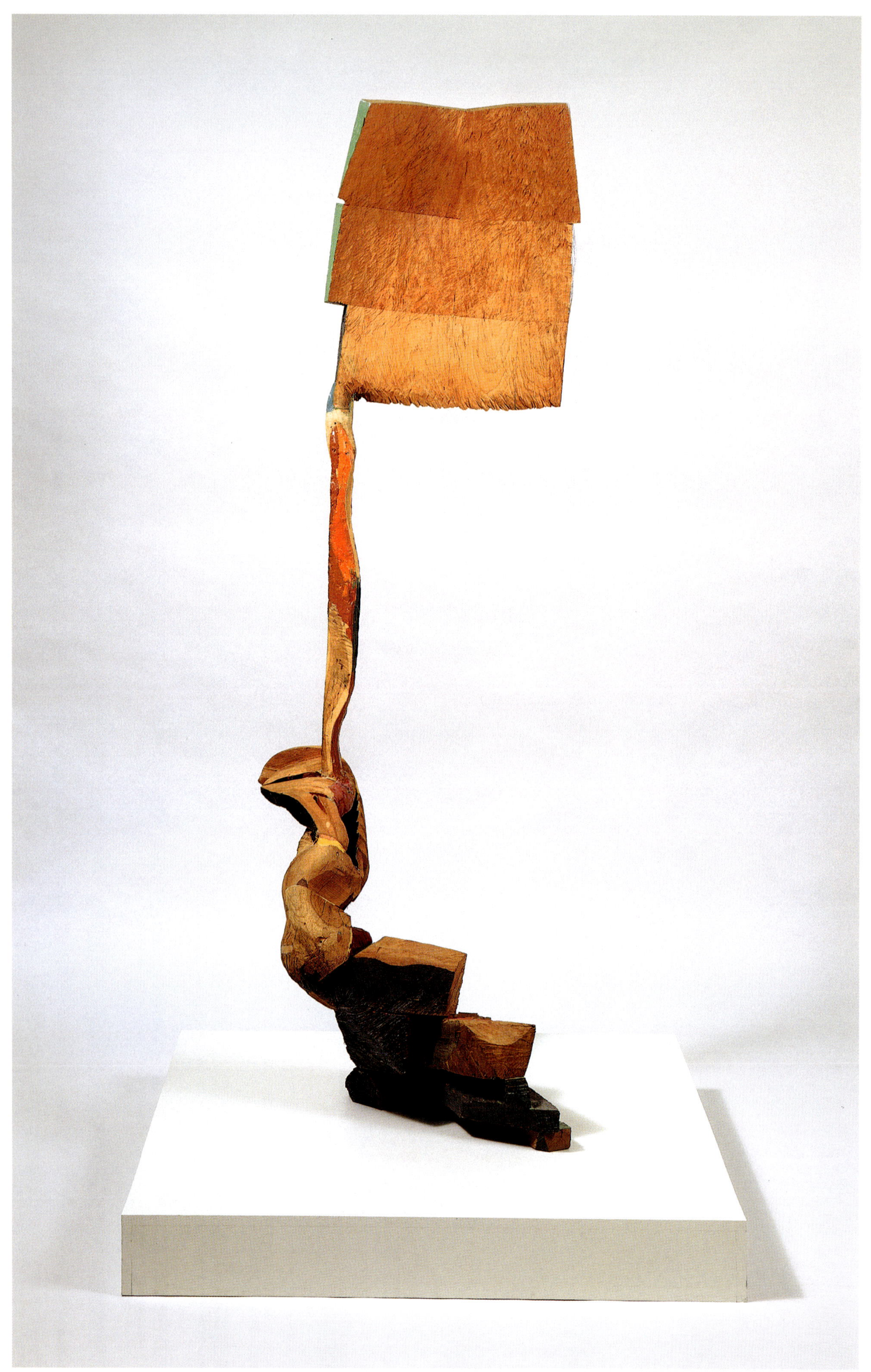

# ALVIN LIGHT

*Untitled* 1980. CARVED AND PAINTED WOOD. 86 × 29 × 17

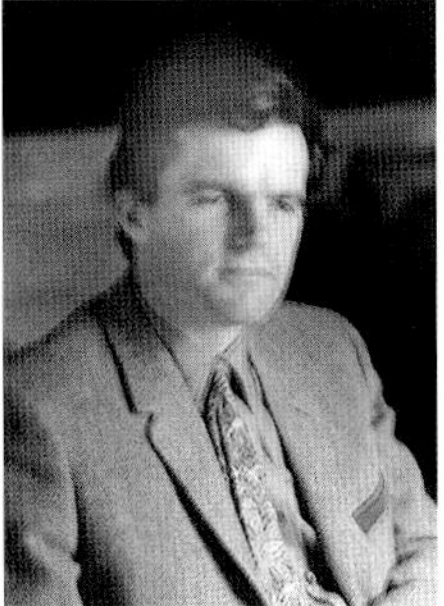

Sculptor Alvin Light was born in Concord, New Hampshire, in 1931 but was raised in central and Southern California. He began his education at the College of the Pacific in Stockton, California, as a pre-med student who also took art courses. In 1951 he began to study intermittently (including time out for military service) at the San Francisco Art Institute (SFAI), where he earned a BFA in 1959 and an MFA in 1961. He taught at SFAI from 1961 until his death in 1980.

Light was one of the first artists in the San Francisco Bay Area, and possibly in the United States, to construct sculptures by adding and subtracting natural pieces of wood, which he sawed, chiseled, chopped, and chipped to create three-dimensional Abstract Expressionist statements. He often used paint for emphasis. While his early sculptures resembled standing human figures, in the 1970s he deviated from this convention through his greater use of found materials.

Writer and artist Knute Stiles commented on his work: "Alvin Light glued and dowelled together lengths, chunks, and branches into a sculptural form which, though still organic, was abstract and nonspecific. Sometimes the pieces looked like vines, but others took on some ghost reference to an ape, or monster—but only a suggestion. Balance was an important element in this work. I'm told he changed pieces of the sculpture, and what had been on the base was later in the middle, each part adding to the equilibrium of the whole."[1]

Art critic Arthur Bloomfield likened Light's 1965 de Young Museum solo exhibition to "a sort of sculptural Seventeen-Mile Drive" with its lordly cypresses.[2]

1. "KNUTE STILES REMEMBERS." THE DILEXI YEARS, 1958–1970. THE OAKLAND MUSEUM, OCTOBER 13–DECEMBER 16, 1984. EXHIBITION CATALOGUE, P. 31.

2. "HIS SCULPTURE CUTS THE AIR." SAN FRANCISCO NEWS CALL BULLETIN, APRIL 6, 1965, P. 26.

# CHARLES LINDER

***Fiat Lux*** 1997, MIXED MEDIA AND FOUND OBJECTS, 83½ × 83½

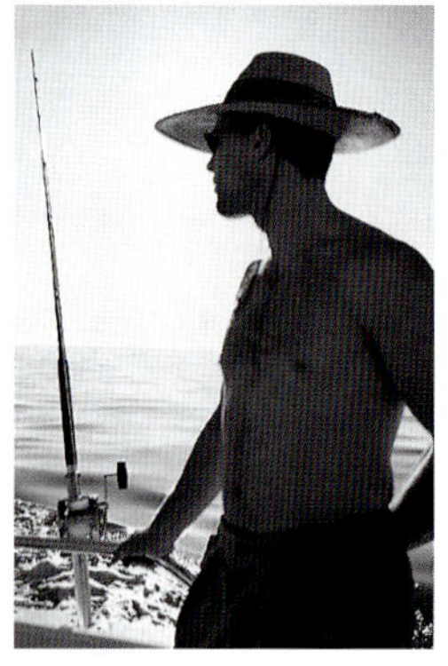

Charles Linder has brought energy to the San Francisco Bay Area as both artist and entrepreneur. In 1990 he founded Refusalon, a gallery he has directed since its opening, to show the works of artists from around the world; in 1993 he began exhibiting his own works in alternative spaces.

As a conceptual artist Linder has used commercial red paper dots, blue fingerprints, and pushpin holes to make beautiful two-dimensional works whose histories of compulsive process evoke time as another dimension. He has also made works whose recontextualizations of appropriated media, from Hans Hofmann paintings to conventional discards, both delight and instruct.

Linder was born in Pittsburgh, Pennsylvania, in 1967 and moved to California in 1985. He received a BFA from the San Francisco Art Institute in 1990 and an MFA from the University of California, Berkeley, in 1997.

*Culling from a vernacular source deep in Agraria, my sculptures come about through the meshing of my suburban youth in Alabama and my developmental years at various Megalopoli elsewhere. The tension between rural and urban and their dichotomies bind my work: conceptualist/craftsman, artist/businessman, city mouse/country mouse. Less illustrative than indicative, my work co-opts political dogmatism for its second cousin, situational opportunism, and asserts a life of artistic ritual in which intention and chance discovery are equally valued.*

Fiat Lux *represents a psychic collision between the worlds of high and low, the life of art and of crime, and the virtues of intention versus chance. Stolen records of a forceful, albeit overlooked, act of futility, the signs echo an agrarian urge to "make one's mark." The formal recombination of the signs as* Fiat Lux *(Latin for "Let there be light," the motto of the University of California) indicates my interest in throwing light onto otherwise overlooked areas of "creativity."*

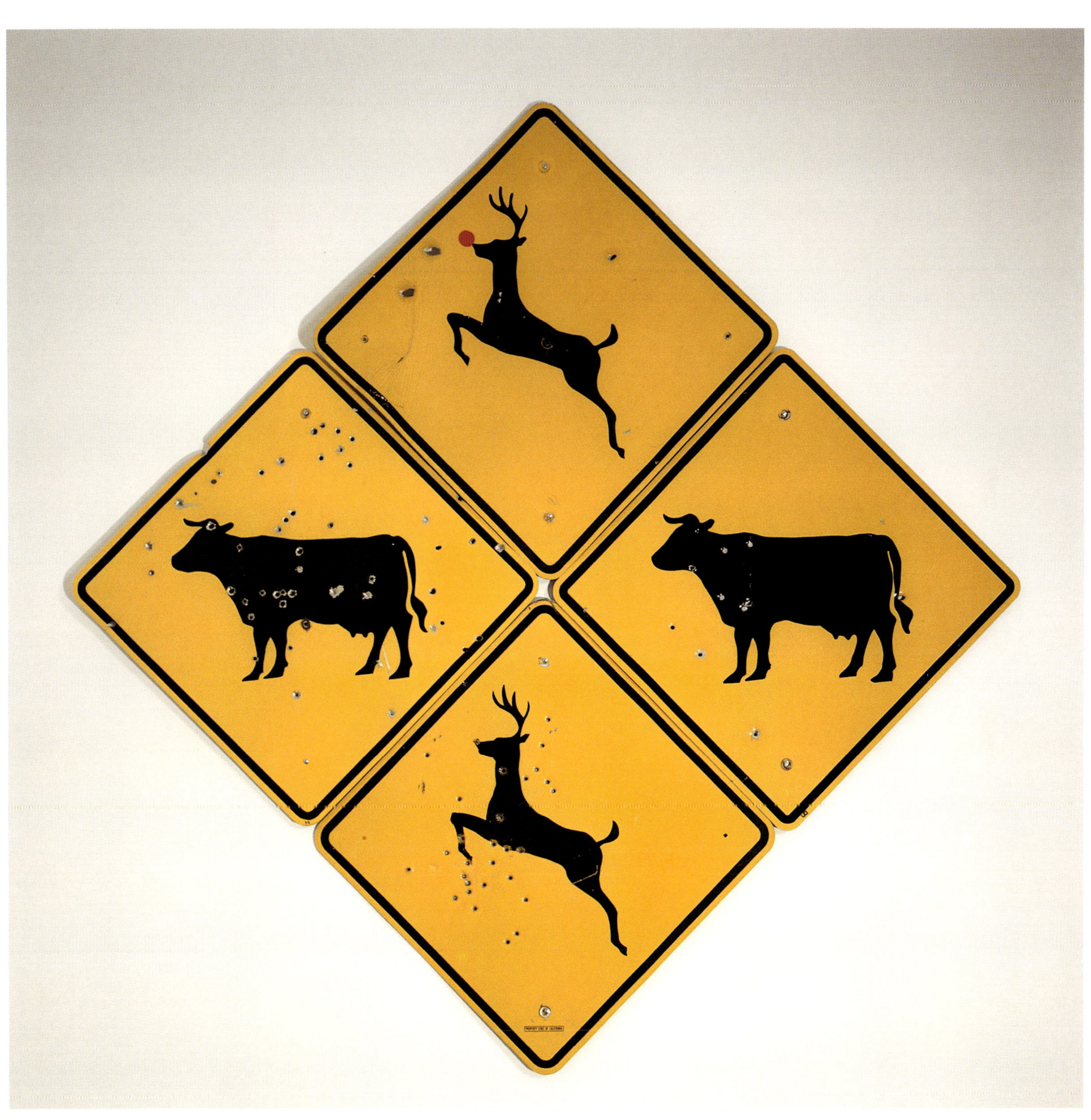

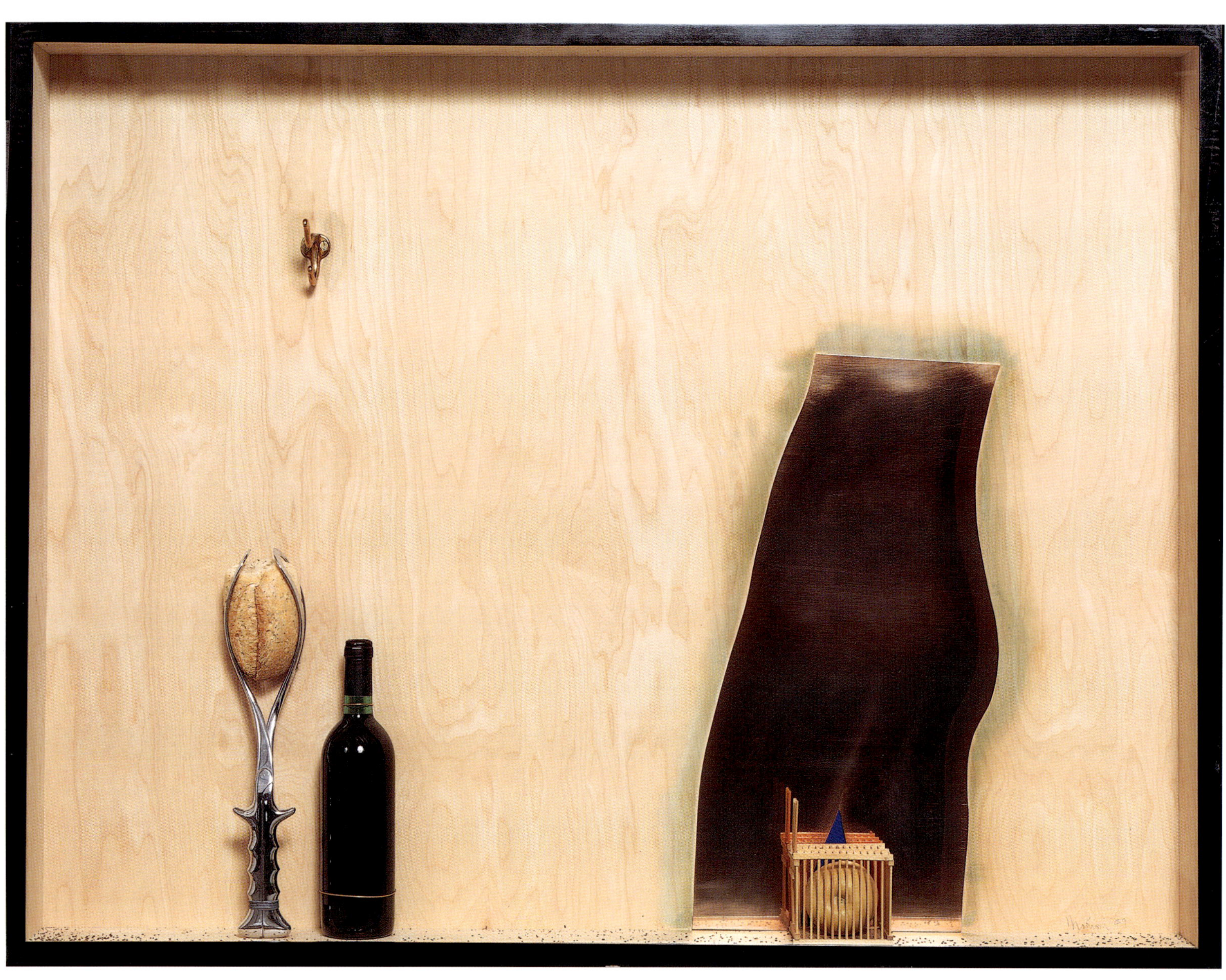

# TOM MARIONI

1989, SHADOW BOX, 36 × 48 × 4¼ ***Friday***

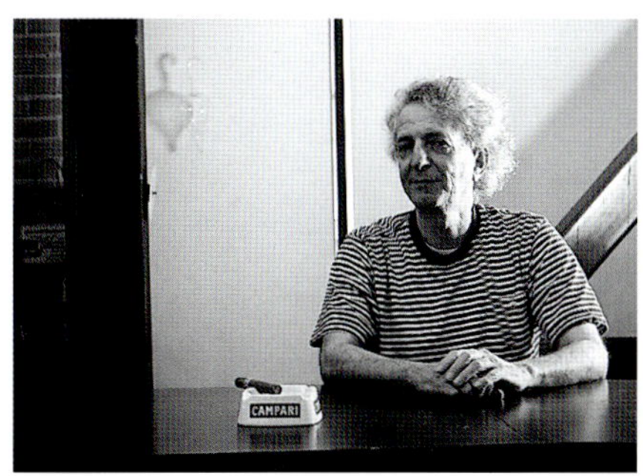


Tom Marioni is one of our most provocative artists, a presence—like a persisting evanescent idea, a phrase, a melody, a vision.

Born in Cincinnati in 1937, he attended the city's music conservatory and then studied at its art academy from 1955 to 1959, when he came to San Francisco. He championed Conceptualism as curator at the Richmond Art Center from 1968 to 1971 and as creator of the Museum of Conceptual Art in San Francisco. A memorable work was his *Piss Piece* in 1970, for which, disguised as a fictive Allan Fish, he drank much beer, climbed up a stepladder, and urinated loudly into a metal container whose pitch rose during the process. Another was *The Sound of Flight* in 1977, for which he repetitively/meditatively used drum brushes to drag gold dust across sheets of paper, producing drawings resembling birds in flight. Continuing to make works of great integrity and beauty, Marioni remains an inspiring, significant force in the maintenance of Conceptualism.

Friday *is one of a series of seven "shadow boxes" named for the days of the week. I don't like to remove all the mystery of the work, but I can tell you each work has a set of clues in it. I used the first pages of the Old Testament as a script for the boxes. Friday is the sixth day of the Creation, so it refers to Adam and Eve. Each work in the series also refers to a great artist that influenced me, in this case Yves Klein.*

*A shadow box is a rectangular frame fronted with a glass panel for simultaneously displaying and protecting merchandise, popular in the nineteenth century.*

# JOCK MCDONALD

***Rene & Gorilla***

1988. GELATIN-SILVER PRINT. 9¾ × 9¾

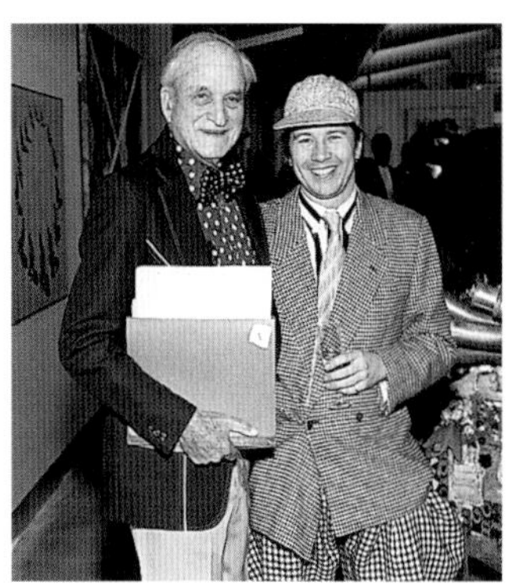

Jock McDonald, who was born in Vancouver, British Columbia, Canada, in 1961, is a self-taught photographer. Having moved to California in 1979, he managed the David Tise photographic studio in San Francisco from 1982 to 1986 while producing a broad range of commercial photographs. In 1985 he created the first of a continuing series of larger-than-life, photo-linen portraits of distinguished artists, which were exhibited at the Fuller Goldeen Gallery in 1986. His subjects included Robert Arneson, William T. Wiley, Roy De Forest, Robert Hudson, and Manuel Neri. That same year he embarked on his career as an independent commercial photographer, shooting in both black-and-white and color.

The hallmarks of McDonald's photographs are their clarity, their classic formal balance and intimacy, their humor, and their feeling. His subjects convey the pleasure—even playfulness—they experience working with him. For example, Dr. Carl Djerassi, inventor of the birth control pill, poses holding his left hand over his distended stomach. In contrast, an elegant image of a dancer approaches pure abstraction in its beauty and energy.

The image of *Rene & Gorilla* originated in Rene and Veronica di Rosa's efforts to protect the Napa Valley by protesting the development of property adjacent to Winery Lake. The couple, dressed in gorilla costumes, picketed the Napa City Hall announcing, "I'm ape for the grape." Veronica di Rosa is not hidden behind this mask, however.

*Vision is not the ability to see. Vision is the desire to see in a way that others usually do not. Humor and feeling are the two things that connect me with my photography.*

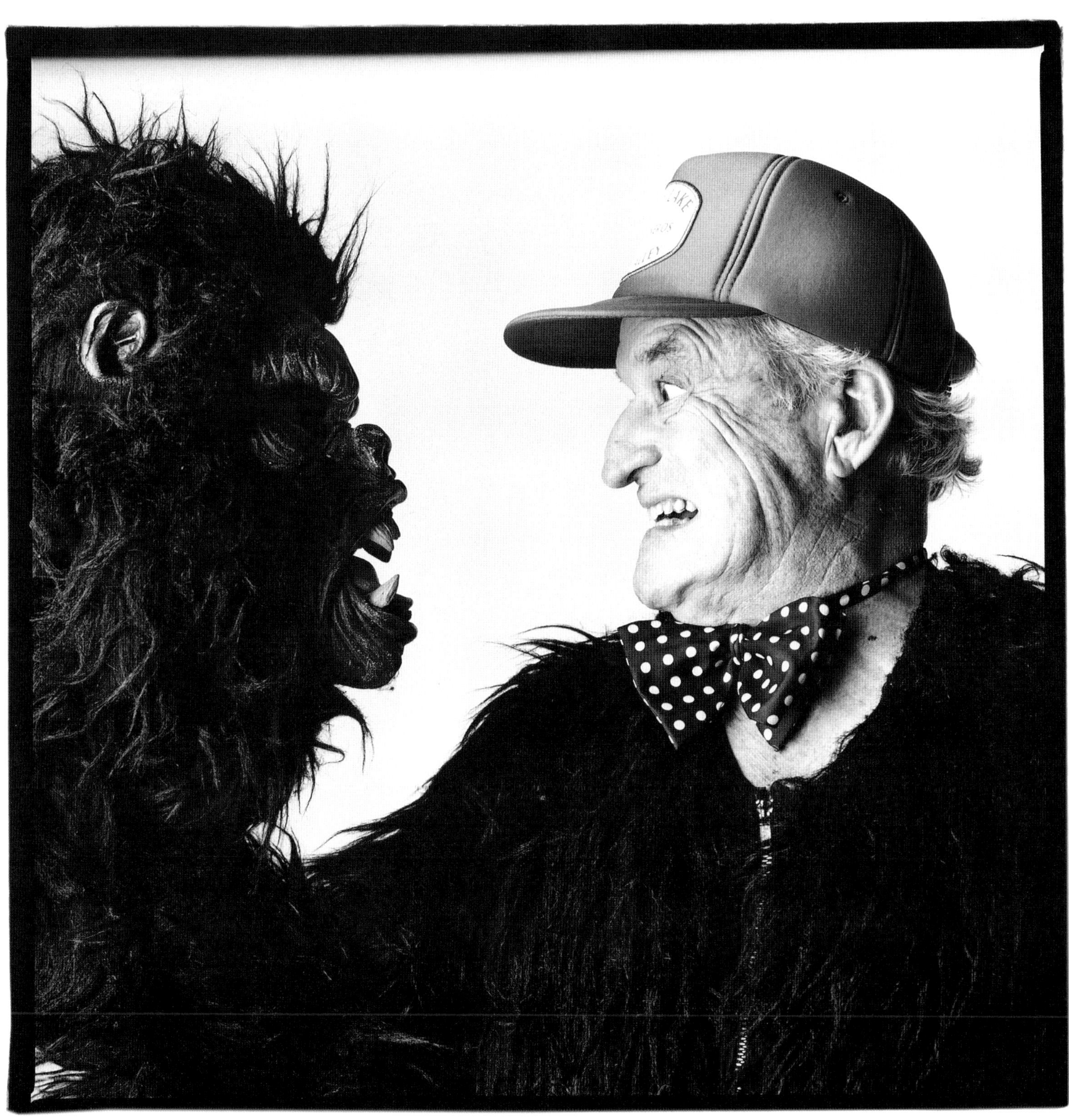

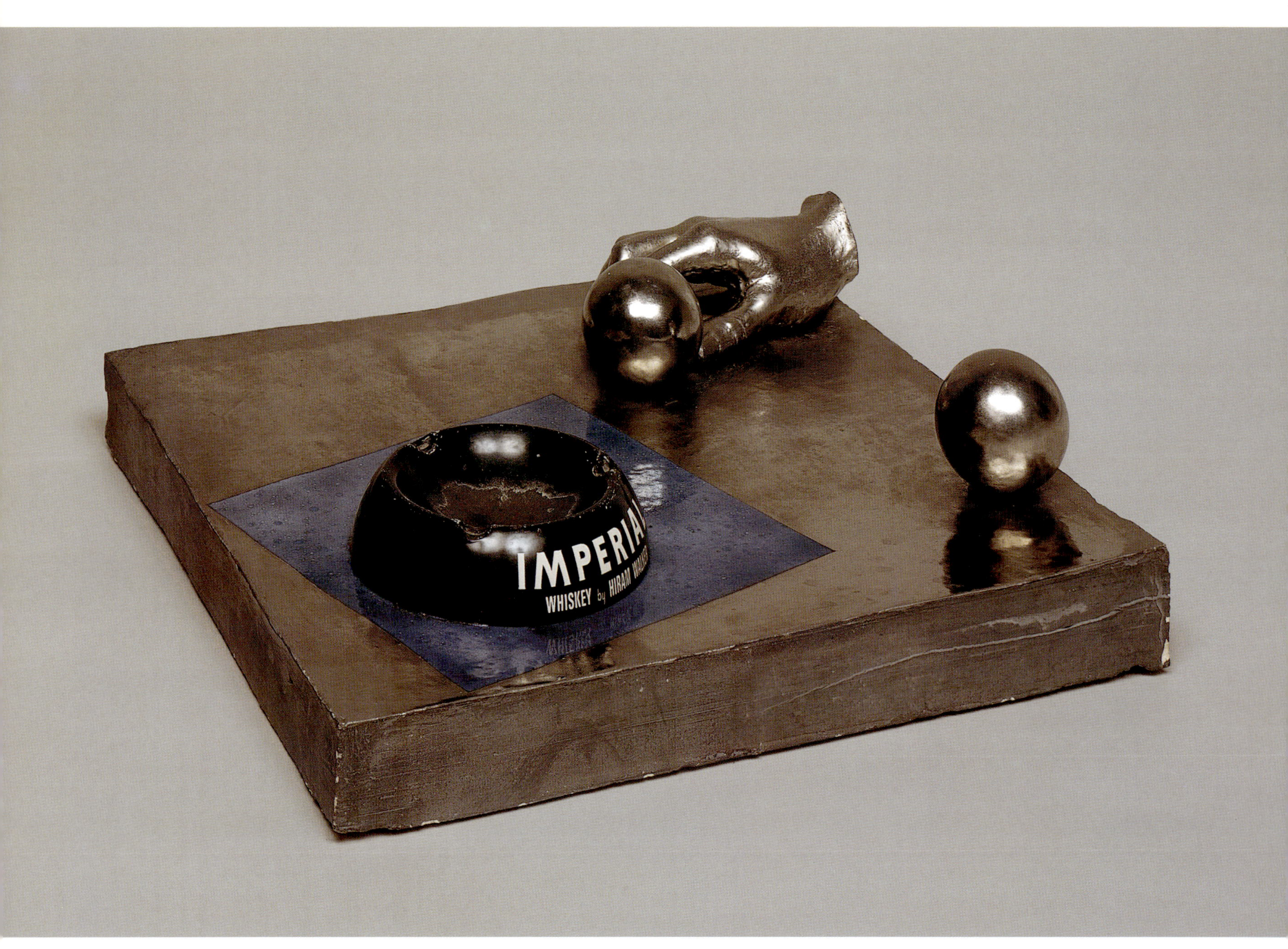
IMPERIAL
WHISKEY by HIRAM WA

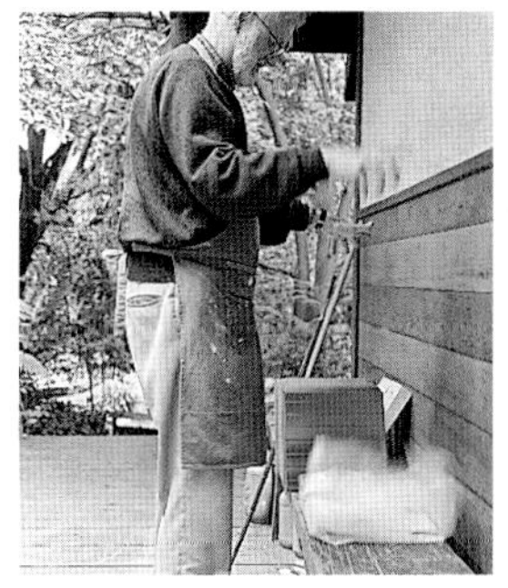

# JIM MELCHERT

1968, METAL, CLAY, AND GLAZES, 4½ × 15 × 15 ***Photo Negative with Metal Ashtray***

Jim Melchert is one of the leading figures in the San Francisco Bay Area artistic community, noted for his openness to experimentation and his encouragement of that of others. While championing the new, with particular emphasis on conceptualism and clay, he also sets standards of integrity and grace among artists—like a patrician hippie.

Melchert was born in New Bremen, Ohio, in 1930 and received degrees from Princeton and the University of Chicago; in 1961, he earned an MA from the University of California, Berkeley, where he studied ceramics with Peter Voulkos. He taught at the San Francisco Art Institute and then at UC Berkeley. He was director of the Visual Arts Program of the National Endowment for the Arts from 1977 until 1981 and of the American Academy in Rome from 1984 until 1988.

*It is essential to know that I made this piece at a time when smoking was so common that you might easily see someone use the ashtray in it.*

*I was thinking about photography when I made this three-dimensional representation of the negative of a photograph. The picture was probably taken in a bar where someone was toying with a couple of billiard balls at a table.*

*As you know, photographers are free to print as much of a negative as they want. In this case, the only part of the film actually printed is the square that contains the ashtray. (The color distinguishes it from the rest of the negative.) The piece is completed when someone's hand is seen entering the realm of the ashtray, alive and moving, the smoke curling into the air in juxtaposition with the frozen state in which the rest of the negative awaits release.*

# RICHARD MISRACH

## *Athena Nike (Column)*

1979. COLOR COUPLER PRINT (1982). 18 5/8 × 21

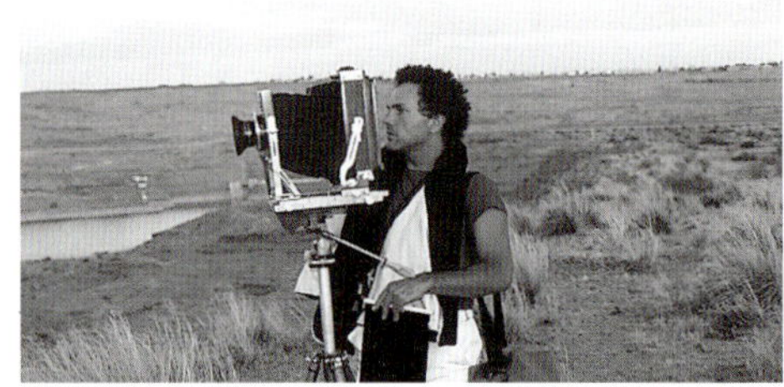

Richard Misrach has spent most of his career photographing landscapes, especially deserts in America. He began to photograph the western terrain in 1969, while he was still a psychology major at the University of California, Berkeley. He took no formal photography classes, except for one from William Garnett, offered by UC's environmental design department.

"I learned by shooting a roll of film, then developing and printing it at [the Student Union, which offered noncredit photography classes and the free use of darkrooms to UC students]. Somebody would be there and say, 'That print's too dark. That print's too light. Go back and change it.'"[1]

Misrach was born in Los Angeles in 1949. He received a BA in psychology from UC Berkeley in 1971. He lives in Emeryville, California.

Athena Nike (Column) *is part of a portfolio of twelve images entitled* Graecism: Photographs of Ancient Greek and Roman Ruins, *a series of dye-transfer prints made at night in 1979 when I was traveling with the aid of a Guggenheim fellowship. The nocturnal studies were an extension of my previous interest in the primal and mysterious qualities of natural sites like the desert and in man-made, archetypical monuments like Stonehenge.*

*In hindsight, the Greek work proved to be a crucial, transitional period in my development. Along with my* Hawaii *series, it represents my very first endeavor in color photography, which has been my sole medium ever since. Nearly twenty years later, some of the discoveries I made working at night in Greece continue to influence my interests today.*

1. ANNE WILKES TUCKER, "A PROBLEM OF BEAUTY," CRIMES AND SPLENDORS: THE DESERT CANTOS OF RICHARD MISRACH, THE MUSEUM OF FINE ARTS, HOUSTON, TEXAS, JUNE 2–AUGUST 23, 1996, EXHIBITION CATALOGUE, P. 17.

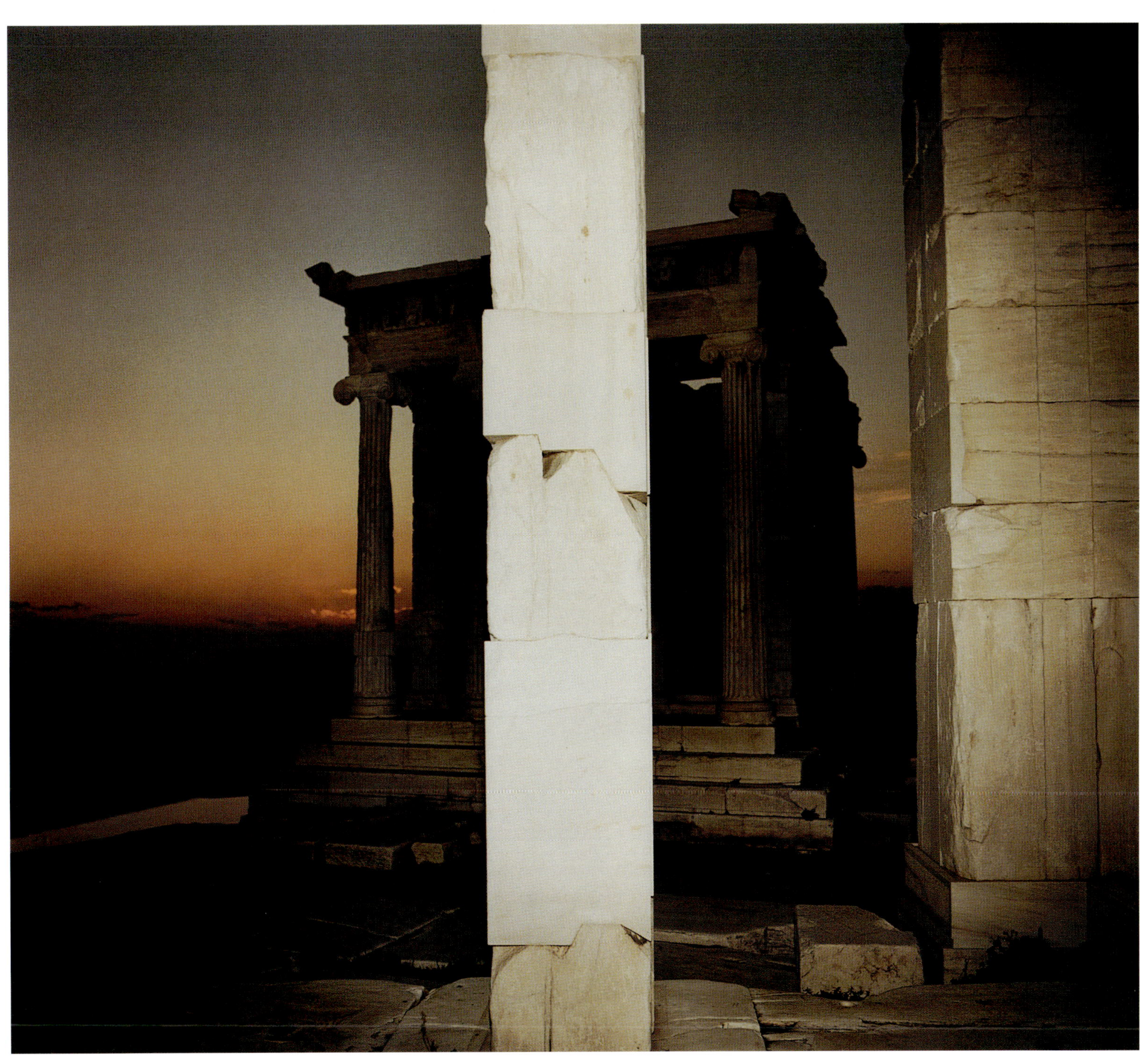

# RON NAGLE

Ron Nagle makes glazed ceramic sculptures whose great presence belies their small scale. While vestigially related to the cup in form and history, they are also three-dimensional paintings. They are

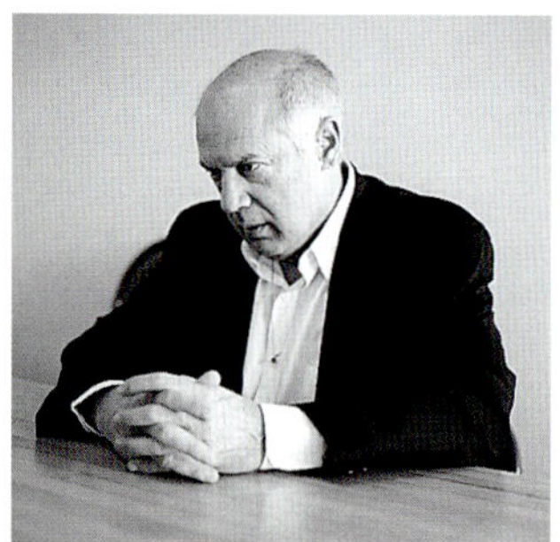

objects for study and contemplation, foci for meditation, and stimuli for synesthetic experiences. They are complex yet minimal, and above all, they are ravishingly beautiful—like great sonnets and art songs. They are works to explore for a greater understanding of art and of oneself.

Nagle is one of the handful of artists, including Peter Voulkos, Michael Frimkess, Kenneth Price, and Jim Melchert, who through mentorship, mutual influence, and cooperation brought about a revolution that reclassified ceramics from craft to art. Nagle glazes and fires his forms twenty to thirty times to achieve "not any one hue, but a mist comprising dozens."[1] His works merit being experienced as fully and intimately as possible. No longer merely cups for consumption, they become cups for communion.

Nagle was born in San Francisco in 1939 and earned a BFA from San Francisco State University in 1961. He has taught at Mills College since 1978, has been a rhythm-and-blues and jazz musician, and has written songs.

*Although my work is part of a ceramic tradition, it is not only the materials or processes that interest me, but the potential for intimacy inherent in the small object and the capability of color to convey emotion. For nearly forty years I have been investigating the cultural, formal, ceremonial, and—sometimes—functional aspects of the cup. Beyond this, it is my hope that the interpretation of my work be as open-ended as possible.*

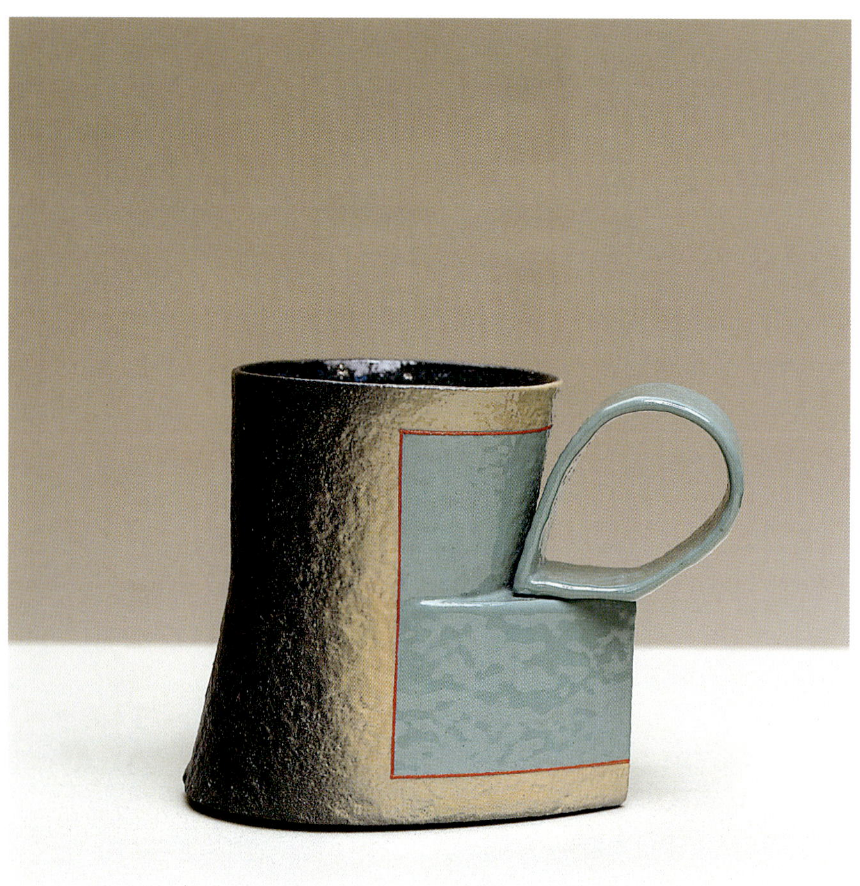

***Anderson Ranch Series—Turquoise*** 1988, PORCELAIN AND OVERGLAZE, 2½ × 3½ × 1⅞

1. MICHAEL MCTWIGAN, "RON NAGLE," AMERICAN CERAMICS, VOL. 2, NO. 4 (FALL 1984), P. 63.

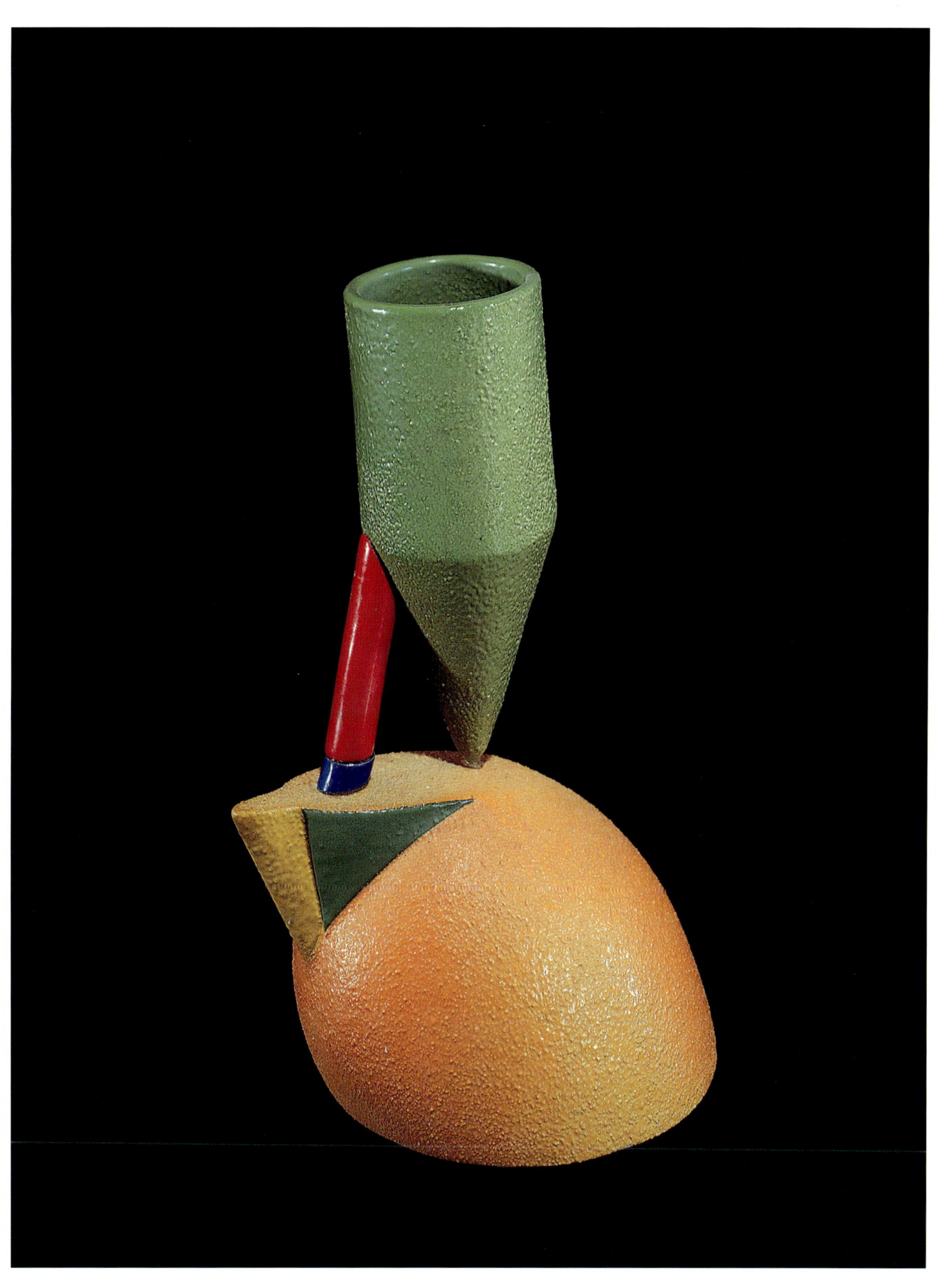

*California Dreamin'*

1975, SLIPCAST LOW-FIRE CLAY WITH OVERGLAZE, 5½ × 3¼ × 2¾

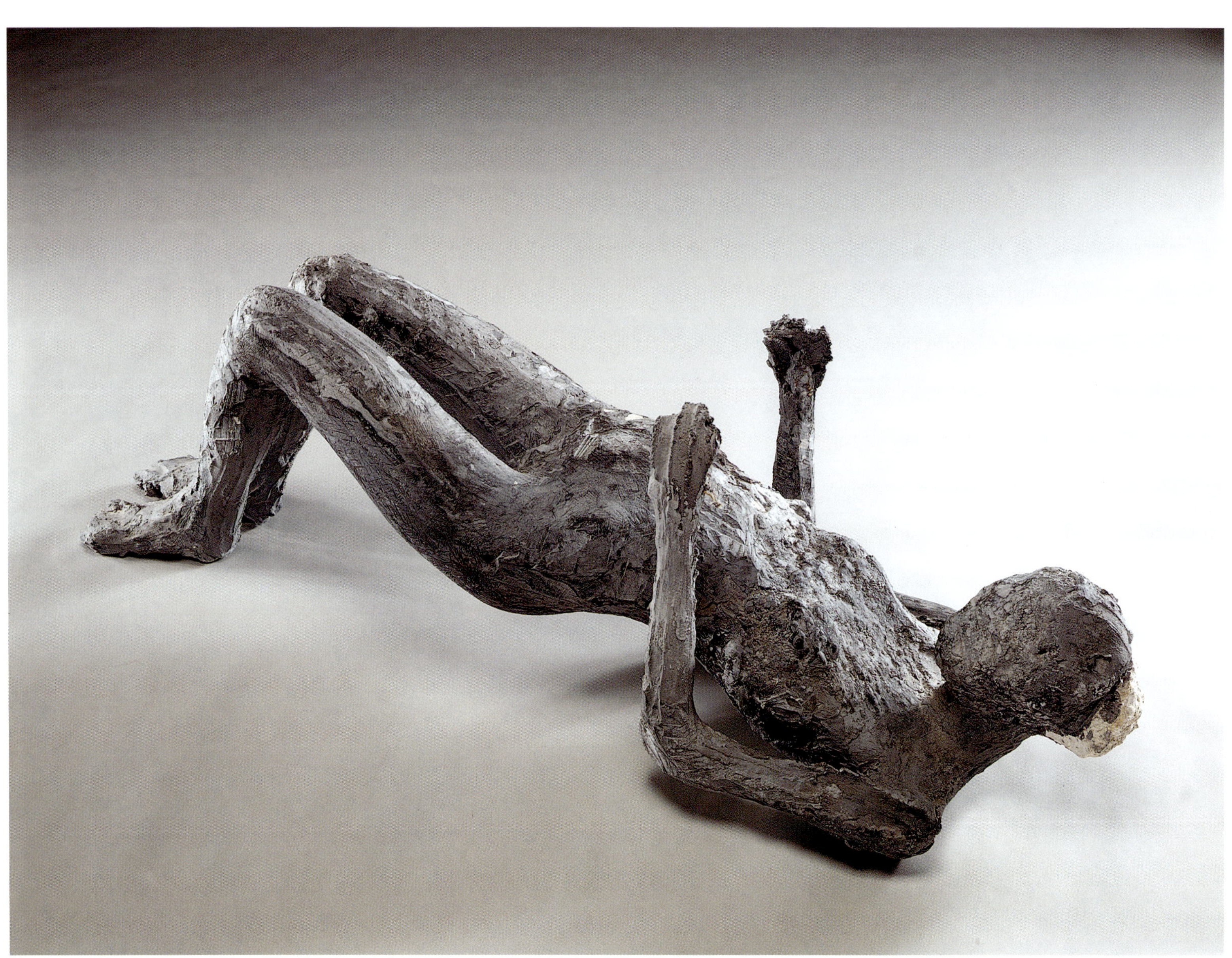

# MANUEL NERI

## *Acha de Noche III*

1975. PLASTER, LAMPBLACK, STYROFOAM, AND BURLAP ON STEEL ARMATURE, 16¼ × 56 × 14¼

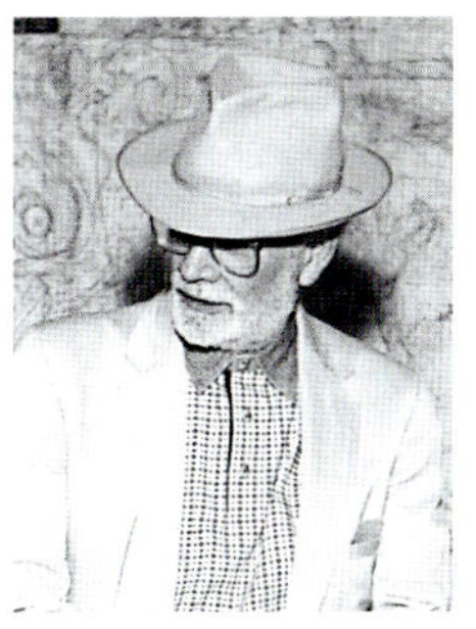

Manuel Neri represents the art of the San Francisco Bay Area to much of the world, in part because of his fidelity to the human figure—in particular the female form—as the source of his inspiration. His life-size sculptures in a variety of media—plaster, cast acrylic, bronze, and marble—have, since the late 1950s, been regarded as analogous to Bay Area Figurative painting. And although he continues to explore a unique and changing vision, the early influences of Abstract Expressionist painting and of Funk nevertheless persist.

During the period represented by *Acha de Noche III,*[1] Neri used plaster to create emaciated women in awkward poses. Their rough surfaces—gouged, hacked, cut, abraded, broken—appeared to have been formed brutally rather than lovingly, revealing the artist's intention to degrade his figures, an effect accentuated by an arbitrary use of color. Although not lifelike in appearance, Neri's sculptures are strongly appealing in character, perhaps because most viewers identify more readily with awkwardness than they do with grace and can empathize with their forms psychologically, if not physically.

Neri was born in Sanger, California, in 1930 and attended several schools, including San Francisco City College, the University of California, Berkeley, the California College of Arts and Crafts, the Archie Bray Foundation in Helena, Montana, and the San Francisco Art Institute. Initially he planned to study engineering, but a course in ceramics with Peter Voulkos influenced him to pursue art.

1. FOR NERI'S SPANISH-ENGLISH PLAYS ON WORDS IN GENERAL AND WITH RESPECT TO THE *HACHA* (WITHOUT THE H) *DE NOCHE* SERIES IN PARTICULAR "NIGHT AXE, ACHE, OR ACTS," SEE JOHN BEARDSLEY, "THE HAND'S OBLIGATIONS," *MANUEL NERI: EARLY WORK, 1953–1978,* THE CORCORAN GALLERY OF ART, WASHINGTON, D.C., JANUARY 31–MAY 5, 1997, EXHIBITION CATALOGUE, P. 107 (NOTE 27).

# NATHAN OLIVEIRA

1983, OIL ON CANVAS, 36 × 27

## *Standing Site Figure*

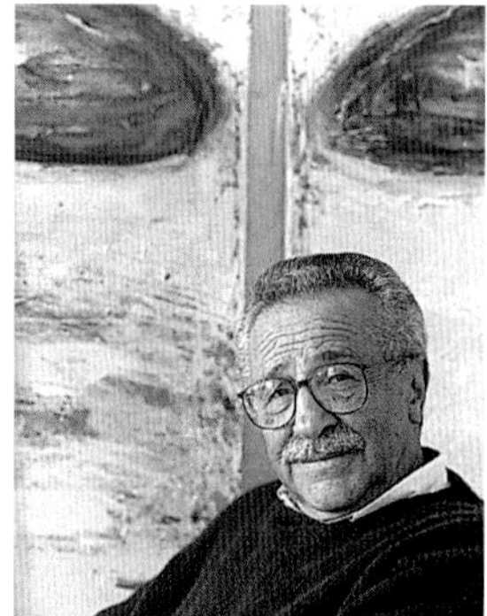

Guided by intelligence and intuition while responding to the sensual pleasures and frustrations of his physical acts, Nathan Oliveira directs his skills toward synthesizing intense passion and sublime vision in his art. During a career lasting nearly fifty years, he has created a world of images whose beauties, as they seduce viewers, instruct them about their singular histories and whose lessons about art and creativity are also a catechism about the nature of humanity.

Exposure to the works of Max Beckmann, Edvard Munch, Oskar Kokoschka, Alberto Giacometti, Pablo Picasso, Henri Matisse, and Marino Marini influenced Oliveira in his natural propensity to be a figurative artist. Absorbing elements of Abstract Expressionism into his personal aesthetic, he developed an affinity for the works of Willem de Kooning in New York and David Park, Elmer Bischoff, and Richard Diebenkorn in the West. Through his masterly conjunctions, he made paintings whose physical dynamism exalts their psychological content and cultural meaning.

Oliveira was born in Oakland in 1928 and received an MFA from the California College of Arts and Crafts in 1953. During the summer of 1950 he studied at Mills College with the great German symbolic figurative painter Max Beckmann. He taught at Stanford University from 1964 until 1996.

*I paint figuratively because "we meet at the figure," a common point, the idea. It is then given over to those who can, or wish to, interact with the vision and then continue the journey for themselves.*

*I cannot write more.*

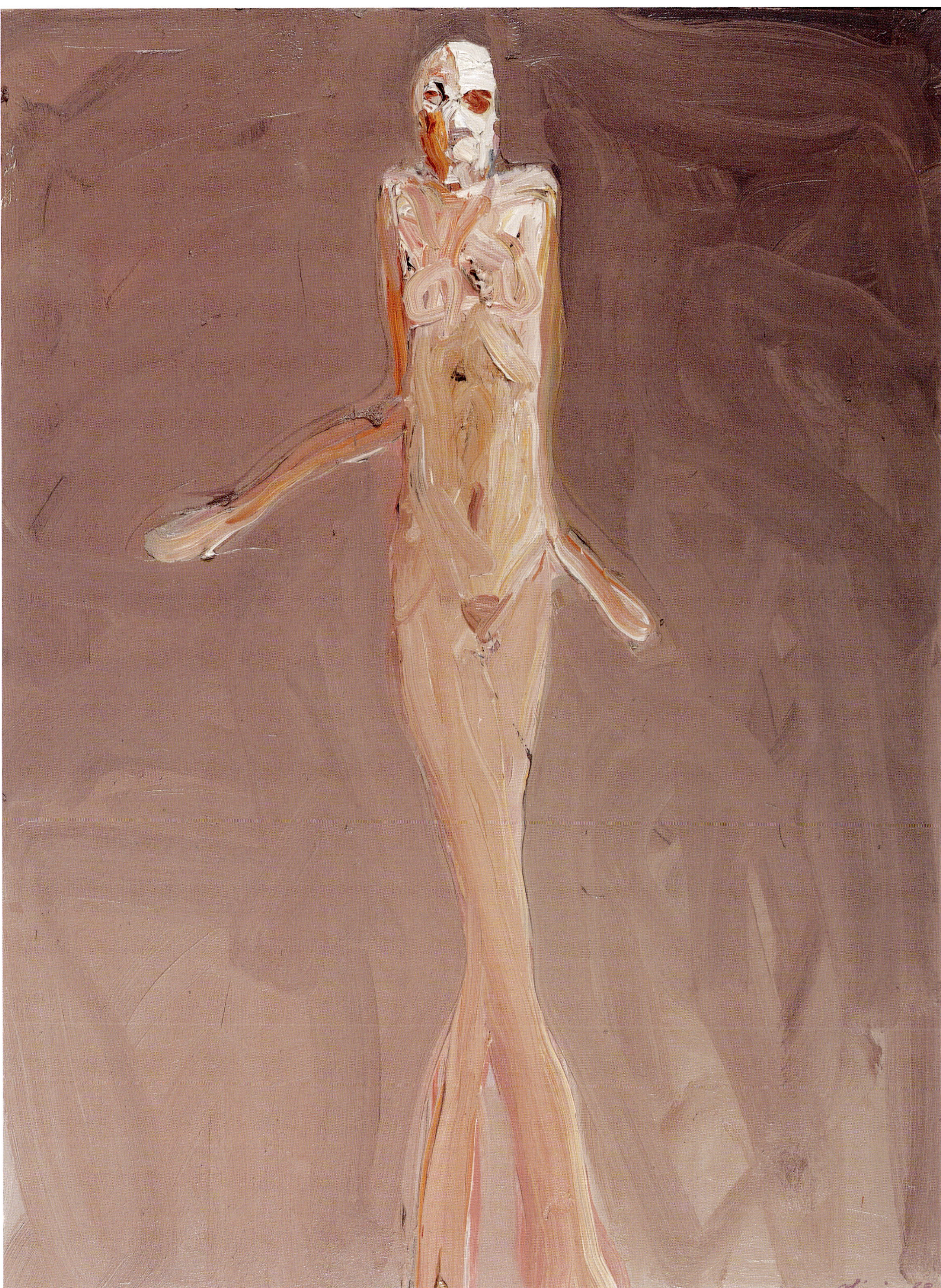

# DEBORAH OROPALLO

## *Untitled (Fox and Skeleton)*

1986. OIL ON PAPER. 39½ × 27¾

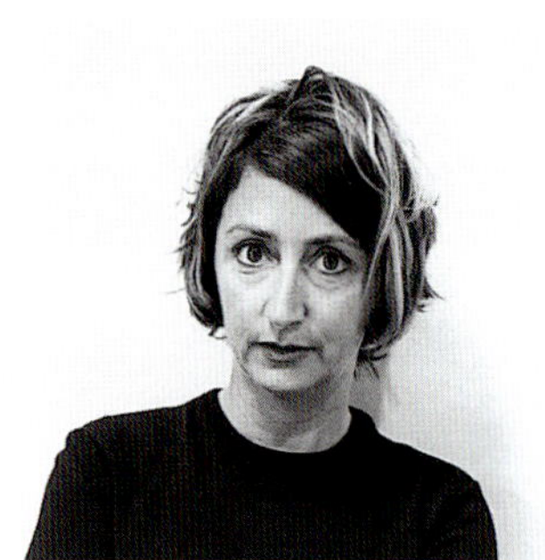

Deborah Oropallo uses images of ordinary things, as Marcel Proust used a madeleine and herbal tea, to enter the stream of consciousness. She, however, moves viewers of her works to explore their own personal histories, not hers.

Karen Kitchen, director of the Institute of Contemporary Art at the Maine College of Art in Portland, succinctly describes the process: "By successfully combining painterly gesture with concrete images, Deborah Oropallo creates compositions that tread the boundary between reality and abstraction. Each painting is an exercise in contradiction, defined by dual but opposing principles of direction and randomness, control and freedom, atmosphere and flatness, movement and stasis. Oropallo composes her paintings through a calculated orchestration of commonly found items such as toys, coat hangers, hair pins, or puzzle pieces. Silk-screened individually or in pairs, the images are applied to the surface in multiple layers over time. Tempering the flat, non-gestural character of the silk-screening process, she scrubs, wipes, or paints over each successive layer, creating a dense and ghostly depth."[1] *Untitled (Fox and Skeleton)* is an early intimation of that "ghostly depth."

Oropallo was born in Hackensack, New Jersey, in 1954. She studied at the Leo Marchutz School of Drawing and Painting in Aix-en-Provence, France, in 1975 and earned a BFA from Alfred University in Alfred, New York, in 1979. She then studied at the University of California, Berkeley, receiving an MA in 1982 and an MFA in 1983. She has taught at the San Francisco Art Institute and the Art Academy College in San Francisco. She lives in Berkeley.

1. KAREN KITCHEN. *DEBORAH OROPALLO: NEW WORK*. SEPTEMBER 25–NOVEMBER 2, 1997. EXHIBITION CATALOGUE. P. 1.

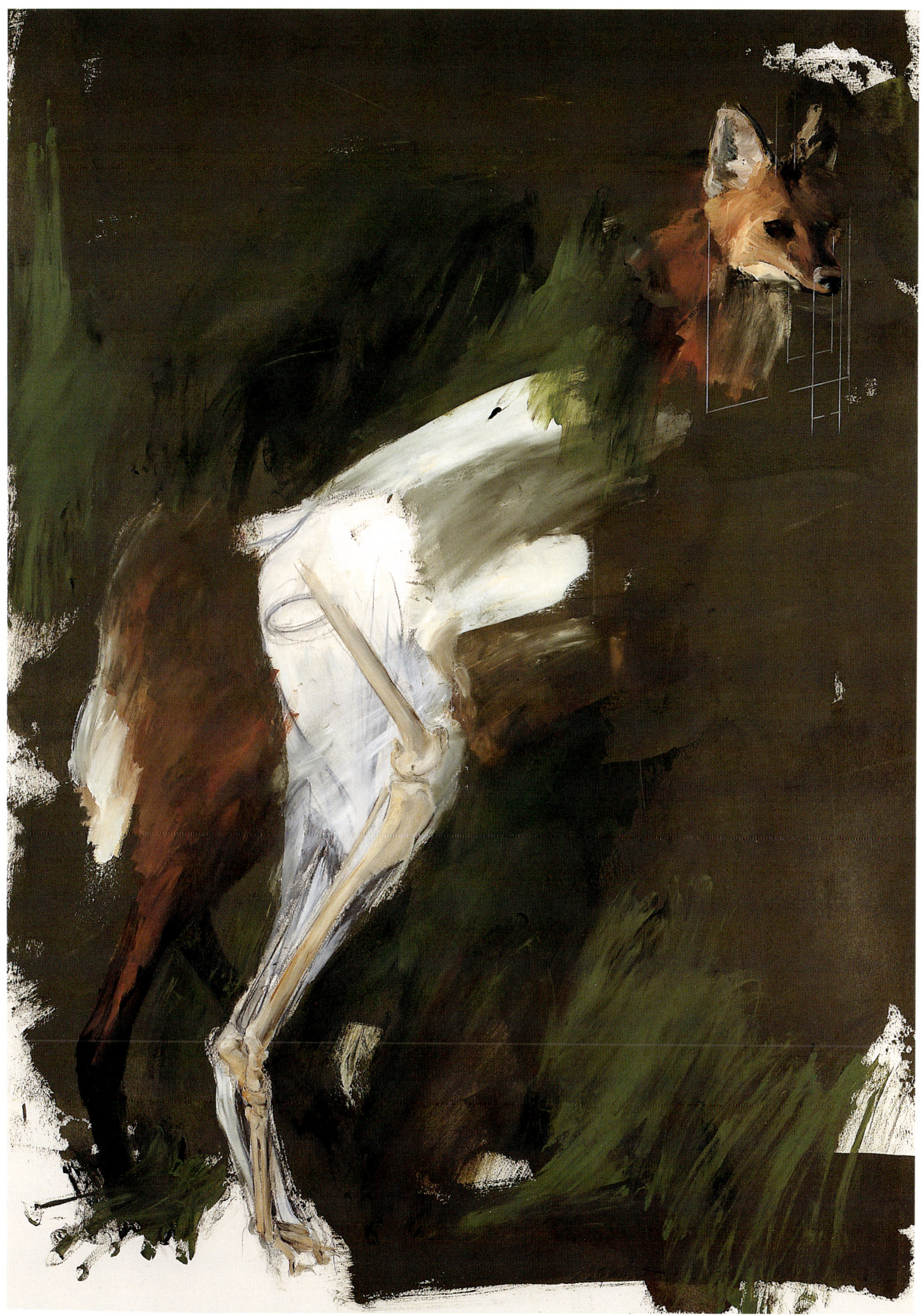

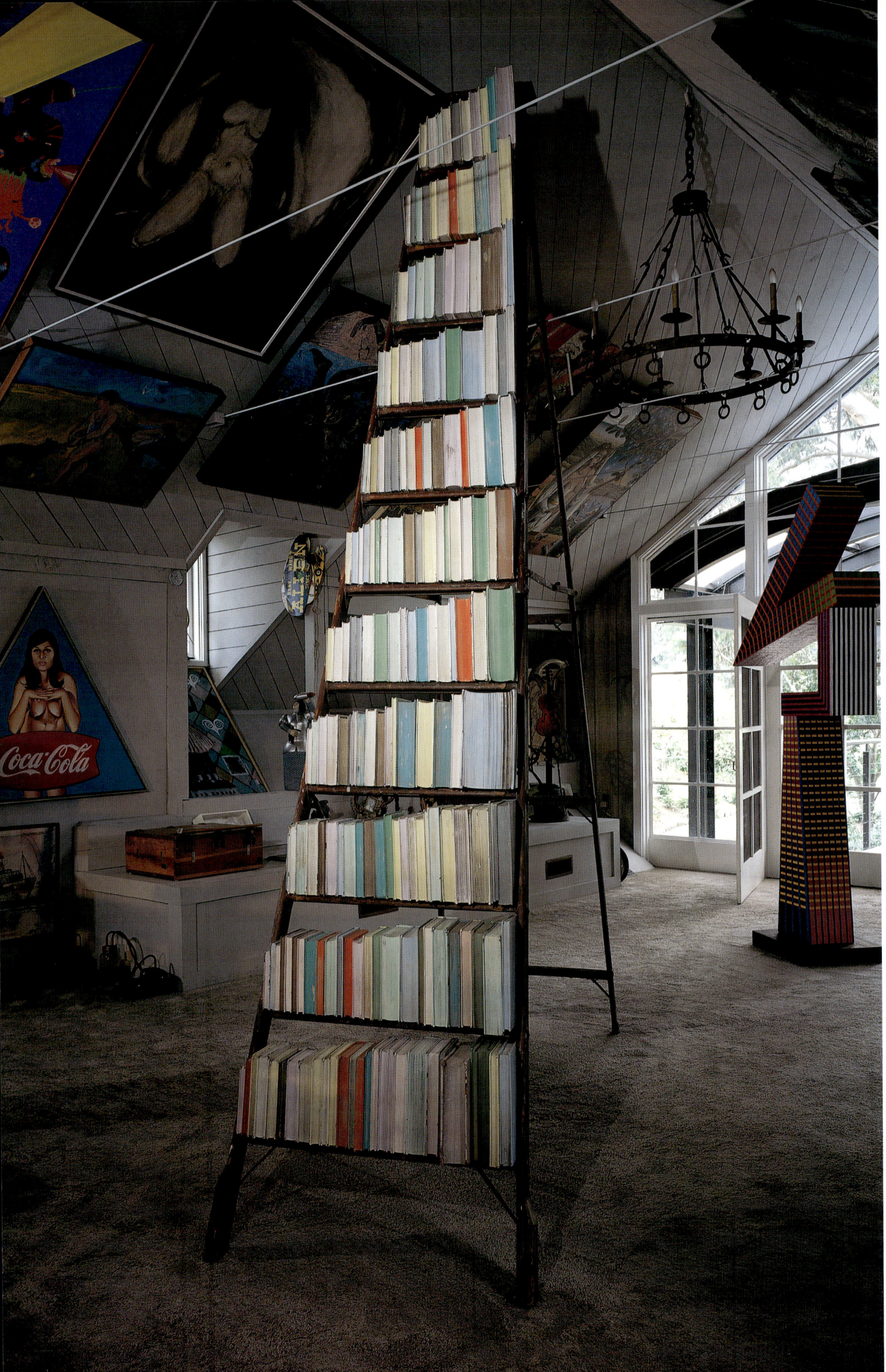
Coca-Cola

# JIM POMEROY

1971. STEPLADDER AND PAINTED BOOKS. 134 × 24 × 93

## *Ladder Day Paints*

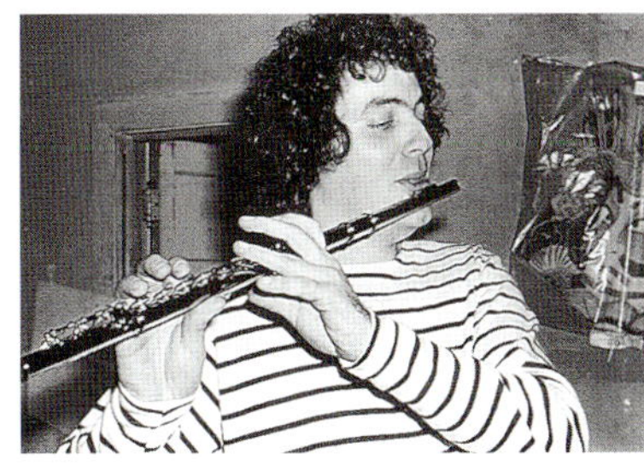

Jim Pomeroy was beyond classification. Through art, he questioned basic assumptions about the way we understand the world. He also questioned notions about the artist's uniqueness and role as a spiritual guide. He worked in many fields, ranging from performance art featuring his body, to audio installations, to stereoscopic exhibitions.

Pomeroy was a tinkerer with things and a poet-punster with words. His *Ladder Day Paints* refers teasingly to the Church of Jesus Christ of Latter-day Saints (the Mormon Church), but is not a commentary about it. In notes at the Preserve he wrote, "I just wanted to see what it'd look like if I got enough books and stacked them on the biggest stepladder I could get hold of." He used secondhand books—"All you can carry for $1"—whose titles he painted out. He appropriated the ladder—a favorite form—from the University of California, Berkeley. It may or may not symbolize the stairway to paradise.

Pomeroy was born in Reading, Pennsylvania, in 1945. He received a BFA from the University of Texas in 1968, and an MA from the University of California, Berkeley, in 1970, followed by an MFA in 1972. He was cofounder of 80 Langton Street, an alternative exhibition space in San Francisco. He died in Arlington, Texas, in 1992 from a brain hemorrhage he suffered when he fell, knocked over by a dog.

*One man's museum is another man's graveyard is another's gold mine is another's dung heap is another's pretension is another's encyclopedia is another's holy shrine is another's balance sheet . . . promotional display . . . conqueror's trophy case . . . cultural atrophy index . . . social registry . . . reliquary . . . hall of fame . . . wall of frames . . . hollow games . . .*[1]

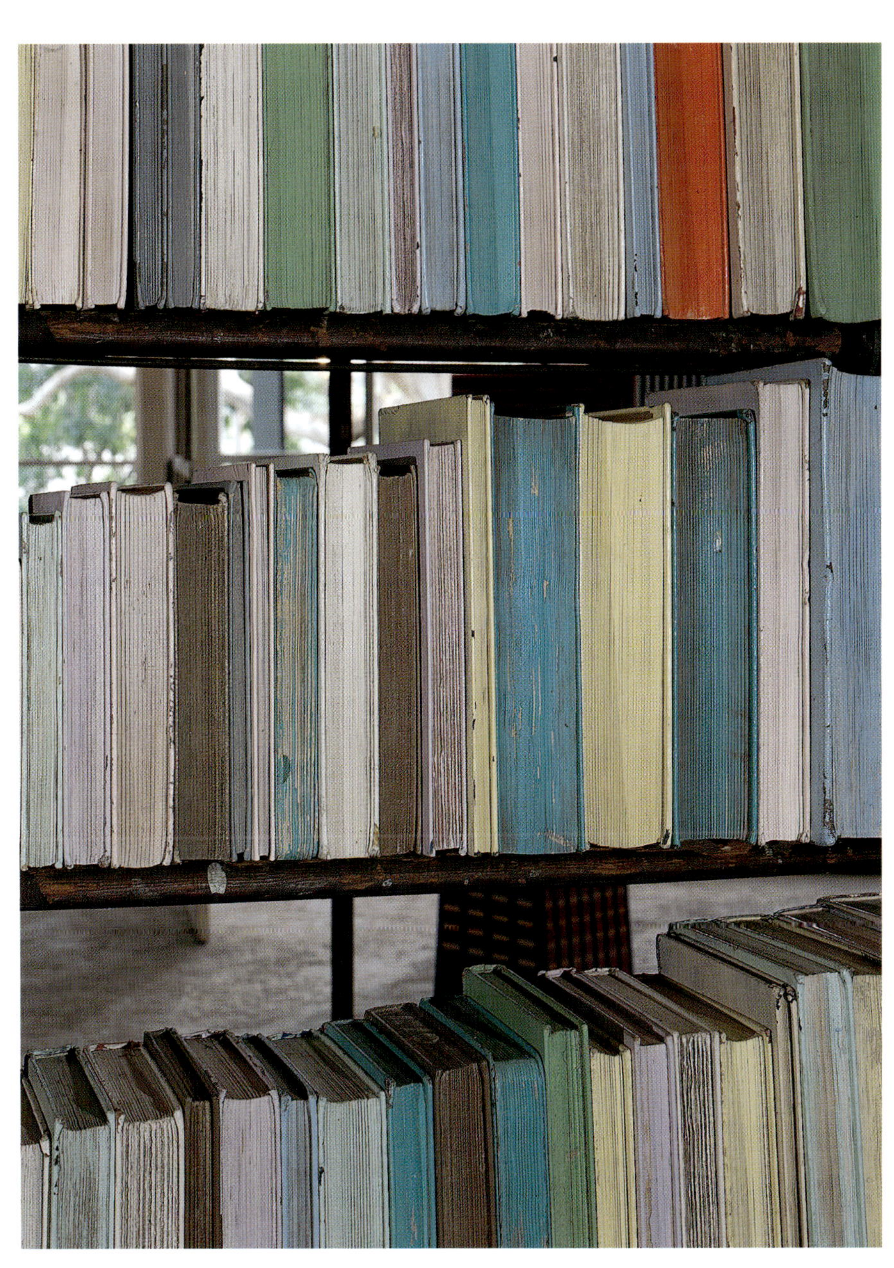

1. JIM POMEROY, *FOR A BURNING WORLD: ESSAYS BY AND ABOUT JIM POMEROY*, EDITED BY TIMOTHY DRUCKREY AND NADINE LEMMON (BROOKLYN, N.Y.: CRITICAL PRESS, INC., 1993), BACK COVER.

# JANIS PROVISOR

1979, OIL, ACRYLIC, RHOPLEX, AND MODELING PASTE ON CANVAS, 22½ × 24 ***Longview***

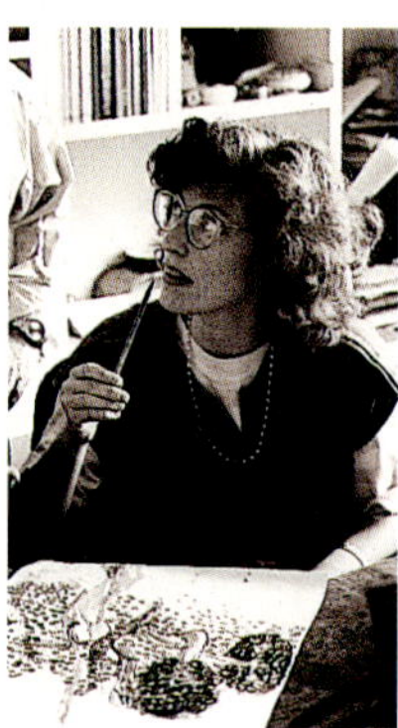

A typical Janis Provisor painting of the *Longview* period is about two feet square with a very thickly impastoed monochromatic surface in which several enigmatic forms seem fixed as if in a gel. Her colors are unusual, the sort you might see in reproductions when things become muddied and sour. For all their peculiarities, however, once you accept them you will have made a breakthrough in your appreciation of color.

Provisor is economical in her use of forms, providing information so scant that it is easy to commit her compositions to memory. Many resemble store-bought cookies and candies, especially the imported, colorful-but-flavorless varieties.

For all the ostensible simplicity of Provisor's paintings, it is impossible to convey the impressions they create: they have an untransmissibility that may be one measure of their strength as visual expressions. The artist finds her inspiration and sources in life, especially religious rituals, and her works have the formality of ritual, in which the displacement of even one element invalidates the whole. If her works are referential at all, it is to the mysteries of life, which are the purviews of religion, science, and art.

Born in Brooklyn, New York, in 1946, Provisor earned a BFA in 1969 and an MFA in 1971 from the San Francisco Art Institute. She currently lives in Hong Kong.

*My work has always been nature based . . . whether obviously so or not. For a few years in the late '70s, I was living in Texas and came under the spell of the Texas hill country. The topography was unlike any other I had experienced before, and it elicited a spiritual, almost mystical, response from me. In time, my work began to map out or become a diagrammatic depiction of this internal experience. I began to title my paintings after Texas towns as a personal marker of this ongoing relationship.* Longview, *the painting, became part of the place.*

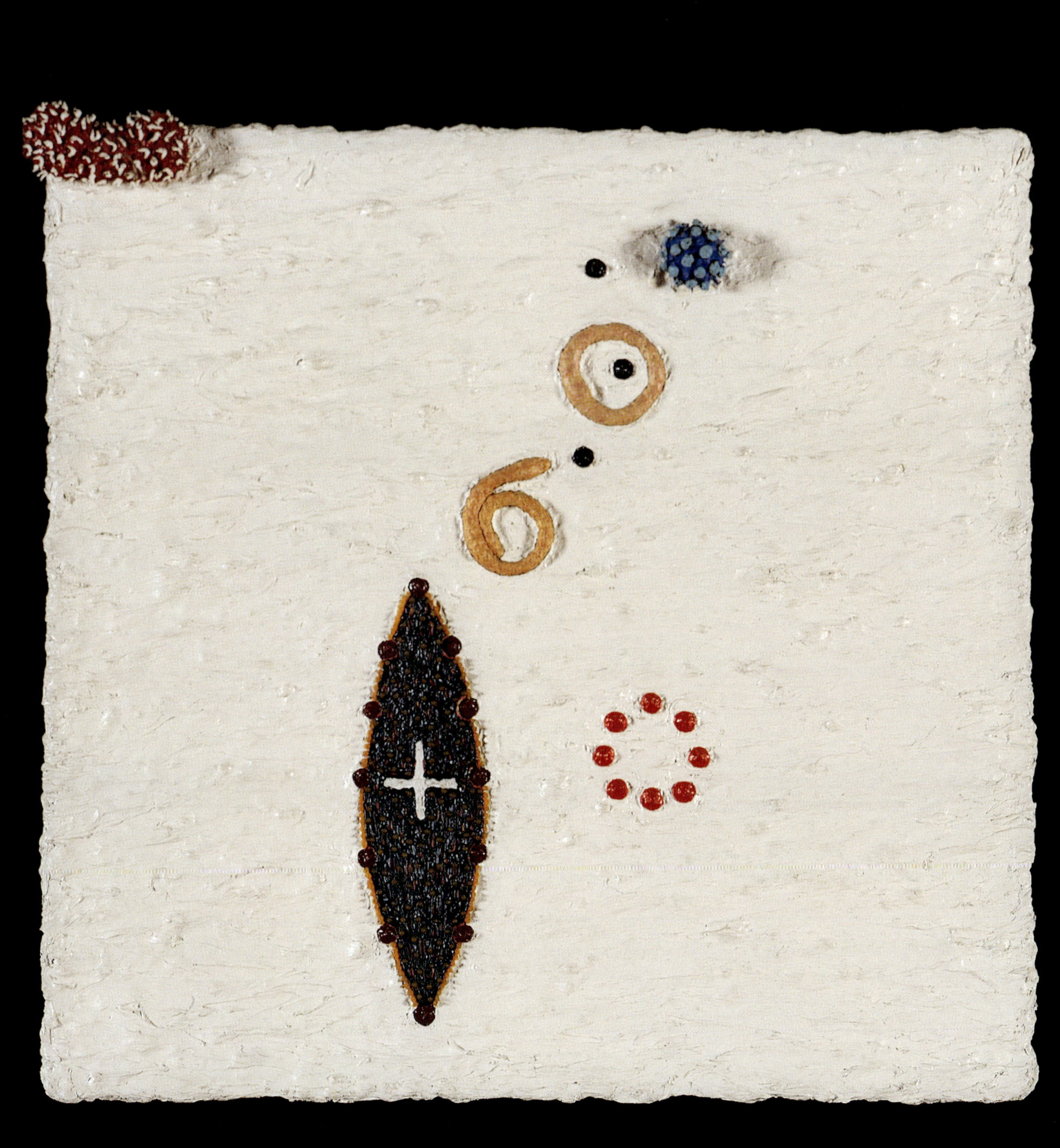

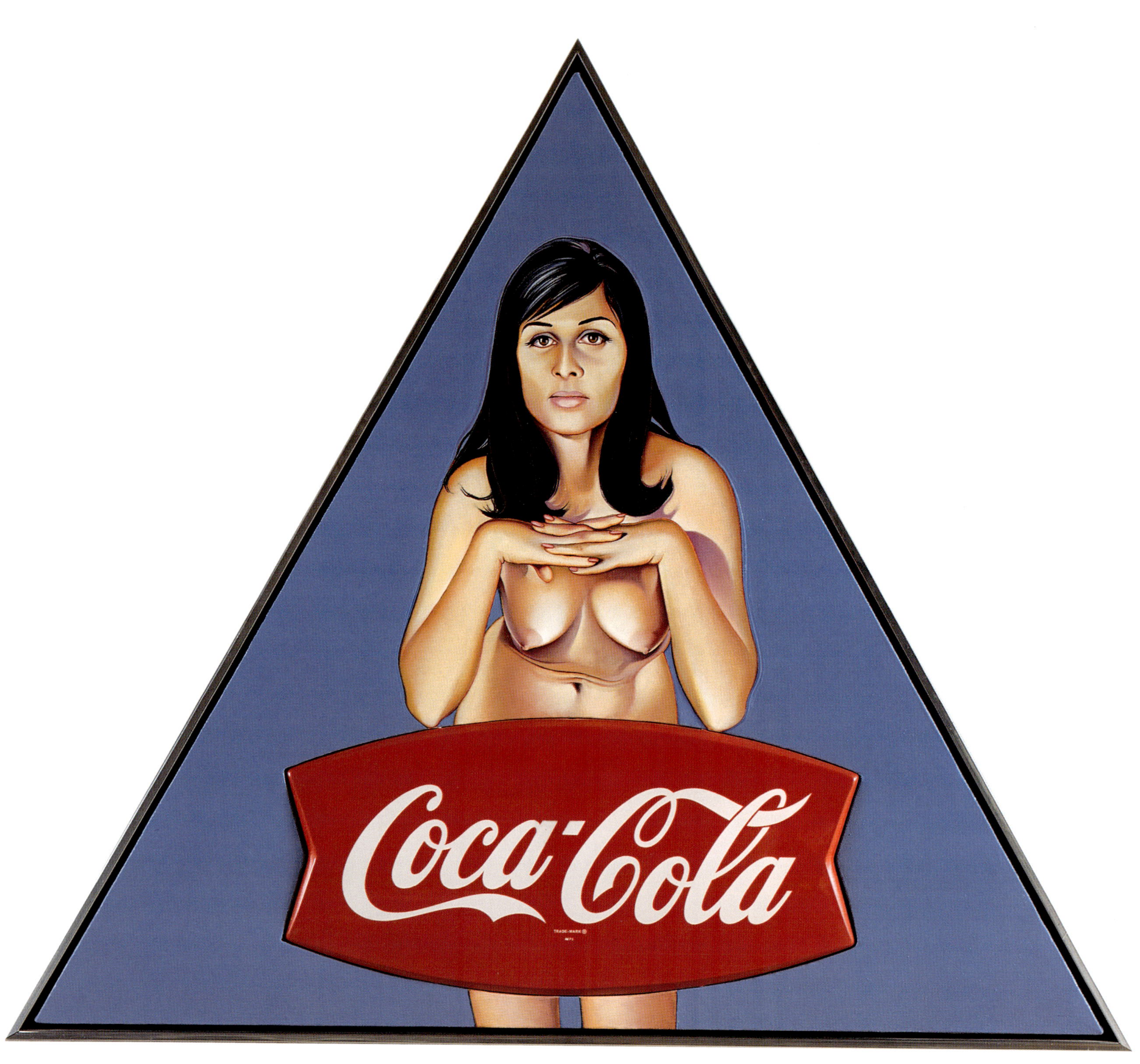
Coca-Cola

# MEL RAMOS *Lola Cola*

1967. OIL ON CANVAS WITH METAL SIGN. 41¾ × 48¼

Mel Ramos is recognized internationally for making works of art that give pleasure. To realize his vision, he may appropriate conventions that he finds useful—for example, those of Pop art in *Lola Cola,* for which his wife, Leta Ramos, posed.

Ramos, born in Sacramento, California, in 1935, received a BA in 1957 and an MA in 1958 from Sacramento State College. After establishing himself professionally, in 1966 he accepted a position at California State University, Hayward, where he remained until his 1997 retirement.

Ramos developed his gifts for representation and use of space under his teacher Wayne Thiebaud, whose initial background was in advertising. He appropriated images from comic books—*Superman, Flash Gordon*—and from girlie magazines and calendars. An alluring blonde *Chiquita* smiles full-face from a half-peeled banana in which she stands, her nude torso in profile. The background is a Chiquita label marked with an "R" in a circle for "Registered"—or maybe "Restricted." In other paintings models pose with representatives of the wild, like a brown bear, and beautiful faces contradict the bodies of quasi-de Kooning women. The versatile Ramos has also made landscape paintings of palm trees against monochromatic fields, and several other series, including *The Artist's Studio* and *Nude Descending a Staircase.*

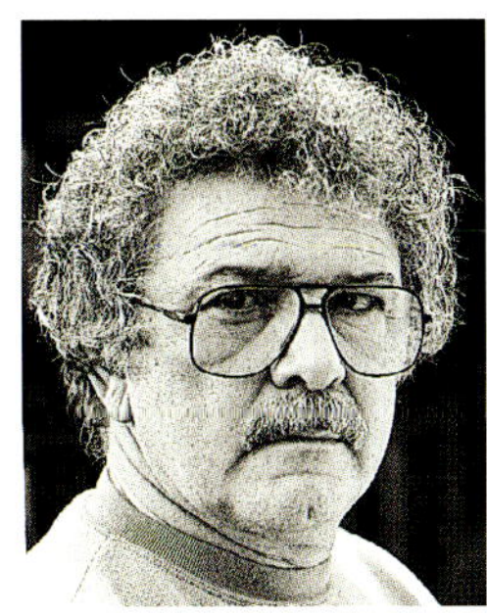

*In 1967 I was preoccupied with the notion of real or physical space as opposed to the illusion of space, which is the primary tenet of painting. I did a series of paintings in which I appliquéd objects to the picture plane. With the painting called* Lola Cola *I embedded an enameled Coca-Cola sign to the surface, which created the effect of bas-relief.*

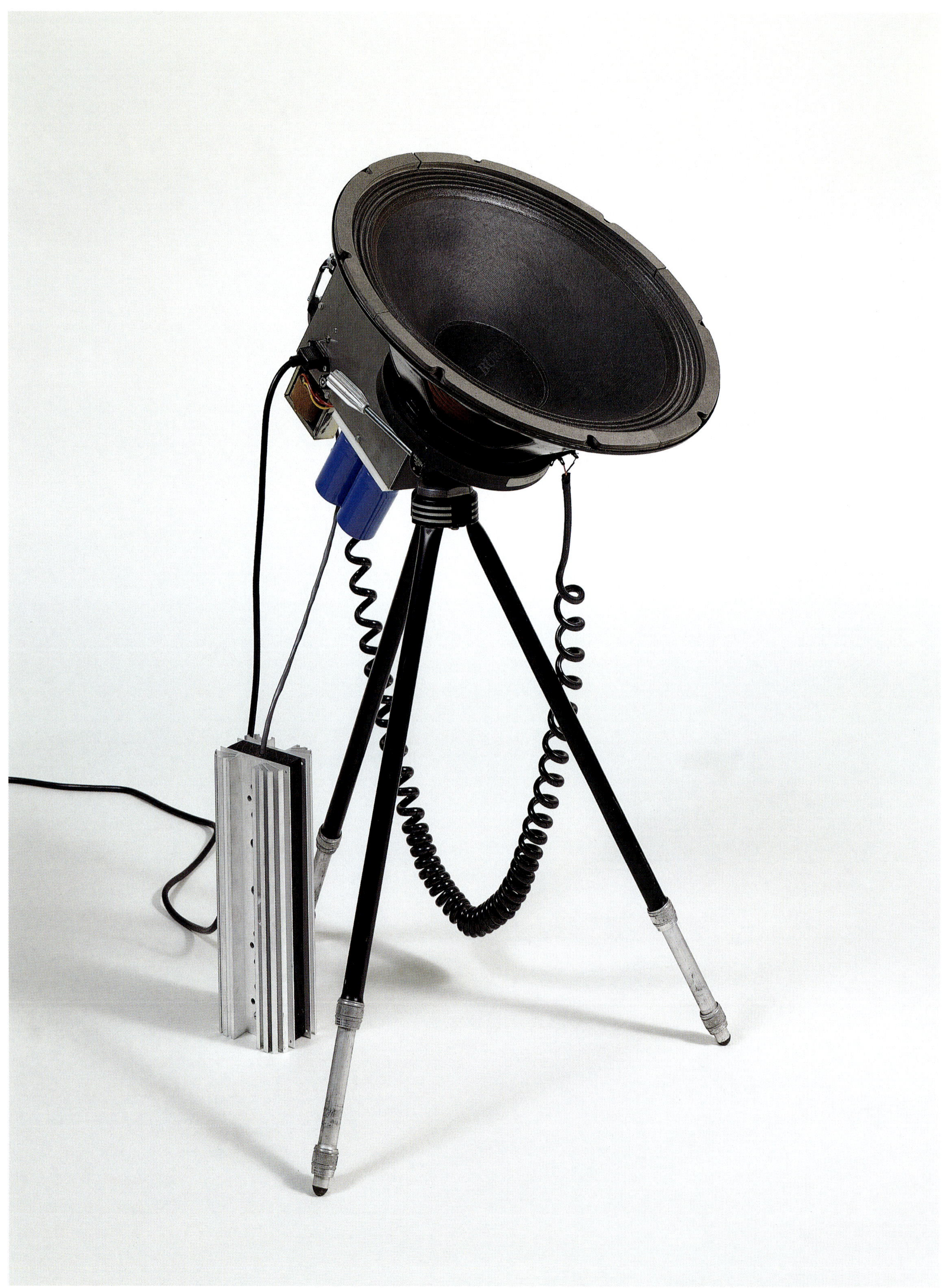

# *Bumper* ALAN RATH

1990. STEEL, ALUMINUM, ELECTRONICS, AND SPEAKER, 37½ × 18 × 34

Sculptor Alan Rath is one of the most successful artists today working to marry art with science. Before assembling a piece, he completely conceptualizes both the aesthetics and the technology of what he wants to do. His sculptures engage viewers through their form, their humor, and their humanism. They pulsate and gyrate; they make sounds; they may even have a human face.

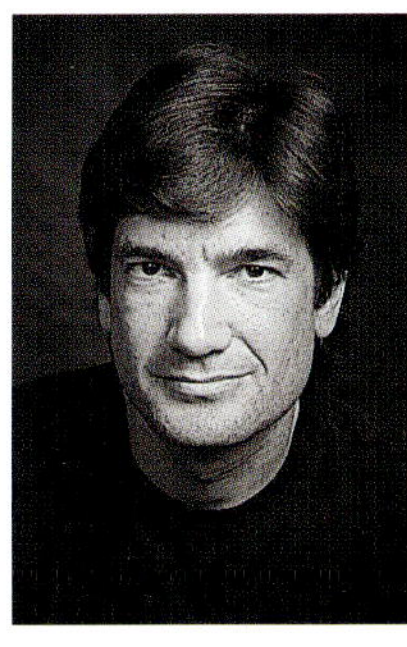

Rath was born in Cincinnati in 1959. At five he experienced the fun of technology when his mother, an artist, helped him assemble a crystal radio set. At six, however, he experienced its dangers when he stuck a hairpin into an electric outlet. At twelve he began building transistorized circuits, and at sixteen he designed the stage lighting for a three-day rock concert.

Rath earned a BS in electrical engineering from the Massachusetts Institute of Technology (MIT) in 1982. Later he experimented with aesthetics and technology at MIT's Visual Language Workshop, Architecture Machine Group, and Center for Advanced Visual Studies. During a visit to Europe he encountered the kinetic sculpture of Swiss artist Jean Tinguely, which profoundly influenced him. In 1984 he left a well-paying job to move to California to be near Silicon Valley. He later moved to Oakland, where he now resides, and worked with light artist Milton Komisar, whom he had met at MIT. In 1985 he built his first digital video sculptures, and since then his career has soared.

*I've always endeavored to build sculptures that do something rather than just sit inertly. The large speaker in* Bumper *inaudibly pulses and throbs at various speeds. Unfortunately, such behavior is difficult to record in a photograph.*

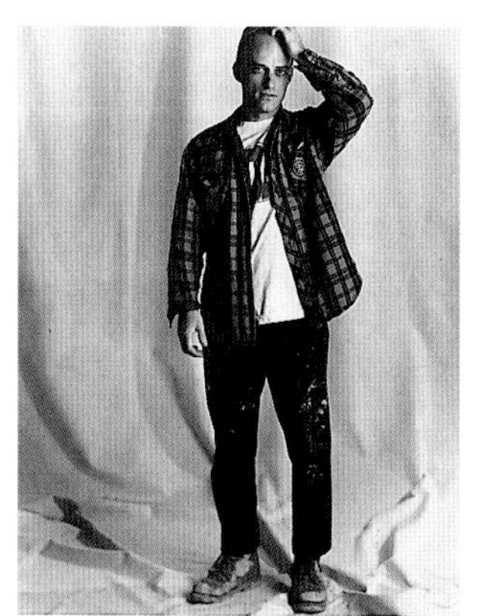

# RIGO 92 *Missile*

1992. PUSHPINS ON WOOD. 48 × 48

Rigo 99 challenges his viewers' visual assumptions and, by extension, all others—economic, social, cultural.

Born in 1966 on Madeira Island, Portugal, Ricardo Gouveia created a protective acronym in high school to avoid the possibility of discipline for a publication. In addition, he changes his name annually—soon he may be Rigo 00. He likes to take risks in his work, especially by choosing to use advertising techniques against themselves.

Rigo received a BFA from the San Francisco Art Institute in 1991 and an MFA from Stanford University in 1997. In that year, under the sponsorship of the Capp Street Project, he created three gigantic murals in San Francisco, each designed to compel passersby to reassess the character of the environment. One was a huge simulacrum of a "One Way" sign on a building at an intersection, seeming to point toward a freeway on-ramp but reading "One Tree." Actually pointing at a solitary tree silhouetted against a bleak wall, it had the potential to surprise drivers speeding by and raise big questions in their minds.

Missile *is part of a series of works dealing with the metamorphosis and disappearance of North America's native peoples from the USA's consciousness. I use the familiar pushpin to create a fragmented portrait of a very disturbing phenomenon, one that superimposes the identity of a people on a piece of equipment/machinery which embodies the very philosophy that led to the near genocide of the former by the creator of the latter.*

*Native American identities are often used in the United States to name military and auto industry output. In 1991* Time *magazine named the Tomahawk missile the Gulf War's hero.*

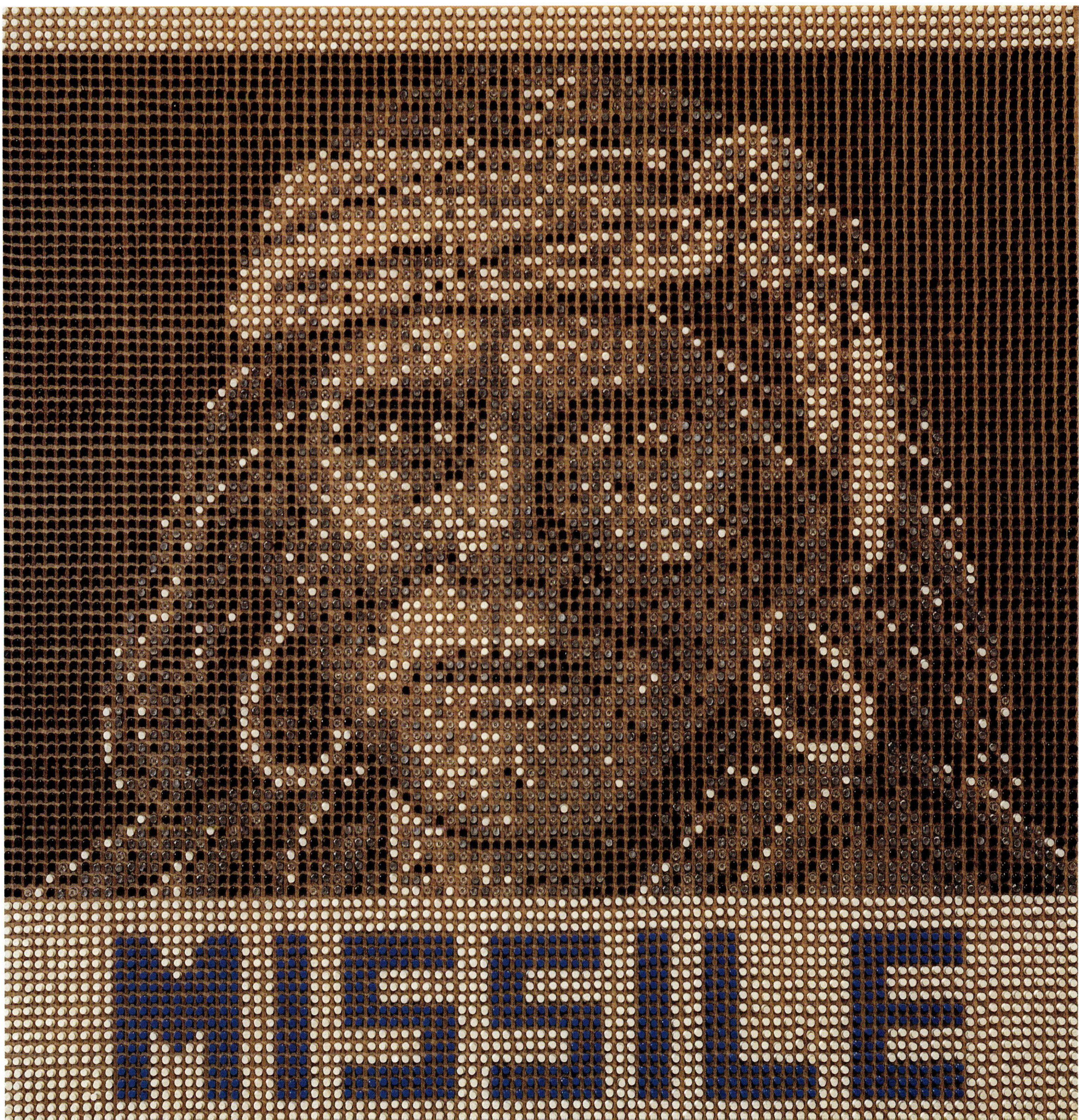
MISSILE

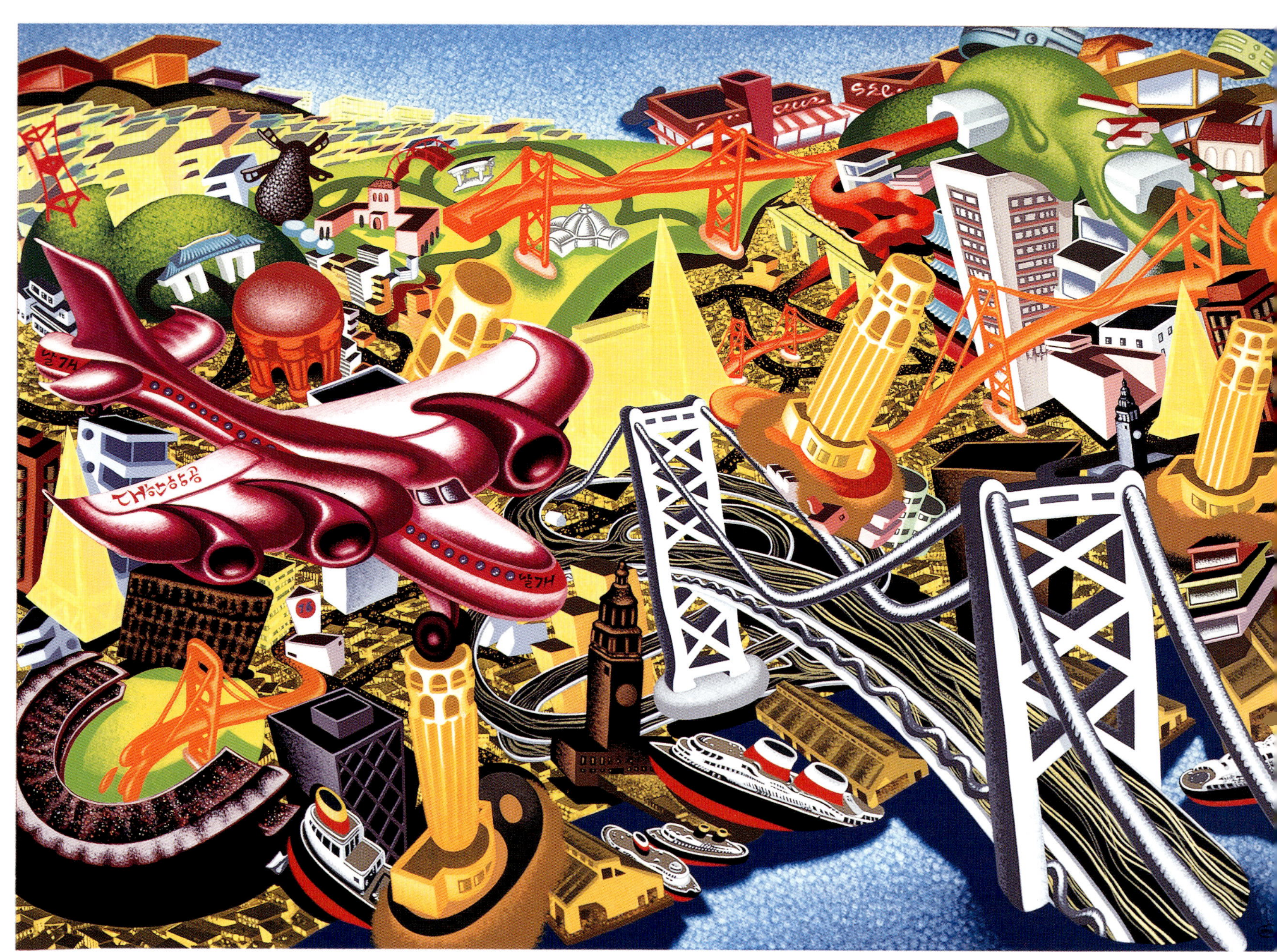

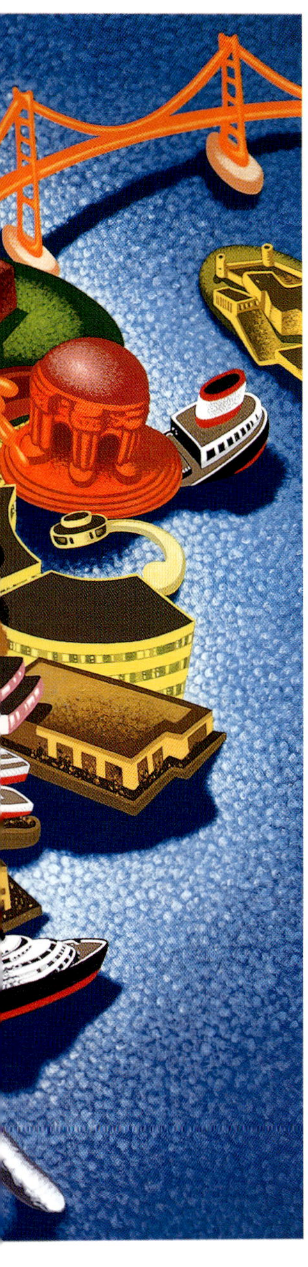

# PETER SAUL

## *View of SF/Red Plane*

1985, ACRYLIC AND OIL ON CANVAS, 67 × 109

In his paintings of the early 1960s, Peter Saul worked in an Abstract Expressionist fashion using cartoonish figuration. As his moral concerns more clearly defined themselves, however, encompassing the war in Vietnam and the struggle for civil rights, he drafted his forms more aggressively and painted them in dazzling hues. He is a reformist and does not equivocate. And yet, in the tradition of the Social Realists of the 1930s, while boldly satirical, he paints as he does because he cares about his craft and about people.

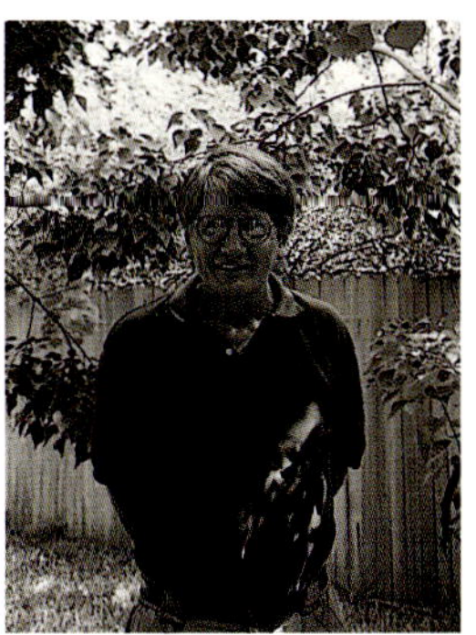

Saul was born in San Francisco in 1934. He completed a BFA at Washington University in St. Louis in 1956 and then traveled to Europe. He now lives in Austin, Texas.

*This picture was made after I moved to Austin, and I was involved in changing my technique to be more "ritzy." This picture is supposed to look real good. It combines the idea of Abstract Expresh (that's the cause of all the extra bridges and chaos) with the idea of an earthquake (also a good reason why there should be chaos) with those menus that downtown tourist restaurants used to have where illustrations of tourist things (Coit Tower, etc.) are superimposed on a simplified street plan. I think they used to have them at the Golden Pheasant Restaurant (Union Square) when I was a child growing up on Octavia Street. Also an inspiration for this picture (there seem to be many) is remembering the commercial cartoon illustrations of some guy named Tolfer, or something like that—wildly exaggerated hills with cable cars shooting off the top, etc.*[1]

1. PETER SAUL, LETTER TO RICHARD REISMAN, APRIL 4, 1988.

# RAYMOND SAUNDERS *Captain Marvel*

1979. MIXED MEDIA AND COLLAGE ON PAPER. 29 × 22

Ray Saunders makes works of art that are vibrant, elegant, personal, and engaging. A gallery of his paintings and drawings is a place of celebration, despite his occasionally solemn comments. In conveying to his viewers the thoughts, feelings, and energy invested in his works, he achieves the directness of communication that moved Walter Pater to assert, "All art constantly aspires toward the condition of music."[1] For Saunders, that music is jazz!

"Raymond Saunders has been at the forefront of color experimentation, collage, assemblage, drawing, and gestural painting in this country," art historian Richard J. Powell observes. "Apart from his career longevity and high level of artistic production, Saunders has successfully merged in practically all of his work the perceptual qualities of paint and other artist's pigments with the psychological qualities of racial and/or cultural pigmentation."[2]

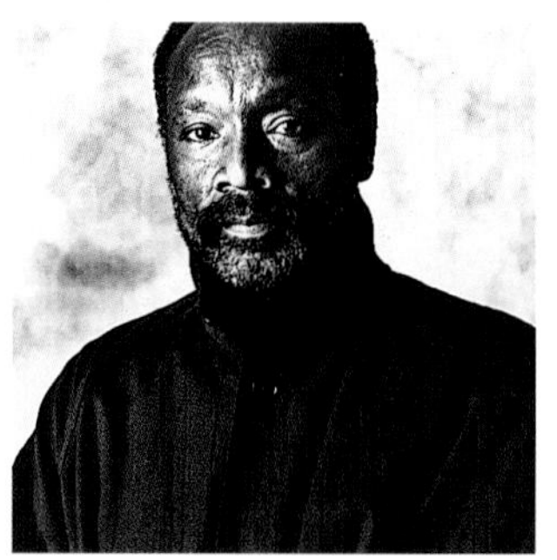

Having seduced viewers through his composition and color, his symbols and words, Saunders compels them (in a nice way) to study his works for instruction—sometimes with rough challenges—about their personal condition and society's. He fulfills a very big, but also a very traditional, order for art in our society.

Born in Pittsburgh, Pennsylvania, in 1934, Saunders became interested in art in the first grade. He received a BFA from the Carnegie Institute of Technology in Pittsburgh in 1960 and an MFA from the California College of Arts and Crafts (CCAC) in 1961. He lives in Oakland and teaches at CCAC.

*In the end, my art is about myself; it's not about being art. It is not about people reading into it what I want them to. Each person comes at my work as themselves, and brings their own experiences to it.*[3]

1. THE RENAISSANCE: STUDIES IN ART AND POETRY, THE 1893 TEXT, EDITED, WITH TEXTUAL AND EXPLANATORY NOTES, BY DONALD L. HILL (BERKELEY: UNIVERSITY OF CALIFORNIA PRESS, 1980), P. 106

2. RICHARD J. POWELL, "THE ART OF RAYMOND SAUNDERS: COLORED," NEW OBSERVATIONS, VOL. 97 (SEPTEMBER/OCTOBER 1993), P. 10.

3. JOLENE THYM, "RAYMOND SAUNDERS: BLACK PAINTINGS," THE OAKLAND TRIBUNE: CUE, FEBRUARY 24, 1995, P. 10.

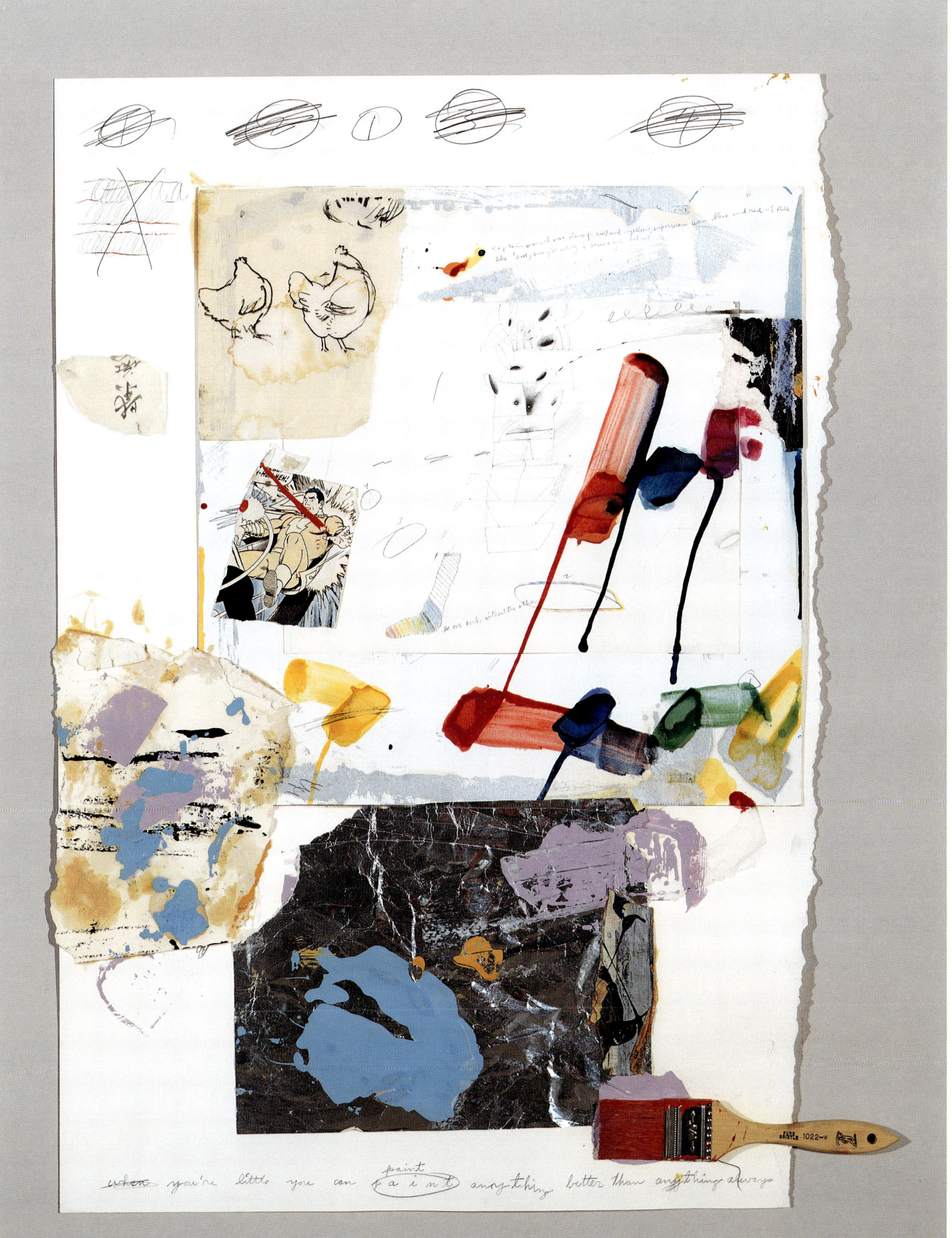
paint
you're little you can paint anything better than anything always

# RICHARD SHAW

## *Sinking Ship in Couch*

1971, PORCELAIN WITH GLAZES, 15 × 36 × 15

Richard Shaw ranks among those artists responsible for the current prestige of ceramics. While his technical skills allow him to create components having

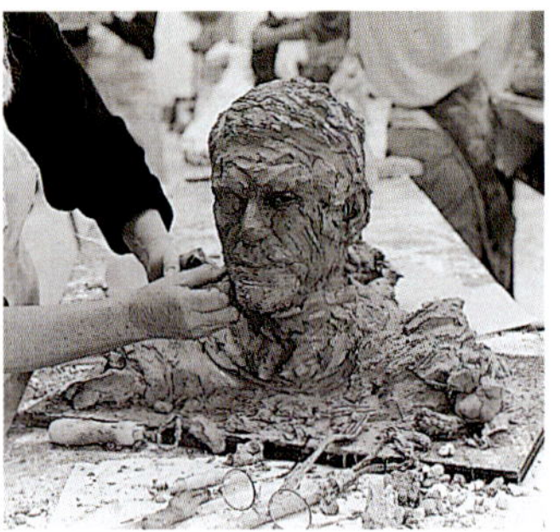

trompe l'oeil verisimilitude, his juxtapositions of them flout reality. "Art is about breaking every rule in the world," he says.[1]

Born in Hollywood in 1941, Shaw was encouraged in art by his parents, who were both artists. (His father was a cartoonist at Walt Disney Studios.) He received a BFA from the San Francisco Art Institute (SFAI) in 1965 and an MFA from the University of California, Davis, in 1968. He taught at SFAI from 1966 to 1987 and now teaches at the University of California, Berkeley.

Sinking Ship in Couch *culminated ideas I had developed since I started using the sinking steamship theme around 1967. I drew endless sinking ships all through junior high and most of high school because I had to read the* Reader's Digest *version of* A Night to Remember *about the* Titanic *every semester.*

*I constructed the* Sinking Ship *in my studio in Stinson Beach in 1970–1971. I painted the seascape right out of the studio window, which faced the ocean and the Farallon Islands. I hand-built the couch and ship—only the smokestacks were thrown on the wheel. It dried too fast and self-destructed in the bisque firing—cracked and fell apart. However, with Bondo and glue I pieced it back together and painted it up.*

*This was the last couch I made. It represents the end of the period when I manipulated materials this way and dealt with these kinds of illusions.*

1. JAN BUTTERFIELD, RICHARD SHAW/ CERAMIC SCULPTURE, NEWPORT HARBOR ART MUSEUM, NEWPORT BEACH, CALIFORNIA, OCTOBER 3–NOVEMBER 29, 1981, EXHIBITION CATALOGUE, P. 2.

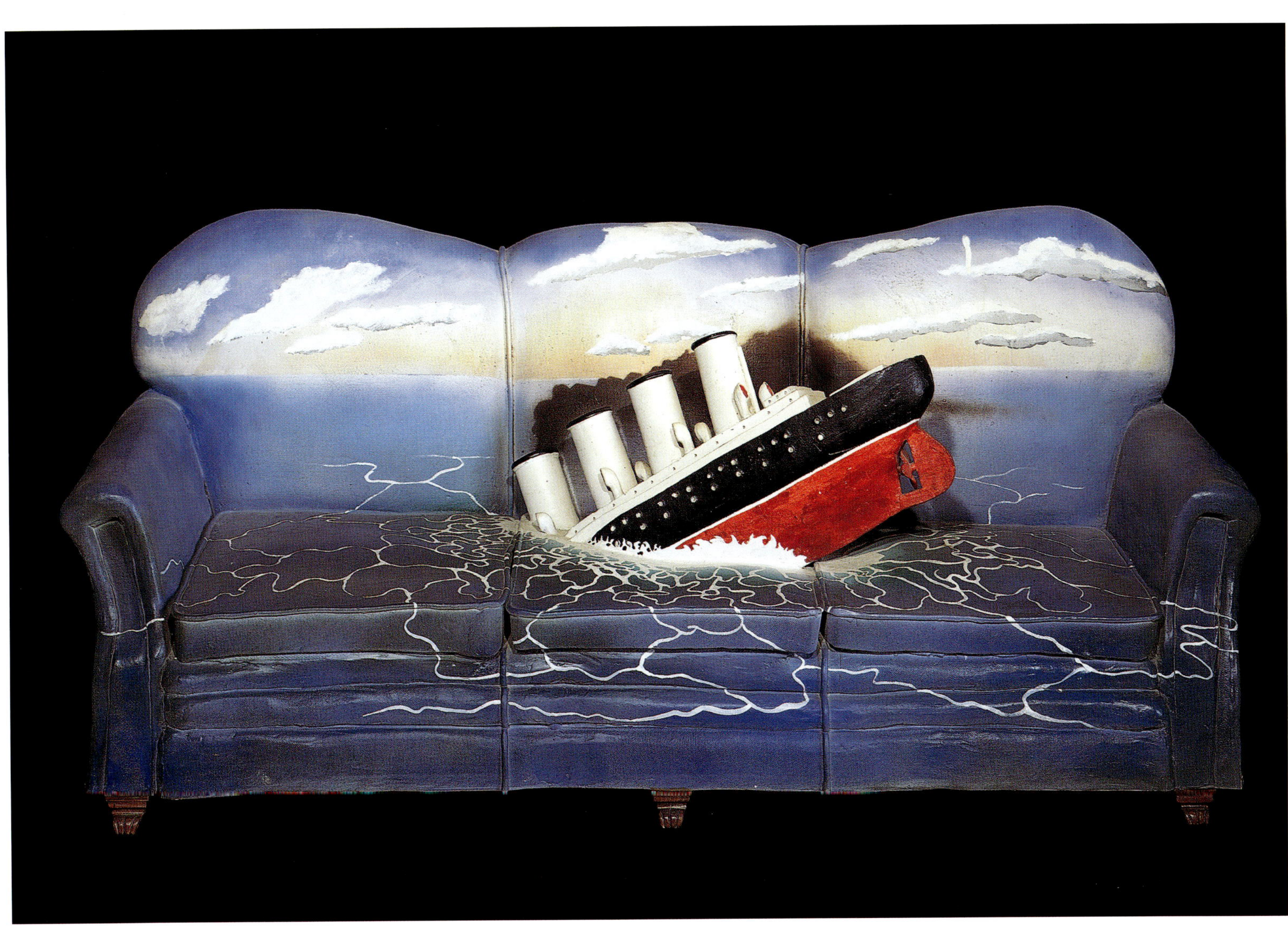

# ALAN SHEPP

1990. GRANITE. 66 × 164 × 49

## *Negotiating Table II*

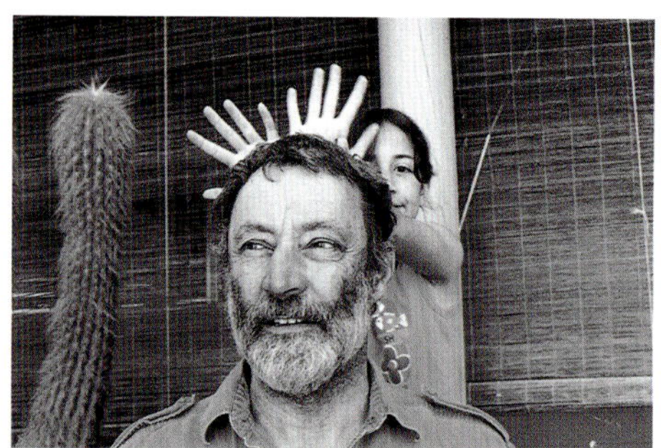

Alan Shepp approaches new materials to learn their inherent qualities and their possibilities for contributing to the development of his artistic vision. After earning his MFA in painting, he traveled in Europe and Asia and then took a studio in London, where he worked with light and kinetic sculpture. In the early 1970s he used lasers in sculptures and computer animation in performance pieces. Despite his successes in art and technology, however, in the late 1970s he turned to more traditional sculptural concerns, working with slate and, in the 1980s, with granite. While his sculptures frequently have a heroic scale and character, they do not overwhelm viewers. Instead, they evoke a sense of connectedness with past and future.

Shepp was born in Cleveland, Ohio, in 1935. He received a BA from Bowling Green State University in 1957, a BFA from the Cleveland Institute of Art in 1958, and an MFA from the University of Washington in 1963. He has taught at California State University, Hayward, since 1971. He lives with his family in Napa.

*At the time I was working on* Negotiating Table II *I was also working on several sculptures that made connections to other cultures and the work of Amnesty International, but* Negotiating Table II *cannot be talked about as a story. It did not evolve in a linear fashion, as from one artwork to the next. It was, like all my art, the result of a cumulative process that encompasses all the stuff I have done in my life, most of which has not been doing art.*

*Because I work in stone, I try not to hit my fingers with the hammer.*

*Thinking about doing sculpture is a lot of work.*

*Making sculpture is a lot of work.*

*Sculpture is a lot of work.*

*I make art for myself, mostly.*

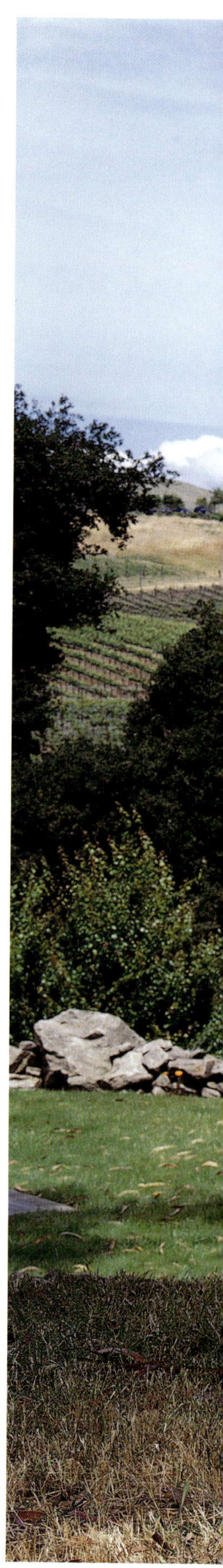

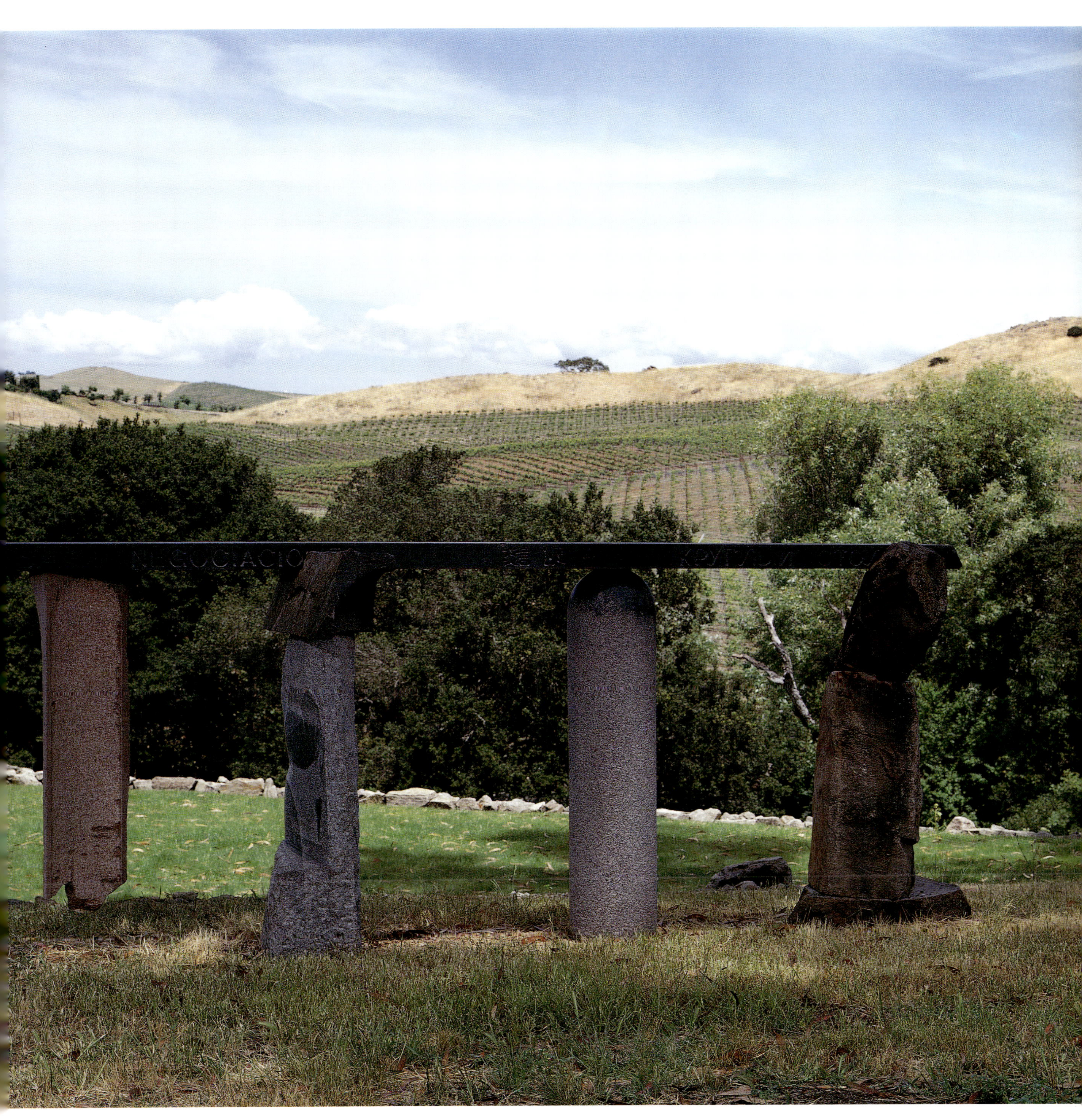

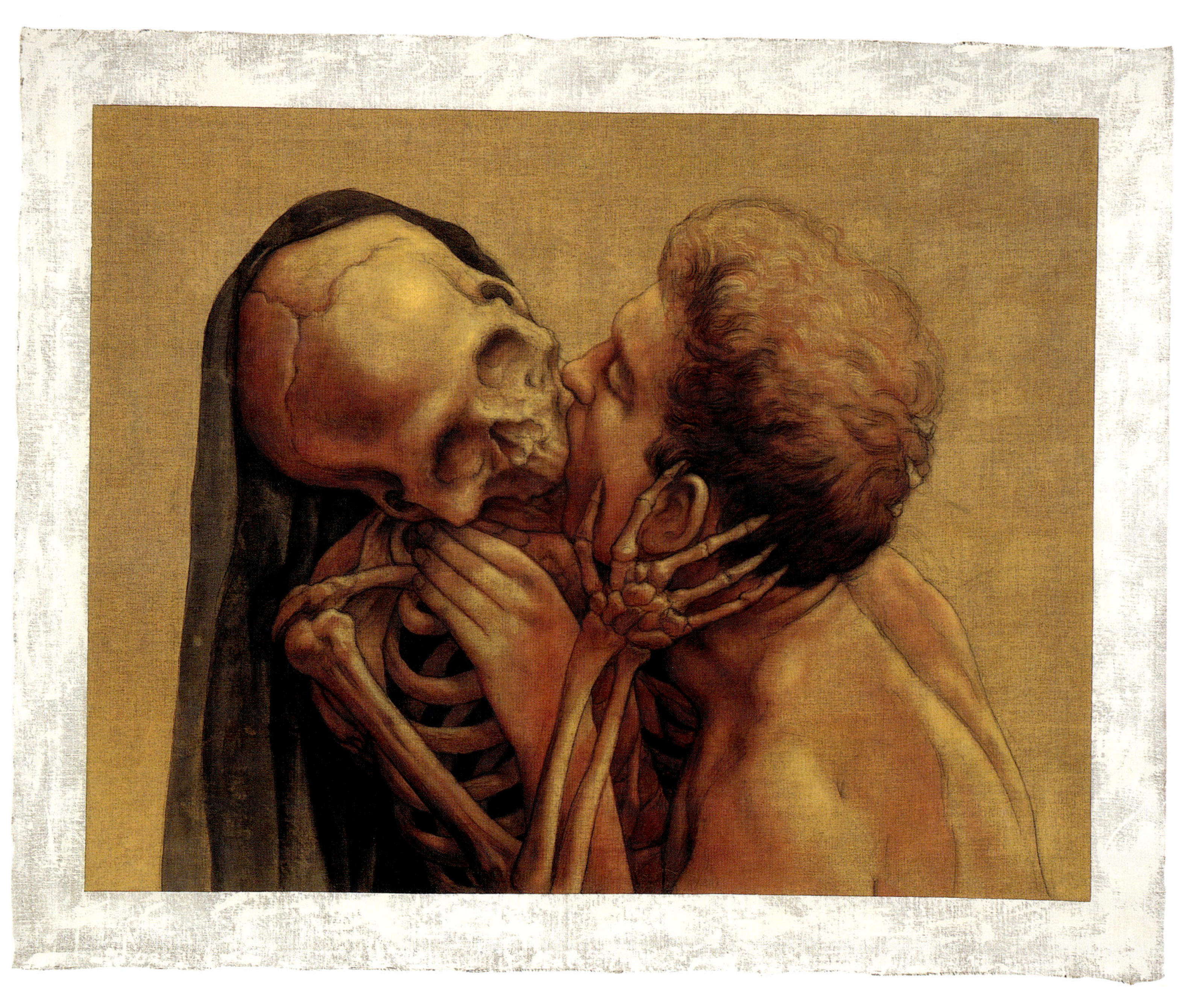

# SCOTT SIEDMAN *First Kiss*

1995, PASTEL AND CHARCOAL ON LINEN, 45 × 57

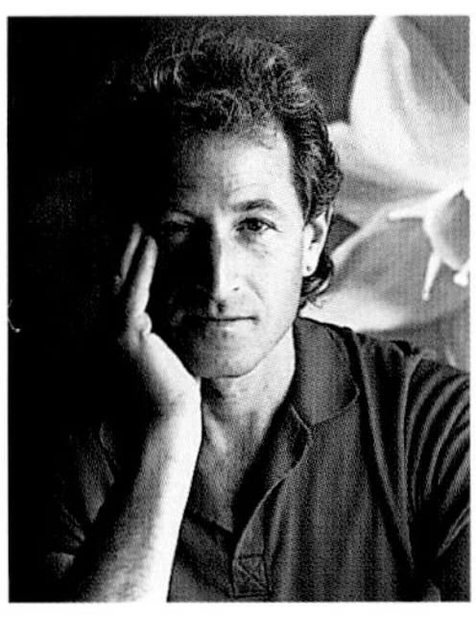

Scott Siedman appropriates and alters imagery from Renaissance paintings, including *The Last Supper,* for idiosyncratic purposes. Using his technical skills as a draftsman and colorist, he creates works of art that are remarkable for their verisimilitude. The most notable of his changes have been additions of exceptional penises to male subjects. The dogmatic principle thus illustrated—and Siedman's own as well—is that although they were holy men, Jesus and his followers were fully human. In other paintings, Siedman's principle has been that gay men and lesbians may be saintly as well as fully human.

Siedman tests our assumptions. Here, a shrouded, androgynous skeleton embraces a handsome, nude young man. AIDS, we conjecture. But the prudent test themselves with other scenarios as well.

The humanistic, enthusiastically heterosexual Siedman especially enjoys making set designs. Born in Los Angeles in 1948, he received a BFA from the California Institute of the Arts in 1971 and claims art saint John Baldessari as his mentor/advisor. Dying is not the problem, he suggests. The problem is living.

*FIRST KISS*

*The terrible moment—a man faces death.*
*The skull stares into his eyes, smiles, holds a secret.*
*A question, answered only in Death's embrace.*
*Suddenly the man is not afraid. He moves forward and*
*places his hand on the chest of Death, which turns its*
*head and welcomes him, tenderly.*
*Bony fingers—around flesh, through hair—hold his*
*precious head for a kiss.*
*They are joined at the mouth, bone and flesh, fear and*
*desire.*
*Love into Death into Love.*
*Not creepy, not the end of life. The end of suffering,*
*of denial.*
*A kiss to honor Death celebrates Life.*
*They are joined.*

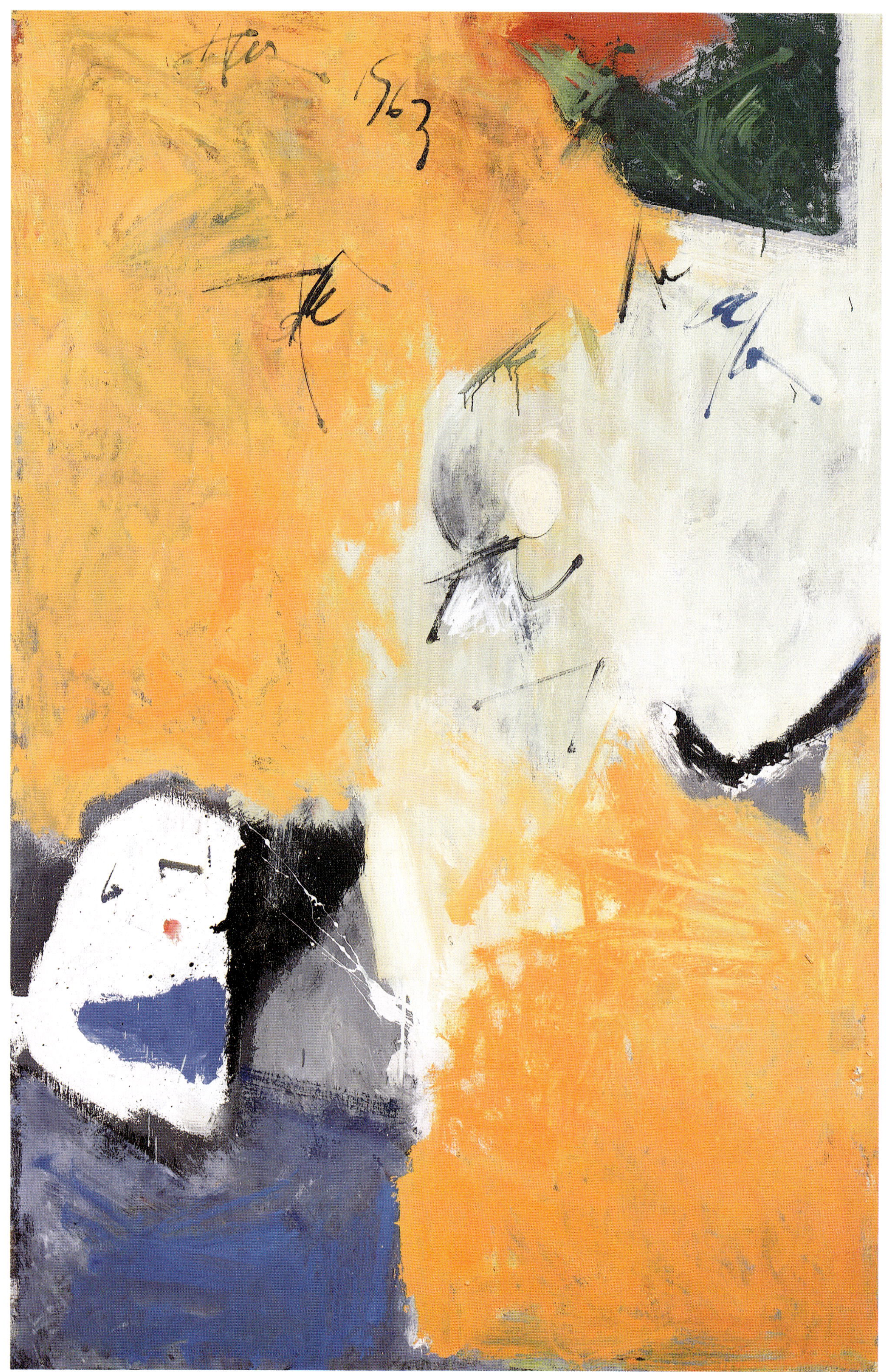

## HASSEL SMITH *Sept. '63*

1963, OIL ON CANVAS, 68 × 46

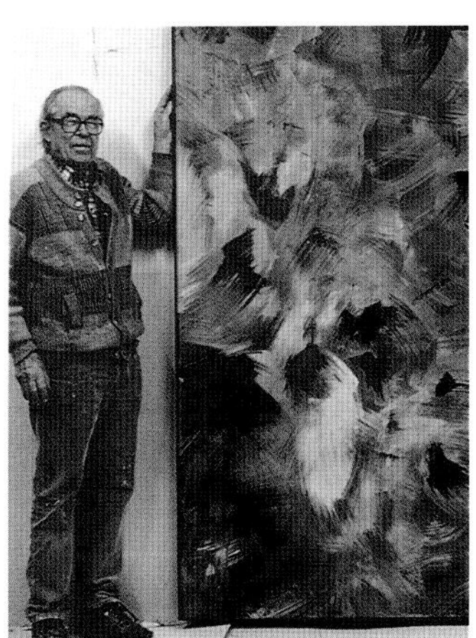

Born in Sturgis, Michigan, in 1915, Hassel Smith attended classes at the San Francisco Art Institute (SFAI) from 1936 to 1938, after receiving a BS in art history at Northwestern University. At the time, Social Realism, regionalism, Cubic Abstraction, and nonobjective painting dominated the scene. For several years he traveled and worked at a variety of jobs while painting landscapes and figures. He taught at SFAI from 1945 to 1952, while the school was under the aggressive direction of Douglas MacAgy (until 1950) and the faculty included artists such as David Park, Elmer Bischoff, Richard Diebenkorn, and Edward Corbett. The greatest influences were those of Clyfford Still and Mark Rothko (a summer-session visitor), who represented contrasting tendencies of Abstract Expressionism as feeling in action and feeling in thought, feeling objectified and feeling transcended, self-assertion and inclusive love.

Smith was bowled over by the works of Clyfford Still he saw in an exhibition at San Francisco's Palace of the Legion of Honor in 1947. The figures he had been making in the fashion of European Expressionists seemed to presage Bay Area Figurative painting, which emerged in the 1950s. But under the influence of Still in the late 1940s, Smith began to make his own distinctive Abstract Expressionist paintings, conveying, in part, his love of dance and of jazz. His works were improvisatory and playful, with thinner surfaces, figural references—often cartoonlike, and sinister as well as humorous—and dancing lines, as in *Sept. '63*.

Smith departed the Bay Area in 1966 to teach in England, but he often returns.

# MICHAEL STEVENS

## *Black Hand*

1988, PINE AND ENAMEL, 77 × 36 × 18

Using pieces of wood, both found and crafted, Michael Stevens conjures up human and animal forms, fashioning companions who are not only visible, but whose spirits are nearly palpable and whose voices and sounds are nearly audible. His enigmatic sculptures articulate human concerns.

Stevens's sculptures in 1969—responses to the war in Vietnam and to the imagery of the Hairy Who—were bandaged lumps of wax resembling human body parts, including hair and blemishes. His career, however, has been based on his elaborate, iconic painted-wood figures. Increasingly he used animal forms as metaphors for the human condition, and his figures conveyed a more sardonic mood as his vision evolved. In the late 1990s, however, his works appeared more playful, reflecting his interest in cartoons, puppets, toys, and theater. Nevertheless, they convey a sense of whimsy with a bite.

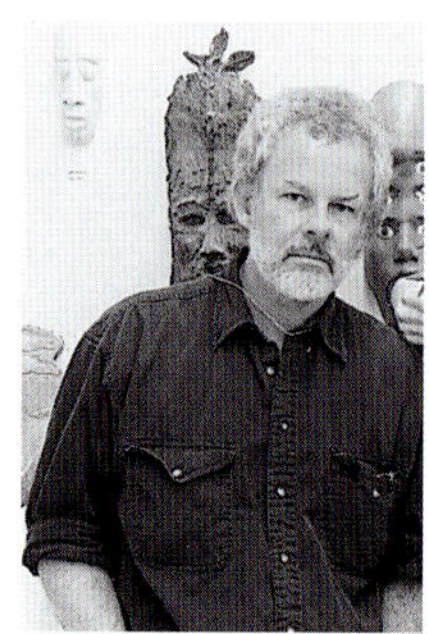

Michael Stevens was born in Gilroy, California, in 1945. He received a BA in painting in 1967 and an MA in sculpture in 1969 from California State University, Sacramento.

Black Hand *comes from a series of life-size figures dealing with the human condition. The body takes on the appearance of an articulated puppet supported with a crutch, while the head is a face with a bird escaping through the nose.*

*Most of my work deals with a storytelling dialogue laced with psychological overtones. I choose to use a variety of textures, including broken sticks, carved and painted pine, found objects, nails, screws, and visual construction methods.*

Black Hand *is about all of these elements coming together to create sculptural theater.*

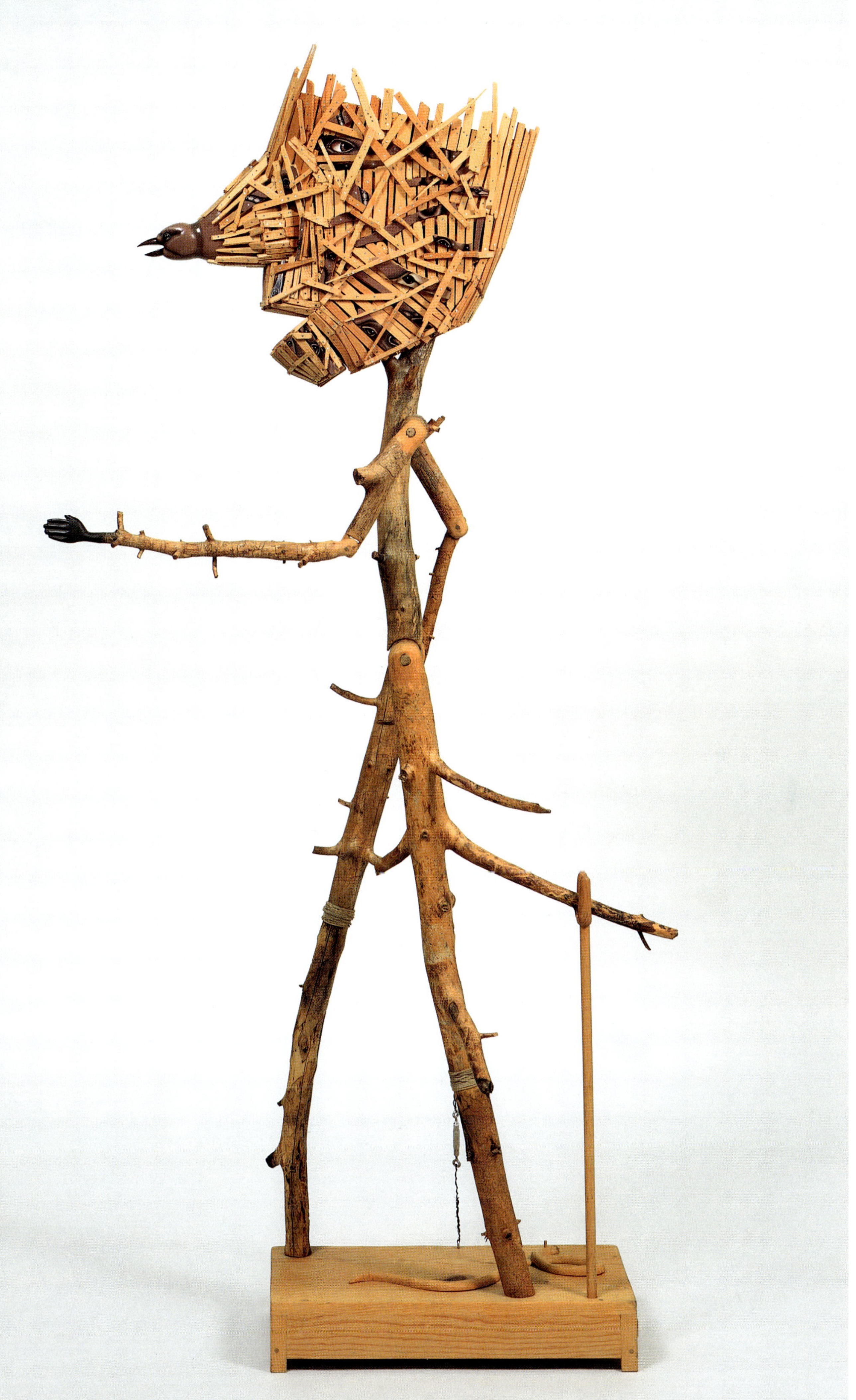

# *Golf Swing* LARRY SULTAN

1989. CHROMOGENIC COLOR PRINT. ED. OF 10. 40 × 50

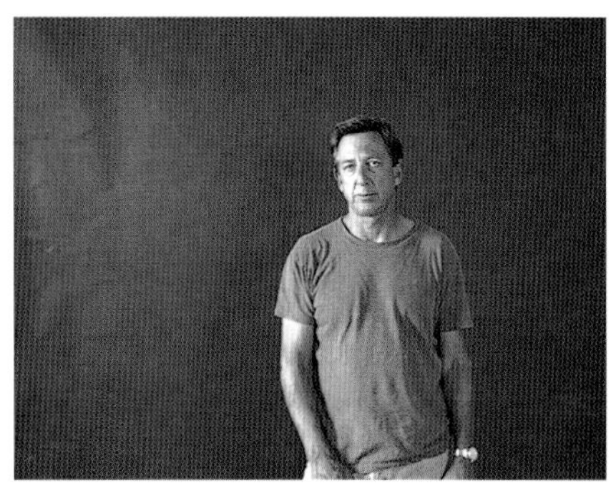

Larry Sultan was born in New York City in 1946. When he was three years old, his family moved to Southern California and realized much of the "American Dream"—a house in Sherman Oaks and a corporate vice presidency for his father.

Sultan first used a camera in the late 1960s to document the student upheaval in Berkeley, where he was enrolled at the University of California. In the turbulent year of 1968 he received his BA in political science.

Since earning an MFA in photography at the San Francisco Art Institute (SFAI) in 1973, Sultan has sought to penetrate the surface of American life. His images, often accompanied by text, have appeared in gallery exhibitions, public venues, books, film, video, billboards, posters, and murals. He has a kind eye, showing that energy mitigates malaise.

Sultan taught at SFAI from 1978 until 1988; since 1989, he has taught at the California College of Arts and Crafts. He lives in Greenbrae, near San Francisco.

*I'll let my father—the subject of the photograph—speak for the picture and himself.*

*He says, "Of all the photographs that you made of me the one I dislike the most is the picture of me swinging the golf club inside the condo in Palm Springs. I hate it even more than the one of me sitting on the bed looking lost. I'm sure you have very high-minded interests in the image and the implications of swinging a club with the television on and the curtains drawn, but for me the picture is pure description. It's such a shitty swing that I cringe every time I see it."*

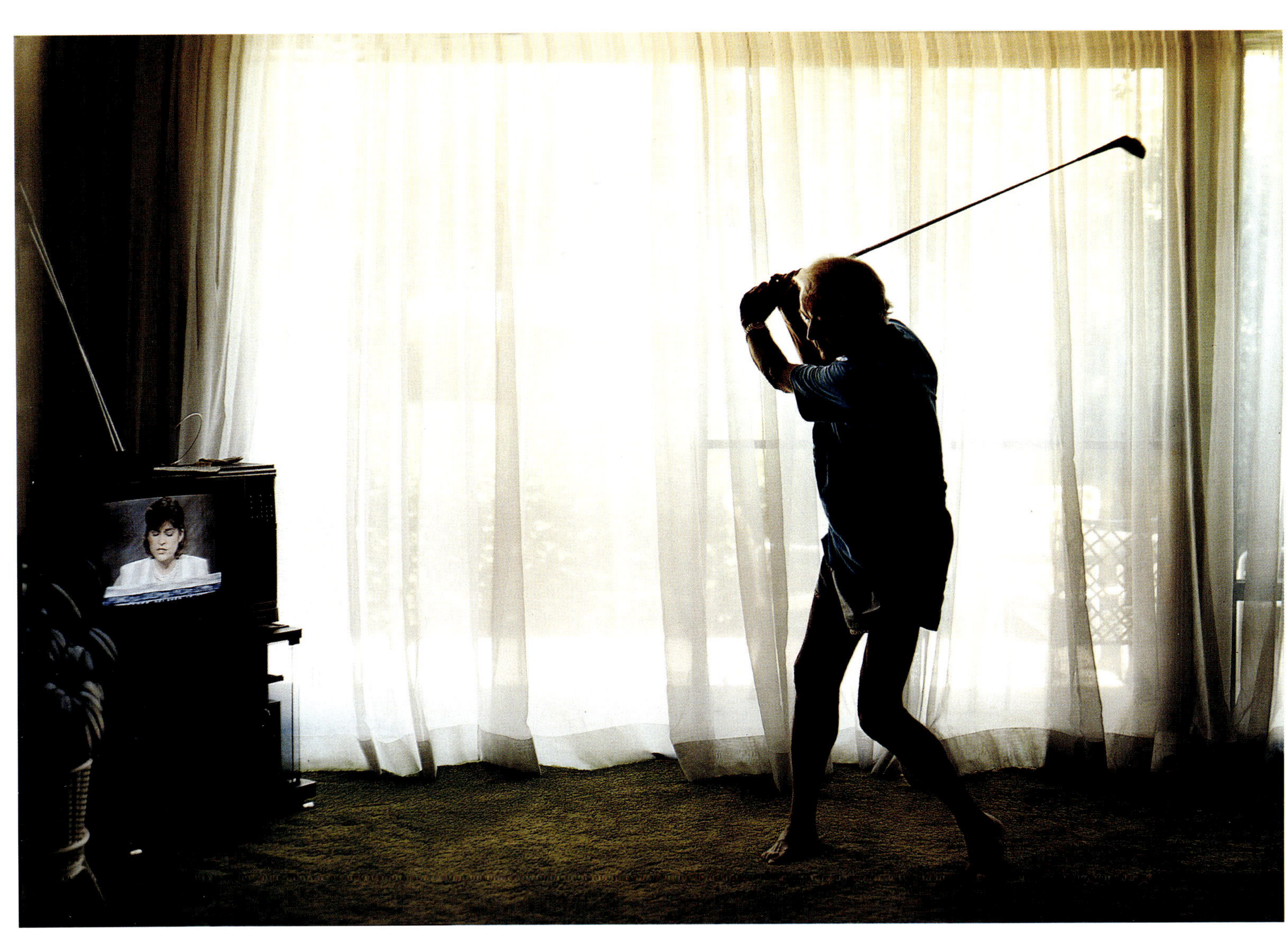

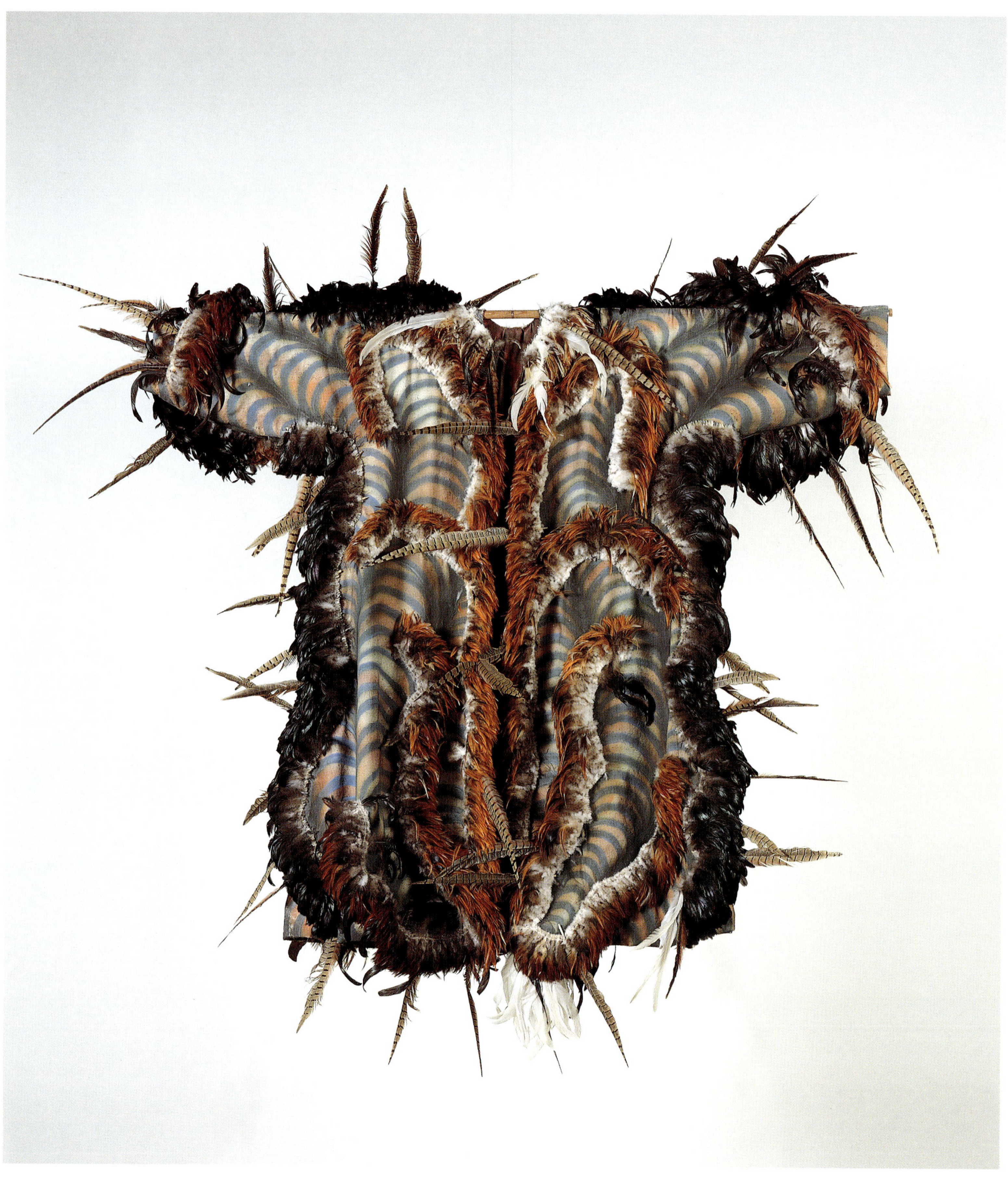

# CARLOS VILLA

## *Third Coat*

1983, CANVAS, TAFFETA, ACRYLIC PAINT, FEATHERS, BONES, AND HAIR, 79 × 80 × 11

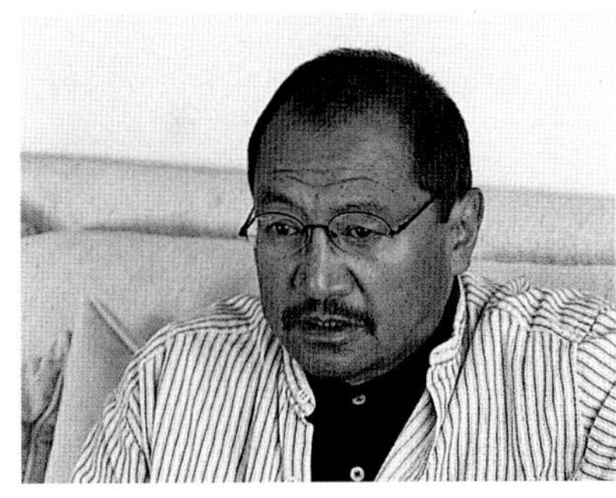

Carlos Villa, born in San Francisco in 1936, received a BFA from the San Francisco Art Institute (SFAI) in 1961 and an MFA from Mills College in 1963, when he departed for New York. At the time, he made lyrical Abstract Expressionist acrylic paintings on unstretched canvas to which he added materials such as feathers and broken glass. In New York, he spray-painted abstractions on canvas and made minimalist sculptures.

In 1969 Villa returned to San Francisco and began teaching at SFAI, where he remains. That same year, inspired by Matisse's vestments for the Vence Chapel and by traditional Hawaiian feather cloaks, he made his first cloak using ethnic fetish materials. He painted and then, using feathers, ornamented the canvas *Third Coat,* which Beverly Berrish had fabricated and lined with painted satin. Learning that it was customary for American Plains Indian shamans to have histories detailed on the interiors of their buffalo robes, he had bone dolls sewn inside this one.

*My mature work began when I returned to San Francisco from New York. My concerns were deepened and inspired by my rediscovery of traditional African, Oceanic, and Aboriginal arts. My issues of identity as a Filipino-American artist were profoundly nourished. A conscious, personal poetic of applying materials such as acrylic paint, blood, feathers, hair, and beads on refigured forms elevated a personal "beyond" from contemporary mainstream aesthetics. From then through the 1990s I matured from my experience as an artist/teacher as well as that of a curator and organizer of exhibitions involved in actions in both mainstream and minoritized communities.*

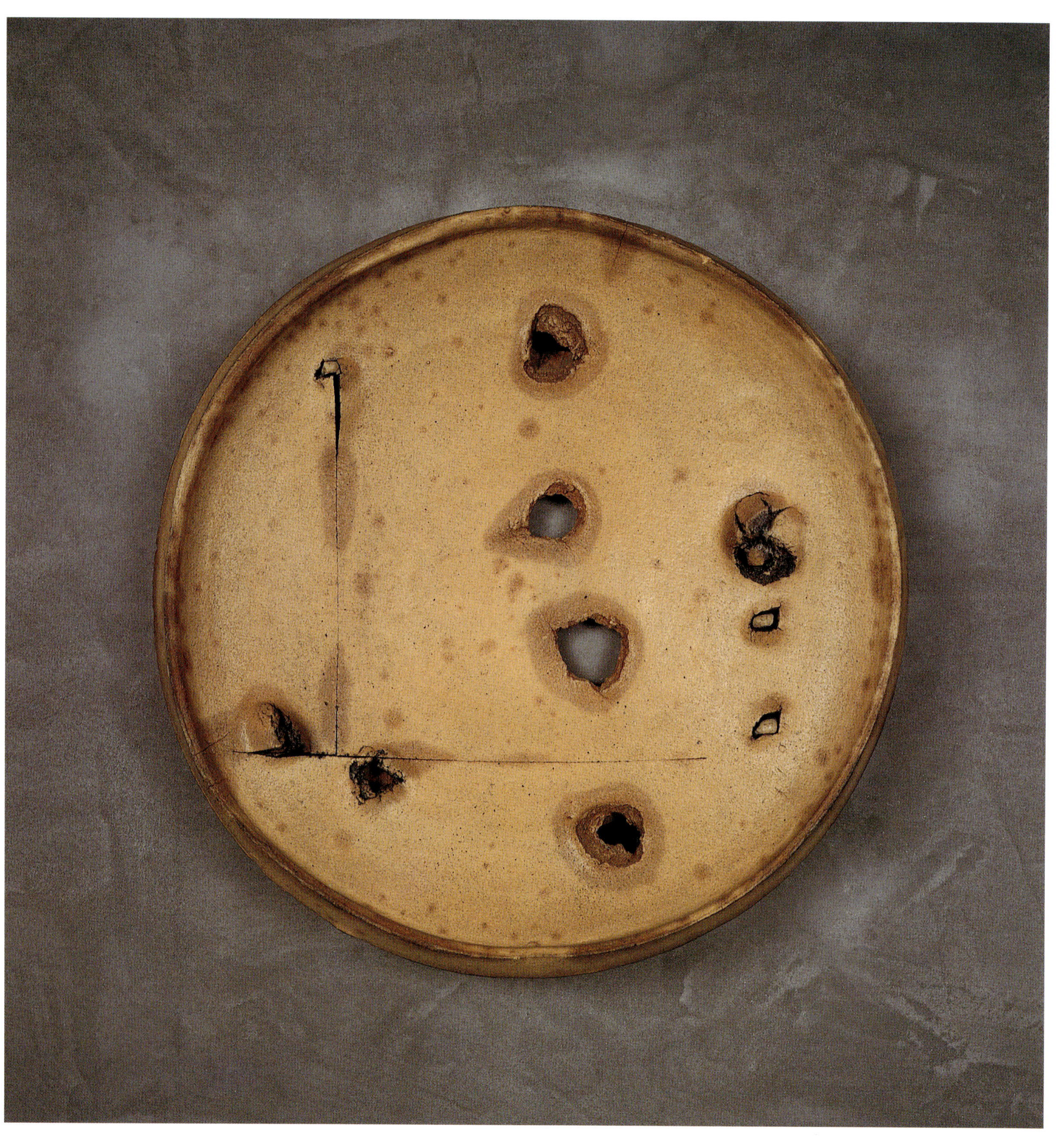

# PETER VOULKOS

*Untitled Plate* 1973, STONEWARE AND PORCELAIN, 21½ × 21½ × 4½

A giant among contemporary artists, Peter Voulkos liberated clay from craft, making it a sculptural material that he used for its expressive possibilities beyond normal utilitarian forms and purposes. At the time he was a vigorous, rough-hewn figure who seemed to convey his own raw energy to his sculptures. His achievements in ceramics paralleled what Jackson Pollock did for painting and led the way for other ceramists to advance their art through further intimate explorations of their medium. *Untitled Plate* is a classic example of his work in clay.

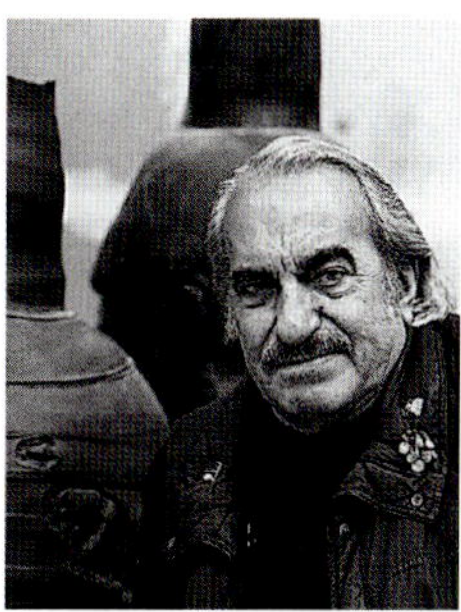

Voulkos brought a fresh, expansive vision with him when he moved from his native Montana to California in 1951. Teaching at the innovative Black Mountain College in North Carolina in 1953 and later at the Otis Art Institute in Los Angeles and the University of California, Berkeley (where, in 1959, he created a ceramics curriculum), he exerted an influence that has shaped generations of ceramic artists. At Berkeley, he also began to work in bronze, combining geometric and twisting, tubular forms.

Voulkos was born in Bozeman in 1924 to parents of Greek origin. He attended Montana State University under the GI Bill, earning a BS in 1951. In 1952, he earned an MFA from the California College of Arts and Crafts. He retired from the University of California, Berkeley, in 1985.

*I first worked with painting, in which I developed a strong interest. Then I took a course in ceramics and fell completely in love with clay. My energy was drained from painting and I couldn't concentrate on it any longer. The work in clay took everything I had.*[1]

1. HENRY HOPKINS, 50 WEST COAST ARTISTS: A CRITICAL SELECTION OF PAINTERS AND SCULPTORS WORKING IN CALIFORNIA (SAN FRANCISCO: CHRONICLE BOOKS, 1981), P. 72.

# CATHERINE WAGNER

1984. GELATIN-SILVER PRINT. 14 × 18¼

## *7th & 8th Grade Science Classroom, Moss Landing Elementary School*

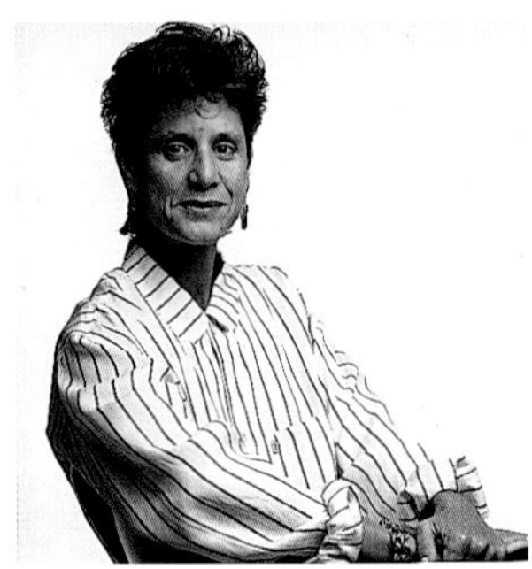

Catherine Wagner is a conceptual artist working with a camera. Uniting the acuity of a scientist with the sensitivity of a humanist, she creates photographs of profound cultural-historical depth. She is a leading figure in erasing the barriers between art and science.

Wagner has commented about art and science, "I think that in terms of funding and the power of science, there is still this idea among the general public that whether they know about science or not, it is something that we need. Especially . . . in terms of advances in medicine. . . . But with art, people don't know that they need it in their lives. Then if you ask people, what are the things that have really mattered to . . . [them] . . . and have really affected . . . [them], people will often [cite] a passage of literature, a piece of music, a work of visual art. This betrays the idea that science is needed and art is expendable."[1]

Wagner was born in San Francisco in 1953. She earned a BA in 1975 and an MA in 1977 from San Francisco State University. She has taught at Mills College since 1978.

*This image is from a series of photographs entitled* American Classroom, *a traveling, solo exhibition with a catalogue published by the Museum of Fine Arts, Houston, in 1988. In the series, the classroom is used as a model of a repository for our collective conscience. Andy Grundberg in the* New York Times *wrote, "As a result, the classrooms seem like archeological sites that, if studied long and hard enough, might yield the keys to understanding our civilization."*

1. LANE BARDEN, "A CONVERSATION WITH CATHERINE WAGNER, PHOTOGRAPHER," ARTWEEK, VOL. 28, NO. 2 (FEBRUARY 1997), P. 18.

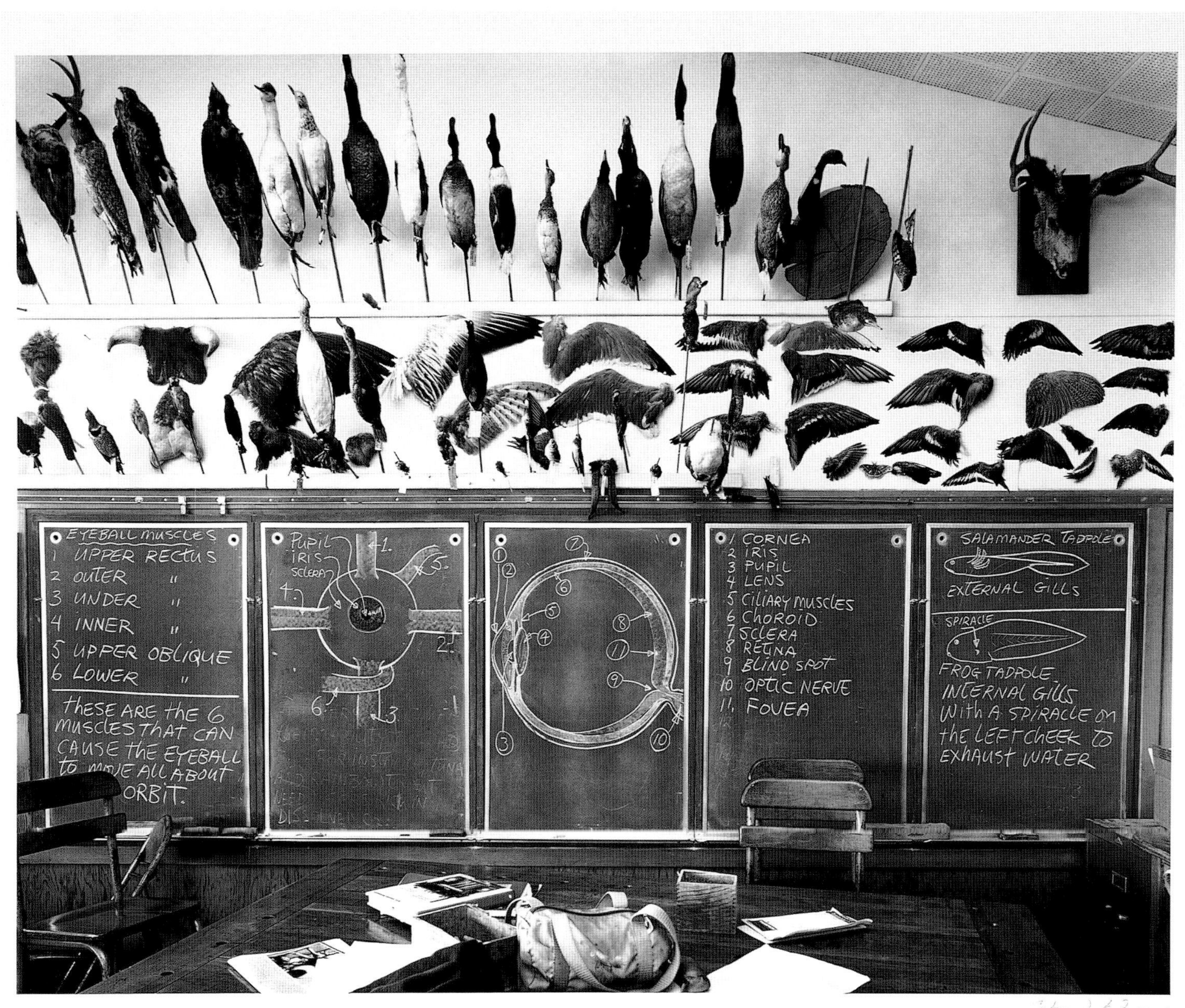
EYEBALL MUSCLES
1 UPPER RECTUS
2 OUTER "
3 UNDER "
4 INNER "
5 UPPER OBLIQUE
6 LOWER "
THESE ARE THE 6 MUSCLES THAT CAN CAUSE THE EYEBALL TO MOVE ALL ABOUT
ORBIT.
PUPIL
IRIS
SCLERA
1 CORNEA
2 IRIS
3 PUPIL
4 LENS
5 CILIARY MUSCLES
6 CHOROID
7 SCLERA
8 RETINA
9 BLIND SPOT
10 OPTIC NERVE
11 FOVEA
SALAMANDER TADPOLE
EXTERNAL GILLS
SPIRACLE
FROG TADPOLE
INTERNAL GILLS WITH A SPIRACLE ON THE LEFT CHEEK TO EXHAUST WATER

# WILLIAM T. WILEY

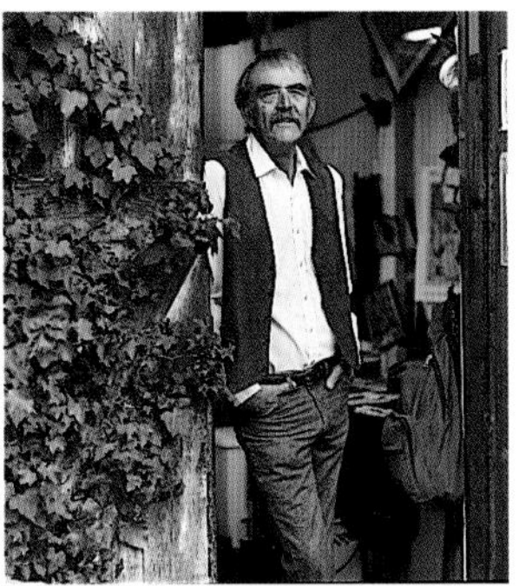

William T. Wiley is a guru of freedom to artists and nonartists of the San Francisco Bay Area and beyond. Through acquaintance with his works, they may learn: "Art! What a concept! It saved my life! A place where you can do as you please!"[1]

Wiley's extraordinarily complex works of art—paintings, sculptures, assemblages, and prints—are generally identifiable through their idiosyncratic mixed media, dense compositions, repetitions of figures and forms, and interweavings of original texts—replete with puns. (Wiley is an accomplished punster but a careless speller.) His paintings, generally on unprimed and sometimes unstretched canvas, look informal, like a restive ego's daybooks, dipping into memories and the unconscious, harking back to archetypes while struggling with a self-improvising life. Wiley enjoys playing in space, adding three-dimensional components to paintings as well as making freestanding works of art such as *Bench Mark,* which includes, on the floor, a black-and-white painting whose parts in some works represent himself, his wife, and their two sons. Wiley has also gone beyond the studio to create earthworks, films, music, happenings, performances, theatrical events, and conceptual works. For all his seriousness and professionalism, Wiley, like Bill Allan and Bob Hudson (friends from his youth), is famous for championing the use of humor in serious art.

Born in Bedford, Indiana, in 1937, Wiley received his initial strong guidance toward art from teachers Thelma Pearson and Jim McGrath in Richland, Washington, where he moved as a boy. Like Allan and Hudson, he acquired an appreciation of Native American art and culture from McGrath, who also helped him assemble a portfolio that brought him a scholarship to the San Francisco Art Institute, where he received a BFA in 1960, an MFA in 1962, and the first of many prizes.

Wiley started out making impressive Abstract Expressionist paintings but soon began to liberate himself from that form of transcendental exercise and to approach art through life as it is

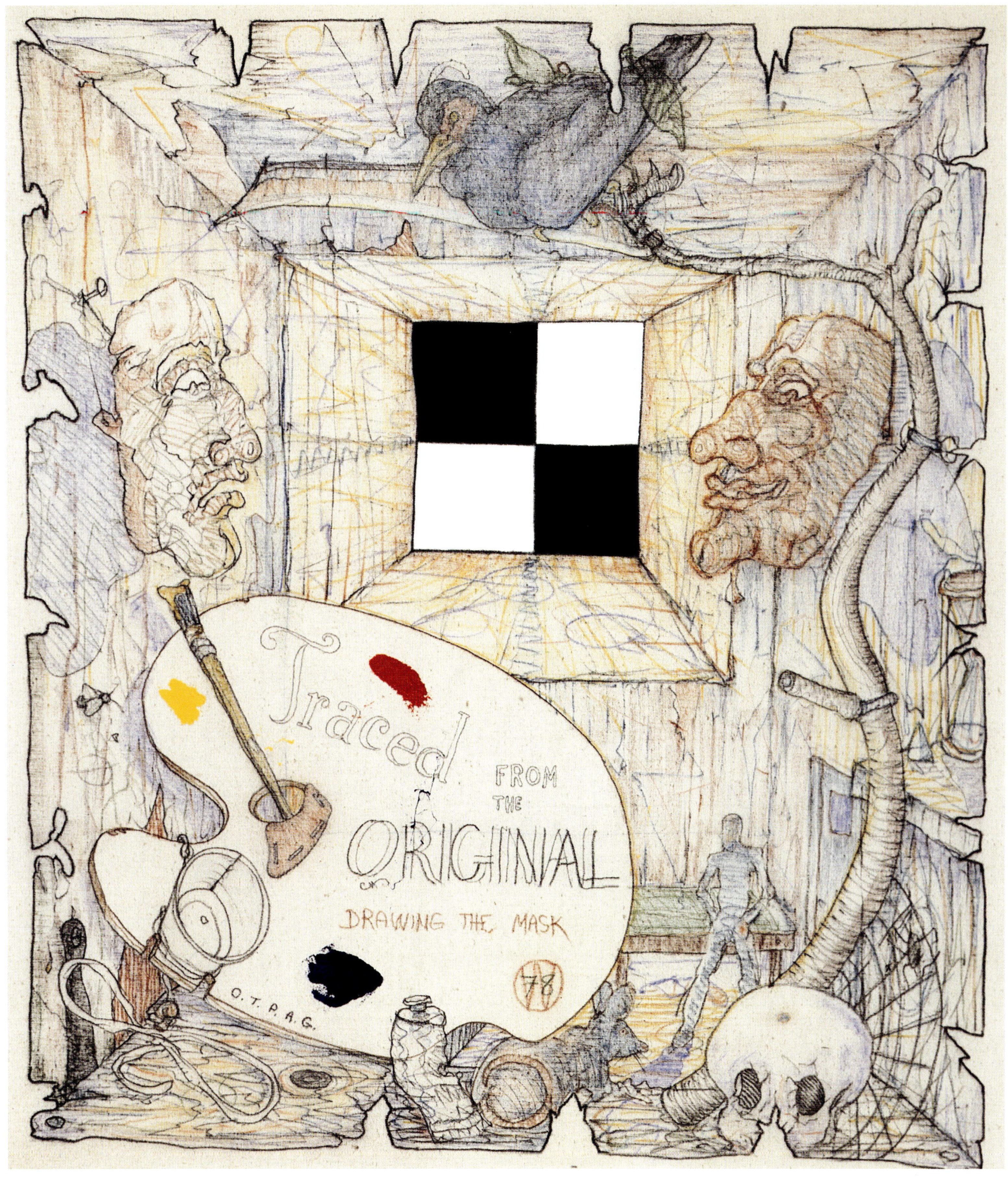


*Traced from the Original*

1978, ACRYLIC AND MIXED MEDIA ON CANVAS, 44 × 39

## *Bench Mark*

1988, MIXED-MEDIA CONSTRUCTION, 66 × 69¾ × 36

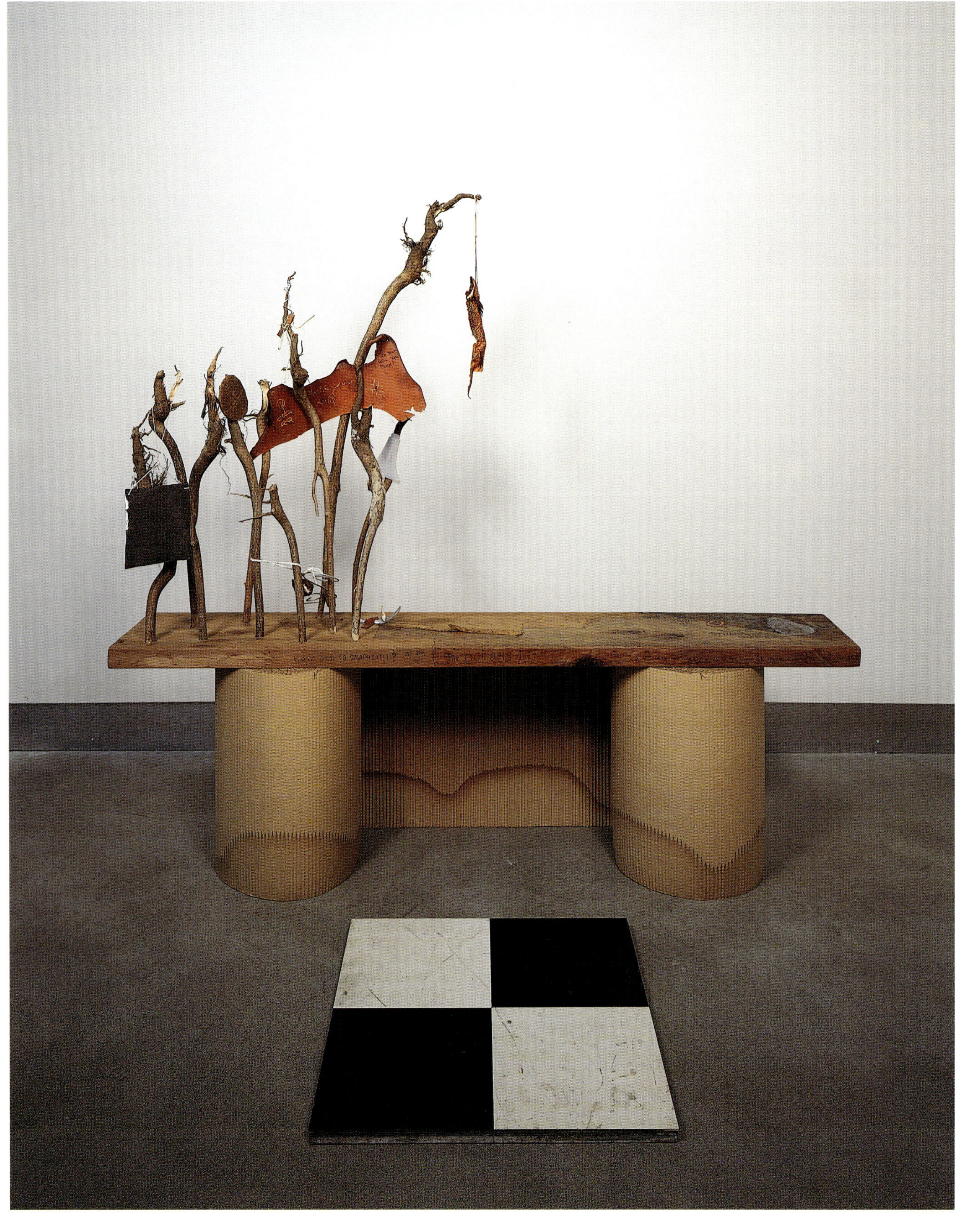

lived and objectified in its artifacts, including its discards. For him, this opened the way to the Funk art of the 1950s and 1960s. He helped to define that aesthetic through his initiation, with Bruce Nauman, of the Slant Step show at the Berkeley Gallery in San Francisco in 1966 and his participation in Peter Selz's important *Funk* exhibition at the University of California, Berkeley, in 1967. That Funk identification was transitory, however—like Funk itself—for Wiley's range of vision became infinitely inclusive, as did his works.

Viewers become engaged with, or disengaged from, this artist's works as they would with a complex personality, musical composition, or novel. The meandering line in some paintings is like a crazy road map for guidance or a net holding things together; the vertiginous microcosms of penciled lines in which seemingly random, recognizable forms appear play a similar role. The purposes of these meshes seem distantly related to the white writing of Mark Tobey, another Washington mystic. And even now, as in Wiley's youth, Abstract Expressionist eruptions may occur.

Wiley has had an exceptionally distinguished career as an exhibiting artist and as a teacher, most recently at the University of California, Davis, from 1962 to 1973. He lives in Marin County.

*So . . . what is not traced from the original? What is not a bench mark viewed by a particular lens or circumstance? These many-minded layers of focus we find, experience, the layers like petals in the mind and heart. Land, love, and art keep opening us up to experience. Leading from dark to light—and back again . . . our dance, as people, humans, artists, spirits across the landscape of our lives, our souls, celebrating it as we can as we go, in story, song, and image.*

*It's really a very ancient form of science, of investigation, imagining ways to encounter and dialogue with the self as other.*

1. HENRY HOPKINS, 50 WEST COAST ARTISTS: A CRITICAL SELECTION OF PAINTERS AND SCULPTORS WORKING IN CALIFORNIA (SAN FRANCISCO: CHRONICLE BOOKS, 1981), P. 74.

## LIST OF PLATES

*All dimensions are given in inches; height precedes width precedes depth.*

**JUDY DATER**

Page 84: *Untitled*, 1983, color coupler print, 15 × 19

Page 85: *Ms. Clingfree*, 1982, Ektacolor print, 17½ × 14

**STEPHEN DAVIS**

Page 86: *Corridor*, 1986, oil and plywood on canvas, 60 × 60 × 8½

**JAY DEFEO**

Page 88: *Isis*, 1972, acrylic and mixed media on masonite, 48 × 24

Page 89: *Geisha I*, 1987, oil on canvas, 84 × 60

**ROY DE FOREST**

Page 90: *One Life to Lead*, 1986, painted wood, 60 × 109½ × 24

Page 91: *Camp of the Landscape Artists*, 1991, polymer paint on linen with wood and mixed media, 87½ × 116 × 10

**STEPHEN DE STAEBLER**

Page 92: *Standing Woman with Yellow Breast*, 1979, porcelain and low-fire clays, 87½ × 14½ × 26½

**VERONICA DI ROSA**

Page 94: *Secondary Cow*, 1988, monotype, 30 × 44½

**MARK DI SUVERO**

Page 97: *For Veronica*, 1987, painted steel, 261 × 422 × 468

**VIOLA FREY**

Page 99: *Homage*, 1987, ceramic, 60 × 96 × 84

**CHARLES GATEWOOD**

Page 101: *Jennifer & Clint*, 1995, chromogenic color print, ed. 2/25, 18½ × 12½

**WALLY HEDRICK**

Page 102: *The Red Boots at Brown Bag Corral*, 1980, oil on canvas, 62 × 54½

**MIKE HENDERSON**

Page 105: *Oldies and Goodies*, 1988, oil on canvas, 70 × 70

**LYNN HERSHMAN**

Page 107: *Constructing Roberta Breitmore*, 1975, chromogenic color print, 19¾ × 12¾

**TOM HOLLAND**

Pages 108–109: *62nd Street Series #43*, 1978, epoxy on paper, 35 × 45 × 2¾

**MILDRED HOWARD**

Pages 110–111: *Memory Garden, Phase I*, 1990, 4,000 bottles, text, and mixed media, 132 × 120 × 96

**ROBERT HUDSON**

Page 112: *Teapot, 1972 (Ceramic #19)*, 1972, porcelain with underglazes and china paint, 17½ × 12¼ × 8½

Page 113: *Untitled*, 1980–1981, acrylic, charcoal, enamel paint, and collage on canvas, wood, masonite, tin, finishing saw, and wire, 76 × 46 × 21

Pages 114–115: *Figure of Speech*, 1984, welded and painted steel, 170½ × 104 × 62

**DAVID IRELAND**

Page 116: *Untitled*, 1994, wood, metal, and Fixall, 35 × 20 × 17

**OLIVER JACKSON**

Page 119: *Untitled No. 6*, 1985, oil pastel on linen, 57 × 70

**JESS**

Page 121: *And It's Jung by a Gnose*, 1955, photo collage, 13 × 21

**DAVID JONES**

Page 122: *They Who Chose*, 1987, mixed media, 89 × 23 × 23

**PAUL KOS**

Page 124: *Chartres Bleu*, 1986/1996, laser discs, players, monitors, and electronics, 180 × 57 × 19

**MARILYN LEVINE**

Page 126: *Brown Drawstring Bag*, 1980, high-fire ceramic with leather laces, 6½ × 5½ × 4½

Page 127: *Blue Hat*, 1971, unglazed low-fire ceramic with blue engobe, 8 × 16 × 15

**TONY LIGAMARI**

Pages 128–129: *Last Supper*, 1991, mixed-media paint on unprimed cotton, 78 × 120

**ALVIN LIGHT**

Page 130: *Untitled*, 1980, carved and painted wood, 86 × 29 × 17

**CHARLES LINDER**

Page 133: *Fiat Lux*, 1997, mixed media and found objects, 83½ × 83½

**TOM MARIONI**

Page 134: *Friday*, 1989, shadow box, 36 × 48 × 4¼

**JOCK MCDONALD**

Page 137: *Rene & Gorilla*, 1988, gelatin-silver print, 9¾ × 9¾

**JIM MELCHERT**

Page 138: *Photo Negative with Metal Ashtray*, 1968, metal, clay, and glazes, 4½ × 15 × 15

**RICHARD MISRACH**

Page 141: *Athena Nike (Column),* 1979, 1982 color coupler print, 18⅝ × 21

**RON NAGLE**

Page 142: *Anderson Ranch Series–Turquoise,* 1988, porcelain and overglaze, 2½ × 3½ × 1⅞

Page 143: *California Dreamin',* 1975, slipcast low-fire clay with overglaze, 5½ × 3¼ × 2¾

**MANUEL NERI**

Page 144: *Acha de Noche III,* 1975, plaster, lampblack, Styrofoam, and burlap on steel armature, 16¼ × 56 × 14¼

**NATHAN OLIVEIRA**

Page 147: *Standing Site Figure,* 1983, oil on canvas, 36 × 27

**DEBORAH OROPALLO**

Page 149: *Untitled (Fox and Skeleton),* 1986, oil on paper, 39½ × 27¾

**JIM POMEROY**

Pages 150-151: *Ladder Day Paints,* 1971, stepladder and painted books, 134 × 24 × 93

**JANIS PROVISOR**

Page 153: *Longview,* 1979, oil, acrylic, Rhoplex, and modeling paste on canvas, 22½ × 24

**MEL RAMOS**

Page 154: *Lola Cola,* 1967, oil on canvas with metal sign, 41¾ × 48¼

**ALAN RATH**

Page 156: *Bumper,* 1990, steel, aluminum, electronics, and speaker, 37½ × 18 × 34

**RIGO 92**

Page 159: *Missile,* 1992, pushpins on wood, 48 × 48

**PETER SAUL**

Pages 160-161: *View of SF/Red Plane,* 1985, acrylic and oil on canvas, 67 × 109

**RAYMOND SAUNDERS**

Page 163: *Captain Marvel,* 1979, mixed media and collage on paper, 29 × 22

**RICHARD SHAW**

Page 165: *Sinking Ship in Couch,* 1971, porcelain with glazes, 15 × 36 × 15

**ALAN SHEPP**

Pages 166-167: *Negotiating Table II,* 1990, granite, 66 × 164 × 49

**SCOTT SIEDMAN**

Page 168: *First Kiss,* 1995, pastel and charcoal on linen, 45 × 57

**HASSEL SMITH**

Page 170: *Sept. '63,* 1963, oil on canvas, 68 × 46

**MICHAEL STEVENS**

Page 173: *Black Hand,* 1988, pine and enamel, 77 × 36 × 18

**LARRY SULTAN**

Page 175: *Golf Swing,* 1989, chromogenic color print, ed. of 10, 40 × 50

**CARLOS VILLA**

Page 176: *Third Coat,* 1983, canvas, taffeta, acrylic paint, feathers, bones, and hair, 79 × 80 × 11

**PETER VOULKOS**

Page 178: *Untitled Plate,* 1973, stoneware and porcelain, 21½ × 21½ × 4½

**CATHERINE WAGNER**

Page 181: *7th & 8th Grade Science Classroom, Moss Landing Elementary School,* 1984, gelatin-silver print, 14 × 18¼

**WILLIAM T. WILEY**

Page 183: *Traced from the Original,* 1978, acrylic and mixed media on canvas, 44 × 39

Page 184: *Bench Mark,* 1988, mixed-media construction, 66 × 69¾ × 36

## ARTISTS IN THE DI ROSA COLLECTION AS OF OCTOBER 1, 1998

Abbott, George L.
Adams, Bobby Neel
Adams, Ginger M.
Adele, Sister, O.P.
Alderette, Bob
Alfe, Michael
Alicia, Juana
Allan, William
Allen, Maxine
Allen, Patrick W.
Allen, Stuart
Allen, Terry
Almond, John
Altoon, John
Amerigian, Gary
Amodio, Angela
Anderson, David
Anderson, Jeremy
Angell, Robert
Arakawa, Patience Lima
Arbus, Diane
Armer, Ruth
Arneson, Robert
Arnold, Sharon
Azaceta, Luis Cruz
Aziz, Anthony
Babior, Daniel
Bailey, Clayton
Bailey, R.
Ballaine, Jerry
Baltz, Lewis
Banks, Ian
Barbieri, Jonathan
Barrish, Jerry Ross
Barry, Colleen
Barsness, James
Bartlett, Freude
Bates, Mary
Battenberg, John
Becher, Bernd and Hilla
Bechtle, Robert
Beech, John
Beery, Gene
Beldner, Ray
Benton, Fletcher
Berger, Richard
Berman, Erica
Bernhard, Ruth
Bernstein, Jeffrey
Berry, John
Best, David
Biever, Margrit
Binnendyk, Marcia
Birk, Sandow
Bischoff, Elmer
Bishop, Michael
Black, Craig M.
Black, LaVerne Nelson
Blake, Nayland
Blankman, Judith
Blondin, Bruce
Bloomfield, Debra
Blott, David
Boel
Bogus, Gary
Bonick, Dona Kopol
Borensztein, Leon
Boyce, Roger
Bradford, Carlton
Bradford, Donald
Brady, Robert
Branscom, Don
Braun, Bill
Breschi, Karen
Briscoe, Stephen
Brody, Blanche
Brooke, Pegan
Broom, Joy
Brotzman, John
Broughton, James
Brown, Christopher
Brown, Joan
Brown, William Theo
Bruce, Martha
Brunson, Jamie
Buck, John
Bufano, Beniamino
Bullock, Benbow
Bullock, Wynn
Bulwinkle, Mark
Burden, Erni
Burris, Bruce
Butler, Frances
Butterfield, Deborah
Byington, Dean
Campbell, Jim
Canada, Alonzo
Cannon, Bruce
Carnwath, Squeak
Carrari, Joe E.
Carrier, Alan
Carter, Bob
Carter, Richard
Cartier-Bresson, Henri
Casella, Alfred
Castano, Carolyn
Caulfield, Gail
Chagoya, Enrique
Champagne, Lee Roy
Chase-Bien, Gail
Chen, Teresa
Chester, Mark
Chihuly, Dale
Chow, Lena
Christensen, Tom
Ciarelli, Doug
Cicansky, Victor
Citret, Mark
Clark, Bill
Clark, Crystal
Clergue, Lucien
Cliff, Wilma Daubenspeck
Coke, Van Deren
Colby, Sas
Cole, Brad
Conner, Bruce

Connor, Linda
Conrad, Dale
Cook, Gordon
Cooper, Tim
Cornblatt, Marque
Costanzo, Betty Jo
Crail, Charr
Crane, Margaret
Crisswell, Lynn
Crook, David
Cucher, Sammy
Culbert, Rae
Cummings, Timothy
Cunningham, Imogen
Dailey, Dan
Dane, Bill
Darwin, Beatrice
Dater, Judy
Davi, Jr., Frank
Davis, Jerold
Davis, Stephen
Dawson, Robert
DeFazio, John
DeFeo, Jay
De Forest, Roy
DeFranceaux, Deidre
De Grazia, E.
de Guzman, Rene
Dekker, Mary Case
DeLap, Tony
DeLorenzo, Angelina
De Marinis, Paul
Demonchy
Dern, Carl
deSoto, Lewis
De Staebler, Stephen
di Rosa, Veronica
di Suvero, Mark
Dickinson, Eleanor
Dittman, Marjean
Doisneau, Robert
Donaldson, Peter
Doogan, Margaret Bailey
Doren, Kelly V.
Dreyer, Clarice
Durant, Mark Alice
Dusenbery, Walter
Eggleston, William
Eichner, L. D.
Eichner, Susan
Elisofon, Elin
Elledge, J. Scott
Ellison, Robert
Elozua, Raymon
Etienne, Serge
Evans, Phill
Evans, Walker
Falk, Ben
Faralla, Richard
Farley, William
Farrow, Al
Felzmann, Lukas
Fenwick, Conrad
Ferris, Andrée
Fillip, J.
Finnegan, James Patrick
F.I.R.E.
Fisher, Shirley
Fitts, Robert
Flyr, Diane
Forrester, Patricia Tobacco
Francis, Sam
Frankforter, Katharine
Frederick, Robilee
Frey, Viola
Fried, Howard
Friedman, Lynn
Fritzius, Harry
Fryer, Finley
Fryling, Dawn
Fulton, Jack
Gallagher, Dennis
Galvez, Daniel
Garland, Terri
Gatewood, Charles
Gay, Garry
Geis, William
Ghioni, Elena
Giambruni, Tio
Gilhooly, David
Gillman, Steve
Gilmore, Cindy
Giulini, Nole
Glaser, Nina
Glover, Tim
Goldbeck, Eugene Omar
Goldyne, Joseph
Golik, Christine Vita
Golik, Jay
Gooch, Gerald
Goodwin-Guerrero, Erin
Graff, Richard
Graigie, Rob
Green, Ian
Green, Susan
Griffin, Norman
Grimmer, Neil
Grover, Marilyn
Gutkin, Peter
Guttin, Bruce
Hall, Barbara
Hall, Dennis
Hall, Douglas
Hall, Judy
Hamilton, Frank
Handelman, Michelle
Hannaford, John
Harader, Andy
Harding, John
Harmon, James
Hasson, Bruce
Hastings, Robert D.
Hatch, Ann
Hedrick, Wally
Held, Archie
Hendee, Stephen
Henderson, Mel
Henderson, Mike
Herms, George
Hershman, Lynn
Hibbert-Jones, Dee
Hill, Bill
Hill, Shelley
Hird, Beth
Hirss, Ivars
Hobson, Charles
Hoefer, Wade
Holland, Tom
Holman, Art
Howard, Mildred
Howard, Robert
Hudson, Robert
Huether, Gordon
Huetter, Bobbe
Hunter, Allan
Hussong, Randy
Hutchison, Jim
Hyder, Frank
Imboden, Clint
Ireland, David
Isaac, Jeffrey
Isaac, Stephanie
Jackson, Oliver
Jag, Tim
Jampol, Glenn
Janssens, Luc
Jess
Jette, Susan
Johnson, Andrea
Johnson, Jae
Johnson, Jerome
Johnson, Karen
Jones, David
Jordan, Larry
Joaquin
Kadonaga, Kazuo
Kane, Linda
Kano, Betty

Karpilow, Shelley
Keller, Vic
Kelly, Leon
Kendle-Saiz, Adrienne
Kerr, Leslie
Kertész, André
Key, Jeff
King, David
King, Hayward
King, Jeffrey
Kingford, Linda M.
Kinmont, Robert
Kishi, Masatoyo
Kling, Fred
Kluge, Gordon
Kokin, Lisa
Kos, Paul
Krims, Les
Kriz, Vilem
Kruzick, Zena
Kwong, Evri
Labat, Tony
Lachowicz, Rachel
Lamanet, Shari
LaMotte, Jason
Lasser, Robin
Lederer, Carrie
Leger, Fernand
Leisure, Jerry
Leivick, Joel
Leon, Dennis
Leonard, Joanne
Leong, Stanley
Levine, Marilyn
Li, Saiman
Ligamari, Tony
Light, Alvin
Linda, Rose
Linder, Charles
Linhares, Phil
Lipofsky, Marvin
Lipzin, Janis Crystal
Little, Connell Ray
Little, Ken
Lloyd, David
Lobdell, Ann
Loverro, Victor
Lucero, Michael
Luckin, Brenda
Lupper, Ed
Lynn, Billie Grace
Mack, Mark
Majdrakoff, Ivan
Makanna, Philip
Malloy, Judy
Mannino, Joseph
Manuel, K. Lee
Marc
Marioni, Tom
Mariscal, Joe
Martin, Fred
Matsumoto, Masashi
Mazzon, Galliano
McClave, Wade
McClellan, Douglas
McDevitt, Genivive
McDonald, Jock
McDonald, Mary
McDowell, Michael
McGrath, Scott
McGraw, David I.
McKenzie, David
McLean, Richard
Meadows, J.
Meadowsweet Dairy
Melchert, Jim
Mendelson, Richard
Mendoza, Hector
Mew, Michael
Meyers, Gilda
Milgrim, Charlie
Miller, Bill
Miller, Ken
Minick, Roger
Misrach, Richard
Modesty, Chuba
Modrak, Judith
Montgomery, John
Moon, Robert
Morgan, Scott
Morris, William
Morsberger, Philip
Moulton, Margaret
Murray, Joan
Murray, Robert Bashasco
Myers, Martin
Nagle, Ron
Natsoulas, Tony
Nauman, Bruce
Navarre, Marie
Nelson, Gunvor
Nelson, Robert
Neri, Manuel
Neri, Noel
Noraas, Knut Jarl
Norman, Irving
North, Judy
Nuzom, Tom
Okamura, Arthur
Oliveira, Nathan
Ollman, Arthur
Olson, Signe
Ongaro, Vittoria
Onslow-Ford, Gordon
Oppenheim, Dennis
O'Rear, Chuck
Orland, Ted
Oropallo, Deborah
Orr, Diana
Osato, Sono
O'Siochain, Tara
Overall, John
Overstreet, Richard
Owens, Bill
Page, Merrily
Palmbach, Ulrike
Parady, Scott
Parini, Shirley Rae
Paris, Harold
Park, David
Parker, Fred
Parks, Judi
Peed, Michael Howard
Peroni, Joe
Perry, Sam
Pettibone, Richard
Phillips, Joyce
Pierson, Jean Louis
Pijoan, Irene
Plumb-Chambers, Mimi
Podmore, Amy
Polos, Iris
Polsky, Benjamin
Pomeroy, Jim
Poole, Wesley
Porter, James
Potter, Dennis
Pratchenko, Paul
Price, Ken
Priola, J. John
Provisor, Janis
Prowler, David
Puls, Lucy
Rabinovich, Marilyn
Raboff, L.
Raffael, Joseph
Rajan, Deva
Ramos, Leta
Ramos, Mel
Rand, Al
Rapoport, Sonya
Rascon, Armando
Rath, Alan
Rawet, Salo
Ray, Man
Reisman, Richard
Remington, Deborah
Reynolds, Jock

Richards, Eugene
Richardson, Judy
Richardson, Sam
Rigo 99
Ringman, Steve
Rivera, Judy
Roberts, John
Roberts, Kent
Robinson, Walter
Rodia, Simon
Roeder, John
Roiceil, Nicholas Pascal
Roldan, Johanna Rudjen
Roloff, John
Ronzio, Angela
Ross, Charles
Ross, Richard
Rubenstein, Meridel
Ruda, Lesley
Ruddell, David
Rummel, Ruth
Runion, Scott
Rutherford, John
Saltero, Emilio
Sam., Joe
Sapien, Darryl
Saul, Peter
Saunders, Raymond
Scarlatta, John
Schneider, Ursula
Schulz, Cornelia
Scolaro, Diane
Selby, Judith
Selter, Carol
Sengstock, Guy F.
Serra, Rudy
Servais, James
Severson, Ann
Shaffer, Mary
Shames, Steven
Shannonhouse, Sandra
Shaw, Leslie
Shaw, Richard
Shearer, Erik
Sheldon, Mick
Shepp, Alan
Shepp, Diane Damé
Siedman, Scott
Simon, Sandra
Simonet, Jean-Marie
Simons, Sheri
Simpkins, John
Simpson, David
Simpson, Samantha
Simpson, Suzanne
Singer, Zhee
Sinton, Nell
Skoff, Gail
Smelser, Sharin
Smith, Hassel
Smith, Maria Dawn
Smith, Meg
Snowden, Mary
Somerville, Travis
Soss, Rick
Splady, Charles
Stackpole, Peter
Stafford, Harvey Bennett
Stayton, Janet
Steiner, Judy
Steinman, Susan Leibovitz
Stern, Gerd
Stevens, Lorna
Stevens, Michael
Stiegelmeyer, Norman
Storer, Inez
Straiton, John
Strong, S. J.
Sultan, Larry
Sunday, Elisabeth
Takamori, Akio
Tanwar, Ram
Taylor, Derrick
Taylor, Gage
Taylor, Yoshio
Tchakalian, Sam
Tchelitchew, Pavel
Tepper, Irvin
Terry, Kerry
Thacher, James
Thollander, Earl
Thoma, Marta
Thomas, Lewis
Thurlow, Erin
Tiffany, Daniel
Titus, Robert
Titus, Sebastian
Trave, Cecilia Kanda
Trave, Horst
Trejo, Ruben
Troxel, Ted
Tsouo-Harvey, Christiane
Turner, Lincoln Hale
Tuteur, Vee
Tyson, Steve
Uelsmann, Jerry
Urban-O
van Krijdt, Nicolas
VanAllsburg, Chris
Vandersteen
Vasquez, Gabrielle
Veraldi, Anne
Villa, Carlos
Voulkos, Peter
Waddell, John Henry
Wagner, Catherine
Walberg, Gerald
Watten, Jane
Wayne, Jim
Webster, Mary Hull
Weeks, James
Weier, Debra
Weintraub, Sheila
Weis, Ron
Wessel, Henry
Westermann, H. C.
Weston, Brett
Whaley, Jo
Wheatley, Dee
White, Jerry
Wibroe, Susanne
Wiener, Daniel
Wight, Gail
Wiley, William T.
Williams, Franklin
Williams, L. G.
Willis, Nancy
Wilmoth, Steve
Wilson, Patrick
Winet, Jon
Winkelman, Jane
Winter, Peter
Wintersteen, James
Witkin, Joel-Peter
Wollard, Robert
Wonner, Paul
Wood, Nicholas
Woodall, John
Worth, Don
Yates, Samuel
Yorba, Norma
Young, Miriam
Zak, Ron
Zecher, Peter
Zepeda, Dian
Zhang, Baochi
Zoller, Richard